FAST
FOOD

THE ROAD AND AMERICAN CULTURE

Drake Hokanson, *Series Editor*
Karl Raitz, *Consulting Editor*
George F. Thompson, *Founder and Series Director*

Published in cooperation with the Center for American Places,
Santa Fe, New Mexico, and Harrisonburg, Virginia

John A. Jakle & Keith A. Sculle

FAST

ROADSIDE RESTAURANTS
IN THE AUTOMOBILE AGE

FOOD

THE JOHNS HOPKINS UNIVERSITY PRESS   BALTIMORE & LONDON

1999

© 1999 The Johns Hopkins University Press
All rights reserved. Published 1999
Printed in the United States of America on acid-free paper
9 8 7 6 5 4 3 2 1

The Johns Hopkins University Press
2715 North Charles Street
Baltimore, Maryland 21218-4363
www.press.jhu.edu

Library of Congress Cataloging-in-Publication Data will be found
at the end of this book.

A catalog record for this book is available from the British Library.

ISBN 0-8018-6109-8

For our daughters

Contents

Preface and Acknowledgments

Roadside restaurants, along with gasoline stations and motels, provide vital services linked to and supportive of use of the automobile. Eating, refueling the car, and staying the night all sustain those traveling by car, whether they are tourists or those with other business or personal destinations. Gas stations (now mainly convenience stores) and roadside restaurants both have everyday implications as well. With the nation's geography firmly reconfigured around automobility, the frequent gas stop has become a necessity as we keep our automobiles energized. So also have we become frequently reliant on restaurant food as a quick source of bodily energy, and, more important, as a means of breaking domestic routines of eating. By some estimates, half the food consumed in America today is consumed outside the home, the restaurant being the prime venue for this activity. Americans are increasingly "on the go," and "fast food" and "quick service" have become emblematic of modern lifestyles.

We use the words "fast food" in our title in relating not only to specific food items, but, more important, to eating and its connection to America's evolving automobile orientation. Although we emphasize what the restaurant industry prefers to call quick service by focusing on such foods as hamburgers, ice cream, and pizza, we do not exclude the likes of the steak or seafood dinner. Our concern is food served by the roadside under conditions of easy automobile access. It is food served in highly programmed settings—settings variously engineered to rapid food preparation and, indeed, to rapid customer turnover, some venues, in relative terms, more quickly paced than others. It is food and setting in harmony with the age of automobile convenience.

We offer here an exploration of the roadside restaurant—its origins, its evolution as a form, its changing geographical distribution, and its changing social meaning. How did distinctly automobile-oriented and automobile-convenient restaurants evolve as a kind of business? How did they take form as architectural expression? How did they spread along America's highways?

What sorts of regional patterns were created? How did roadside restaurants, and the food they served, evolve as cultural icon? These are the sorts of questions explored herein. Our emphasis is the entrepreneur. We view restaurants as an industry with distinctive products and services specially packaged for consumption. The story we tell is one of origins, emphasizing, accordingly, the people, and the kinds of people, who created and ran roadside eateries. And, as well, we consider those who created the corporate chains. What was the nature of their successes? Their failures? From entrepreneurial activities we can infer something of customer satisfactions. And from those apparent satisfactions we can say something about the customers themselves and their changing society. We can imply something about cultural values.

This book, on the roadside restaurant in America, continues exploration of two organizing themes explored in our earlier studies of gas stations and motels: place-product-packaging and corporate territoriality. *Place-product-packaging* describes commercial places formed through coordination of architecture, decor, product, service, and operating routine across multiple locations—the chain of stores that conforms to a set business system. *Corporate territoriality* refers to the trade territories created as different corporations compete with one another for market share using place-product-packaging. Through the two related processes, the American roadside has been substantially homogenized—roadside selling thoroughly rationalized through standardization. Automobile convenience has been the critical impulse, the packaging and repackaging of roadside places taking into account ease of customer access by motor car. Americans may view themselves as enjoying wide degrees of freedom in making such routine decisions as to what and where to eat. Yet corporate America in its commodifying of life may have limited such choices more than we might suspect.

In the introduction we consider our own discovery of roadside restaurants. We use our own experiences to suggest just how restaurants can impact individual lives as important places of social reference. We see ourselves, like most Americans, as dependent on restaurants in everyday life. More important, reminiscence helps explain how it is we approach our subject, enabling readers to better understand our orientations and our preoccupations as scholars. Chapter 1 outlines the rise of quick-service restaurants, focusing on the era before widespread automobile use. Emphasis is placed on the form, layout, and functioning of such diverse eating places as hotel coffee shops, confectionery stores, main-street cafés, and diners. Chapter 2 outlines the transition brought to quick-service eating with the arrival of the automobile. In this chapter we focus on the rise of roadside tearooms, wayside stands, coffee shops, drive-ins, and outdoor and indoor "walk-ups," as well as the latest in restaurant fad, the "double drive-through." Chapter 3 treats business format franchising and the rise of the large restaurant chains through adoption of place-product-packaging. Brief histories of selected coffee-shop chains, like Howard Johnson's and Denny's, illustrate.

What follows in subsequent chapters is a linking of the various restaurant formats with specific food emphases. Architectural change is discussed in relation to evolving market segments defined by food group. In chapters 4, 5, and 6 we focus on the hamburger, the quintessential road food. Respectively, we deal with the rise of the early diner chains like White Castle and White Tower, the later growth of giant corporate chains such as Burger King and Hardee's, and, of course, the rise of McDonald's, the giant of them all. McDonald's has become not just an industry dominant, but a kind of cultural icon for much of what America has become. The introduction of the McDonald's chain into a new country (over 100 now) is taken as a sign of spreading American influence worldwide. Chapters 8 through 14, in turn, link roadside restaurants with ice cream, breakfast food, chicken, seafood, pizza (and other Italian food), tacos (and other Mexican food), and steak. In chapter 15 we consider so-called concept restaurants programmed around selected themes. In concept restaurants, "sense of place" is fully emphasized. In these restaurants food is linked with decor to speak forcefully of lifestyle. Chapter 16 presents a case study—a look at Springfield, Illinois—in order to illustrate the changing restaurant geography of a typical American city of modest size. Finally, in the conclusion, we offer synthesis. Just what might the roadside restaurant mean in the American experience? Where might future scholarship be directed?

We consider the restaurant to be a kind of place. Our emphasis is on the quick-service roadside restaurant that offers what Americans have come to call fast food. Such places reflect broad social forces as repositories of social meaning. As behavior settings frequented by the vast majority of Americans, they contribute much to society's changing formulations. As places, restaurants both construct and are constructed, borrowing some currently fashionable social science jargon. For example, African-Americans were traditionally denied access to lunch counters and other kinds of restaurants before the sit-ins of the 1960s redefined restaurants as public places. That restaurants were targeted by the leaders of the civil rights movement only demonstrated their importance to everyday life. No one denied access to their products and services could be a part of the American mainstream. Restaurants say much about who we have been and who we are becoming as a nation.

Geography and history are enriched through the first-hand accounts of those who participated in events studied and those who share private or archival materials. For their time and generosity we are deeply indebted to the following: Vic Abshier; Pearl Ahrenkiel; Patricia Baer; Doris Baker and the Grundy County–Jewett Norris (Missouri) Library; Debra Lee Baldwin; Betty Bartley and the Hendrick County (Indiana) Historical Society; Tim Barton and the Department of Planning and Development, Landmarks Division, City of Chicago; Robert Bastian; David Becker; Mary Bledsoe; Phil Bloomer and the *Champaign-Urbana (Ill.) News-Gazette*; Dale Brown; Grady Copeland; Cy Copra; Merle Davis; Sheila Davis and the Livingston

County (Missouri) Library; Dale J. Diamond; Emil Epoh; Mary Etzel; Armando and Lucille Falzone; L. B. Felkey and the Kokomo–Howard County Public Library; Emma H. Fisher; Steven Gordon and the Ohio Historical Society; Joseph Grave; Martha Gregg and the Wichita Public Library; Betty Halsey; Richard E. Hattwick and the Illinois Business Hall of Fame, Western Illinois University; Sheila E. Heiflin and the Owensboro–Daviess County (Kentucky) Library; Arthur Hepworth; Donald and Arabella Hill; Jacqueline Hughes; Mark Johnson; W. Dwayne Jones and the Texas Historical Commission; Howard Kelley; Velma Kelley; Stewart Kull; Barry J. Locher and the *State Journal-Register;* Barbara A. Love and the Marion (Ind.) Public Library; Ray W. Luce; Jack Luer; Leslie Kenyon; Robert Knowles; Herbert Leonard; Jacob McCutchan; Michelle McNabb and the McLean County Historical Society; Forrest Niedholt; P. J. O'Brien; Martin C. Perkins; Frank P. Piontek and the Beverly Hills Public Library; Susan L. Poludniak and the Springfield Sangamon County Regional Planning Commission; H. Wayne Price; William Rennie; Edward C. Roark; Everett Roberts; James Rollett; Susan Roth and the Minnesota Historical Society; Edward J. Russo, Melinda Garvert, and Curtis Mann, and the Sangamon Valley Collection, Lincoln Library; Henry Schroeder; Randolph Shaw; Wiley and Betty Shott; Chris Shovey and the San Bernardino Public Library; Brooks Shows; Frederick Slater and the *St. Joseph (Mo.) News Press;* Brian Spangle and the Knox County (Ind.) Public Library; Caroline Stevemer and the *Minneapolis Star Tribune;* Lemuel L. Stroud; Michael Sublett; Victoria D. Swadley and the River Bluffs Regional Library; Ralph Tandy; James Van Meter; Dominic Vitale; Vigo County Public Library; Richard Warren; and Raymond Zien.

Corporate administrators and archivists deserve special recognition. Business pace does not permit many to cooperate with scholarly research; however, the following were kind to take time from their regular work to answer the authors' questions and provide material: Tom Amberger and the Galardi Group; Stuart B. Barnhill, John S. Carty Jr. and Hardee's Food Systems, Inc.; Ben and Jerry's Homemade, Inc.; Blue Chip Cookies, Inc.; Bojangles Restaurants, Inc.; Richard Bowen, Jackie Pedini, and Honey Dew Associates, Inc.; John Brinker and Chili's Grill and Bar; Suzi Brown and Carl Karcher Enterprises, Inc.; Lori Burns and Runza Restaurants; Lane Cardwell, Sheri Bennett, and Brinker International; Sonja Castillo and Pizza Hut; Mary Cusick and Bob Evans Farms; Richard A. Failey and Texas Pig Stands, Inc.; Marylou Flynn and Cinnabon; Friendly Ice Cream Corporation; Grandy's; Mary Jane Hughes and the Sonic Corporation and Subsidiaries; Jean Litteret and the KFC Corporation; Melanie Macary and Carvel Ice Cream Bakery; Jared Nixon and Subway; Robin Pearlman and Kenny Rogers Roasters; Perkins Family Restaurants; Maggie Proctor and Domino's Pizza, Inc.; Rally's Hamburgers; Red Lobster; Jennifer Rosenberg and Dunkin' Donuts; Charles Chip Rosencrans and Stuckey's Corporation; Sizzler International, Inc.; Charles A. Stuppy and the Original Cookie Co.; Deborah Trager and Heartland Food Systems; Cathie Weinberg and The Olive Garden; Wendy's International, Inc.; Whataburger; Victor F. Yeandel and Steak 'n Shake; Albert F. Zehnder

Preface and Acknowledgments

and Zehnder's of Frankenmuth; Ellen Zimny and the Coca-Cola Co.; and Nicholas W. Zuk and the White Castle System, Inc.

Cartographer Jane Domier, Department of Geography, University of Illinois, produced the maps for this book. Kathryn M. Harris and Janet Noecker, Illinois Historical Library, Springfield, rendered invaluable bibliographical and interlibrary loan assistance. Without the tireless patience and competence of Barbara Bonnell, the manuscript for this book could not have been typed for publication.

Two people have emerged as especially helpful in our partnership for books about the roadside service industries. For the opportunity to bring these books in manuscript form to the attention of the Johns Hopkins University Press, we are indebted to George F. Thompson, president of the Center for American Places, and his vision in landscape studies. For the patience to edit this book while honoring the intentions of our prose we are again indebted to Therese D. Boyd. She also edited *The Gas Station in America.*

Wives Cynthia Jakle and Tracey Sculle continue to share both their husbands' time on the road and support their absence writing while at home. The road has been richer for the time together.

FAST
FOOD

Introduction

We begin by asking our readers to indulge some personal reminiscing and some preliminary defining of key concepts.[1] Shared recollection serves not only to introduce our subject—America's roadside restaurants—but to acknowledge the cultural and social orientations that we, as interested scholars, bring to our endeavor, a social history of eating out in America's evolving automobile age. Although our individual experiences are quite particular, they are, we suspect, not atypical and that, indeed, despite the different personal specifics, they reflect general involvements quite common to the majority of our readers. We are, all of us, subsumed in an evolving and increasingly effervescent popular culture built substantially around the use of automobiles. As for basic definitions, it is always helpful for authors to share with readers the special meanings assigned to common words—words like *landscape* and *place*.

Eating out several times each week constitutes an important part of most Americans' routine. The places as well as the foods consumed in eating out play an important role in fulfilling lifestyle aspirations. The food sought varies from expensive meals taken in upscale restaurants to snack foods eaten in relatively unpretentious emporiums. Eating out runs the gamut from steaks and seafood dinners to hamburgers and fish sandwiches, to coffee and bagels, and to ice cream and other desserts. Of course, when Americans travel, a near total dependence on restaurants prevails. Indeed, one of the highest pleasures of tourist travel is that of eating out. The restaurant looms as an important way to experience new localities, even, paradoxically, when the tourist relies on chain restaurants that are very much alike from one locale to another.

Restaurants and their uses are all very familiar, and may seem hardly worth scholarly contemplation. They may not seem to merit the grand abstractions that scholars tend to foist on readers. But not long ago the "commonplaceness" of America's restaurant scene, especially its orientation to highways and the uses of automobiles, was largely unknown to most Americans. How times have changed! The roadside restaurant is now a major fixture of American landscape. Roadside restaurants not only reflect changing society but, as places inviting to and supportive of categories of normative behavior, they sustain change and may even precipitate it. Restaurants are symptomatic of our times and lessons can be learned from them about who we are as a people. That is the principal assumption upon which we base our work.

FAST FOOD

John Jakle's World of Eating Out

What stands out in my memory about growing up in the decade after World War II was the dedication with which my family persistently ate at home. We did not "eat out" in the course of normal routines. We usually ate at the kitchen table, the more formal dining room being reserved for the special entertaining of relatives and friends. My mother, whose career as a teacher did not begin until after I left home for college, prepared all of our meals. My father, the "breadwinner," occasionally helped with cleanup until I was old enough to "pitch in." A patterned menu developed which I, as a child, found quite confining: fried chicken every Sunday noon, meatloaf Monday night, pork chops on Thursday, fish on Friday, and so on. Occasionally, inserted by my request, was something (now viewed in retrospect as awful) first encountered in a school cafeteria—regrettable adolescent enthusiasms like mushy chipped beef on toast or even fish sticks as dry as they were hard. It was, after all, the beginning of the dried and frozen food revolutions, and there was no novelty not worth trying at least once at home. Things my family relished more in vacation travel also intruded at home: hot dogs and hamburgers, for example. My mother was an ice cream aficionado and needed no encouragement in the dessert department.

My mother's cooking was "heavy," built around meat and potatoes, a "cuisine" rooted in both the rural Belgian / French background of her family and the German background of my father's people. It was the sort of fare a family might aspire to on achieving some measure of wealth and security in the world. It spoke of middle-class aspirations, being very high in protein and carbohydrates. It was also bland, being rarely seasoned for excitement. And the meat and potatoes were invariably overcooked by today's standards. It was a culinary standard against which the highly spiced, heavily salted, and usually fried "fast food" of restaurants came to stand in sharp contrast. For my parents, however, whose families had known degrees of deprivation in earlier generations, what was important was quality and abundance.

Only an emergency or a special occasion would incline us to eat out. Probably for the infrequency of experience, many of my earliest restaurant meals in the years following World War II remain vivid in memory. For example, I link a certain soda fountain with my family's purchase of a house in suburban Detroit where I would grow up through my elementary and high school years. That house was resold over a quarter of a century ago, but I can return to that restaurant in Detroit and still get a strong feeling of being home. It is a stronger feeling than when I stand on my old street before the house that now belongs to people I do not know. Cars were angle-parked along the curb out front, the restaurant occupying a common storefront sandwiched between a fruit market and a hardware store. A large room, finished in elaborate wood paneling, held a series of sales counters down one side backed by shelving, and an elaborate soda fountain backed by mirrors on the other. Customers sat on stools that swiveled at a low marble counter, uniformed waitresses serving sandwiches, soft drinks, and various ice cream concoctions. The soda fountain is still there, although it has been "modernized" over the years. The pendant lamps still hang against the knotty pine over the soda fountain. Of course, the candy counters are gone, replaced by self-serve racks and a cash register near the door. Nonetheless, the basic outline of the place remains and I can go there and feel anchored across a half-century of time. I can go there and buy a sandwich, and get a sense of still belonging in a community that once was but is no longer my own.

Sociologist Ray Oldenburg would identify my experience as that of a "great good place," the third realm of satisfaction (after home and work) in the organizational scheme of any society.[2] In these places the stranger feels at home. Without them even the native feels alienated. It is the place where social interaction appears relatively unplanned, unscheduled, unorganized, and unstructured. It is a place where people can mix unobtrusively, a sense of social leveling resulting. One can sit back and watch and feel a part of a surrounding. One can obtain a sense of being anchored in a locale. I go to my old haunt not only for food, but for a sense of rootedness as I look around to see who I might recognize and who might recognize me despite my years away.

When we traveled, which as often as not was to visit relatives in southern Illinois, we occasionally returned to Detroit by way of Urbana, where my mother had graduated from college in the 1920s. In 1967, I moved to Urbana with my wife and two daughters to become an assistant professor of geography at the University of Illinois. A block from my office was, and still is, a campus eatery into which I innocently wandered my first week in town. The impression was profound—one of immediate *déjà vu*—for I had been there previously as a child. The place was little changed, the distinctive look that of a Spanish plaza. Rough-plastered walls simulated stucco; decorative roofing tiles evoked Mediterranean spirit. Chairs and tables were placed around a small central fountain and wooden booths were arrayed down the walls of the room (see fig. I.1). Waitresses provided service from a kitchen hidden behind swinging doors.

Today I start nearly every morning in this place which is now a coffee house, the latest excitement in campus eateries as well as elsewhere across the United States. A decade ago this restaurant was converted into a "copy shop" operated by a national chain. Some of the Spanish motif was stripped away to accommodate display shelves for paper, and, of course, the copy machines. But a small café was also installed and that was the business that proved most profitable. The stacks of paper and the machines are gone in favor of tables and chairs once again. The prism glass of the 1920s has been re-

FAST FOOD

FIG. I.1 Prehn and Babcock Confectionery, Urbana, Ill., ca. 1946. A scene from childhood.

stored across the building's facade. Here I can sit at a major campus intersection, watch the early morning commuting, and gather my thoughts for the day. How many Americans my age can claim the privilege of daily anchoring one's life in a "public" place first known in childhood?

As Oldenburg asserts, the course of economic growth in America has been hostile to informal public life, and hostile to such third places as I have just described.[3] The American restaurant, especially what Americans today call fast-food restaurants, are to many people inherently alienating in a social sense. They attract customers through standardized physical formats, ply them with standardized food, and hurry them along so that others may take their place. Customers are not invited to tarry. The restaurant experience is orchestrated almost solely to corporate profit-taking, the turnover of customers foremost. Only with difficulty are such places colonized by those who would linger to see and be seen. Only with some difficulty do customers assert a sense of possession.

My first "drive-in" was at Terre Haute, Indiana, where my parents had grown up and where, accordingly, we also made frequent visits. How exciting this new kind of eating place was to an impressionable boy already enamored with automobiles. One could drive under a cantilevered canopy behind a building "streamlined" with large curving plate-glass windows set in tile which, of course, glittered at night when floodlit. Teenaged girls, whom I quickly learned to call "carhops," took orders and returned with food on trays. But my parents were too conservative for such license, and so we went inside to sit in a booth where I delighted in playing my first jukebox. It was 1947 and I had a sense of visiting the future. But usually we ate in downtown or main-street cafés whether in Terre Haute or elsewhere. Most of these places included lunch counters along one wall, but with tables and booths

4

filling the remainder of the space. Upscale places kept the kitchen "out back"; in others food was prepared at the front counter, offering a kind of theater for waiting customers.

When we traveled in New England in 1948, I discovered Howard Johnson's "coffee shops" with their orange roofs and turquoise trim. I did not realize it at the time, but here was a commercial packaging of roadside place brought to an early level of high refinement. At Howard Johnson's, I could count on lunch built around hot dogs (Johnson's insisted on calling them "frankfurters") and, of course, chocolate milkshakes to which I became addicted as a boy. At night we turned to restaurants recommended by *Duncan Hines Adventures in Good Eating,* a book that my mother carried on her travels like a Bible. These were restaurants individually owned and managed, each unique to a degree in terms of decor and menu. For travelers, as strangers from away, restaurant expectations were often built around guidebook descriptions. Otherwise, the look of a building's facade, its sign, or some other physical cue to quality had to suffice when choices of where to eat were made. Vacation dinners went upscale, usually in hotel dining rooms.

Growing up a teenager in the Motor City involved automobiles in a big way. Dating required a car, either one's parents' car or one's own. As often as not a drive-in movie followed by a drive-in restaurant constituted an evening's entertainment. I ate my first pizza at a drive-in with the girl who eventually became my wife. Raising one's own family while still in college did not lend itself to extravagant luxury. Occasionally, my wife and I treated our two daughters to hot dogs, french fries, and root beer at a drive-in. In Bloomington, Indiana, it was usually to the Dog "N" Suds located near the Indiana University campus that we resorted on a Friday or Saturday evening. Dog "N" Suds, I would later learn, was the creation of several high school teachers from Champaign, Illinois—Urbana's twin city. Indeed, they taught at the high school where my wife now serves as librarian.

Today, with two of us working, and our children moved out and raising families of their own, my wife and I now eat out at least two or three evening meals per week, besides morning breakfasts and frequent lunches out. Our tastes have turned nostalgic. A 1950s diner is a regular lunch spot. Several vintage "bar and grills" (taverns with expanded menus) are on the regular game trail. McDonald's, Hardee's, Wendy's, Friendly's, and other chain stores are stops of convenience primarily while traveling. Dated and now anachronistic White Castles, Dairy Queens, Carvels, Howard Johnson's, and other like restaurants stop me in my tracks for photo taking. I search for (but only infrequently find) the traditional luncheonettes, main-street cafés, and hotel coffee shops.

My interest in restaurants as a geographer, especially roadside restaurants, evolved from previous writing on gasoline stations and motels. A 1982 article in the *Journal of Cultural Geography* concisely outlined the evolution of roadside restaurant architecture.[4] Considerably expanded and updated, that article represents the essence of chapter 2 which follows. In publishing *The Tourist: Travel in Twentieth-Century North America,* I focused on the kinds of places where automobile tourists ate.[5] The quick-service restaurant before widespread automobile use, the changes introduced in response to widespread automobility, and the rise of what has come to be called place-product-packaging came to fascinate me. Much change I had witnessed myself. All I had to do was make sense of it as a scholar.

Keith Sculle's World of Eating Out

I was born and raised on Chicago's Southside and the city's immediate western suburbs in the 1940s and 1950s, where quick-service restaurants were integral to growing up. Hamburger joints and hot-dog carts abound in memory of the street side well before highway-oriented chain drive-ins. These places seemed all-encompassing. They were more than places to eat. They were places of deep psychological satisfaction: focal points of social interaction with others, blended aromas and special sounds, and signals of parental approbation—no small thing for a child. Food was eaten at these stool-and-counter hamburger stands or beside hot-dog carts after some other equally pleasant recreation, often a streetcar ride on the Western Avenue line and hours spent at the Riverview Amusement Park or a movie. Clear are memories of exiting Riverview in the early evening, of the wafting scent of steaming hot dogs with relish sold from carts on the sidewalk, of pleading with my mother for yet another purchase that day.

The eateries of my childhood were small places, each imparting its own distinctive atmosphere. They seemed self-contained and self-satisfied, excluding all beyond them, whether the imaginary perimeter within which one stood to eat at the hot-dog cart or outside the hamburger stand's huge plate-glass "picture window" displaying satisfied customers inside to prospective ones outside. Euphoria welled up from the totality of the space, size, location, and associated activities of these places for eating. How could I come to grips with my "hometown" otherwise? Chicago had always loomed too big and dizzyingly hectic to be possible of comprehension as I whirled through it on public transportation, but felt somehow accessible on a human scale in these restaurants. There I at once came to ease with the sprawling and dynamic city at the same time as I confronted it directly, feeling not unlike some character of a half century before coming to Chicago in a Theodore Dreiser, Upton Sinclair, or Frank Norris novel.[6]

While Chicago's visitors in fiction were ambivalently lured, often in views from railroad passenger cars, I had the advantage of periodically alighting in my travels from streetcars and buses, thus coming to understand "my" city principally in places like quick-service restaurants. They mediated between the stony-cold landscape of manmade concrete, rails, and skyscrapers and the alternative of small talk with strangers, or the satisfactions of closely watching people. Such self-affirming experiences proved essential to my early view of life. There was something fundamental in those restaurants, a tangible, knowledgeable, external dimension giving rise to my faith in a real world.

As an upperclassman at Northern Illinois University in DeKalb, I recall occasional short walks from my residence hall to the McDonald's nearby and, as a graduate student family at the University of Illinois in Urbana, we occasionally treated ourselves at the Dog "N" Suds, the Steak 'n Shake, and other like places, especially McDonald's.

By the early 1970s, my interest in roadside restaurants turned scholarly. Responsibility for surveying 27 Illinois counties for prospective landmarks to be designated in the National Register of Historic Places (1972–75) and administering the registration (1976–88) and survey process (1983–88) for the Illinois historic preservation program focused my attention on many common places as genuine historic "resources," in the vocabulary of the historic preservation community. Roadside businesses, and especially its restaurants, were at once places of affection within many communities, but usually also places very short-lived. Should such ephemerality be preserved? Was it even worthy of inventory? A group of roadside restaurants drew my attention, those of small or defunct chains like Geri's, Hill's Snappy Service, the Jack Robinson System, Maid-Rite, and Prince Castle. My research agenda required access to records both written and photographic, and to respondents with immediate and reliable information. I needed evidence of restaurants extant, and of their surroundings at various stages of evolution. Reading the landscape as a kind of archive became both an important data-collecting strategy and a source of inspiration. Why had roadside restaurants located where they did? Why and how frequently had they changed location? How had they originally looked? Such questions required intimate knowledge of specific changes in specific locations.[7]

For several weeks in 1988 I worked at a fast-food restaurant in Springfield, and, accordingly, came away with a more balanced view of the fast-food business than academic pursuits alone allowed. My time was on the early evening shift as a part-time worker, as I continued to attend to my professional duties at the Illinois Historic Preservation Agency during the day. A week's training introduced me to restaurant standardization. I picked the "back line" when asked where I wanted to work, meaning that I worked in the kitchen preparing food and, as time permitted, cleaning up. I preferred this to the "front line" where one waited on customers. Back-line workers were schooled in the sequences by which each sandwich was made—the hamburger, then bacon, salad dressing, tomato, all topped by lettuce, for example.

Kitchen routine was learned from its chief, a grill man who also worked almost full-time for a competing fast-food chain across town. A man in his late twenties, he seemed exhausted every evening when he started work, but was a patient teacher. The other back-line workers were uniformly males in their late teens or twenties with neither aspirations for further schooling nor ascension into the ranks of management. Shortly after I began work, a new manager walked onto the job. I had observed much already—one was paid regularly, volume was master, workers helped each other through difficult times, and there were opportunities for advancement (but they were seldom taken). Most workers left for other work or were fired. Turnover was very high. Labor cycled through as rapidly as any other commodity in mass culture industry.

The new boss pushed the back line relentlessly and without discrimination between those who worked hard and those who worked indifferently. Anyone of us was called a "deadbeat" who did not anticipate the new manager's orders and work ceaselessly, even repeating a particular chore when it had been done only a very short time before. In his own rude manner the new manager was trying to structure a sense of teamwork among survivors—all in the name of corporate profit. One evening, however, several workers called in sick on my shift as well as on the shift following with the result that I worked from 6 P.M. to 6 A.M. Realizing that this might happen frequently, I thought it best to leave the restaurant, my career in fast food coming to an abrupt end that very morning. I returned fully to my professional life having had a taste of the very real world of restaurant work. I also reaffirmed that moral judgments about mass culture were class-based and that understanding the fast-food industry required suspension of my upper-middle-class values.

Eating out in recent times has represented as much a quest both for distinctive settings as for distinctive food. Several chain restaurants on Springfield, Illinois's southwest side, however generic in style, have offered congenial places to catch up with my grown daughter's busy life as she passes from Chicago through her old hometown. Lately, my wife and I have enjoyed seeking out small family-run restaurants, those definitely not standardized by menu or format.

Of what significance are such personal experiences? We think that there are at least three preliminary conclusions to be drawn from our collective remembering. First, the quick-service restaurant served us in youthful years as an "alternative" place. Soda fountains, drive-ins, and diners, for example, offered contrast to childhood home, although in retrospection restaurants and home seem closely linked. The quick-service restaurant became a testing place for comprehending the world beyond normative routines of residence and workplace. Second, restaurants attracted people not so much according to the food available as to the sense of place they offered. Food was often incidental to the other attributes of place, especially those attributes that engendered socializing, and the opportunities to watch others socializing. Karl Marx observed that we are "what we eat." But, we suggest that we are as well "where we eat."[8] Third, restaurants mean something very different to workers than to customers. The romance of the roadside, nostalgic or otherwise, pales for the average hourly employee. And the laborer's perspective is not that of management.

The World of Scholarship

Much has already been published about restaurants in America, including and especially those places of the quick-service or fast-food variety. Our favorite books include the following. Excellent overviews are offered by geographer Richard Pillsbury in his *From Boarding House to Bistro: The American Restaurant Then and Now* and by journalist John Mariani in his *America Eats Out*. The rise of the lowly diner, early located outside factory gates on streetcar lines and then later along highways, is treated in John Baeder's *Diners* and Richard J. S. Gutman's *American Diner, Then and Now*. Paul Hirshorn and Steven Izenour, both architects, offer an insightful case study focused on one of the earliest restaurant chains in their book, *White Towers*. The rise of the coffee shop is developed in Alan Hess's *Googie: Fifties Coffee Shop Architecture*. The idea of the "drive-in," covering a spectrum of building types and marketing ideas, is given overview in popular writer Michael Witzel's *The American Drive-In: History and Folklore of the Drive-In Restaurant in American Car Culture* and Jim Heimann's *Car Hops and Curb Service: A History of American Drive-In Restaurants, 1920–1960*. The rise of modern fast-food restaurants is surveyed in Philip Langdon's *Orange Roofs, Golden Arches: The Architecture of American Chain Restaurants*. Finally, Stan Luxenberg examines restaurant franchising in his *Roadside Empires: How the Chains Franchised America*.[9]

A reading of these books would give one no small education focused on restaurants in America. As the titles imply, focus has been given to selected building types, marketing systems, and firms. It is our intent, however, to draw together these and other considerations around the related concepts of landscape and place. We are concerned with the food offered and the distinctive ways in which it has been delivered to restaurant customers. We are concerned with spatial design and architectural decor as restaurants have been constituted as built environment, especially in response to the nation's rising automobility. We are interested in marketing, especially the ways in which restaurants are packaged as places in restaurant chains. We are interested in restaurants as behavior settings insofar as they invite categories of ongoing activity. In short, what have Americans expected from roadside restaurants over the years? What have they received?

What, therefore, is the social or culture import of the roadside restaurant as an aspect of landscape in America?

Evolved over the past 40 years is a diverse scholarly literature organized around the "landscape" idea. Increasingly, those concerned with landscape have come to use the concept of "place" as an integrating idea. As this book is conceptualized around these two basic notions, landscape and place, it seems appropriate to define these terms, and to relate them directly to the study of restaurants. Just what do we mean when we call a restaurant a place? And, how do restaurants contribute to landscape?

LANDSCAPE

Landscape is a term whose meaning continues to change.[10] In English the word originally described what could be seen when one looked out over an area of some broad geographical extent. It implied not only what could be seen, but, as well, what existed to be seen. Indeed, landscape was closely allied with the word *scene* (that seen) and with the word *scenery* (that to be seen). Landscapes were depicted in paintings often following standard compositional devices that were imitated in the creation of real places, especially landscaped estates for European elites. Thus the verb "to landscape" was heavily charged with social class as well as artistic implication. Landscape and landscaping carried strong social status implication since creation of landscapes, real or on canvas, cost money.

In many minds today, the term *landscape* carries natural implication, places where nature has been spared in especially spectacular if not pristine states—at Yosemite or at Yellowstone, for example. At first, only the more affluent could afford to experience first-hand the nation's new national parks although photography, as a new medium for portraying landscape, did bring the experiencing of such places to the masses.

Eventually, the automobile enabled Americans of even modest means to seek and enjoy landscape as scenery, especially in the pastoral scenery of open countryside. Shown in the vintage postcard is the Grand View Hotel and Restaurant on the old Lincoln Highway in Pennsylvania (see fig. I.2). Customers could look out over parts of three states. Americans, as perhaps people everywhere, found the most visually exciting landscape to be where views were down and across broad expanses—the sense of prospect reinforced by succeeding horizons. Important was the exaggerated third-dimension which, in the case of the Grand View, was provided by topographic relief where the Lincoln Highway topped the crest of an Appalachian ridge.

Through the nineteenth century, most Americans lived in rural places on farms and in small towns. As the nation industrialized and became increasingly urban, the demand for nostalgic landscape paintings depicting

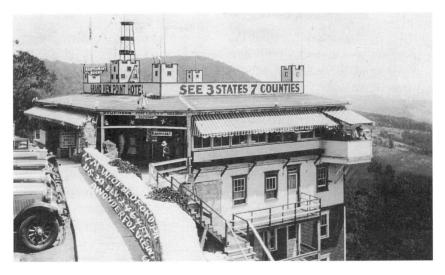

FIG. I.2 The Grand View Hotel and Restaurant east of Bedford, Pa., on U.S. 30, ca. 1930. This roadside establishment took advantage of a view available out over a mountainous landscape.

rural locales increased. Prints displaying barnyards, wood lots, orchards, or country lanes adorned many a parlor wall in houses closely built on narrow city streets substantially devoid of greenery. These were scenes not unlike those to be glimpsed from the Grand View. More affluent urban Americans moved to "suburbs" with tree-lined streets, dooryard gardens, and access to nearby open country. Through the twentieth century, first with the help of the railroads and then, more especially, automobile technology, American cities have been virtually remade in a pastoral image, sprawling subdivisions organized around curvilinear streets and cul-de-sacs.

Commercial as well as residential infrastructure was decentralized in sprawling cities which, in reality, were neither urban nor rural, but a mix of the traditional elements of both. Although it may be argued that the United States has always had an anti-urban bias culturally, the nation nonetheless created and continues to sustain some of the world's most urban (or urbane) places, cities like New York City, Boston, San Francisco. Traditionally, terms like *city scape* or *town scape* were used in lieu of *landscape* in considering such urban environments. Prime among today's urban landscapes are what we designate as "roadsides."

With the widespread adoption of the automobile for personal transportation, commerce spread out along the peripheral highways of suburbia. Central-city streetcar-oriented commercial strips, given over to buses and cars fully, also were modified substantially. To the fore came new breeds of commercial building—not general-purpose storefronts as before, but purpose-built buildings that spoke clearly of their specific functions. The gasoline station was one of the first such building types to emerge. The motel was another. By the 1930s, retail establishments were closely tied to automobile parking—angle parking on widened thoroughfares or, more important, off-street parking lots. After World War II, retail structures, now primarily single-story, drew back from city and suburban streets to face onto sprawling parking lots. Stores were increasingly configured in commercial complexes or shopping centers. Large electric signs rose near curbsides providing visual anchor. Like the "strand" of a popular beach resort or the "midway" of a fair (which both provided prototypes for the automobile strip) the commercial roadside became a glittering advertising extravaganza where buildings, signs, and buildings-as-sign competed for motorists' attention.

Shown in another postcard (one panoramic in scope) is a complex of buildings typical of contemporary interstate highway interchanges (see fig. I.3). A restaurant and gasoline station complements a motel at the Shepherd Hills Truck Stop near Lebanon, Missouri. Here is a landscape created around the needs of automobile travel. Driveways, parking lots, canopies, signs, and building layout and orientation, among other characteristics, speak of a pervasive automobile convenience.

It was difficult for many scholars, especially those whose interests in landscape turned on traditional elite orientations, to embrace commercial strips and the other kinds of seemingly "tasteless" breeds of built environment brought to the fore by automobility. Led by such observers as editor, author,

FIG. I.3 The Shepherd Hills Motel and Restaurant at Lebanon, Mo., ca. 1970. This commercial enterprise combines landscape elements usually developed separately although frequently in close geographical assoçiation. As a functionally integrated landscape it forms a kind of place more than the sum of its parts.

and teacher John B. Jackson, the landscape idea was broadened. Jackson defined landscape as "a concrete three-dimensional shared reality" and focused attention on what he called "vernacular landscape."[11] Advocated was concern with the popular and the commonplace. In emphasizing the "shared reality" aspect of landscape, Jackson and others focused on comprehending landscape function. Landscape meaning was seen to lie primarily, if not exclusively, in landscape use, in the place utility that landscape implied. Yet we will ask our readers to remember that restaurants, as most kinds of places, tend to be experienced in the first instance as visual display. For restaurant customers, place meaning is cued in its initial approximation by what is seen. That is why buildings by the roadside sport exaggerated signs, and why commercial strips exist as loud visual displays.

PLACE

Places are meaningful contexts for behavior.[12] They exist at various scales of contemplation—from whole landscapes (vistas and scenes, for example) to aggregates of structural forms (a complex like that at Shepherd Hills), to specific structures (the Shepherd Hills restaurant or the restaurant parking lot). The advertisement for Pete's Café in Gallup, New Mexico, illustrates (see fig. I.4). On Route 66 in Gallup in the 1950s was a specific location easily identifiable through an automobile windshield where, it was claimed, good eating satisfaction could be obtained. One had only to seek and to find. Places may be thought of as nesting in landscape, and, indeed, of nesting within one another. Inside Pete's Café there was a lunch counter, itself a distinctive place. So also the patron's stool, as he or she leaned forward to read the menu, constituted a place in the hierarchy of places engendered. Places may not even be seen to exist, that is they may not be defined by special structure. The location where two people accidentally meet in a parking lot can take on profound place implication for those briefly involved.

In understanding how places work as behavioral settings, it may be useful to define their salient characteristics. Although not every dimension need be present in every circumstance, outlined below are the characteristics that define places.

Every place has a location. Places exist within a geographical or spatial frame of reference that establishes the "here-ness" and "there-ness" of life. Location was emphasized in the 1950s vintage postcard that advertised the Trent Diner (see fig. I.5). Geographers traditionally have emphasized location in their scholarship, striving to understand why some things are here and not there, why distinctive patterns of geographical distribution occur. Human geographers emphasize the social processes that operate to organize the human world spatially, and the ways that socialization is influenced, in turn, by spatiality. Questing universal laws (or, at least, universally applicable generalizations), some geographers focus on the geometric qualities of geographical "space." In the process of developing "spatial science," with its emphasis on the normative behavior of population aggregates (people and things numerated by region or area, for example), the unique characteristics of place have been ignored as, indeed, the spatial behavior of individuals making such geographical decisions as where to live, where to shop, where to eat.

In the past, geographers rarely thought beyond mere location as a defining criterion of place. But places have meaning for reasons other than mere geographical situation conceptualized in two-dimensional "map-like" frames of reference. Places are actually three-dimensional. Architects work to physically structure places as three-dimensional envelopes or containers for human activity. But even when we restrict ourselves to considering only two-dimensional maps or even floor plans for buildings, it is clear that places have spatial extent as well as location. This spatiality carries territorial implications—for example, an area of centrality (or core) versus a peripheral zone ending with a boundary.

Places involve entrance and exit behaviors that recognize the crossing of a "boundary." The entrance to a restaurant's parking lot, the door to its dining

FIG. I.4 Advertisement for Pete's Café, Gallup, N.M., on U.S. 66, ca. 1950. "This Is the Place!" The restaurant has a vividly painted facade with a sign raised high above. It attracts the eye as a meaningful location.

FIG. I.5 Advertisement for the Trent Diner east of Trenton, N.J., on U.S. 1, ca. 1940. Every restaurant is a function of its location, both site (its actual footprint by the roadside) and situation (its relative position vis-à-vis other sites).

room, the edge of an occupied booth—all carry implications for conduct. The transition between inside and outside (and between private and public space) was deliberately emphasized at Howard's Restaurant in Gatlinburg, Tennessee (see fig. I.6). The door, clearly marked by an electric sign, was easily accessible to the sidewalk and to the street, where cars could be parked close by. But in warm weather the restaurant also functioned outdoors on a terrace, an enticement to ease of customer approach and ease of customer participation. In a restaurant, some spaces are open for everyone's use while circulation in other spaces is restricted to employees. Restaurants may be divided into "front and back regions," where different people and different behaviors occur.[13]

Time is another dimension of place. Places open and close, usually with predictable regularity. Business hours are usually posted on restaurant doors. Many places, like restaurants, function for set durations usually with cyclical pattern—preopening preparation, morning rush, midmorning doldrums, noon rush, midafternoon quiet, dinner rush, closing, and after-hours maintenance. Places change over time as things are added or taken away. Places have life cycles—birth, maturation, old age, death. Some places may be deliberately contrived and advertised, as at the Pioneer Grill in Washington, Pennsylvania, to seem old or historical (see fig. I.7). Permanent closing is usually brought on by technological or social change rendering a restaurant obsolete.

Places reflect change both short- and long-run. Historians in their quest to understand social change emphasize the grand and the monumental in seeking historical significance. They focus on the significant personages and events of the past. Only in recent decades has social history brought to the

Introduction

FIG. I.6 Advertisement for Howard's Restaurant, Gatlinburg, Tenn., ca. 1955. "Meet us at Howard's," the postcard reads. Promoted is a place for socialization beyond the mere consuming of food.

FIG. I.7 Advertisement for the Pioneer Grill, Washington, Pa., ca. 1940. Historical time has been made a theme around which a distinctive place imagery is formed.

fore emphasis on the common and the ordinary. Yet it is to a relatively few social scientists (sociologists, social psychologists, and anthropologists) that one turns to understand the short-run patterns of change in ordinary places such as restaurants.[14]

Every place contains, and thus invites, ongoing behavior viewed as normal. What has gone on before—what appears appropriate—predisposes

15

continuation of the same although the use of any place is, in fact, a continuing negotiation (what might be called a symbolic interaction) through which behavioral change or modification accrues. Eating, relaxing, carrying on conversations, watching people—all these activities are normal to restaurants generally. Exchanging greetings with friends, ordering favorite dishes, or watching a particular fry cook at work may characterize the regular activities of a specific patron in a specific restaurant. Certain kinds of behaviors are recognized as normal in every place, such definition usually sustained by the regulars of a place, especially those with delegated jurisdiction. Owners and managers arbitrate appropriateness in restaurants as "public" places. The police powers of government, of course, provide an environment for management. Restaurants must abide by health and safety codes and civil rights laws.

Places are sought and used according to satisfactions anticipated (if not dissatisfactions avoided). Stereotyped "person-types," if not people actually known to some degree, are seen to be engaged in predictable activities. From these actions expectations can be set regarding the individual's felt needs. Based on previous experience in the same or in similar places, the person, according to his or her intended role with others, forms expectations fitting him- or herself into the ongoing drama of the setting. It might be useful to think of places, restaurants for example, as a kind of theater stage onto which individuals insert themselves as actors. Restaurants contain both customers and those who work to serve customers. Patrons may be strangers or persons known from regular patronage. Workers usually are stratified socially—the manager, the cook, the hostess, the waitress, the busboy. Clear social stratification is evident in the photography of the Plantation Inn at Lake Wales, Florida (see fig. I.8). Employees play different roles in the functioning of this restaurant as place, the relationships engendered varying spatially and temporally in the operation of the restaurant as a behavior setting.

The people who occupy a place use specific props. Places are furnished and arranged to encourage ongoing behaviors. At the Plantation Inn, an atmosphere of aristocratic elegance was cultivated through the use of fine silverware, china, and linen in the front region of the dining room. Other than location, the physical manifestations of place are what most people usually think of when specific places are described. People engaged in various ongoing activities serve to establish place meaning. Behind the scenes, the fry cook is surrounded by vats of boiling grease. The dishwasher manipulates a conveyor belt that feeds dishes into the appropriate machinery. Or, perhaps, a restaurant's kitchen is open to view rather than hidden. Behind the stainless-steel counter, with its implications for sanitation, the operations of cooking and cleaning are placed fully on view to amplify a sense of theater for customers. Furnishings foster utility but also stand symbolic.

PLACE IMAGES

It may be helpful to differentiate between place as object-reality (physical place) and place imagery (symbolic place). Places do exist outside of one's

FIG. I.8 The Plantation Inn, Lake Wales, Fla., ca. 1960. Customers are invited to partake of the "Old South" of clearly stratified class and race relations. "The Inn is famous for the friendly service furnished by an efficiently trained staff—all costumed in the dress of the era of the old Southern Plantation," reads the postcard caption. "The Inn radiates contentment and hospitality of a by-gone day," it emphasizes.

direct experiencing to the extent that they have physical existence. However, places are known to human beings only through impressions garnered through the senses, impressions construed as meaningful on the basis of past experiencing. This knowing is formed around memories obtained through both direct and indirect contact. It is not what a place is so much as what it is thought to be that matters when behavior is formed. It is from assessing the symbolisms of location, time, and people in a place (and their props and activities) that places are known. Relevant comprehensions hinge both on using places first-hand, and on the second-hand information that comes from casual conversation, reading magazines, watching television, and the like. Most important in today's world is the advertising with which we are constantly bombarded. The depicting of commodities in place, and the depicting of places as commodities, substantially fosters our sense of being in the world.

Place images may be thought of in terms of belief, attitude, icon, and intentionality.[15] A belief is an understanding that something does or does not exist. A town does or does not have a drive-in restaurant. Attitude has to do with how a thing is valued pro or con. A town's drive-in may be good, bad, or indifferent. It does or does not serve good food. Service is or is not adequate. Decor is or is not attractive. Beliefs and attitudes are represented or symbolized by things seen or otherwise experienced. Icons are the physical things that symbolize such realities. A cantilevered canopy, a carhop on roller skates, or trays hanging from car windows may stand for the larger collective that is the drive-in. In the careful "packaging" of McDonald's restaurants in the 1960s, as we will emphasize in a subsequent chapter, the "golden arches" came to provide profound symbolic shorthand as icon. Today's American needs no instruction as to its referent.

The beliefs and attitudes that people attach to the icons of places—the overall expectations or place meanings that places engender in their reading or assessment—are a function of behavioral intentionality. People come to the same place (or to the same kinds of place) for a variety of reasons and can take away with them, accordingly, differing notions of place. Intentionality is a function of both past experience and immediate and long-term objectives—internalized values brought to the fore and acted upon in the context at hand. American tourists in Europe immediately identify the golden arches not only with familiar food from home, but as signifying a clean and convenient public toilet, an amenity not easily arrived at in many European towns and cities.

Geographer Robert Sack, in *Place, Modernity, and the Consumer's World*, outlines a strategy for assessing places within the larger context of advertising and media place-promotion generally. We will not elaborate Sack's conceptual scheme, but we will acknowledge several of his basic comprehensions regarding the significance of consumerist places, like roadside restaurants. Consumption is basic to living in today's world, he writes. "Places of consumption are central to modernity. . . . Consumption is a place-orienting and place-altering act," he asserts.[16] As social beings we are a function of the things that we consume which, in turn, depend substantially on the "whereness" of that consumption. Thus, sense of place is used to sell things. Places are packaged as advertising devices and linked through the media to the consumer's pursuit of a particular lifestyle. Modernity is lived and felt through commodified place.

It is helpful to think of people as living in environments fraught with symbolism.[17] Meanings are loaded onto commercial places to guide behavior. Thus restaurants denote the functions that they perform, but often carry as well very strong thematic connotations to tap the dreams and even the fantasies that drive self-actualization. Restaurants are made suggestive of satisfactions that exceed mere eating. Places are designed to be readily read, allowing the customer to draw rapidly on a repertoire of competencies self-satisfying as they effectively knit him or her into wide social practices.[18] Every commercial place, restaurants included, stands as a set of "to whom it may concern" messages to be variously interpreted.

Landscapes and places are more than mere backdrops, mere containers of social life. Rather, geography—organized as landscape and place—is integral to human socialization. Social agendas play out through organization of the built environment, the realities of a spatially differentiated material world, in turn, influencing social formation through the defining of possibilities, the defining of behavioral options. The roadside represents a kind of landscape central to emergent American modernity. Along the roadside the restaurant sits as a kind of place central to the organization of modern life.

The restaurant, like the gas station and the motel, is a form of commodified place, most of which follow the strict formatting of one or another corporate chain. Such places are highly rationalized as they are highly standardized. And yet new restaurant forms continue to emerge, to embrace and encourage social change.

Everything takes place. Geography is not merely incidental to human behavior given that all behavior must necessarily be somewhere contained. Rather, place-orientation is a substantial dimension of human behavior. Expectations that lay the basis for socialization are always place-specific. Society forms around places as places are formed through socialization. With degrees of regularity, we all use places in structuring our lives. In modern America certain categories of place have evolved, a function of a highly materialistic consumer society. The roadside restaurant is one such place. We all have developed varying relationships with restaurants of the roadside. We have learned to "read" them in the seeking of varieties of satisfaction in life. Experiences in these places well up in the forming of personalities to greater or to lesser degrees individual to individual. Most of us have assumed these meanings to be entirely personal. Few of us have thought that some images of place engendered might be widely shared. However, the roadside restaurant is too widespread, and too ingrained in American dietary and recreational habits, not to be an institution of considerable public importance.

Our restaurant behavior (our predisposition to choose, our actual choosing, and our use of restaurants) reflects past personal history anchored in social context. Some restaurants, and some kinds of restaurant, stand out in memory to guide decisionmaking. Other experience, on the other hand, lies forgotten or, perhaps, even repressed in memory. Our relating to common places has much to say about who we have become—who we are—as individuals. But our relating to common places is not strictly personal. Rather, it is anchored in codes of conduct learned and constantly renegotiated in our interactions with others. Thus beyond personal history there are lessons to be learned about society, and the cultural values that underpin society. Let us, therefore, turn from personal reminiscence and the defining of key concepts to exploring and interpreting the roadside restaurant as a place-type significant in the American experience.

CHAPTER 1

The Rise of the Quick-Service Restaurant

W e consider here the development of quick-service restaurants in the United States. Although our emphasis in this book is the automobile-convenient restaurant, such eateries did not suddenly appear created, as it were, without prior context. Rather, roadside stands, drive-ins, and all the other kinds of latter-day roadside restaurants came out of a well-established tradition of offering food quickly to hurried customers. Formats such as the soda fountain and luncheonette, main-street café, and the diner readily come to mind. Our emphasis in this and the next chapter, which does focus on roadside eateries, is building form. What form did quick-service restaurants take over the past 100 years? To what extent did distinctive design vocabularies emerge to define the quick-service restaurant as a unique kind of place? As we will establish, much that came to characterize roadside eating had its origins in the pre-automobile era.

By "architecture" we mean the physical form that restaurants took as places defined at the geographical scale of the retail store—furnishings, their spatial arrangement, the building as structural container, its orientation to the public way, and its facade and signage among other characteristics. Our purpose here is to identify structural designs (and even prototypes) with which restaurant food came to be closely associated. Following chapters will emphasize the growth of restaurant chains whereby lookalike restaurants of various configurations were used to establish local, regional, and national trade territories—the rise of place-product-packaging in the restaurant business. Later chapters will focus on the kinds of food served in restaurants. As we will outline, different architectural forms were variously used by different chains in offering menus built around different focal foods.

Restaurants

As common as restaurants have become, it is difficult to conceptualize life without them. And yet, the restaurant as we know it is a relatively recent innovation in the American experience, truly flourishing only since the Civil War. The word "restaurant" was borrowed from the French, who used it to designate in the 1760s a form of bouillon, a soup of sheep's foot in white sauce.[1] In the nineteenth-century United States the term came to designate "eating houses" as well as "dining rooms," "coffee houses," and "oyster houses." Less popular was the verb "to restaurate"—to eat at a restaurant, to take a meal, or, in a more general sense, to restore.[2]

Before the Civil War, food outside the home could be found in a variety of places. Travelers could obtain drink and "victuals" in the coaching inns and taverns. Hotels maintained dining rooms that catered not only to transients but to long-term residents renting rooms by week, month, or year. Boardinghouses, many catering only to bachelor males, also offered meals to nonresidents on a contractual basis. But it was the coffee house, which served as a center for socializing and conduct of business, and the oyster house, which specialized in oysters preserved and shipped in salt brine, that provided templates for a new kind of freestanding eating place not specifically tied to overnight accommodation. The craze for coffee reflected both its ready availability, a cheap import from South America, and the American aversion after the Revolution to customs English, such as drinking tea. The craze for oysters reflected their cheap abundance (before industrial pollutants destroyed the oyster beds of New England and diminished those of the Chesapeake Bay) and the ability to ship them quickly over long distances, especially with development of the nation's railroads. Oysters served as a kind of exotica in otherwise bland diets. Neither the coffee house nor the oyster house operated on a strict schedule where people entered, sat, and ate by the sound of a bell. Rather, during business hours, customers could enter and order on a "come and get it" basis.

Members of the Del-Monico family, perhaps more than any other entrepreneurs, popularized the restaurant idea, applying the name to several Manhattan eating establishments in the 1830s. Introduced was a French "Parisian" cuisine that brought immediate approval from New York City's social elites. As with many words of high status or class implication, the term *restaurant* was quickly expropriated to common use, reflecting the leveling instincts of a new popular culture built around democratic political ideals. Although some restaurants, like the various Delmonico's, catered to the affluent, most catered to the working man, both the lowly hourly industrial laborer and the up-and-coming salaried clerk employed in store or office.

The saloon was another place where a light meal could be obtained, at least at noontime—what came to be called "lunch." Free or very inexpensive food was made available as a kind of "loss leader," saloonkeepers taking their profits from the beer or other drinks consumed. Such lunches, usually grabbed on the fly, fit the needs of workers regulated by the clock. Once Prohibition was introduced, first state by state and then nationwide in 1919, saloon food disappeared, giving the quick-service restaurants a substantial boost.

Because the restaurant idea was applied to different kinds of establishments decade by decade, it is difficult, even for recent years, to estimate the numbers of establishments or to estimate levels of patronage. In 1958, the U.S. Bureau of the Census counted 229,815 eating places and 114,925 drinking places; the figures stood in 1982 at 301,700 and 80,000 respectively.[3] In 1967, over $91 billion was spent by Americans on food, $22 billion (or 24 percent) on food and beverage bought and consumed outside the home in places other than clubs, schools, hospitals, prisons, and on trains and airplanes. Included, besides restaurants, were hotels and drugstores.[4] In 1978, the food-service industry generated sales of some $70 billion, making it the third largest American industry, and the nation's largest employer with some 4 million employees earning some $15 billion.[5] In 1983, quick-service restaurants featuring fast food constituted some 40 percent of the nation's eating and drinking places.[6] Americans were spending nearly 40 percent of their food dollars at restaurants, the average person eating out 3.7 times a week.[7] By 1990, the estimated number of "limited menu" restaurants had grown to 188,755.[8] In 1992, the top 200 restaurant chains accounted for more than 50 percent of all domestic restaurant sales, surpassing independent restauranteurs for the first time.[9] By 1996, the restaurant business in the United States was a $212-billion industry.[10]

Not only have Americans become more dependent on restaurant food, but the very nature of the American diet has been changed by eating out. Not only did restaurants appeal through speedy service, made possible by frying and the introduction of frozen and other "convenience" foods, but restaurants came to promote highly flavorful "novelty" foods, the taste for which came to alter American dietary habits even at home. Between 1960 and 1976, beef consumption rose from 64.3 to 95.4 pounds per year per person. One restaurant chain, McDonald's, was selling over 6 million hamburgers a day in 1976. Like the oyster before, the hamburger, the hot dog, the french fry, and the pizza slice were introduced originally as mere novelties. But, unlike the oyster, the supply of these latter foods increased decade to decade until they became a dietary norm rather than an exotic indulgence. Thus did consumption of frozen potatoes jump from 6.6 to 36.8 pounds a year per person between 1960 and 1976, as did the use of hard cheese from 8.3 to 15.9 pounds, and tomato sauce and paste from 7.6 to 13.3 pounds.[11]

Not all Americans enjoyed equal access to restaurants. The less affluent, as we have implied, were restricted largely to limited-menu establishments where the price of food remained a prime attractor. Originally, restaurants were primarily masculine places, customers being overwhelmingly male, as were cooks and counter and table help. First in the kitchen, then as waitresses out front, did women come to the restaurant scene. And as women provided more and more of the labor, restaurants opened to unescorted women as customers. In the American South, and to lesser degrees elsewhere in the nation, African-Americans were regularly denied service in restaurants before the Civil Rights Act of 1964. In the South, blacks were either excluded entirely or, if admitted to white-patronized restaurants, required to enter by separate doors and sit at separate tables. Many black communities supported their own restaurants accordingly.[12] Although segregation kept blacks and whites from eating together, it did not keep them from eating the same kinds of food separately. Of course, much of the kitchen labor in white-only restaurants was African-American.

Restaurants reflected the larger social contexts into which they were embedded. As a kind of place important in everyday socializing they became important targets for social reformers. When African-Americans set about to confront segregation laws, they organized sit-ins at lunch counters. Traditional social symbolism ultimately was changed through the "violation" of traditional behavioral norms. Eventually, restaurants of all kinds were opened to everyone. The common restaurant proved an ideal place to demonstrate and partially remedy a deprived minority's discontent.

Our purpose in this chapter is to explore the kinds of restaurants that ordinary Americans used in living, working, and traveling in the United States before the era of the automobile. We also describe briefly the continued influence that these places enjoyed after the nation's reorientation to motor cars and highway travel. We start, therefore, with hotel dining rooms and coffee shops, soda fountains, luncheonettes and lunchrooms, cafeterias and automats, and diners as the prevalent quick-service restaurant types before the era of automobile convenience.

Hotel Dining Rooms and Coffee Shops

The hotel in America grew out of the stagecoach inn, reoriented to travel by railroad and streetcar, and finally to travel by automobile. By 1900, leading big-city hotels were mammoth structures with hundreds of guest rooms (and sometimes thousands) with large public spaces including ballrooms and, of course, formal dining rooms. They echoed the grandeur of the European palace, with a preponderance for French rococo or Italianate baroque or Beaux Arts classicism in interior ornamentation. Flowered carpets, brocaded wallpaper, crystal chandeliers, and gilded mirrors were very much in vogue in dining-room decor, all articulated in emulation of European aristocracy. Shown is the dining room of the Rosslyn Hotel in Los Angeles, a large room of classical motif that echoed, as well, Arts and Crafts influence in tiled floor, woodwork, and furniture design (see fig. 1.1). Serving primarily businessmen, hotel dining rooms featured heavy meals built around red meat and an abundance of alcohol.

For lighter meals, guests might repair to a hotel bar and grill or, especially for breakfast or lunch, to a hotel coffee shop. To make up for lost dining-room and bar trade with the coming of Prohibition, hotels catered more specifically to women and to family groups through lighter fare, more female employees, and simplified interior decor more feminine and more "home-like."[13] Hotel coffee shops reflected the increased informality of relaxed social codes driven forward, substantially, by the increased geographical mobility of automobile travel. New automobile entrances and new coffee shops were often located side by side as, for example, at the Hotel Pittenger at Centralia, Illinois (see fig. 1.2). Small towns like Centralia could only emulate

FAST
FOOD

FIG. 1.1 Dining room of Rosslyn Hotel in downtown Los Angeles, ca. 1910.

FIG. 1.2 Hotel Pittenger, Centralia, Ill., ca. 1930.

remotely the big-city grand hotel and the Pittenger's coffee shop, therefore, was scaled down to fit the town. One side of the small room was configured as a soda fountain where drink and food was prepared. The remainder of the room was given over to tables and chairs. Ornamentation was minimal, but reflected big-city tastefulness. A kitchen beyond contained stoves and ovens, additional food-preparation counters, sinks for dishwashing, and storage cabinets.

In 1928, the Albert Pick Corporation, a hotel outfitting company, estimated that the average 75-room hotel, like the Pittenger, generated $57,480 from guest-room rental (based on an assumed 70 percent occupancy), and $52,600 (or 42 percent of total revenues) from food service.[14] For 150- and 225-room hotels, the proportion of revenues obtained from dining rooms and coffee shops stood at 41 percent. Hotel restaurants, therefore, represented an important revenue source for the hospitality industry. Indeed, the typical hotel traditionally made most of its profits from its public spaces, room rentals providing an "in-house" clientele for restaurant and other services.

In the early era of motoring, the automobile tourist looked to old railroad hotels for both overnight accommodation and food. Included were the resort hotels that catered especially to more affluent women who, with their children, escaped from city heat in summer months. In the more progressive towns and cities, investor syndicates, often formed through a chamber of commerce or booster club, promoted new upscale hotels with automobile entrances and nearby storage garages. There especially did dining rooms and coffee shops coexist as complementary formal and informal spaces, the coffee shop reflecting directly the relaxed dress codes appropriate to motoring. The hotel restaurant greatly eased the traveler's problem of deciding where to eat in a strange locality.

Soda Fountains, Luncheonettes, and Lunchrooms

A variety of quick-service restaurants embraced, in whole or in part, innovations brought forward in the nation's "soda fountains." The soda drink, compounded of carbonated soda water blended with flavored cream syrup, originated in 1839 at the shop of Eugene Roussel, a perfume dealer in Philadelphia.[15] The idea spread quickly, with small but highly ornamented dispensing mechanisms for table- and countertops, called soda fountains, manufactured by a host of companies. When proper amounts of sulfuric acid, carbonic acid, and water were filtered through marble dust, carbon dioxide gas was released, the liquid produced charged with harmless bubbles. Mixed with extracts of fruit, flavored soda water was sold under a variety of generic names—birch beer, pepsin, ginger ale, sarsaparilla. In 1874 Robert Green, at the Franklin Institute of Philadelphia, added ice cream to soda water to produce the first ice cream soda.[16] Stores with soda fountains quickly added iceboxes in which to store ice cream, and ice with which to cool drinks. It was not until 1903, however, that the now-familiar soda-fountain prototype emerged with its two units—a large high-back section

FIG. 1.3 Advertisement for the Russ Company. (*Source: The Soda Fountain* 14 [Dec. 1915]: 2.)

FIG. 1.4 The Palace, Knoxville, ca. 1915. The back of the advertising card reads: "The Palace. Knoxville's Finest Soda Grill. We make our own candies. Quick lunch for Busy Folks."

heavily ornamented with a large mirror or painting, and a companion low front section configured as a counter at which customers could sit on stools (see figs. 1.3 and 1.4). These fountains mimicked the bar fixtures of saloons, employing wood or other heavy materials such as Italian marble or Mexican onyx. By 1908, there were an estimated 75,000 soda fountains located in a variety of different kinds of stores, especially drugstores and confectionery shops.[17]

The Rise of the Quick-Service Restaurant

Beginning in the 1880s, many stores with soda fountains began to add light food, especially sandwiches, to complement their soda drinks and ice cream desserts. And, with the coming of counters at which customers sat, the luncheonette was born. Food increased trade, especially at noontime when specialty desserts were in low demand. Sandwiches, soups, and other light fare also increased business beyond the warm-weather months. In Houston, the Rouse's Drug Stores advertised, "In order to maintain the operating expenses of our enormous Soda Fountains during the Winter months we have inaugurated a Light Lunch Service at the Fountains every day."[18] Perhaps drugstores, more than any other type of business, embraced the soda fountain/luncheonette in largest numbers. However, fountains and lunch counters also commonly appeared in department stores, in the new dime stores, and in railroad stations. Only the fancy passenger trains carried dining cars, most railroad travelers dependent for food on lunchrooms in depots. Perhaps the most celebrated were the Fred Harvey restaurants operated for the Atchison, Topeka, and Santa Fe Railroad. The hurried railroad traveler came to personify the lunch-counter customer, but the railroad station was but one place where early fast food flourished. With the coming of Prohibition, many saloons became soda fountains and luncheonettes. The soda fountain also drove establishment of "lunchrooms," eating places less oriented to the dessert crowd and more oriented to seekers of cheap and quick meals morning, noon, and night.

The habits of quick eating, built around coffee, soft drinks, and novelty sandwiches like hamburgers, brought condemnations. Wrote one anonymous medical doctor quoted and pilloried in an industry trade journal: "The good, old fashioned American meal of ham, cabbage and potatoes . . . is being rapidly supplanted by sugary concoctions of the soda jerker's ingenuity." "This indiscreet eating," he continued, "with almost a total lack of exercise, now features the life of the average businessman. Up at 8 in the morning; a hasty breakfast, ride downtown in an automobile; a ten minute lunch, of miscellaneous sugary drinks in the quick lunch or drug store, back to the office, home in an automobile—they call that a day. . . . The consequences are indigestion, bad nerves, decaying teeth, restless nights and cutting down the span of life," he argued.[19]

The layout of soda fountains and luncheonettes varied, but always employed the basic organizing device of counter and stool. At the U-shaped lunch counter diagrammed, customers sat facing one another across a kitchen galley (see fig. 1.5). The cash register at the top of the U, like everything else in the layout, was operated from the service aisle. Glasses and chi-

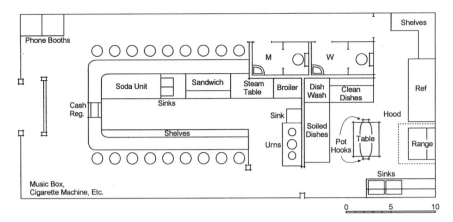

FIG. 1.5 U-shaped counter plan. (*Source:* Ernest M. Fleischman, *The Modern Luncheonette* [Stamford, Conn.: Dahl Publishing Co., 1947], plate 2.)

naware were cleaned in an adjacent room. Here was a highly efficient plan that minimized movement. No wonder the counter formula came to thrive in a host of restaurant venues. Lunch counters remained central to the restaurant idea in America for over 50 years. They continue in certain kinds of restaurants today.

From early soda fountains came America's most popular soft drinks. Atlantan John S. Pemberton concocted a syrup of sugar and other flavorings, including kola leaf and kola nut extract, and a small amount of artificial synthetic caffeine.[20] Pemberton, in and out of the wholesale drug business throughout his business career, previously had perfected such fanciful products as Indian Queen Hair Dye, Triplex Liver Pills, and Globe Flower Cough Syrup. His new syrup was marketed by an Atlanta druggist who combined it with soda water to create a new drink under the name Coca-Cola. Local businessman Asa Candler organized the Coca-Cola Company and launched an aggressive advertising campaign across the American South featuring signs of red, white, and green. Quickly, Coca-Cola began to supplant locally concocted syrups in soda fountains nationwide. Indeed, the Coca-Cola sign, when hung over the front door of a drugstore or other business, became perhaps the clearest cue to soda-fountain services ever developed.

Pepsi-Cola was the invention of Caleb D. Bradham, a New Bern, North Carolina, druggist in search of a cure for dyspepsia. Patented in 1903, Pepsi-Cola contained pepsin, a digestive enzyme marketed as a stomach soother.[21] However, it was entrepreneur Charles Guth who created the Pepsi-Cola Company, turning, as did Cola-Cola also, to marketing a soft drink in bottles through a system of bottling franchises organized territorially across the United States. Royal Crown Cola originated in Columbus, Georgia, in 1905, the work of another pharmacist.[22] Dr. Pepper originated in a Waco, Texas, drugstore in 1885.[23] The Dr. Pepper Company's lemon-lime soft drink proved so successful that the firm changed its name to the Seven-Up Corporation in 1929. There were, of course, many imitators, especially of the Coca-

Cola idea, including the now-forgotten Ameri-Cola, Cola Queen, Dixie Cola, Its-A-Cola, Kiss-Kola, and Taka-Cola.

Out of the luncheonette evolved the lunchroom, most retaining the lunch counter as a principal feature. By 1920, chains of lunchrooms were well established in most large cities, although most chains comprised only two or three establishments sharing a name and advertised as "a system." Larger chains also shared central commissaries as well. The Thompson lunchrooms in Chicago and the Baltimore Dairy Lunch Rooms in that city both numbered over 100 stores by 1920; Waldorf Lunch operated a total of 75 stores spread from Springfield, Massachusetts, where the company was headquartered, to New York, Boston, Buffalo, and Providence.[24] The lunchrooms operated by Child's Unique Dairy Lunch in New York City occupied, as with all the chains, standard storefronts. Locations were pedestrian-oriented and were sited, accordingly, along streetcar lines or near subway station entrances. Each restaurant was long and narrow, its axis perpendicular to sidewalk and street. Down one side ran a long counter, with a line of stools, tables, and chairs filling the remainder of the room. Customers on stools sat facing the countermen (eventually replaced by waitresses), and, of course, a rear counter where food was prepared. On entering, customers received a ticket to be stamped, paying a cashier as they left.[25] However, at Waldorf locations, as well as at Baltimore Lunch locations, food supplied from central commissaries was dispensed at counters in the rear of each store and carried by customers on trays to one-armed chairs or to small booths.

Schrafft's, developed by Frank Shattuck, originated in Boston in 1898. By 1915, the company had nine stores in Manhattan, one in Brooklyn, and one in Syracuse besides its Boston facility. By 1923, the chain had grown to 22 stores, and by 1934 to 42.[26] The company was originally, and remained, a candy manufacturer, its confectionery–soda fountain stores created as sales outlets for its candy. The firm targeted as customers women as well as men, and was one of the first to employ women managers. "Many of our customers are secretaries and stenographers . . . who must watch their pocketbooks," Shattuck reported in an industry trade journal.[27] A journalist writing in *The Soda Fountain* found the Schrafft stores "equipped with fine fixtures and decorated with dignity and taste." "In most of the stores fine selected walnut has been used for wood work and the decorative scheme carried out in early American period furniture."[28] Schrafft's, and the other luncheon chains, were early attempts at place-product-packaging, the replicating of lookalike stores in chains defining sales territories.[29]

We should emphasize that most lunchrooms, like most of the soda fountains and luncheonettes that they closely emulated, were not chain-operated. The lunch-counter business, certainly before World War I, was often linked in a "mom and pop" operation to confectionery sales—candies, bakery goods, and, sometimes, fruit sales. Candy and baked goods were usually made on the premises in a back room or basement work space. It was the kind of business that many immigrant families could aspire to early in the twentieth century. Although entrepreneurial and managerial talent was

✷ ✷ ✷ **NOW OPEN** ✷ ✷ ✷

The **HACIENDA**

106 East Front Street

15c Plate Lunch 15c

CHOICE OF MEATS, POTATOES, SALADS & DESSERT

MENU CHANGED DAILY

Variety of Sandwiches   **BEER**
Hot and Cold   Bottled or Draft

FIG. 1.6 Advertisement for the Hacienda Café, Bloomington, Ill., ca. 1915.

FIG. 1.7 Tingles' Café, Asheville, N.C., ca. 1935.

FIG. 1.8 Ellis' Café, Huntington, Ind., ca. 1935.

FIG. 1.9 Derby's Café, Chamberlain, S.D., ca. 1950.

drawn from many different ethnic groups, varying, of course, from one part of the country to another (and even from one city to another within a region), Greek-Americans made an impact almost everywhere in the United States. The "Greek" confectionery shop with its soda fountain and candy counter was an important urban fixture across the United States.

Main-Street Cafés

Small-town main streets and city business districts came to sport small restaurants usually called cafés. They, too, used the soda fountain and lunch counter as an organizing idea, but placed more emphasis on table service. Booths, which provided some privacy for customers and were easy for proprietors to maintain, won rapid acceptance. Main-street cafés promoted both quick service, especially at breakfast and at lunch, as well as more leisurely dining, especially in the evening. Usually a wider menu was available than at lunchrooms, and rarely were candies and bakery goods sold. Food—breakfasts, noon lunches, or dinners, and both light and heavy evening meals—were the emphasis (see fig. 1.6). Occupying an ordinary storefront was Tingles' Café in Asheville, North Carolina, pictured about 1935 (see fig. 1.7). Although little had changed inside the restaurant since its opening in 1918, the exterior facade displayed a new neon sign configured in the "modern" style. Banks and other sources of finance capital encouraged restaurants in standard retail spaces. Should a restaurant fail, as Tingles' surely had not, its space could be readily occupied by another business, even of a very different kind.

Standardized commercial space in main-street and downtown business blocks—rectangular in shape with one narrow end to sidewalk and street—set a template driving much standardization in restaurant arrangement town to town, city to city. Space was organized similarly at Ellis' Café in Huntington, Indiana, depicted in a 1930s postcard, and at Derby's Café in Chamberlain, South Dakota, depicted in the 1950s (see figs. 1.8 and 1.9). Ellis' was recommended by the American Automobile Association and listed in its guidebook.

Beginning in the 1930s, and accelerating after World War II, main-street cafés "modernized." Not only were signs upgraded, but whole facades were replaced. Adopted were "open fronts" with wide expanses of glass. Brightly lit, interiors were opened to street view, especially at night. An interior, replete with fixtures streamlined in light-reflecting materials, showed like a kind of sign to be read easily by passing motorists. The storefront had to accomplish several objectives, wrote one promoter of glass reconstruction. "It must be the medium that identifies the restaurant and sets it apart from others. It must reflect character, quality and cleanliness to the potential patrons. It must present easy access to the interior."[30]

Main-street cafés were important places for socializing, counter and stool and table and booth offering seating arrangements conducive to categories of social interaction. The café became so well known to so many that novelists, like Sinclair Lewis, could regularly place characters in fictional café settings without need of explaining social implications. In Lewis's 1926 novel *Oil!*, a young boy, the narrator of the book, enters the Elite Café with his father. "Dad was in his element in a place like this. He liked to 'josh' the waitress; he knew all kinds of comic things to say, funny names for things to eat. He would order his eggs 'sunnyside up' or 'with their eyes open, please.'"[31] Today, the once-ubiquitous main-street café has all but disappeared. Journalist Gary Thatcher has offered a guide to their discovery, at least in his part of the country, the American South.[32] Look for a family name, he writes. "Watch out for any place that starts with 'La' or 'El,'" he warns. A sign near the door advising that the Rotary Club meets there is a good omen. Somewhere will be displayed a photo of the owner's family. On counters and tables, glass sugar dispensers, with screw-on pouring tops, stand erect. Look also for bottles of ketchup and vinegar. William Least Heat Moon, in his classic travel narrative, *Blue Highways,* identifies calendars—no fewer than five clearly displayed—as the critical cue to quality café tradition.[33]

Cafeterias and Automats

Emulating the factory assembly line, customers pushed trays along elongated counters, putting together their own meals as they moved along a cafeteria line. The all-male Exchange Buffet, opened in New York City in 1885, may have been the earliest restaurant utilizing self-service.[34] The Young Women's Christian Association (YWCA) operated some of the earliest serving lines at its downtown facilities in eastern cities. William and Samuel Childs, at several of their lunchrooms, also innovated buffet counters with customer cues about 1898.[35] The cafeteria idea spread so rapidly that people in various parts of the country came to claim the cafeteria as their own. So

FIG. 1.10 The Blue Boar Cafeteria, Cleveland, ca. 1940.

popular did the new restaurant form become along the Pacific Coast that California was dubbed "the Cafeteria Belt."[36] It was in Los Angeles that Helen Mosher opened her cafeteria in 1905 with all female cooks. But it was in the American South and Southwest that cafeterias enjoyed persisting popularity well beyond World War II. As John Mariani points out, the cafeteria struck "just the proper balance of formality and traditionalism, serving a solid old-fashioned Southern cooking—hot biscuits and gravy, fried chicken, turkey with corn-bread dressing, fried catfish, mashed potatoes, numerous vegetables, and congealed salads."[37] Southern hospitality played out with waiters carrying customer trays.

Required was a large-scale operation to bring costs per serving down to profitable levels. The typical establishment, as, for example, Cleveland's Blue Boar Cafeteria (shown about 1940), occupied a large room, along one end of which ran a cafeteria line (see fig. 1.10). Most cafeteria lines were organized with trays and silverware first, then desserts, salads, entrees, and drinks. The hungry customer was tempted by dessert before common sense or a tray loaded with other food intervened. Clearly, cafeterias were for heavy meals rather than light fare. Yet, with assembly-line speed, even a full repast could be obtained and consumed in relatively little time. Cafeterias remained popular with older Americans living on fixed incomes.

Although most cafeterias were independently owned and operated, the cafeteria format also lent itself to chain development. A Blue Boar Cafeteria, for example, also operated in Louisville, both establishments part of the larger Britling chain. Britling Cafeterias in 1940 were located in Memphis, Tulsa, and Oklahoma City, as well as Birmingham where the firm originated. Among the earliest and largest chains were the Boos Brothers Cafeterias (established first in Los Angeles in 1906 and spread to other Pacific Coast cities), Morrison's (established in Mobile in 1920 and spread across the South),

FAST FOOD

FIG. 1.11 Morrison's Cafeteria, Ocala, Fla., ca. 1970.

Laughner's (also established in 1920 but at Indianapolis and spread across the Middle West), and S&W (established at Asheville in 1929 and thus expanded across the South).[38] Large chains in the 1990s, most still only regional in geographical reach, included Furr's (of Lubbock, Tex.), Morrison's, Piccadilly (of Baton Rouge), Luby's (of San Antonio), Wyatt (of Dallas), and S&S or Smith and Sons (of Macon, Georgia). The cafeteria, at first introduced in downtown storefronts, has long moved to the shopping mall and other roadside locations. The chains, like Morrison's, developed, beginning in the 1950s, self-standing highway-oriented restaurants with off-street parking (see fig. 1.11). In the 1950s, the buffet—often called a smorgasbord (thus given Swedish implication)—enjoyed limited popularity, a revival of the cafeteria idea. In the 1990s, the buffet format revived again. Among the largest cafeteria operations today are the Old Country Buffet and Home Town Buffet chains (Table 1.1).

Cafeterias were more impersonal than main-street cafés, customers cuing and helping themselves. Perhaps the most impersonal restaurants of all were the automats developed by the Horn and Hardart Company first in Philadelphia in 1902, and then in New York City 10 years later (see fig. 1.12). The automats took the self-service of the cafeterias one step further. Borrowed was an idea previously perfected in Sweden for dispensing food through banks of small windows. Configured along the walls of the restaurant were hundreds of small glass compartments, six by eight inches in size, each with a coin slot and a knob. Through the glass the customer could see the food—a sandwich, a salad, a dessert—placed there from behind by a kitchen employee. The customer inserted the appropriate coin, lifted the glass door, and removed the dish. In 1950, the firm operated 85 automats supplied by commissaries.[39] In 1979 there were only two automats left, the

TABLE 1.1 Leading Cafeteria Chains, 1996

Chain	Headquarters	Units Worldwide	Sales (in millions)	Sales Rank Top 300
Old Country Buffet	Eden Prairie, Minn.	259	$526	54
Luby's	San Antonio	204	450	60
Piccadilly	Baton Rouge	130	277	81
Morrison's	Atlanta	155	270	83
Furr's	Lubbock, Tex.	108	189	118
Home Town Buffet	San Diego	84	170	125
K + W	Winston-Salem, N.C.	33	95	176
Fresh Choice	Santa Clara, Calif.	56	76	209
MCL	Indianapolis	28	56	256
Country Harvest Buffet	Bellevue, Wash.	28	53	265

Source: Restaurants and Institutions 107 (July 15, 1997), 66.

The Rise of the Quick-Service Restaurant

FIG. 1.12 Horn and Hardart's Times Square Automat, New York City, 1939.

firm having converted most of its locations to Burger King outlets. Indeed, Horn and Hardart, as we will discuss subsequently, became one of the nation's largest restaurant management firms adopting at its locations, as a franchisee, the brands of other companies.

The automat was an early form of vending. Vending by machine was made popular after World War II, but only for soft drinks and packaged snack foods. In the late 1950s and early 1960s, several companies, including White Tower with its Tower-O-Matic restaurant idea, experimented unsuccessfully with fully automated eateries.[40] Vending in restaurants proved too impersonal, even in the big metropolis where eating anonymously in the "lonely crowd" of an automat could be taken as a sign of urban sophistication.

Diners

Perhaps the most highly personalized restaurants of all were the diners. Organized tightly around the lunch-counter plan, most diners placed employees and customers in almost intimate proximity. The diner was born of the lunch wagon, then evolved into a vague simulation of the railroad dining car (some early diners actually were converted railroad cars), and then into a narrow range of distinctive building forms through restaurant chain development. The term *diner* was expropriated, especially in the Northeastern section of the United States, to signify a range of small restaurants from main-street cafés to highway cafés. Our focus here, however, is on the diner as an architecturally distinctive restaurant form.

In 1872 in Providence, Rhode Island, Walter Scott launched his Pioneer Lunch, a wagon stationed at a downtown intersection after 8 P.M. Sandwiches were sold to night workers through a side window.[41] In 1887, Samuel Jones of Worcester, Massachusetts, created a lunch wagon where customers could enter and stand at a small counter out of the weather. In 1891, Charles Palmer patented his "Owl" lunch wagon, which featured a small counter with stools, putting several of these wagons onto the streets of Worcester each night. Night lunch wagons quickly appeared in many cities, especially in New England and the Middle Atlantic states. In Manhattan, the Church Temperance Society distributed free coffee and 10-cent meals from a dozen wagons in an attempt to keep men out of saloons. Thomas Buckley, whose New England Lunch Wagon Company operated in some 275 towns and cities, held the title of "Lunch Wagon King." He introduced in 1897 a wagon prototype with nickel-plated coffee urns, tile mosaics, and lamps on ebony pedestals. More important, he moved the diner industry from the custom-making of wagons one at a time to large-scale production on speculation, a path followed by a host of emergent wagon manufacturers. Buckley also built the White Home Café in Worcester, an immobile lunch stand with soda fountain.[42]

The term *diner* was coined by Patrick Tierney of New Rochelle, New York, who sought to upgrade the lunch wagon into something resembling more a railroad dining car. He incorporated into his modular buildings, constructed to be fixed on off-street sites, more restaurant amenities—lengthy counters with stools along one wall, booths along the other, enlarged kitchen and storage spaces, and toilet facilities. Beginning in the 1930s, most diner manufacturers "streamlined" their buildings, adopting simplified modern designs suggestive of speed. Reflecting changes in aircraft design, the streamline look was given to railroad trains, automobiles, and a host of household appliances such as stoves and refrigerators (see fig. 1.13). The streamlining of diners called for "smooth, tear-drop packages" with "surfaces and textures brushed, polished, rounded, or wrapped."[43] Also in the 1930s, these new

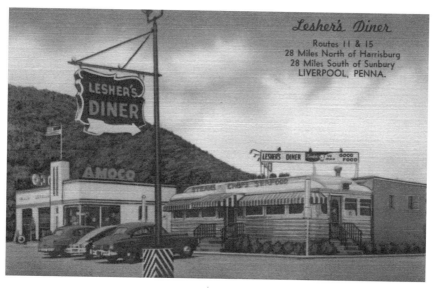

FIG. 1.13 Lesher's Diner, Liverpool, Pa., ca. 1950. The back of the postcard reads: "Breakfast, Luncheon, Dinner. Specializing in steaks, chops, seafood. Homemade pastries baked in our kitchen. Have your car serviced at adjoining AMOCO station while dining in our delightful diner. 24 hour service."

deluxe diners began to appear along the nation's highways, the diner previously primarily a fixture of factory-gate and streetcar-stop locations.

Operating in the United States in 1932 were an estimated 4,000 modular lunchrooms.[44] Twenty years later the number had grown to an estimated 5,000. In 1952, the Jerry O'Mahoney Company of Elizabeth, New Jersey, then the nation's largest manufacturer of diners (producing some 30 per year), offered units ranging in price from $36,500 (for a 48-foot model), to $60,000 (for an 80-foot building).[45] Customers paid one-fourth of the diner's price as down payment, the rest in installments. Towed to construction sites by truck, diners were not taxed in most communities as real property, but at lower rates as personal property. That, and the ability of owners to take accelerated depreciation on buildings, made for significant tax advantage. Relatively cheap to buy, build, and maintain, the modular diner, if unsuccessful, could be partially disassembled and moved to a potentially more profitable location.

The diner came to symbolize a kind of commonplace theater. Author Joseph Manzo described breakfast at the typical diner as follows: "A cacophony of sounds, smells and sights would start the customer's day. The rattling of cups and the rustling of newspapers mixed with the chatter of customers, snappy talking waitresses and a manager greeting people provided the backdrop for the diner's food."[46] The cook juggled orders at the grill, performing a kind of ballet. Waitresses scurried to refill coffee cups when not delivering plates or cleaning away dishes. The smell of coffee and frying bacon permeated the air. At the counter sat business proprietors, construction workers, clerks, and truck drivers—a cross-section of America, the na-

FIG. 1.14 Advertising tag illustration, White Castle System Eating Houses Corporation, ca. 1935.

FIG. 1.15 White Tower Restaurant, Dayton, 1995.

tion's democratic ideals apparently validated. At the diner, wrote another journalist, "one may swing democratically on a revolving stool and watch the chef do miraculous things."[47]

Various restaurant chains emerged in the 1920s to employ the diner idea. Here was the first large-scale embrace of place-product-packaging in the restaurant business, the use of duplicate buildings in the creation of a distinctive business system. Foregoing a broad menu, these new chains—with names like White Castle, White Tower, Little Tavern, and Toddle House—focused on the hamburger sandwich. After five stores were opened in Wichita, the White Castle System of Eating Houses expanded to Omaha (1921), Kansas City (1924), St. Louis (1925), Minneapolis–St. Paul (1926), Cincinnati, Louisville, and Indianapolis (1927), Columbus, Detroit, and Chicago (1929), and Newark and New York City (1930).[48] By 1931, the chain had 115 units.[49] The company developed a white brick, and later porcelain-enameled, castellated prototype building, carefully replicating it from city to city (see fig. 1.14). The castle image was intended to symbolize "strength, permanence and stability," and the white "purity and cleanliness."[50]

The White Castle image prompted immediate imitation. In 1926 the White Tower System was launched in Milwaukee, the firm also adopting a small, white, castle-like building.[51] Surface ornament was kept to a minimum, the medieval motif suggested by a tower, pseudo-buttresses along the sides of each building, and arched tower. Subsequent porcelain-enameled buildings were fully streamlined (see fig. 1.15). Everything was bold and offered sharp contrast with older neighboring buildings, especially when lit at night. As with White Castle, the White Towers functioned as signs—sign-like buildings readily identifiable and readily associated with their distinctive food. From Milwaukee, White Tower spread to Chicago, Detroit, Cleveland, Pittsburgh, Philadelphia, New York, and Boston among other cities. In the mid-1950s, White Tower had grown to some 230 stores.[52] Other chains that spread from city to city included Little Tavern (founded in Louisville in 1927), Toddle House (Houston, 1929), Krystal (Chattanooga, 1932), White Hut (Toledo, 1935), and Royal Castle (Miami Beach, 1938).[53]

Although we tend today to equate quick-service eating with automobile convenience, the fact is that many important attributes of the fast-food restaurant were worked out long before automobile use became widespread. Save for excluded minorities, the American restaurant by 1910 had come of age, catering to customers from across society's spectrum. The principal organizing device was the lunch counter with stools. At the counters of America's confectionery stores, hotel coffee shops, drugstores, dime stores, main-street cafés, and diners, Americans sat rubbing elbows. Beyond the counters in many restaurants ranged tables and booths arrayed to offer more privacy. By the 1920s, the format varied hardly at all from restaurant to restaurant except, as in the case of the smallest diners, tables and booths were eliminated. Only the cafeteria and the automat offered a different option, discounting for the moment the formal dining room. But, self-service formats were not widely adopted across the United States, being restricted primarily to big cities, and, in the case of the automats, adopted only in two cities. Many of the pre-automobile restaurant types continued to flourish after the automobile's arrival. Some, like the main-street café and diner, evolved along the nation's new highways little modified. However, as we explore in the next chapter, customers arriving by motor car made new demands and opened new possibilities. The quick-service restaurant changed.

CHAPTER 2

Quick-Service Restaurants in the Age of Automobile Convenience

T he automobile appeared in America in the 1890s and remained for decades primarily a sporting device and a status symbol for the nation's well-to-do. In 1908, however, Henry Ford produced his first Model T, and William Durant founded General Motors. Inexpensive cars for a mass market revolutionized transportation in the United States, fostering substantial reorganization of the nation's geography. Streets and roads were widened, hard-surfaced, and otherwise improved, and new kinds of highways created. New building types evolved, oriented specifically to automobile use through off-street parking, drive-through windows, and other automobile-convenient contrivances. Gasoline stations and motels and, of course, new kinds of restaurants helped engender a new kind of landscape—the commercial roadside. Automobility enabled a new kind of city—suburbia comprised of spread-out subdivisions, shopping centers, and office parks all connected by strip thoroughfares.

Begun in the 1920s, but slowed during the Depression and World War II, the nation's new automobility did achieve clear dominance in the 1950s. In 1921, there were some 8 million automobiles registered in the United States, and 10 years later some 23 million.[1] By 1955, the number was 60 million, and by 1990 143 million.[2] The automobile promised not only speed in movement, but the convenience of door-to-door travel, something that the railroads, for example, could not provide. And one's car could be used whenever need dictated for travel was not tied to corporate timetables. The motor car offered privacy in travel. It was also a prized possession, tangible proof through ownership—and the geographical mobility implicit in ownership—of one's personal value.

We continue in this chapter discussion of quick-service restaurant architecture, turning directly to the changes that automobile travel wrought in restaurant layout and design. At first, traditional restaurant venues, provisioned with parking lots or other automobile-oriented amenities, were used in intercepting customers in cars beyond big-city downtowns and beyond small-town main streets. But then new restaurant forms began to evolve, forms even more accommodating to customers arriving in cars. New services were introduced that were inviting to innovative infrastructure—site arrangements, facade treatments, sign configurations, internal arrangements. Distinctive restaurant prototypes evolved to capture the American imagination—building designs that, in retrospect, symbolize the nation's emergent automobility.

Tea Rooms

As early automobile travel remained the privilege of the well-to-do, the earliest roadside eateries catered especially to the gentry. As a recreation, motoring required destinations—places to go. Tea rooms evolved, especially in the Northeast, as leisure-time destinations for those motoring in search of rural retreats. Effie Gladding, who drove the Lincoln Highway to write a travel book, described the typical tea room as an old farmhouse at whose gate hung a quaint sign. It might read "The Sign of Green Tea Pot," for example. "It is a charming little place, kept by a woman of taste and arranged for parties to sup in passing by," she wrote. "We admire the simple, dainty furniture, the home-like little parlor. . . . Views about the place are charmingly pastoral."[3] The tea room represented a "family ideal," according to historian Warren Belasco. It provided a pleasant atmosphere, an uncontroversial menu based on tea, coffee, light entrees, and desserts, and an absolute proscription of alcoholic beverages.[4] The tea room was a homelike, feminine place in its informality, comfort, and domestic air. Travelers, especially women, venturing from home without the encapsulating assurances of public transport, could find reassurance there.

Tea rooms were not restricted to farmhouses, but could be found in restored taverns, grist mills, and other rural structures. The attraction as destination related not only to the urban resident's search for the rustic, but for the old-fashioned as well. As Belasco wrote: "Although the automobile was a modern machine, it was frequently perceived in nostalgic terms. To a generation raised on the railroad, the train—not the car—represented Modern Times." Thus the car "promised a suburban-style escape to a pre-industrial golden age. Traveling as a close unit in a cramped space along winding, bumpy roads, many tourists hoped to relive the adventurous trials of the supposedly well-knit pioneer family."[5] Prized were interesting places with exposed ceiling beams, old fireplaces, and antique furnishings, such as cupboards, spinning wheels, quilts, and old mirrors and brass.[6] Obtained at tea rooms was quick, courteous service, customers treated rather like guests in a private house. Tea-room prices were often twice that charged in main-street cafés, but patrons gladly paid the premium in buying a "sense of place," and not merely food.

Tea rooms, once popularized along rural highways, opened in traditional city storefronts and in hotels (see fig. 2.1). Others thrived in suburbia. Tea rooms not only served a largely female clientele but also represented an im-

FIG. 2.1 Cozy Corner Tea Room, Maumee, Ohio, ca. 1920.

portant avenue into the business world for women entrepreneurs. "There is perhaps no business more preeminently a woman's field than that of feeding the public," argued Josephine and Jeannette Ware in 1924 in the *Journal of Home Economics*. "There is no barrier, no prejudice, no tradition against woman's activity in the eating world." "That woman's place is in the tearoom," they concluded, "has been accepted as an inevitable corollary of 'woman's place is in the home.'"[7] Women's suffrage, the women's temperance movement, Prohibition, and the nation's new automobility all seemed to come together in the new tea rooms.

Roadside Stands

As automobile ownership increased to embrace even the lower middle class, the market for "road food" grew, inviting contexts for roadside eating less pretentious than the tea rooms. The roadside stand evolved as the most unpretentious of all eating places. Shed-like refreshment stands—or stalls or booths—were common to fairs and carnivals, and to public parks and beaches. Many foods, now basic to the American diet—the hamburger and the hot dog, for example—were first popularized at fairs as exotic dishes served at stands. At Coney Island, ice cream, soft drink, and hot-dog stands were numerous. The Luna Park attraction had two soda fountains and six orangeade and lemonade stands, the latter configured as giant ice pails.[8] But it was the plain rectangular one-story, wood-frame shed that typified the early roadside. At least one wall of the typical building contained a service window, a horizontal band of open space above a ledge or counter secured by a pull-down shutter after business hours (see fig. 2.2).[9]

At first, roadside stands tended to be placed flush with sidewalks or with highway shoulders, but in time most were set back from roadways and serviced by driveways and parking lots. Most stands were seasonal since, until the late 1920s, motoring was primarily a warm-weather proposition. Only in mild-winter states like California or Florida did stands operate all year. Highway selling was ideal for entrepreneurs willing to experiment with limited capital. The roadside stand, like the tourist cabin court, was hailed as one of America's last "frontiers" for independent businessmen. Most stands were built by their owners, the capital invested largely that of "sweat equity." Driveways, to the extent that they were improved, were usually covered with gravel spread by proprietors.

After 1910, soda-fountain operators in many localities began to offer "curb service," fountain personnel responding to motorists who stopped and honked at curbside. Such was the case with the Pig Stand Company's first store in Dallas. Orders were taken, and food subsequently delivered on trays. The company's second store in 1923, the first of some 60 developed within the decade, was a roadside stand with off-street parking.[10] Also in 1923, Roy Allen and Frank Wright opened their first A&W Root Beer stand in Sacramento. There "tray boys" brought orders out to customers who ate sitting in their cars. A precursor of the drive-in, the roadside stand took its place among a variety of early roadside eateries using "carhops." Travel writer Cecil Roberts wrote of Florida in the 1930s:

> Everywhere one sees "Joe's Barbecue" or "Tom's Barbecue." It may be an elaborate pseudo-Spanish bar, with gay awnings and aluminum stools, a soda fountain, or a mere wooden shanty on the roadside. . . . You need not get out of your car. You draw into the kerb, sound your horn, and a white-jacketed, sailor-capped youngster brings you your lunch on a tray that he clamps to the door of your car.[11]

Architectural experimentation was a hallmark of the late 1920s and early 1930s. Stands were built as giant oranges, lemons, milk cans, inverted ice cream cones, and milk cartons (see fig. 2.3). "Dutch windmills" may have been the most popular of the exotic building types. "The American people like novelty and are invariably attracted by the unusual," editorialized *Soda*

FIG. 2.2 Prototype stand for the Maid-Rite Company, an early restaurant chain.

FIG. 2.3 Freda Farms Stand, Hartford, Conn., 1933.

Fountain magazine in an article entitled "Unusual Places That Get the Business." The purpose of unusual design, the article asserted, was "to arrest the attention of the speeding public."[12] Southern California, inspired by Hollywood fantasies, led the way. "Here stands a monstrous white pup with a beautiful little soda fountain inside of him; there sits a bright-eyed green frog with a door in his belly; yonder a hoot-owl with green lights for eyes peers out on the road," wrote another traveler.[13] Called programmatic architecture (and sometimes "Hansel and Gretel" architecture), more fanciful Los Angeles buildings included the Hoot Hoot Ice Scream stand, the Tail O' The Pup stand, and the Big Do-Nut. As intriguing as these buildings were, it is important to remember that the giant coffee pots, chili bowls, and root-beer kegs did not constitute the norm; rather, they were playful deviants.[14] Roadsides, in fact, were dominated by quite ordinary, and quite utilitarian, buildings.

Relatively few roadside stands, judging by the commentary of the day, were considered attractive. Their flimsy construction and functional aspect, compounded by unimproved driveways, lack of landscaping, and garish signs, brought widespread condemnation. By 1926, there were tens of thousands of stands operating along American highways, the vast majority, according to one critic, "disreputable shacks" built of "old boards" and covered with "hideously colored signs" giving "unfavorable effect."[15] The derisive descriptor "hot-dog kennel" was widely applied. Planners began to criticize openly. Wrote one, "Where an enterprise of this kind causes annoyance and discomfort to adjoining property owners, it may be declared a nuisance and abated as such."[16] The American Civic Association sponsored several design contests in an attempt to improve stands, but to small avail. Good design, a gentry impulse, was doomed from the beginning. Americans were not about "to clean up the miscellaneous hodgepodge of unsightly 'hot dog' stands and the accompanying riffraff of roadside markets and what-not that clutter the roadside throughout the country."[17] Organized was the National Standowners' Association to serve the new "roadside refreshment industry." The idea was to improve the roadside stand by encouraging better waste disposal, restroom construction, improved parking lots, and better night-time lighting.[18]

Highway Cafés

Some improvement came to roadside eateries through the café idea, configured, as on main street, around the counter and stool format augmented by tables and booths. As one tourist from England wrote:

> I had grown familiar with these places, each one so like the other, with its warm smell, compounded of hamburger and hot milk and cardboard and central heating; its armory of intimidating machines, steaming for coffee or freezing for ice cream; the bright but timeworn plastic "leather" of its bar stools and booths; its slot machines . . . its racks with such enticing magazines as *Lincensored Confessions* and *Daring Romances;* and to accompany all, the monotonous muted psalmody of the juke box, canned and unchanging from coast to coast.[19]

Like the roadside stands, highway cafés came in assorted sizes and styles. Some were self-standing, occupying a site by the side of the road as an independent business. Bico's Café at Kearney, Nebraska, was such a place, occupying as it did a white frame building with hip roof (see fig. 2.4). Windows across the front opened the interior to view. Helpful also in attracting atten-

FIG. 2.4 Bico's Café, Kearney, Neb., ca. 1955.

FIG. 2.5 Half-Way House, Waddy, Ky., ca. 1955.

tion were the two signs, one placed on the restaurant's roof and the other on a tall pole beside the building. Parking was out front, the parking lot a kind of extension of the road itself.

Cafés were frequently linked with gasoline stations. John Steinbeck described such a place in his novel *The Wayward Bus*. "There was a little lunchroom in back of the gas pumps, a lunchroom with a counter and round, fixed stools, and three tables for those who wanted to eat in some style." In setting a mood for action to follow, Steinbeck detailed the place.

> On the first shelf behind the counter were sweet rolls, snails, doughnuts; on the second, canned soups, oranges, and bananas; on the third, individual boxes of cornflakes, riceflakes, grapenuts, and other tortured cereals. There was a grill at one end behind the counter and a sink beside it, beer and soda spouts beside that, ice cream units beside those, and on the counter itself, between the units of paper napkin containers, juke-box coin slots, salt, pepper, and ketchup, the cakes were displayed under large plastic covers.[20]

The Half-Way House at Waddy, Kentucky, on U.S. 60 was one such place (see fig. 2.5). Located midway between Lexington and Louisville, the café was, as shown in the mid-1950s, quite popular with truckers. The message written on the back of the postcard reads: "This is where we had a cup of coffee. Roads are good, no trouble. Many trucks. Scenery good. Love Mom."

Highway cafés were frequently linked with motels, and often with both motels and gas stations—offering thus "one-stop accommodation." The

FIG. 2.6 Lee-Jackson Tourist Court, Gas Station and Café, Winchester, Va., ca. 1935.

FIG. 2.7 I-55 Motor Plaza, Pevely, Mo., ca. 1970.

Lee-Jackson Tourist Court at Winchester, Virginia, was one of the latter (see fig. 2.6). "Inspect this strictly modernized tourist court. Open the year round and serving meals that have built our reputation," read the caption on the postcard's back side. After 1960, restaurants and gas stations, save in truck-stops, rarely shared buildings. Rather, two separate structures were clustered, as at the freeway interchange pictured at Pevely, Missouri (see fig. 2.7). The caption on this postcard read: "Robinhood of the Highway Restaurant features complete menu of finest foods, man-satisfying portions at modest

FIG. 2.8 Lincoln Court and Hitching Post Restaurant, Cheyenne, Wy., ca. 1955.

FAST FOOD

FIG. 2.9 New Perry Motel, Perry, Ga., ca. 1960. The postcard caption read: "Famous for delicious Southern food and flowers on each table."

prices. Magnificent decor." Beginning in the 1990s, certain fast-food chains and certain petroleum companies partnered in reinventing the integrated "tie-in." Latter-day gas station/restaurant combinations included Burger King restaurants in Amoco, Chevron, and Mobil convenience stores in Florida, and Dunkin' Donut shops in Amoco, Citgo, Exxon, Mobil, and Shell stations in various states.

In the late 1930s nearly half of the nation's motels included restaurants, usually cafés.[21] One such place was the Lincoln Court and Hitching Post Restaurant on the old Lincoln Highway in Cheyenne, Wyoming (see fig. 2.8). Another was the New Perry Motel and Restaurant "right on your way" in Perry, Georgia (see fig. 2.9). The postcard view at the New Perry is across the "Garden Room" and through the window outside to the motel swimming pool. Sometimes a motel's restaurant was leased out and run as a separate business. Sometimes it was not. Trade journals advised limiting restaurant seats to half the number of guest rooms.[22] Motel owners could expect that half their restaurant's clientele would be local, the other half transient from the motel. When corporate motel chains like Holiday Inn evolved, their highway motor inns featured dining rooms and coffee shops in replicating traditional hotel services. Beginning in the 1980s, however, economy motel chains eliminated restaurants.

Highway-Destination Restaurants

One other kind of restaurant deserves brief mention here. Highway-destination restaurants catered not to transients seeking security and convenience, but to discerning customers seeking the unusual. Included were upscale restaurants like Christy's on the Baltimore Pike near Glen Mills, Pennsylvania (see fig. 2.10). Like the tea rooms, such restaurants attracted more affluent customers motoring out for pleasure from cities and towns. Unlike the tea rooms, however, they offered full menus. Christy's postcard caption read: "One of the most beautiful restaurants on U.S. No. 1. Serving daily lunches, dinners, a la carte, soda fountain service. Choice wines and liquors. Really a place for mother, wife, sister or sweetheart. Once you stop at this magnificent place it will always remain in your memory." Other restaurants were less pretentious such as Sam's Sea Foods at Seal Beach, California (see fig. 2.11).

Customers sought dining experiences removed from the ordinary. "Atmosphere" was expected with exterior architecture and landscaping, interior design, furnishings, and table appointments calculated as place-defining. Of course, the same fads and fashions tended to be used everywhere, making many of these restaurants, in fact, very similar one to another, at least in broad outline. After Prohibition ended, the sale of alcoholic beverages set the highway-destination restaurant apart from other roadside eateries. Indeed, profits usually came more from the sale of alcohol than from the sale of food. A rural highway location was often selected in order to place a restaurant beyond restrictive municipal liquor laws.

FIG. 2.10 Christy's Restaurant, Glen Mills, Pa., ca. 1935.

FIG. 2.11 Sam's Sea Foods, Seal Beach, Calif., ca. 1940. "At the Sign of the Swordfish."

Highway Coffee Shops

A new kind of restaurant appeared along America's highways in the 1930s. Called "coffee shops" or "family restaurants," they had many of the amenities of the destination restaurant, but alcoholic beverages were not available. It was a place where families could come with children. In tone, entrepreneurs like Howard Johnson sought to merge the informal soda fountain with the more formal dining room. The motorist parked and entered through a vestibule: the dining room was to one side of the entrance and the soda fountain to the other. Although desserts and sandwiches were prepared at the fountain, other food originated in a large kitchen which served the dining room most especially. The cashier's counter just inside the door served as a "pivot point" where customers selected their preferred seating, and where bills were paid in departing. Several firms innovated the new venue, including the Interstate Company with its Glass House Restaurants in the Middle West and South with its "art moderne" form of streamlined architecture.

It was the Howard Johnson's chain, however, that early epitomized the highway coffee shop. Howard Johnson pioneered franchising as a means of rapid expansion. With previous restaurant chains—Schrafft's and White Castle, for example—outlets were completely owned by the corporation. Johnson, on the other hand, evolved a partial-ownership franchising system. He retained half-ownership of each new restaurant. A local investor bought into Johnson's place-product-packaging scheme, supplied half the capital needed for building construction, and agreed to manage the restaurant upon its completion. Johnson had 130 locations operating by 1940.[23] Bankers were still reluctant to mortgage highway restaurant buildings, considering them "speciality buildings" not easily converted to other uses should a restaurant fail. Lenders still thought of restaurants in terms of multipurpose commercial storefronts. With his franchising agreements, Johnson tapped local sources of capital not otherwise available. But he also obtained local managerial talent, thus insuring higher quality operation.

Johnson's buildings were designed for instant visibility and intended to instill customer loyalty through ready brand recognition. Unmistakably, they were restaurant buildings belonging only to the Howard Johnson's chain. Originated in New England, and spread southward through Virginia before World War II (with two outlying restaurants in Florida), Johnson adopted a pseudo-colonial design for his buildings, structures intended as reminiscent of New England town halls/churches (see fig. 2.12). White stucco or clapboarded walls, turquoise-blue cupolas, and orange roofs, coupled with large driveway signs (featuring the company's "Simple Simon meets the Pieman" logo), spoke with clear distinction.[24] Gas rationing during World War II closed all but 12 of Johnson's restaurants, forcing him to rebuild his chain after the war. Food-service contracts for the Pennsylvania Turnpike and other turnpike authorities fully linked the company with progressive road building and modern automobility.

To the soda, shake, and sundae concoctions based on his 28 flavors of ice cream, Johnson added hot dogs, hamburgers, chicken, steaks, and clams. As in most other roadside eateries, food was fried in order to speed service. Stephen Kurtz noted that Johnson's food was consistent with his interior decor. "Nothing calls attention to itself," he wrote; "it is all remarkably unremarkable. The sense of *déjà vu*, so strange in other circumstances, is commonplace here."[25]

It was the informal side of the highway coffee shop that dominated after 1950, new design ideas emanating especially from Southern California.

FIG. 2.12 Howard Johnson's Restaurant, Richmond, Va., ca. 1940.

FIG. 2.13 Sailee's Coffee Shop, Burbank, Calif., ca. 1960.

Sailee's Coffee Shop in Burbank was an early example (see fig. 2.13). Bold roof silhouettes were incorporated into buildings—roofs made to appear disjointed as if hanging in midair, suggesting a kind of "antigravity" architecture. "Googie" architecture, named after a small coffee-shop chain with such exaggerated design, sought to bring outdoors indoors. Cantilevered ceilings, resting on rough stone or unfinished concrete pylons, broad expanses of glass, space-age lighting fixtures, and multiple floor levels spoke of a new "organic" architecture somehow "western" in inspiration. The tenets of modern architecture provided rationale. Buildings needed to express their times;

FIG. 2.14 The Parasol Coffee Shop, Torrance, Calif., ca. 1965.

materials and structure needed to express their inherent natures and functions; nature needed to be integrated into buildings; technology—especially the automobile—needed to influence design.[26] Signs out front were also exaggerated—parabolas, boomerangs, giant amoebas, rockets, and stars, all in gaudy colors brilliantly lit at night.

Philip Langdon, in describing coffee shops designed by the Los Angeles architectural firm of Armet and Davis, wrote: "Walking into some of their coffee shops meant entering under a low canopy and then finding the space exploding upward to a high sloped ceiling and then back down to a lower scale at the counter area, where a canopy was suspended in any of a number of shapes."[27] Rather than use predictable right-angled floor plans, Armet and Davis produced layouts with aisles meeting in a series of 30- or 60-degree angles. Customers sat in U-shaped booths, or at a serpentine or otherwise irregularly aligned counter. Other architects turned completely away from rectilinearity to embrace circular, hexagonal, and octagonal floor plans (see fig. 2.14). Most coffee shops, especially those built beyond Southern California, were rarely as innovative. Yet even in the more staid coffee shops of the 1960s and 1970s in the Middle West, Northeast, or South, some California ideas found expression, for example, emphasis on "exhibition cooking" (where activities in the kitchen could be glimpsed through wall openings), reliance on heavily padded booths, or the use of curving lunch counters (see fig. 2.15). At its best, "coffee shop modern," concluded John Mariani, exemplified "the casual, comfortable, witty, unpretentious, and accessible." At its worse, it "blighted the landscape with awkward shapes and cheap materials."[28] The California coffee shop, much watered down, fostered in the 1960s and 1970s creation of several large restaurant chains, including Denny's, Sambo's, and Coco's.

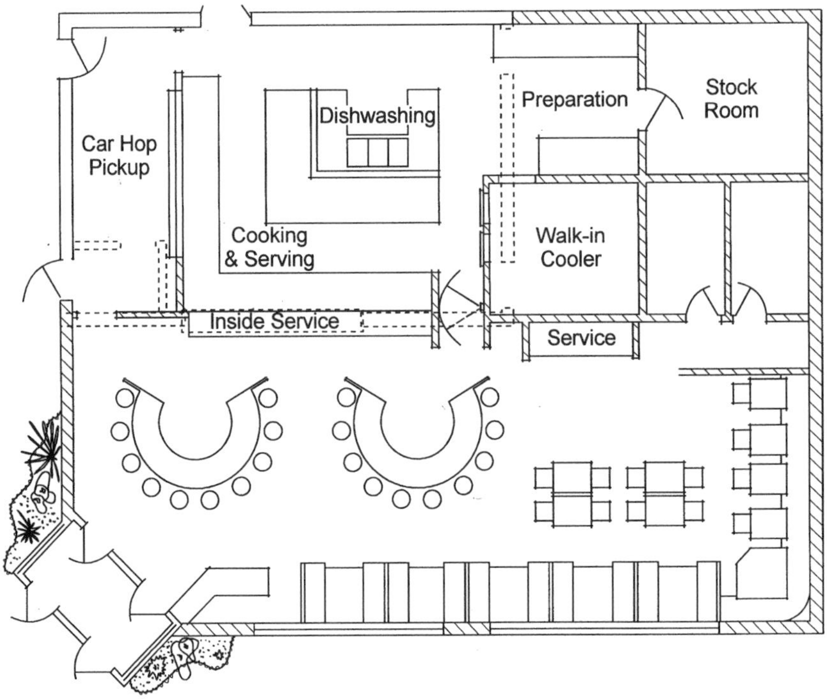

FIG. 2.15 Coffee shop floorplan. (*Source:* Lawrence Witchell, ed., *Drive-In Management Guidebook* [New York: Harcourt Brace, 1968].)

Drive-Ins

The drive-in grew out of the roadside stand and into the highway coffee shop, the term thus representing a variety of restaurant forms. After World War II, drive-ins came to share one important architectural feature—the canopy. And the canopy served one important purpose—to shade in-car eating where food was delivered on trays by carhops. What truly set drive-ins apart as a kind of place, therefore, was carhop service. "Service in Your Car" is what Spokane's Top Hat Drive-In championed (see fig. 2.16). The postcard's caption read: "Delicious food, reasonable prices, quick service, inviting atmosphere." The carhops, undoubtedly, provided much of that "atmosphere."

Perhaps "exploitation" is too strong a word. Nonetheless, central to the drive-in idea was a linking of female sexuality and the automobile. As machine, the motor car was still largely a male preoccupation. Put simply, girls were hired and attired as an attraction in the defining of place. As an article in *Life* explained:

> That a dimpled knee, a shapely thigh, a fresh young mouth smiling prettily has a stimulating effect on the male appetite is a truism which has been practiced ever since eating in public became an accepted social custom. For centuries, kings and princes and men-in-the-money have mixed their gustatory pleasures with the visual delights of comely young ladies.

FIG. 2.16 The Top Hat Drive-In, Spokane, Wash., ca. 1955.

For the price of a hamburger customers at drive-ins could enjoy a kind of beauty contest. At Sivil's Drive-In in Houston, carhops in 1940s worked 7½-hour shifts, six days a week, for which they received no pay but kept their tips, which averaged some $5.00 a day.[29] At Winstead's Drive-In in Kansas City, carhops in 1957 worked for minimum wage, keeping tips as well. In theory, one carhop could handle some 130 cars in an eight-hour shift, servicing upwards of 400 people.[30]

By 1964, there were an estimated 33,500 restaurants in the United States calling themselves "drive-ins," but only 24,500 offered hot food, the remainder being ice cream and soft-drink stands primarily.[31] Layout varied from drive-in to drive-in, but three principal spaces could always be found: a canopy-covered driveway adjacent to the building, a kitchen, and a carhop station linking kitchen and parking lot.[32] The smallest drive-ins offered carhop service only, but many also featured indoor lunch counters and booths, sometimes on the scale of the coffee shop. Carpenter's Drive-In in Santa Anita, California (along with the three Henry's Drive-Ins in Alhambra, Glendale, and Pasadena under the same ownership) were twinned drive-in/coffee-shop combinations (see fig. 2.17).

Rectangular shapes dominated most drive-ins, although round, octagonal, and hexagonal forms were popular as well. Architect Wayne McAllister pioneered the circular plan at Simon's Drive-In in Los Angeles in 1935, and then at other Southern California locations including the many Herbert's, Robert's, and Van de Kamp's drive-ins. McAllister's designs featured tall ver-

FIG. 2.17 Carpenter's Drive-In, Santa Anita, Calif., ca. 1955.

tical pylons centered on rooftops and broad, overhanging canopies cantilevered out over adjacent driveways. Circular buildings extended the
sense of facade around all sides, no motorist forced to park "behind" a
building.[33]

Drive-ins varied in size. Casey's three drive-ins in Abilene, Texas, employed 14 people at each location—seven carhops, two waitresses, two
cooks, and a dishwasher, maintenance man, and cashier.[34] Atlanta's Varsity
Drive-In (which persisted for decades in calling itself the "world's largest
drive-in") employed 150 people in three shifts in the early 1950s. The parking
lot held 200 cars, all serviced under canopies, with indoor seating for an
additional 100 people.[35] The Park and Eat Drive-In in Gulfport, Mississippi,
in 1958 employed 33 people in two shifts—eight carhops, two "expediers,"
six waitresses, two counter girls, two cashiers, four dishwasher-busboys, six
cooks, a maintenance man, an assistant manager, and manager.[36]

Labor costs at drive-ins were high, averaging approximately 25 percent of
sales through the early 1960s. Thus various innovations were introduced to
trim labor requirements. For example, the Track Drive-In in Los Angeles featured a cumbersome system of tracks and service boxes (called a "Motor-
mat") to connect the kitchen and parking stalls, negating the carhop completely. Telephones and speaker boxes were more commonly used to speed
service and reduce the number of employees required. At Forton's Drive-In
at Muskegon, Michigan, carhops carried "French phones" to be plugged in at
each stall; orders were called to a kitchen switchboard. At Bill's Drive-In in
Butte, Montana, "speaker phones," permanently mounted on posts, enabled
customers to call in their own orders, the food subsequently delivered by
carhops. Numerous call-in systems were patented with names like Aut-O-
Hop, Dine-a-Mike, Electro-Hop, Fon-A-Chef, and Ordaphone. Other drive-

ins installed conveyor belts to link food preparation areas with their carhop stations, as at the Driv-O-Matic Drive-In in Hammond, Indiana.[37]

The drive-in fit nicely into "cruising" routines where youngsters followed set routes between drive-ins to see and be seen after school and during evening hours. Adolescents had (and have) a heightened sensibility to their peers, one's identity hinging on peer acceptance, itself a function of appropriate social display. Drive-ins were places where teenagers could congregate largely outside adult supervision for display purposes, manipulating the symbolisms of automobility especially.[38] Cars came to have strong sexual overtones. For males, cars were ideal expressions of manhood—power and freedom implicit. For couples, cars afforded privacy for sexual experimentation, manhood's (and, perhaps, womanhood's) ultimate test. For most drive-in operators, however, teenagers became increasingly problematical, noise from racing motors, reckless driving in parking lots, litter, and vandalism driving away other customers.[39]

The Outdoor Walk-Up

Originally considered a fixed cost, labor came to be viewed as a variable cost to be reduced by mechanizing the food preparation process and by eliminating personnel. New "walk-up" restaurants evolved when drive-in buildings were stripped to their bare essentials—kitchen, service window, and restrooms. Served from windows, customers ate in their automobiles, sat at picnic tables provided, or took their food to eat elsewhere. Service windows were protected by portable glass vestibules during the winter months. Many buildings were prefabricated steel-frame structures covered with glass and porcelain enamel. As such, they were ideal for restaurant chain development.

What truly set the outdoor walk-up apart from the traditional roadside stand was its highly mechanized kitchen. Restaurants were geared to rapid, large-scale sandwich, drink, and dessert production. Electric frying vats and grills, and automated ice cream, shake, and drink machines, as well as cup and plate dispensers, were all arranged to effect assembly-line production.

Although most drive-ins had sported large electric signs, the outdoor walk-up became a kind of sign in itself.[40] Franchise chains sought distinctive architectural forms, color schemes, and ornamentations to stimulate ready customer recognition. The age of place-product-packaging, launched along the roadside by Howard Johnson, came fully of age. McDonald's was the most successful competitor for public attention. Each red and white McDonald's building sported a pair of "golden arches" easily recognized from the highway (see fig. 2.18).

The history of McDonald's has been told and retold to the point of assuming mythic, even mystical qualities. To some, Ray Kroc, the franchiser of the restaurants, stands as an entrepreneurial wizard in a league with Henry Ford. As Ford is believed to have mechanized automobile manufacture, so Kroc is thought to have put hamburger-making on assembly lines.[41] Time and motion studies at McDonald's did produce a system capable of delivering a hamburger, fries, and a shake every 50 seconds.[42] At most drive-ins carhop service was slow and food was rarely delivered hot. At McDonald's, the food was not only hot, but the elimination of the carhops substantially reduced labor costs with lower prices passed on to the customer. The McDonald's system, fueled by careful organization, a comprehensive training program (including the famous "Hamburger University" with degrees in "Hamburgerology"), and extensive advertising (especially on television), became the nation's largest restaurant chain. Over 4,000 units were in operation when the company celebrated its twentieth birthday in 1975.[43]

But McDonald's was not alone. Many traditional drive-ins had added "take home" departments in the early 1950s.[44] And numerous franchisers promoted chains of the new walk-up restaurant prototype. For example, Burger Chef developed a building with cantilevered gable-roof supported by an illuminated trapezoidal arch. Burger Chef's fast service featured a conveyorized infrared broiler that prepared hamburgers at a rate of 800 an hour.[45] At Burger King the process of hamburger manufacture was separated into discrete tasks. Buns of bread and patties of meat traveled at precise speeds on conveyors through the broiler to fall into small chutes where they were sandwiched.[46] Burger Queen, Burger Jet, Whataburger, and numerous other chains developed variations on the automation theme.

Building prefabrication was a means of trimming construction costs. Salesmen emphasized that, as with diners, prefab units could be moved to new locations should highway relocation or other problems arise. The Biff-Burger system developed a "Port-A-Unit" which could be erected and furnished in less than a week.[47] Ice cream vendors were more reliant on prefab units than the purveyors of hamburgers. Ice cream cones, Eskimo Pies, and Popsicles had been joined shortly before World War II by "soft" ice cream or

FIG. 2.18 McDonald's Restaurant, East Lansing, Mich., 1976.

"frozen custard." Dairy Queen, Tastee-Freez, Carvel, and other chains grew rapidly by featuring the new specialty food.

Cheap labor was the key to profits in what now was being called the "fast-food" industry. The entrepreneur substituted capital equipment for labor by mechanizing. The high degree of specialization through adoption of limited menus and the use of unskilled labor through job specialization allowed for greater use of part-time, minimum-wage employees. As a result, absenteeism and labor turnover became significant problems in the 1960s, with turnover as high as 300 percent per year for some chains.[48] Employees confronted arbitrary shifts, long hours, and drudgery work. Most considered restaurant employment to be only temporary. Besides reducing costs, the indoor walk-up helped solve the "teenager problem" since the carhop was eliminated. McDonald's took the carhop's demise one step farther by hiring only male counter help in the early years.

The Indoor Walk-Up

Many early roadside restaurants were attention-getters. From the Dutch windmills and inverted ice cream cones to the turquoise and orange Howard Johnson's to the golden arches of McDonald's, entrepreneurs sought to achieve maximum visibility. Bold forms, gaudy colors, and garish signs brightly illuminated at night had combined to contrast restaurants sharply with their surroundings. In the mid-1960s, negative public reaction to the excesses of roadside huckstering brought restraint. New designs sought to blend buildings with their surroundings. The late 1960s was a period of relative affluence and Americans were spending approximately 4 percent of their incomes on restaurant food.[49] Franchisers sought to make their fast-food stores more attractive and more comfortable to better compete for the restaurant dollar. Dining rooms—enclosed eating areas—were added to renovated walk-up restaurants. Although dining rooms were included in new units, customers continued to order at walk-up windows (see fig. 2.19).

McDonald's led the new trend toward tasteful restraint and stylishness. After 1968 McDonald's red and white exteriors were replaced by dull-brown brick and plate-glass facades, capped by double-mansard, shingle roofs (see fig. 2.20). Mansard roofs not only contributed to a more picturesque design motif, but they proved handy for masking ventilating, air conditioning, and other rooftop equipment. "The pulsing, exuberant Golden Arches were streamlined into subdued, nonbiodegradable yellow plastic logos that reared more gently from the road."[50] McDonald's decor changed inside as well as outside, restaurants boasting such amenities as plastic seats and tables, tile floors, and indirect lighting. Decoration varied from unit to unit. Local franchisees and managers were encouraged to adopt "escape" motifs appropriate to their localities. Again, McDonald's was not alone. Burger Chef introduced a new building type with eight alternative design "theme" motifs: colonial, rustic wood, rustic stone, Granada, New Orleans, Monterey, Tudor, and nautical.[51] The new indoor walk-ups were larger than their outdoor

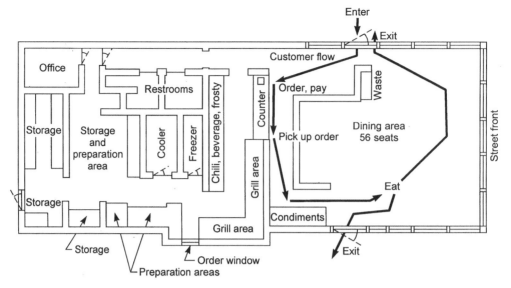

FIG. 2.19 Floorplan for Wendy's prototype building. (*Source:* D. Daryl Wyckoff and W. Earl Sasser, *The Chain-Restaurant Industry* [Lexington, Mass.: Lexington Books, 1978], 99.)

FIG. 2.20 McDonald's Restaurant, Groveport, Ohio, 1995.

walk-up predecessors. McDonald's restaurants increased from an average of 1,500 square feet in the early 1960s to 2,400 square feet in the late 1970s.[52] Also, "drive-through" windows were included in most restaurants after 1970, greatly increasing driveway needs.

The Double Drive-Through

Carryout business is as old as the delicatessen, and, for that matter, the restaurant. However, the first large promotion of carryout food dates from the White Castle, White Tower, and other diner chains that configured their small hamburgers especially for the take-home trade. Not until paper cups, dishes, and cartons became available was carryout truly feasible.[53] During the 1950s, most drive-ins developed take-home departments, some chains creating trademarks around which to advertise their service, Steak 'n Shake's "Takhomasak," for example. Pizza and chicken, rather than hamburgers, dominated carryout food sales after 1960. In the late 1980s, a number of restaurant chains, like Boston Chicken (now Boston Market), evolved to emphasize take-home food. Pizza, unlike other foods, was commonly delivered. After 1980, a number of pizza chains, like Pizza Hut, established delivery kitchens oriented to delivery trucks. Most of these facilities also had carryout counters. In 1990, 61 percent of the food-to-go market was carryout, 8 percent delivered and 31 percent picked up at drive-through windows.[54]

The drive-through window originated in the early 1930s. Pig Stand Number 21 in California experimented with the idea in 1931, customers driving to a small window where orders were taken and food handed out in sacks.[55] Many drive-ins added "drive-up" windows, for example, the five-unit Beverlee Drive-In chain of Columbus, Ohio, in the early 1950s.[56] The idea of ordering through a speaker phone located some distance from the window, thus giving personnel more time to assemble orders, had its start in the 1950s, as, for example, at the Driveateria at Columbia, Missouri.[57] Jack in the Box and Wendy's were the first large chains to integrate drive-through windows into their indoor walk-up restaurants. One chain, Der Wienerschnitzel, adopted an A-frame structure where motorists quite literally drove through the building. By 1988, some 51 percent of McDonald's sales were through the chain's 7,000 drive-through windows. The hourly capacity at a McDonald's window was 144 cars, or one every 25 seconds.[58]

The double drive-through originated in the 1980s, a small building, usually with small indoor lobby with carryout counter but no sit-down eating space, and two drive-through windows serving driveways on either side of the structure (see fig. 2.21). Several regional chains evolved including Central Park (Chattanooga), Checker's (Tampa), Rally's (Louisville), and Skooters (Birmingham). Cheaper food and faster take-home service provided rationale. At indoor walk-up restaurants, drive-through customers actually subsidized eat-in customers, takeout food being much cheaper to sell, yet costing the same. By eliminating the eat-in trade, cost savings could be passed along. Also, the double drive-through format was cheaper than standard buildings to construct. A lot of some 12,000 square feet was sufficient compared with the 40,000-square-foot lot needed for the average Burger King. Central Park's two-story prototype required the least space. Only 12 feet by 12 feet in size, the kitchen was downstairs, and a storage room, manager's office, and toilet upstairs.[59] Most double drive-through restaurants priced hamburgers about 30 percent below that of the major chains. Menus were deliberately kept limited, insuring that customers were served in about 45 seconds.[60]

Drive-through windows fostered in the 1990s emphasis on food held in the hand such that drivers easily could eat and drive simultaneously. Car manufacturers began to equip front seats with cup holders to facilitate dash-

FIG. 2.21 McHugh's Double Drive-Thru, Mattoon, Ill., 1995.

board dining. Thus Taco Bell marketed a folded tortilla that would not crumble and KFC introduced a chicken pita sandwich with a holder to prevent dripping. Market analysts determined that in 1996 the average American ate 13 meals in a car, up from 11 in 1990.[61]

Other Roadside Restaurants

Travel by automobile and motor bus, and the carrying of freight by motor truck, encouraged still other kinds of restaurants along American roadsides. Although they tended to be imitative of restaurants already described, their mention is important if only to make our overview complete. Not everyone traveling by highway did so by car. Less-affluent travelers used intercity buses and ate in bus stations. Americans on vacation, and especially those traveling by automobile with children, patronized tourist stops, restaurants linked with candy and souvenir sales. Truckstops serviced over-the-road haulers, but welcomed other customers as well. The new turnpike highways restricted roadside commerce, service plazas and their restaurants located only at intervals under the aegis of a toll-road authority. Deserving brief mention as well were restaurants established in shopping centers and shopping malls not of the highway but nonetheless oriented to automobile use.

Beginning in the 1930s, buses began to supplant trains as scheduled transportation. By 1950, Greyhound, the largest of the new transcontinental bus lines, had established a chain of "Post Houses" coast to coast, 70 owned and 20 franchised.[62] Shown is the Post House built at Effingham, Illinois (see fig. 2.22). Inside, the soda fountain, booths, and walls were finished in knotty pine. Buses came and went, restaurant personnel trained to deliver food with dispatch. The largest Post Houses, like the one at Cleveland, could handle upwards of 175 people in 15 minutes.[63] By 1960, most of the Post House lunchrooms had been changed to cafeterias, which quickened service even more. Like Horn and Hardart, Greyhound's Post House subsidiary became a management company, converting most of its restaurants, especially those in big city terminals, to Burger Kings. Through another subsidiary, Dobbs House, Greyhound also established restaurants in many of the nation's largest airports.

Tourists traveled for pleasure. By 1960 tourists were spending an estimated $20 billion for food, gas, and lodging, an estimated 27 percent for food.[64] Many restaurants in resort areas and along major highways evolved to cater to vacationists, especially families traveling with children. In the typical highway tourist restaurant, fast food combined with the selling of souvenirs and candy. Horne's (for a period of time also a Greyhound subsidiary) originated just after World War II at Bayard, Florida, as a praline shop. In eight years the chain grew to 17 stores in eight states, replicating a distinctive yellow-roofed, A-frame building at the roadside (see fig. 2.23).[65] "Look for the Yellow Roof—Your Highway Host for One-Stop Service" was the chain's slogan.

Stuckey's originated just prior to the war as a pecan stand in Eastman, Georgia. By 1948, there were 29 stores, and 124 by 1964 when the chain was sold to Pet Incorporated, then also the owner of Schrafft's.[66] Stuckey's originally adopted an A-frame with teal-colored roof, but later replaced it with a more traditional building with turquoise roof. Nickerson Farm's stores sported a steeply pitched red-orange gable roof, the buildings' white walls given a kind of Tudor ornamentation. The chain, based in Missouri, promised "to have the cleanest, friendliest, most courteous stops on the nation's highways. To sell the finest products available at the best prices possible and to give fast efficient service to all of our customers."[67] Dutch Pantry, headquartered in the "Pennsylvania Dutch" country, adopted a red and white gambrel roof for its buildings. Counter and table service was available as at early Horne's, Stuckey's, and Nickerson Farm's stores, but, unlike its competitors, Dutch Pantry also used the salad buffet.[68] Gasoline pumps were located in front of all these "one-stop" places.

FIG. 2.22 Greyhound Post House, Effingham, Ill., ca. 1950.

FAST FOOD

FIG. 2.23 A Horne's Restaurant, location unknown, ca. 1960.

The sign of good highway food was a parking lot filled with trucks, or so the cliché held through the 1940s. By 1960, however, over-the-road rigs had become so large that truck drivers were restricted to where they could eat by where they could park. With the new interstate freeways, the large interchange truckstop became the stopover place of choice, most trucking companies putting drivers on strict schedules and, indeed, restricting them to specific refueling stops (see fig. 2.24). The trucker became the captive of the truckstop restaurant, and, as a captive, vulnerable to indifferent food, the truck-filled parking lot rarely a sign of good taste. By 1970, there were an estimated 2,000 truckstops in the United States. Many were chain-operated. The Pure Oil Company, for example, established by 1968 a network of 305 truckstops, 50 of them at interstate interchanges.[69]

Beginning with Connecticut's Merritt Parkway and the Pennsylvania Turnpike just prior to World War II, toll roads came to represent the ultimate in high-speed driving. Complemented by freeways of the new interstate system beginning in the 1950s, turnpikes continue to serve motorists in New York, New Jersey, Pennsylvania, Ohio, Indiana, and a number of other states. An important feature of these roads was the service plaza, state-owned but leased out to private service providers. When the New York State Thruway opened, restaurant concessions were won by Hot Shoppes of Washington, D.C., and Union News and Restaurants Associates of New York City. As one trade journal reported:

> The Authority provides the necessary permanent kitchen equipment, including refrigerators, ovens, ranges, permanent tables, and shelving, dishwashing machinery, counters and stools. The concessionaires provide what are termed expendables, including cash registers, drink mixers, cooking utensils, meat slicers, cream dispensers, silverware, toasters, small deep fryers, 20-quart food mixers, beverage dispensers, office equipment, draperies and other interior decorations.[70]

Each building contained a dining room seating 128 people, a lunchroom with counter and booths seating 64, and a "stand-up snack bar." Several corporations specialized in toll-road eateries: Fred Harvey expanded from locations along the Santa Fe Railroad to operate in Illinois Tollway "oases." Interstate Host introduced Glass House Restaurants to Oklahoma's turnpikes (see fig. 2.25).

Restaurants in shopping centers and shopping malls, including "food court" complexes, are oriented to pedestrians, but to pedestrians who arrived by automobile in the first instance. Such restaurants range from small walk-up counters dispensing orange juice to indoor walk-ups purveying hamburgers to full-service coffee shops to cafeterias. The same restaurant chains seen along the roadside came to dominate large shopping malls and shopping centers as well. But in many small suburban shopping centers the café, facing onto a parking lot, came to thrive anew with both general and specialty menus, including Italian, Chinese, and other "ethnic" foods.

Quick-Service Restaurants and Automobile Convenience

The needs of motorists drove substantial innovation in restaurant design. Borrowed from the traditional quick-service restaurant were counter and stool and booth and table arrangements. Innovation emerged from full embrace of carhop and "curb service." The drive-in, where customers ate in their cars, was something new and distinctly American. The drive-in was fully symbolic of its time—an era of rapidly growing automobile dependence and thus an era when owning and using cars came to carry profound social and personal meaning. Largely to cut labor costs and increase competitiveness through lower prices, new restaurant chains emerged to promote the outdoor walk-up, eventually expanding the idea into the indoor walk-up.

FIG. 2.24 Deck Plaza, Geneseo, Ill., ca. 1980. Besides its refueling facility, the complex contained a coffee shop, dining room and cocktail lounge, gift shop, and 120-room motel.

FAST
FOOD

FIG. 2.25 Service plaza on the Will Rogers Turnpike near Vinta, Okla., ca. 1960.

Then "drive-ins" became "drive-throughs" as more and more the fast-food chains came to emphasize carryout food handed to motorists through windows. It was the fastest food of all.

The roadside restaurant has come of age as a distinctive kind of place important in the daily lives of most Americans. It is a place-type familiar in its many forms to all. As the majority of Americans reside and work in automobile-convenient landscapes, roadside eateries have come to provide the standards by which the food-service industry abides. The popularity of roadside "fast food" is a function of many factors. Traditionally, "road food" has been prepared and consumed quickly and at relatively low prices. It has been attractive to people on the move in a society highly mobile geographically. The roadside with its sense of informality conveys an aura of glamour, especially the glamour of the traveler enjoying easy, free, and independent adventure. Place-product-packaging has served well the needs of a highly mobile society. People find in roadside restaurants places of comfort where standardized environments, products, and services provide security as well as nourishment away from home. Anxiety from adventuring is contained by the familiar.

Place-product-packaging is a "total design" idea. As behavior settings, roadside restaurants are carefully contrived to attract and satisfy customers traveling by automobile. Little is left to chance, for customer expectations must be validated. Kind of location, opening and closing hours, menus, service, decor, and prices must be consistent as a total place product. Restaurants must look like restaurants. Since 1920 a succession of standardized building types evolved, with each type prevailing for a short period of time. Building types have changed primarily in response to new production and merchandising techniques intended to cut labor costs. Restaurant chains have sought to establish clear brand identities through both architectural styling and distinctive logos. Yet no chain willingly deviates too far from place-product-packaging norms for fear of alienating customers. Thus roadside restaurants contribute much to the standardization of highway-oriented landscapes.

*Quick-Service
Restaurants and
Automobile
Convenience*

CHAPTER 3

Restaurant Chains

Increased homogeneity characterized roadside restaurants after World War II, many influences contributing to the use of a relatively few building types, and to the adoption of a relatively few service formats and menu emphases. First, a mature restaurant industry evolved, replete with trade organizations to host annual conventions and shows, publish trade journals, and lobby at various governmental levels—consensus-building activities designed to set, if not raise, the standards of independent restaurant operators. As well, national suppliers of restaurant equipment came to copy one another's initiatives in the standardization of food-delivery systems, thus giving restauranteurs fewer degrees of freedom in setting menus and configuring physically their restaurants. Second, place-product-packaging came to the restaurant industry, especially through the rise of business format franchising. Created were chains of lookalike restaurants to define, in their varied geographical alignments, evolving corporate-based market territories. Franchise chains sought distinction through specially configured signage, building design, and food-product delivery. Yet deviance was moderated through careful imitation chain to chain, "difference-in-sameness" the ruling marketing principle.

The rise of the roadside restaurant chain, especially through franchising, is the focus of this chapter. We emphasize the service-oriented "coffee shop" or "family restaurant" chains like Howard Johnson's, Big Boy, Denny's, Shoney's, and the now-defunct Sambo's. We treat as well the tourist-oriented highway restaurant, looking briefly at the Stuckey's chain. Nonetheless, it is our intention to outline in this chapter the whole of restaurant franchising, alluding to other chains, and to chains in general, as discussion merits. In subsequent chapters we elaborate the story of restaurant place-product-packaging by focusing on market segmentation, not by service orientation, but by category of food emphasis—hamburgers (McDonald's and Burger King among other brands), sandwiches (Arby's, Subway, for example), chicken (KFC, Popeye's), pizza (Pizza Hut), Mexican (Taco Bell), breakfast food

(IHOP), seafood (Red Lobster). How did franchising come to the restaurant industry? How did it play out in the marketing of different kinds of food products? In what kinds of places could hamburgers most readily be sold? Or pizza? Or pancakes? How and why did the fads and fashions of restaurant "place-appropriateness" change over time?

Franchising

The earliest restaurant chains were ownership chains—White Castle and other similar diner operations, Schrafft's and other confectionery/luncheonette companies, and Morrison's and other cafeteria chains. Restaurants were totally owned by their respective companies. Success hinged on a corporation's embrace of one or another management system built around a distinctive product line or food-delivery scheme. Helpful was the central purchasing of supplies in bulk, and the pre-preparation if not total preparation of food at central commissaries. Given the logistics of central supply, most ownership chains were highly localized, few growing beyond any one region of the country. Critical also was the quality of management brought to bear at the local level. Where careful training and generous compensation encouraged competent local management, chains thrived. But when local management faltered, chains disintegrated.

Successful restauranteurs, wanting to expand beyond the market base of one location, faced a dilemma—how to be in several places at once thus to insure everywhere the same food quality, service integrity, and facility upkeep? Absolutely necessary was access to and a continuing supply of reliable, competent, and aggressive local managers. Necessary as well was a foolproof accounting system whereby a restaurant's operations could be monitored from afar. Ideally, each restaurant in a chain needed to be financed as a separate business thus to negate the impact of branch failure. Successful chain development hinged on shared reputation—the image of a shared name or brand identity calculated to market expansion territorially. Poor management at several locations could damage the whole, a chain being only as strong as its weakest links.

Many of the problems inherent in ownership chains could be avoided through franchising. By franchising to others the right to copy a successful restaurant venue, an entrepreneur could obtain the local managers needed, people energized by proprietary self-interest. Each franchise operation represented a related but nonetheless financially autonomous operation. The franchisor, by charging license and other fees, and by sharing in franchisee earnings, could profit with little direct risk. The franchise arrangement carried with it accountability while at the same time it insulated the franchisor from direct involvement in actual day-to-day branch operations. To the extent that operating procedures were carefully prescribed (covering, for example, the procurement of supplies and the management of personnel), franchise agreements could foster quality control. Franchising also represented an important source of capital useful for expansion.

Franchising was well established in the American economy when Howard Johnson launched his chain of restaurants in the 1930s. Franchise agreements had been used to sell farm implements, sewing machines, automobiles, and gasoline among other products. Here was a method of organization that combined separate business interests into a single administrative unit. A parent company granted or sold to other companies, partnerships, or individuals any or all of the following: the right to distribute its products, use its trade names, and use its business methods. Franchise contracts usually extended for set periods of time with conditions prescribed for renewal. Contracts sometimes carried territorial implication, the franchisee's specified business activities confined geographically and, thereby, protected geographically from the competition of other franchises. Two principal types of franchising are recognized: product franchising and business-format franchising.[1]

Under product franchising a manufacturer markets its output through agents who, in turn, usually are required to buy exclusively from the manufacturer. The agent configures a place of business and operates by whatever business methods prove effective, using, of course, the trademarks identifying the manufacturer's sales system. Critical to success is the quality of the product sold, the dependability of product supply, and the effectiveness of advertising and other marketing activities conducted by the manufacturer in bolstering consumer demand. Some companies support their agents by financing customer purchases at the retail level. Outlined, of course, is the system by which automobile manufacturers have traditionally sold cars in the United States.

With business-format franchising, the outlet itself and its operating procedures, together with a package of support services, combine under the trademark as a comprehensive business concept. It is not so much the product sold as the context or place for selling the product, and the manner of its selling, that matters. The architectural structuring and styling of buildings, the equipping and organization of interior space, and the methods of operating, as well as trademark use, comprise the contractual obligation. Place-product-packaging is the goal. In the restaurant business, it is the total systematizing of business conduct through the coordination of building design, signage, interior decor, food production and delivery systems, division of labor, management procedure, and, of course, the particular food products served.

The legal basis for franchising has emerged over the past century and remains subject to judicial reinterpretation. For example, in a series of court decisions involving the Carvel Ice Cream Company, the Federal Court of Appeals and the Federal Trade Commission recognized the trademark license as a central element in the legal structure of a franchise agreement and established that restrictions on franchise business practice, rather than constituting illegal tying or restraining actions, were reasonably necessary to protect the trademark and a franchisor's integrity.[2] In restaurant franchising, franchisees often were required to purchase food and other supplies from parent companies at substantially inflated prices. Subsequent litigation involving the Chicken Delight Company partially reversed this position, the courts establishing that a franchisor's trademark, as merely a representation of product quality, was separate from other operational aspects of a franchise and could not shield required purchase agreements.

In 1980, in *Principo vs. McDonald's Corporation,* the judiciary recognized business-format franchising as a distinct type of business arrangement separate from product franchising. Accepted was the idea that business-format franchising represented a comprehensive package or bundle of "goods" that needed to be sold as a complete unit.[3] At work at McDonald's, the courts assessed, was a "formula," the integrity of which was seen as crucial to system-wide success and thus the viability of the corporation. McDonald's sold not only food, but distinctive food services set in distinctive places. Customers came not only to eat, but to consume specific food products uniquely served in unique settings.

Franchising's geographical implications vary from chain to chain. Some companies allow franchisees to operate literally anywhere. Such agreements are common where risk of market saturation in any given locale is low. Other companies restrict franchisees to one or more fixed locations. Still other companies allow franchisees to operate anywhere within a prescribed territory. At the end of the 1960s nine out of ten franchisors in the United States provided franchisees with territorial guarantees, over half extending protection in terms of a radius of miles.[4] In assigning territories, however, many franchisors early on were not interested so much in protecting franchisees or, for that matter, bringing efficiency to product or service distribution, but were motivated merely to excite the selling of licenses. Especially when subfranchising was allowed, a parent company could extract an upfront licensing fee and then delegate the costs of chain expansion to franchisees.

The pyramiding of territorial licenses was common in restaurant franchising in the 1960s. Licensees, holding a franchise for a broad territory, sublicensed their rights to others, collecting franchise fees up front with each transaction. Subfranchisees, in turn, could sell parts of their territories to third-level operators, and so on. Such practices encouraged exploitation—franchisors turning quick profits by selling restaurant concepts they had no real intention of operationally supporting. One secret to McDonald's success was the company's general avoidance of territorial franchises.[5] Ray Kroc, McDonald's founder, came very quickly to a policy of single-store franchises sold relatively cheaply. Kroc intended McDonald's to profit from the success of its franchisees in selling hamburgers, not from speculation in licenses. Most chains that licensed franchisees territorially found it difficult to maintain quality. Where subfranchising operated it was almost impossible to exert central authority. Kroc's putting the needs of franchisees first led McDonald's into store financing, the company becoming, through lease agreements, landlord to most of its licensees. As landlord, the company was able to exert quality control across the breadth of its franchise operation.[6]

The typical franchise package offered a range of services and obligations. Franchisor assistance might cover any of the following: site selection, mortgage financing or lease negotiation, architectural design, equipping and furnishing, training for owner/managers and employees, door-opener promotions, local advertising, operating instructions, recordkeeping and accounting systems. Such services were covered by a range of fees usually including an upfront franchise fee, an assessment to support chain advertising, and an annual royalty payment usually calculated as a percentage of gross sales. In addition, a franchisee might be required to lease equipment and signs, and buy from the parent company food products and paper and other supplies used in daily operations. In 1974 restaurant franchisors sold to franchisees food ingredients valued at $206 million, paper supplies worth $81 million, and equipment worth $38 million.[7]

Ray Kroc licensed McDonald's franchisees for $950 in 1955.[8] By 1969, the cost of starting a McDonald's outlet stood at approximately $53,000, a sum that covered all fees, equipment installation, and startup supplies. The franchise fee itself was $10,000. A service fee of 2.8 percent of the gross volume was required semimonthly.[9] Twenty-year leases required rent payments equal to 8 percent of annual gross sales, which in 1967 averaged some $300,000 across the company's chain of 1,137 restaurants.[10] In 1969, Burger King required franchisees to sublease a fully equipped restaurant costing some $70,000, Burger King financing half, the franchisee the other half. The company took a 2.9 percent royalty fee based on gross sales, and a 4 percent advertising fee to cover chain promotion.[11] Franchisors, including McDonald's and Burger King, advertised for franchisees in trade journals and established promotional booths at conventions and trade fairs. The Wee

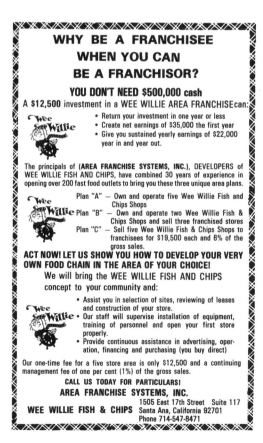

FIG. 3.1 Advertisement for Wee Willie Fish and Chips. (*Source: Franchise Journal* 2 [September 1969]: 51.)

Willie Fish and Chips ad that appeared in *Franchise Journal* illustrates the type of appeal made (see fig. 3.1). Promoted in the ad is a pyramiding scheme encouraging to subfranchising.

Franchising carried advantages and disadvantages both for franchisors and franchisees. For restaurant franchisors, franchising became an important source of financial capital, enabling more rapid chain expansion. A chain's franchisees could tap local sources of investment capital otherwise unavailable to a franchisor. Indeed, many chains sought to grow without assuming any financial commitment, driving forward chain expansion solely on the basis of franchisee obligations. Of course, franchising represented a way of obtaining and controlling managerial expertise. Also, the franchisor could spread the costs of promotion, development of advertising, and media purchase. Disadvantage hinged primarily on an inability to control quality across the breadth of a chain, usually a failure of management system.

Franchising gave the franchisee a head start on the "learning curve" of the restaurant business. Purchased was an established product defined in outlet design, business system, market reputation. When franchisees bought into a proven corporate system, the likelihood of failure was reduced. Some 65 percent of all new businesses failed in their first five years according to the Small Business Administration in 1983. But the failure rate of franchise holders had been less than 4 percent over the previous decade according to the Department of Commerce.[12] Indeed, through the 1980s franchising was promoted as the "last and best hope for independent business in an era of growing vertical integration." Franchising helped small entrepreneurs to "compete with the giants."[13] On the negative side, franchise agreements could prove overly restrictive for a franchisee, preventing an enterprising restauranteur from responding to market conditions special to his or her locality. Franchisees were vulnerable to parent company indifference, individual restaurants rising and falling according to overall chain success or failure.

What kind of person did franchise agreements attract? In 1981 the typical Burger King licensee was a small investor, white, male, and 30–45 years old with 10–15 years previous business experience (but not necessarily in the restaurant industry). He had $150,000 in net worth excluding home ownership.[14] A decade earlier, a franchisee across the economy generally was reported to be male, 45.3 years old, and married 21.1 years with 2.4 children. He owned 1.8 automobiles, was a high school graduate with some college, and had 15.5 years of prior work experience.[15] These were people who wanted to own a business thus to be their own boss, and make more money. Only after the civil rights legislation of the mid-1960s were African-Americans actively recruited as restaurant franchisees. From four black McDonald's licensees in 1969, the number grew to 50 at the end of 1972.[16] Whereas over 15 percent of the American population was nonwhite, fewer than 3 percent of all businesses were black-owned.[17]

HOWARD JOHNSON'S

Among the earliest franchise chains was Howard Johnson's. The company began in 1925 when Howard D. Johnson took over a failing drugstore in Wollaston, Massachusetts, and, with a loan of $500, turned it into a soda fountain and sundries store. Within the year he also opened a refreshment stand at a nearby beach, and a full-menu restaurant in a downtown Quincy, Massachusetts, bank building. Thus Johnson experimented with a number of restaurant venues before launching the first of his highway-oriented restaurants at Orleans, Massachusetts, on Cape Cod in 1935. Already overextended financially, Johnson hit upon the idea of franchising, a friend footing the bill for the Orleans operation in exchange for franchise rights. Four additional roadside restaurants were ready by the start of the 1936 tourist season, all configured in pseudo-Georgian style with orange roofs and cupola and trim in turquoise (see fig. 2.12). By the end of the year, Johnson's chain had grown to 39 units, most of them co-owned under franchise. Johnson, in retaining half-ownership, controlled each store's menu and operational system, his franchisees providing day-to-day management, each being required to purchase ice cream and selected other food ingredients, and certain supplies, from the company. By the end of 1939 there were 107 Howard Johnson's restaurants in a half-dozen states. By 1941 there were 150.[18]

Prior to World War II, the chain's buildings actually varied by size, shape, and detailing, although each carried the "roadside cathedral" look reinforced by logo and color scheme. Designs were modified to fit particular sites and the anticipated scale of business at each location. As business increased, buildings were variously enlarged—a wing to one side, wings to both sides, a rear projection. The grandest restaurant of all was the "palace" built on Queens Boulevard in New York City which seated 1,000 and was promoted as the largest roadside restaurant in the world. After World War II gas rationing, Johnson set out to rebuild his chain using a series of simplified or "modernized" versions of his icon building (see fig. 3.2). By 1951 there were

FIG. 3.2 Howard Johnson's building prototype, ca. 1950.

Locations by County

- ·   1
- ⋆   2-4
- △   5-9
- ▢   10-19

n=255

FIG. 3.3 Howard Johnson's Restaurants, 1951.

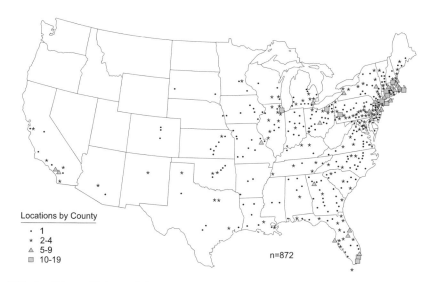

Locations by County

- ·   1
- ⋆   2-4
- △   5-9
- ▢   10-19

n=872

FIG. 3.4 Howard Johnson's Restaurants, 1970.

255 Howard Johnson's "coffee shops" in operation, each featuring both counter and booth and table service built around expanded lunch and dinner menus and ice cream desserts.

Howard Johnson's was concentrated geographically in the greater Boston, New York City, and Philadelphia areas (see fig. 3.3). In addition, a string of restaurants stretched westward from Philadelphia along the line of the new Pennsylvania Turnpike. Constructed at roughly 50-mile intervals were buildings clad in gray stone designed to set a regional tone for the new superhighway. By connecting his name and logo with the turnpike, Howard Johnson vastly enhanced his chain's appeal. As historian Warren Belasco observed, "This partnership with 'America's Dream Road'—the nation's first superhighway—proved a public relations coup, for it identified Johnson with the forces of progressive engineering."[19] Although Johnson retained partial ownership in most of his chain's restaurants, he profited most as a manufacturer and as a jobber, a fleet of refrigerated trucks transporting ice cream and frozen foods out from the company's Wollaston commissary.

By 1970 the Howard Johnson's chain had grown to 872 restaurants located primarily east of the Mississippi River (see fig. 3.4). Early penetration of the lucrative Florida market had been solidified, especially in the greater Miami–Fort Lauderdale area. Restaurants had been established across the Middle West, especially around Cleveland and Chicago, and in Southern California, new commissaries developed to serve them. Important also were new turnpike facilities in New Jersey, New York, Kansas, and Oklahoma. But, Howard Johnson's area of highest concentration remained the New England and Middle Atlantic states, making the chain, even at the height of its development, highly regionalized. In the 1960s, the company's fortunes began to wane. Critics noted that the firm had grown too fast with too little attention paid to organization and administration.[20] Lines of supervision were hazy or tangled, Johnson himself administering the company from a desk still lodged behind the soda fountain of his original store. The company tried diversifying, opening higher-priced Red Coach Grill and Ground Round restaurants, and branching into packaged grocery foods. However, by 1970 the older restaurants in the Howard Johnson's chain had become worn with use and their highly standardized menus suffered the competition of newer chains. In 1979, the franchising rights to 870 Howard Johnson's, 139 Ground Rounds, and 31 Red Coach Grills, as well as 520 hotels and "motor lodges," were sold to the British Imperial Group. A conglomerate, Imperial's interests worldwide ran to hotels, restaurants, beer, wine, prepared and canned foods, and packaging.[21] Imperial, unable to turn the company's fortunes around, sold the firm in 1985 to the Marriott Corporation which intended to convert many of the Howard Johnson's locations to Big Boy restaurants.

The Howard Johnson's chain suffered not only from aging restaurants, but as well from a decaying market niche. Built originally around ice cream, chicken, clams, and hot dogs, the chain's commissary system, especially its dependence on the reheating of frozen food, lost ground to other systems. Whatever Howard Johnson's served, some other chain, like Friendly's, Kentucky Fried Chicken, or Long John Silver's, opened nearby to specialize in it. Be it ice cream, chicken, or fish, competitors served it quicker and better. "They'd come in with better concentration of a product, and maybe a lower price," lamented the junior Howard Johnson whose role it was to sell off the legacy inherited from his father.[22]

BIG BOY

Robert Wian opened the 10-stool Bob's Pantry in Glendale, California, in 1936. Looking for a sales novelty, he took the ordinary hamburger bun, split it twice rather than once, and placed between the respective parts two meat patties, garnishing the whole with mayonnaise, lettuce, cheese, and relish.

Born was what he originally termed the "fat boy," but what quickly came to be the "big boy."[23] By 1964 18 Bob's Coffee Shops were operating in the Los Angeles area. The Bob's Big Boy chain included 103 branches, most located in Southern California, when it was purchased by the Marriott Corporation in 1975. Marriott also bought the Big Boy franchising rights. Wian, like Howard Johnson, had used franchising to expand but, unlike the Howard Johnson's chain, the Big Boy system was built ad hoc through the piecemeal granting of territorial licenses to other restauranteurs, several of whom, in turn, functioned as subfranchisors. Established was not an integrated company so much as a set of loose contractual relationships that funneled to Wian royalties (most set at 2 percent of gross sales) in exchange for use of the Big Boy logo and the sandwich that it represented. At all Big Boy restaurants stood a twelve-foot statue of a bright-eyed, chubby kid with a brown cowlick and the words "Big Boy" spread across his chest (see fig. 3.5).

In 1975, the country was divided into more than a dozen franchise regions (except for Oregon and the northern New England states, which remained unassigned, and California and parts of Arizona, Maryland, and New Jersey which Marriott operated outright) (see fig. 3.6). Franchisees varied in size from Shoney's, Elias Brothers, and Frisch's (with 194, 137, and 127 locations respectively) to Bud's and TJ's (with 2 restaurants each). In 1979, the average Big Boy restaurant seated 143 with both counter and booth and table service, buildings occupying some 5,600 square feet on an acre of land. The cost of building a new store stood at some $500,000.[24]

David Frisch started his first drive-in in Fairfax, Ohio, in 1939. Visiting in Los Angeles in 1948, he inspected Wian's operation and was persuaded

FIG. 3.5 The "Big Boy," Springfield, Ill., 1990.

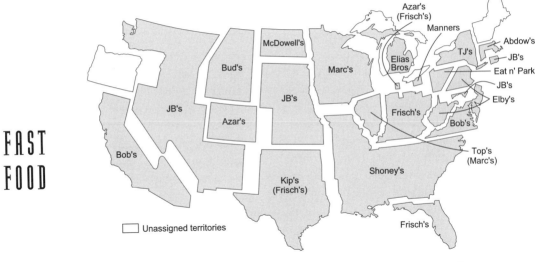

FIG. 3.6 Big Boy franchises, 1975. (*Source:* "Meet the Big Boys from Big Boy," *Restaurant Business* 74 [June 1975]: 76.)

to purchase a Big Boy franchise.[25] Frisch's Big Boy chain quickly developed around a central commissary in Cincinnati. Like the other Big Boy franchisees, Frisch was free to experiment with building designs and equipment, and free as well to offer menu items beyond the Big Boy sandwich. Frisch's Big Boy drive-ins featured both inside waitress and outside carhop service, the latter eliminated only in the mid-1970s when a strictly "coffee house" format was adopted. Approximately half of the restaurants were owned and half subfranchised. Frisch spread his risk by becoming a Roy Rogers franchisee as well, opening 19 stores by 1975. Ben Marcus, owner of a Wisconsin movie-theater chain, opened 14 drive-in restaurants in 1949, the number standing at 36 when they were renamed Marc's Big Boys in 1958.[26] The Marcus Corporation also moved into hotel ownership and eventually developed the Budgetele motel chain. Jack Broberg, who founded JB's Big Boy in Salt Lake City in 1961, had his first Big Boy sandwich as a teenager in Glendale, California, his hometown. Both JB's Restaurants and the Marcus Corporation broke the Big Boy association when Marriott sold the chain's trademark and franchising rights in 1988 to Elias Brothers, the Michigan Big Boy franchisee since 1951. Shoney's, Big Boy's representative across the Southeast, had defected five years earlier.[27]

SHONEY'S

Alex Schoenbaum opened a small 50-stall drive-in in 1947 in Charleston, West Virginia. Located next to his father's bowling alley, it was an outgrowth of the bowling alley's in-house snack bar. Success led to expansion at several other locations across the city. Dave Frisch, met at a trade convention, convinced Schoenbaum to become the Big Boy franchisee for West Virginia, a territory later expanded to Tennessee, Virginia, and North and South Carolina. Later, rights to Maryland and Washington, D.C., were traded for Georgia, Alabama, Mississippi, and Louisiana.[28] Originally called the Parkette Drive-Ins, the Shoney's Big Boy name was used after 1951. Most of the Shoney's expansion involved subfranchising. Ray Danner, the Nashville subfranchisee, built a chain of some 50 restaurants, ultimately buying out Schoenbaum in 1971 in a merger of operations. This was not the first or only instance of a franchisee (or subfranchisee) proving more successful than a parent firm, leading thus to a parent's buyout.

Ray Danner had managed a variety of businesses (a grocery store, a drive-in movie theater, a bowling alley, a gasoline station) before forming his restaurant chain. Danner Foods, besides being a Shoney's subfranchisee, operated a 22-store Kentucky Fried Chicken operation in Louisville sold in order to avoid conflict of interest when Danner built up his own 200-unit Lee's Famous Recipe Chicken restaurant chain. Danner also launched the Captain D's chain of seafood restaurants with its 330 outlets (as compared to Shoney's total of 320) by 1980.[29] In 1994, 936 Shoney's Restaurants (minus the Big Boy label) were in operation, most concentrated in the Southeast, reflecting the company's original Big Boy territory (see fig. 3.7). Clearly evident, however, was a nationwide chain in the making with penetration of the Middle West well established. Through the 1970s and 1980s, Shoney's, Inc. doubled its size every four years.

Shoney's sought to own most of the real estate on which its restaurants stood, financing land purchase internally.[30] Franchising was used to finance building construction and the equipping of restaurants. Among Shoney's largest franchisees was TPI Enterprises of West Palm Beach, Florida, operator in 1995 of 188 Shoney's Restaurants as well as 69 Captain D's.[31] Shoney's

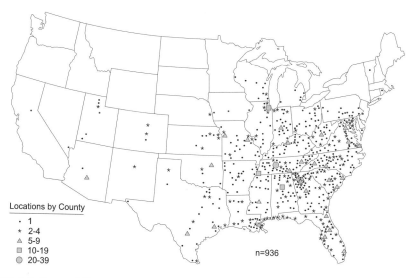

Locations by County
· 1
★ 2-4
△ 5-9
▣ 10-19
◉ 20-39

n=936

FIG. 3.7 Shoney's Restaurants, 1994. Counties with the largest number of Shoney's locations were: Davidson (Nashville), Tenn. (22), Cook (Chicago), Ill. (12), and Shelby (Memphis), Tenn. (11).

FIG. 3.8 Shoney's Restaurant, Chillicothe, Ohio, 1995.

FAST FOOD

followed the Big Boy chain's move into sit-down coffee shop or family restaurants. Adopted was a building format reminiscent of the Southern California googie coffee shop, but simplified to suit more conservative Southern and Middle Western tastes (see fig. 3.8).

DENNY'S

Denny's was founded in 1959, the Buena Park, California, firm operating 81 coffee shops by 1964, most of them in Southern California adjacent to motels at or near new interstate-highway interchanges. Single-site franchising was used to drive the firm's expansion, franchising fees varying from $12,000 for a 42-seat unit to $40,000 for a 102-seat restaurant.[32] The company assumed a "turnkey" responsibility for opening each restaurant, buying the land, constructing and outfitting the building, and training personnel. Franchisees committed to monthly rental payments of 7 percent of gross sales. In addition, most paid a trademark fee, covering use of the Denny's sign, equal to 10 percent the value of weekly invoices for food and supplies. Each restaurant was required to order food ingredients and supplies from vendors approved by the chain. Food had to be prepared, presented, and served in accordance with chain-wide standards. Restaurants were to be operated and maintained according to chain management codes. Each franchisee was required to participate in chain advertising promotions and follow standard bookkeeping and accounting procedures. Dress, appearance, and conduct of employees had to conform to chain rules and regulations.

Denny's purchased the Winchell's Donut chain in 1978, its founder, Verne Winchell, assuming the presidency of the combined company. Under Winchell, a new decor was adopted, the jarring pink and orange colors appropriate early in Southern California thought less attractive to customers elsewhere in the country. Introduced were quiet wood veneers, subdued color schemes, and indirect lighting. "Hanging planters soften the interiors. Handsome hooked rugs based on nature's forms—suns, trees, leaves—inject a sophistication that goes with the wine kegs and upgraded menus," reported one trade journal.[33] By 1977, the chain had grown to 614 restaurants. Under Verne Curtis, Winchell's successor, expansion continued through the opening of new company-owned stores and the buyout of other chains (such as the 35 VIP Family Restaurants of Northern California, Oregon, and Washington). Denny's solidified its entrance into Florida by purchasing units of the disintegrating Sambo's chain. In the 1980s, Denny's targeted more affluent customers by casting aside many of the attributes of the traditional coffee shop. "Gone are the oversized, plastic menus splattered with color pictures of hamburgers and hot fudge sundaes. In their place are menus which bear no resemblance to the 'coffee shop image' Denny's wants to shake," reported another trade journal.[34]

Like Howard Johnson's, with the Red Coach Grill and Ground Round restaurants, or Shoney's, with the Captain D's and Lee's Famous Recipe restaurants, Denny's promoted several secondary restaurant concepts in addition to Winchell's. The El Pollo Loco and Colony Kitchen chains were bought in 1983 and 1984 respectively. In 1987, Denny's was purchased by TW Services, a franchisee of over 400 Hardee's restaurants, and owner of the 200-unit Quincy's Steak House chain and the Canteen Corporation, a firm with vending machine and airline food-service businesses. The sale followed an earlier leveraged buyout by Denny's top managers who had taken the company public. In 1985, Denny's had only 41 franchised restaurants, having discontinued its franchising operation in 1970. However, franchising was resumed in order to raise capital thus to cover the buyout. Restaurant renovation ceased and by 1990 operational standards had declined across the chain's 1,200 restaurants. Sale of Denny's and its sister chains to the Flagstar Companies in 1993 prompted revitalization, including the adoption of both a new logo and a new prototype building (see fig. 3.9). There were 1,470 Denny's in operation in 1994, the highest concentration by far in California, the region of the chain's origin (see fig. 3.10). Denny's led what was now called the family dining segment of the restaurant market, a segment comprised mostly of regional coffee-shop chains (see Table 3.1).

SAMBO'S

The Howard Johnson's, Big Boy, and Denny's chains each used a different franchising scheme—co-owner, territorial, and site-specific franchises respectively. Sambo's, another major player in the coffee-shop or family dining field, used another system which sought, like franchising, to generate a steady supply of competent local managers by offering ownership incentives. Sambo's was launched in 1957 by Sam Battistone and Newell Bohnett as a beachfront pancake house in Santa Barbara, California. Battistone and

FIG. 3.9 Denny's Restaurant, Elk Grove Village, Ill., 1996.

Locations by County
· 1
★ 2-4
△ 5-9
▫ 10-19
● 20-39
▲ 40-79

n=1470

FIG. 3.10 Denny's Restaurants, 1994. Counties with the largest number of Denny's Restaurants were: Los Angeles (73), Maricopa (Phoenix), Ariz., and San Diego (35 each), Orange, Calif. (32), and King (Seattle), Wash. (28).

Bohnett extended to their store managers a buy-in plan which transferred to them equity ownership by stages. The plan was described in a 1966 trade journal as follows. When a new unit manager obtained his store (after a training period of five to eight months), he received a salary of $6,000 for the first year. Each month he also received a cut of his store's profit pie—20 percent of the action. In the second year the base salary jumped to $7,200 with an option to buy a "fraction of the action," 5 percent, in one of the new Sambo's about to open.[35] A version of this compensation scheme was first used by J. C. Penney in building his chain of clothing stores. At Sambo's, each store in the system came to be owned 50 percent by the company itself, 20 percent by its own managers, and 30 percent by six different partners who were managers of other stores, each with a 5 percent interest. Ideally, managers who had been with the chain for 10 years would enjoy the equivalent of 70 percent of their store's profits in terms of fraction ownership, their own plus 10 of the 5 percent shares in the profits of other units.[36] The scheme hinged, of course, on the chain's ability to expand continually.

In 1966, there were 60 Sambo's Restaurants across seven far western states, the vast majority in California. By 1974 there were 345 restaurants in 32 states, and by 1978 883 in 47 states.[37] But already the chain was in difficulty. When the chain's growth rate declined, its "fraction of the action" compensation program faltered, depressing manager morale. Then the Securities and Exchange Commission, following an inquiry into the chain's questionable accounting procedures, forced Sambo's to abandon its shared ownership scheme. By 1980 the chain was suffering from an estimated 100 percent turnover of managers each year.[38] Quality control declined sharply just as the chain's restaurants were beginning to show age. In addition, the Sambo's name came under attack as racist, playing as it did on the "Little Black Sambo" theme. Thus the company entered Chapter 11 bankruptcy,

TABLE 3.1 Leading Family Dining Chains, 1996

Chain	Headquarters	Units Worldwide	Sales (in millions)	Sales Rank Top 300
Denny's	Spartanburg, S.C.	1,596	$1,933	13
Shoney's	Nashville	844	1,209	24
Big Boy	Warren, Mich.	825	970	31
Coco's	Irvine, Calif.	466	710	41
Marie Callender's	Orange, Calif.	147	263	87
Village Inn	Denver	206	251	90
Country Kitchen	Minneapolis	253	235	96
Carrows	Irvine, Calif.	160	217	106
Bakers Square	Denver	154	204	110
Eat 'n Park	Pittsburgh	68	150	135
Lyons	Foster City, Calif.	80	130	149
Shari's	Beaverton, Ore.	96	114	160
JB's	Salt Lake City	95	95	175
Thads	Brigham City, Utah	75	85	193
Kettle Restaurants	Houston	99	81	202
Bill Knapps	Battle Creek, Mich.	53	75	210
Great Harvest Bread Co.	Dillon, Mont.	117	57	252
Kings	McKeesport, Pa.	31	55	260
Howard Johnson's	S. Weymouth, Mass.	56	54	263
Le Peep	Littleton, Colo.	60	46	286
Buffalo Café	Marietta, Ga.	41	44	298

Source: Restaurants and Institutions 107 (July 15, 1997): 66.

closing some 447 of its 1,114 restaurants immediately.[39] The chain began a steady disintegration. The Denver-based VICORP, owner of the Village Inn restaurant chain, bought 183 units in 1986.[40]

Market Segmentation and Franchising

The restaurant market is variously segmented for market research and planning purposes.[41] As diagrammed, the coffee shop or family restaurant, epitomized by Howard Johnson's, Denny's, and the other chains of like restaurants, have represented a middle ground measured along two related scales: service level and menu variety (see fig. 3.11). Low on both scales were the early drive-ins and what subsequently evolved as fast-food restaurants (with outdoor walk-up and indoor walk-up counters), restaurants targeted today to customers of modest taste if not modest wherewithal. Menus are limited, being based on only a few complementary foods served in attractive but nonetheless functional surroundings. At the high end on both scales are the "tablecloth / gourmet" restaurants that target customers able to pay for fine dining experiences built around conspicuous consumption both of food and atmosphere. At the one extreme is the deliberately commonplace. At the other extreme is the deliberately unique and highly contrived if not pretentious. Through the 1970s, most restaurant chains were built around market venues in the diagram's top two rows. During the 1980s and 1990s, however, chain development moved into segments represented by the diagram's lower row.

Early roadside restaurant chains were not only built around the coffee-shop idea but around the drive-in, outdoor walk-up, and indoor walk-up formats. Another, perhaps simpler way of segmenting the restaurant market in the United States involved focus on food product or menu line. Thus, which restaurant prototypes were successfully associated over time with various food emphasis? That question, of course, is exactly what we ask in subsequent chapters as we turn from one menu orientation to another. The aggregate of leading brands variously categorized by food group for 1973, 1979, and 1985 are given in Table 3.2. The trend toward specialty food and wider-menu restaurants is clearly evident. Shown for 1972, 1981, and 1990 is change in total chain restaurant sales, as well as change in the aggregate number of chain outlets operational, the whole broken down by food group (see Table 3.3). Clearly, the trend was one of growth overall but favoring the specialty food and wider-menu chain venues.

In the early years of franchising, many chains were promoted through the name recognition of entertainment and sports celebrities, most focusing on a single food line. For example, country-western artists Minnie Pearl and Eddie Arnold promoted fried chicken, and Tennessee Ernie Ford steak and biscuits. Television shows not dominated by a single personality, or a real personality, also inspired franchise packaging, the Laugh-In Restaurant chain promoted its Bippyburgers, and the Yogi Bear chain its honey-fried chicken. DiMaggio's and Broadway Joe's honored specific sports heroes

FIG. 3.11 Segmentation
of the restaurant market
by service level and menu
variety.

		Menu Variety		
		LOW	MEDIUM	HIGH
Service Level	LOW	Drive-ins Fast Food Restaurants	Diners	Cafeterias
	MEDIUM	Specialty Restaurants	Coffee Shop/ Family Restaurant	Casual-Dining Restaurants
	HIGH	Concept Restaurants	Upscale Dinnerhouses	Fine-Dining Restaurants (Tablecloth/Gourmet)

Restaurant
Chains

TABLE 3.2 Franchise Companies by Food Speciality

Food Specialty	1973	1979	1985
Hamburgers, hot dogs, roast beef sandwiches	104	112	105
Chicken	21	32	30
Pizza	30	73	102
Mexican	14	28	36
Seafood	11	11	14
Specialty sandwiches	6	33	53
Steak, full menu (including pancakes)	59	110	130

Source: Robert L. Emerson, *The New Economics of Fast Food* (New York: Van Nostrand Reinhold, 1990), 62.

TABLE 3.3 Franchise Restaurant Market Segmentation by Food Specialty

Food	Sales (in millions)			Number of Units		
	1972	1981	1990	1972	1981	1990
Hamburgers, hot dogs, roast beef sandwiches	3.8	14.3	33.9	19,324	26,945	38,241
Chicken	1.0	2.8	5.6	4,561	7,388	9,334
Pizza	0.3	3.2	12.0	2,385	9,334	23,277
Mexican	0.1	1.1	4.3	906	3,002	5,593
Seafood	0.1	1.0	1.6	487	2,226	2,969
Pancakes, waffles	0.2	1.0	1.4	735	1,500	2,137
Steak, full menu	1.3	6.6	12.4	3,893	9,406	11,324
Specialty sandwich	0.5	0.5	2.2	247	1,684	8,414
Ice cream	-	-	4.4	-	-	14,681
Donuts	-	-	1.6	-	-	4,197
TOTAL	7.3	30.5	79.4	32,538	61,485	120,167

Source: Ralph Peterson, "Franchising in the Economy, 1975-1977: An Update," *Restaurant Business* 76 (March 1, 1977): 154-55; Andrew Kostecka, "Restaurant Franchising in the Economy," *Restaurant Business* 82 (March 1, 1983): 136-37; Marilyn Alva, "Franchise Relations," *Restaurant Business* 90 (March 20, 1991): 106-8.

while other chains promoted sports in general, for example the Our Hero chain which featured big-bun sandwiches. Entrepreneur John J. Hooker Jr. of Nashville launched several celebrity-based chains including Minnie Pearl's. The comedienne, with price tag dangling from her straw hat, met every new franchisee to present them an autographed picture of herself inscribed "I care." Minnie Pearl's franchises cost $10,000 and by the end of 1968 Hooker had sold 405 of them.[42] Of the 202 Minnie Pearl restaurants operating in 1970, only a few were profitable. Hooker, who had taken the company public, announced losses for 1969 in excess of $30 million. Hooker sold an investment idea but not a functioning franchise service. The launching of chains solely on the basis of collected "one-shot" license fees came to be called "Minnie Pearling it."[43]

Corporate Consolidation

Few franchise ideas evolved beyond a prototype facility, a marketing plan, and a handful of stores actually open. Attracted to restaurant franchising were scores if not hundreds of unscrupulous promoters cognizant of the many investors willing to speculate in franchise licenses, especially licenses that carried territorial rights, and, as well, the many would-be restauranteurs looking for a shortcut to business ownership. Surviving chains found themselves locked in intensive competition for local, regional, and national markets. Market realities favored the large, better-financed companies, and, as we will emphasize in succeeding chapters, especially the firms that serviced their franchisees rather than merely raking in fees or milking franchisees through food and supply purchase requirements. The 1970s brought much consolidation to the restaurant industry and, more important, a high degree of vertical integration through corporate buyout and merger.

MARRIOTT

The Marriott Corporation's rise as a purveyor of hospitality—restaurants, institutional food service, and motels and hotels—stands as one of corporate America's great success stories. J. Willard Marriott opened a root-beer stand in 1927 in Washington, D.C., securing an A&W franchise, but also adding chili, hot tamales, and sandwiches to sustain clientele beyond the summer months. The name Hot Shoppe was adopted. Within two years three drive-ins, each painted bright orange, were operating, food delivered to waiting cars by curb boys working for tips. Airline passengers on their way to National Airport began stopping at the Fourteenth Street location to buy coffee and sandwiches. This led Marriott into contracts with Capital and Eastern Airlines to supply in-flight meals. Eventually a sizable food service business evolved, oriented to factory vending and hospital and office building cafeterias as well as airports. A large food commissary was established in suburban Washington, D.C., with additional commissaries built across the country as Marriott's airline business spread to airports nationwide.[44]

By 1950 there were 20 Hot Shoppe restaurants, 15 in the Washington, D.C.,

FIG. 3.12 Hot Shoppe prototype building, ca. 1940.

area, 3 in greater Philadelphia, and 2 in greater Baltimore. Venues varied (Hot Shoppe Mighty Mo Drive-Ins, Hot Shoppe Char-broilers, Hot Shoppe Juniors, and even a Hot Shoppe Cafeteria), but most followed a prescribed Hot Shoppe prototype, an orange-roofed building containing a coffee shop indoors and an outdoor carhop service at one end (see fig. 3.12). In 1957, the company opened a large luxury motel in Arlington County, Virginia, adjacent to National Airport, the first in what would grow into one of the nation's largest motel/hotel chains. In 1970, Marriott owned and operated 35 Hot Shoppes and 35 Hot Shoppe Cafeterias, and operated 16 airport and toll-road Hot Shoppes in leased quarters. The new celebrity-based Roy Rogers' Western Roast Beef Sandwich chain was launched with 45 restaurants owned and operated by Marriott and 92 operated by licensees under franchise. Marriott owned and operated 35 Bob's Big Boy coffee shops in the East, and controlled the Big Boy franchising rights covering all 541 Big Boy restaurants nationwide.[45]

The Gino's chain, centered on Baltimore, was purchased in 1982, with 180 of its 313 locations quickly converted to the Roy Rogers' brand.[46] Gino's had been the sole franchisee of Kentucky Fried Chicken in Washington, D.C., Maryland, Delaware, New Jersey, and parts of Pennsylvania, Virginia, and North Carolina. Gino's also had operated the 160-unit Rustler Steak House chain. Marriott's Roy Rogers' brand was further strengthened through the purchase and rebranding of 11 Hardd's Restaurants on Long Island, and 13 Burger Chefs in the Washington, D.C., area. Also launched was Marriott's chain of Farrell's Ice Cream Parlours, with 76 company-owned and -operated units and 31 franchised units.[47] The Howard Johnson's chain was acquired in 1987 with the idea of converting owned locations to other Marriott brands, or to still other brands for which the company held limited franchise rights—Popeye's, Dunkin' Donuts, Burger King, and Dairy Queen.

Also in 1987, Marriott unsuccessfully sought to buy Denny's and the El Pollo chains. Marriott also experimented with two new chain ideas—Wag's and Brickford's.

Another brand, Allie's, was introduced in 1988 with the intention of consolidating the company's diversity of coffee-shop formats under a single name. Featured was a food-bar or buffet venue. As the experiment faltered, Marriott took the opportunity to reassess its food business, deciding in 1990 to divest itself of all restaurants, its in-flight catering business having been sold the previous year. Soon brought to a close was a 60-year corporate presence in the restaurant field. Marriott viewed the restaurant industry as mature with opportunities for sustained growth accordingly limited. As Christopher Muller assessed, industry maturity was characterized by

> impending market saturation, customers being able to choose among a selection of leading brands, limited product differentiation among competitors, competition waged through mass advertising, players engaging in price competition and dealing, shakeouts of major players, strong cyclicality of revenue streams, generally falling prices, and lower profits and margins for all players.[48]

As an initial step in divestiture, the Roy Rogers' chain was sold to Hardee's.

Enter the Food Conglomerates

In the early years of expansion—during the industry's drive to maturity rather than its later era of maturity—many of the nation's giant food corporations entered the chain restaurant business. With increased income and leisure time, Americans were eating out more each year. Concerned to maintain, if not increase, their share of the total food market, many packaged-food manufacturers bought restaurant chains or initiated new chains of their own. "For a major food processor feeling the pinch of steady or falling sales of packaged casseroles or breakfast cereal," wrote journalist Robin Ashton, "a natural growth solution is to buy a restaurant chain, a likely source of the stagnant sales in the first place."[49] Thus General Foods bought Burger Chef, Pillsbury bought both Burger King and Steak and Ale, Heublein bought Kentucky Fried Chicken, United Brands bought A&W, and Quaker Oats bought Magic Pan. PepsiCo developed both Pizza Hut and Taco Bell. Royal Crown launched Arby's. Pet, Inc. purchased both Stuckey's and Hardee's. Ralston Purina took over Jack in the Box. General Mills developed the Red Lobster and Olive Garden chains. Hershey Foods bought the Friendly Ice Cream chain.

Buyout brought additional investment capital to restaurant chains struggling to grow. For the food processors came promised share of the restaurant dollar not only through potential chain earnings but also through the selling of their original products as chain supplier. However, as we will outline in subsequent chapters, few of the large food manufacturers proved successful in the restaurant business. Highly structured companies, producing set products packaged and delivered to retailer shelves, found it difficult to adjust to the "freewheeling" restaurant trade with its emphasis on customer service and place-product-packaging formatting.[50] Few chains fared well as corporate subsidiaries. Many were cannibalized in a selling off of chain real estate and other assets. Pet, Inc.'s treatment of Stuckey's is a case in point.

STUCKEY'S

W. S. Stuckey Sr.'s pecan stand, opened in Eastman, Georgia, in 1934, featured pecan logs prepared from a family recipe. Three additional stands—actually stores incorporating café and gas-station functions—were operating by the time the war began. After World War II, a series of prototype buildings emerged as Stuckey launched his chain in earnest, targeting highway travelers, many heading south to resort destinations in Florida. Most of his "one-stop" facilities sported canopy roofs extended forward to shade the gas pumps (see fig. 3.13). Inside was a lunch counter, supplemented by booths, and racks for the display of packaged candy as well as rubber snakes, moccasins, and other souvenir trinkets. With the coming of limited-access interstate highways, Stuckey's expanded to interchange locations, first across the Southeast into Texas, then into the Middle West, and finally across the central Great Plains states into the Rocky Mountains.

The company was sold to Pet, Inc. in 1964, Stuckey becoming a member of Pet's board of directors. Through Stuckey's oversight the chain continued to expand, but more slowly, operating at 314 locations in 1971 (see fig. 3.14). Pet, Inc. was a subsidiary of IC Industries, which was itself consumed with divesting the Illinois Central Gulf Railroad. As the railroad was cannibalized, its parts variously sold off, so also were Stuckey's restaurant assets liquidated, especially the chain's most profitable interstate interchange properties. IC Industries renamed itself the Whitman Corporation after Pet's popular brand of chocolate candies, Stuckey's pecan candies having been the real fo-

FIG. 3.13 Stuckey's Candy Shoppe, Chiefland, Fla., ca. 1940.

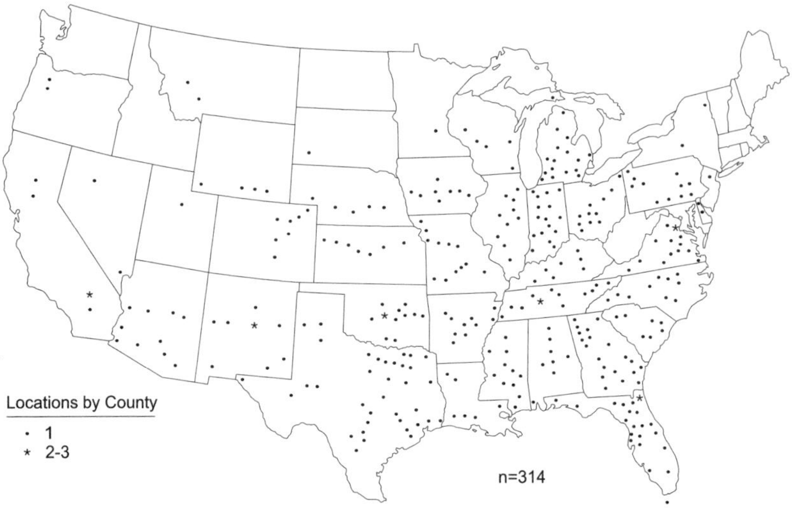

FIG. 3.14 Stuckey's, 1971.

FIG. 3.15 Stuckey's, 1989.

cus of the Stuckey's acquisition originally. "Milked" of assets, the residual Stuckey's chain was resold to W. S. Stuckey Jr., an ex-congressman determined to rebuild the image of his father's legacy. In 1989, the new chain operated 107 owned and franchised units, a much diminished operation compared to the firm's glory years (see fig. 3.15). Stuckey's maintained a commissary in Atlanta from which refrigerated trucks supplied the much-reduced system. Many Stuckey's locations were cobranded with Dairy Queen in the 1990s.[51]

Chains within Chains

The large corporation came to dominate the restaurant business. The most successful franchisor of all, McDonald's, grew into an autonomous corporation. Many other franchisors, Burger King for example, operated as subsidiaries of large food-processing companies as described. But a third kind of corporate giant emerged as well, the management company—the large-scale franchisee with one or more brands operating hundreds of stores. These companies operated not under their own brands but under the brands of others. They operated, in other words, as chains within chains. Indeed, owning and operating restaurants could prove very lucrative, several management companies actually buying out the licensing firms under which they operated. Emergent through the 1970s and 1980s, therefore, was a convoluted pattern of equity relationship tying franchisors and large franchisee companies together (see Table 3.4).

Lack of early success with their own chains led several restaurant companies into management. Horn and Hardart, faced in the 1960s with the decline of their automats, became Burger King's franchisee for New York City and, later, for parts of Florida.[52] The firm also obtained Arby's Roast Beef and Cedric's Fish and Chips franchises for various parts of the country. In 1982, it bought the Bojangles chain of chicken restaurants centered on the Carolinas, putting Horn and Hardart in business belatedly as a franchisor. Chart House, developers of a steakhouse chain centered on Louisiana, became Burger King's largest franchisee, operating 238 Burger Kings in 1976, and subfranchising 39 more.[53] The firm bought the franchising rights to Godfather's Pizza in 1984. In the 1990s, other large Burger King licensees included the Jordan Company (178 restaurants in the East and Middle West), and the Carrol's Corporation (200 restaurants in upstate New York).[54]

Franchising drove the chain restaurant to the forefront of the restaurant industry. Today, chain restaurants substantially dominate America's eating out. Not only do chain-affiliated eateries outnumber independent restaurants, but collectively they set the standards by which all restaurants tend to be judged. Central was place-product-packaging, the formatting and networking of lookalike facilities in the defining of trade territories—a business strategy first brought to the roadside through chains of gasoline stations and then through motel chains. As with the petroleum and hospitality industries, the very rapid emergence of the chain restaurant, especially after 1955, reflected an industry dynamic highly speculative in nature but also logically sound. Competing companies rushed to build restaurant chains as much to deny others market penetration as to meet established demand, producing saturated markets. On the other hand, larger-scale operations meant cost savings in the procurement, preparation, and distribution of food, especially where central commissaries were at work. But, most important, growing chains were inevitably more profitable than nongrowing ones. New locations were usually superior to old locations, given the nation's rapidly chang-

TABLE 3.4 Ten Largest Management Companies, 1990

Name	Headquarters	Brands	Outlets
1. Collins Foods	Los Angeles	KFC Sizzler Taco Den	932
2. Spartan Foods	Spartanburg, S.C.	Hardee's Quincy's	678
3. DeNovo Corp.	Utica, Mich.	Tastee Freeze Dog 'n Suds Dairy Isle BK Root Beer	588
4. TW Services	Spartanburg, S.C.	Denny's El Pollo Loco Hardee's	437
5. National Restaurant Management	New York, N.Y.	Pizza Hut KFC Dunkin' Donuts Häagen-Dazs	373
6. Horn and Hardart	Las Vegas	Burger King Arby's Tony Roma's David's Cookies Bojangles	280
7. TPI Restaurants	Memphis	Captain D's Shoney's	242
8. Scott's Food Services	Austin, Tex.	KFC	185
9. Carrol's Corporation	Syracuse, N.Y.	Burger King	163
10. Restaurant Developers	Independence, Ohio	Mr. Hero Mr. Philly	136

Source: James Tierney, ed., *1990 Directory of Chain Restaurant Operators* (New York: Lebhar-Friedman, 1990).

ing highway system. And a chain's managers—management being the critical key to chain success—needed to be compensated in part through promise of professional advancement, a promise that only chain expansion could assure.[55]

By the increasing use of financial leverage, either through incurring debt obligation or, as was very common in the restaurant industry, through the leasing of property, companies expanded beyond normal returns on equity.[56] Substantial overbuilding was sustained nearly everywhere. High rates of entry into the chain restaurant sweepstakes turned into high rates of fallout as only the very strong could survive. Within each market segment only a few successful chains could thrive, sustained variously by a combination of assets—effective management at all levels, access to investment capital, focus on a few food concepts, use of simplified restaurant formats, and quality of food product and service among other variables. Important was an ability to change, to sense market trends and update marketing strategies. Unsuccessful chains did not change so much as disappear, at best cannibalized for still potentially profitable locations.

The coffee shop was, of course, but one of several roadside restaurant formats successfully used in chain development. Through the 1950s, drive-in or carhop service often complemented coffee shops, as at many Big Boy locations nationwide, the potential of eating in one's car made integral to chain promotion. After 1960, however, the car became more a means of access than a focus of identity, the off-street parking lot treated as a commonplace necessity rather than as a special business promotion. Coffee-shop interiors, once open to the road as visual display, became increasingly obscured to outside view, although buildings as signs, as, indeed, building signs, continued to shout at passing motorists loudly. Building profile, color scheme, and logo—orchestrated as corporate livery—played out across the respective chains, customer expectations and loyalties cued in commercial landscapes substantially automobile-oriented and thus roadside contained.

The franchise chain greatly amplified numerically the automobile-convenient, quick-service restaurant in the United States. Along with the gas station, the motel, and other "drive-in" commercial building forms, the roadside restaurant contributed substantially to a sense of landscape homogeneity in almost every locality across America. A relatively few building formats—programmed by a relatively few menu / service orientations—came to characterize a relatively few restaurant chains. How did specific restaurant brands rise to dominance? What marked successful versus unsuccessful place-product-packaging? We have offered tentative answers in regards to the coffee shop or family restaurant chains, a topic we will return to briefly when we discuss what we term "breakfast food." We turn next to focus on the lowly hamburger, and the emergent commercial empires based thereon. What did it take to sell a hamburger to customers arrived by car? Much coffee-shop business hinged on hamburger sales. In the coffee shops, however, hamburgers usually were subordinated to other foods. What happened when the hamburger was king?

CHAPTER 4

Hamburger Places, Part 1

amburgers, especially when complemented by french fries, are the
preeminent roadside food, developing early among the foods served
through the restaurant chains that came to encapsulate much of the
traveler's experience and still dominating roadside food sales. How did
place-product-packaging and corporate territoriality help guide people to
these foods? Which restaurant forms—which restaurant venues—were important? Who were the entrepreneurs who initiated the hamburger's roadside dominion? By what stages did they rise to preeminence? Why were
some experiments with hamburger eateries successful? What experiments
were initiated only to be abandoned and others not? What at different times
generated the greatest profits? Make no mistake about it—hamburgers are a
business. They are made and served ultimately to maximize investor profit,
in some cases at the expense of consumer health and worker income. This
chapter opens with a brief examination of the cultural and demographic un-
derpinnings of the hamburger's supremacy on the roadside. We then focus
on the forms that developing hamburger eateries took. What kinds of
places came to cater to America's hamburger lust?

The Social Setting

At the end of the nineteenth century, America underwent a series of
converging and often mutually reinforcing fundamental reorientations,
each of profound importance in its own right, whose cumulative effect rendered an essentially new America. Industrialization, urbanization, and ethnic diversity were the transforming forces. Those channeled people's ways
of eating toward places and their products packaged in integrated design
systems diffused through territorial networks of corporate identity. How industrialization, urbanization, and ethnic diversity were rationalized in
America was very much a cultural matter, the symbolic relationships that
emerged and reign to this day:[1] specifically, we understand America's eating

habits occurred within a general culture of consumption made automobile-convenient.

Goods and services have not only an intrinsic value—as in eating food to sustain life—but they have social value communicated visually. Perhaps most notable is the automobile itself. One's identity in relating to others in modern America depends in part on what kind of automobile one owns. Wearing an automobile like a social cachet was the essence of Sloanism, General Motors' "packaging" its automobiles to be consumed variously by people of differing social standing. Customers were encouraged to "move up" from Chevrolet to Cadillac as their wherewithal improved. Americans became "other-directed," as David Riesman explained; they were determined to succeed by getting others to like them rather than by hewing to preconceived courses yielding self-satisfaction. What one ate and where one ate in public helped connote one's status as well as what kind of car one drove.[2] Consuming food with preferred associates carried its own social implications.

The quickest way to capture others' attention seemed to be in the way things were made to look. Hence, restaurants were self-consciously developed to project a particular ambiance. Designs were contrived for effect. In the American economy overflowing with goods and services for most people, competitors had to distinguish their products by some easily and widely grasped means. Packaging thus arose. By arranging colors and shapes in distinctive ways associated with their goods or services, entrepreneurs could set their enterprise apart from others in the consumer's eye at the point of sale. The way a thing looked became paramount, of equal weight if not more important than the consumer's satisfaction with the good or service itself. Slogans—words, after all—were secondary reinforcements appealing to the visually besieged consumer. This visual orientation originated with the packaging of food stuffs for consumption at home. Lessons learned were not lost on the purveyors of food prepared along the roadside, as shall be shown.[3]

Industrialization and urbanization also upset traditional patterns of food preparation and eating, opening new opportunities for convenience starting at the end of the nineteenth century. Perhaps most important was the changed role of women in the workforce. Before industrialization and urbanization, women normally remained at home, where, among their many tasks, food preparation was principal. Women's share of the national workforce, however, jumped from nearly 15 percent in 1870 to 22 percent in the half-century to 1930, most of it due to their burgeoning factory, clerical, or sales work. A widespread need consequently developed for others to prepare and serve food. It became too much to expect women to work outside the home and also make meals at home, at least *all* the meals. With the onset of industrialization, men too were employed outside the home and often sought opportunities to eat and socialize with other male laborers on the way to and from their jobs. Income increased with industrialization's waged-based economy; consequently expendable money was at hand to purchase the foods others prepared and served. Urban restaurants catering

FIG. 4.1 Hill's Snappy Service in Streator, Ill., a small industrial center, typifies the early diner setting.

FAST FOOD

to factory workers traveling streetcar lines and, later, buses, formulated the place types initially used along the automobile roadside on the urban fringes.[4]

Workers in these streetcar- and bus-convenient restaurants largely were drawn from unskilled jobs elsewhere. Industrial jobs, with which the new cadre of restaurant employees were faced as alternative income sources, set the pattern for working. Tasks were specialized in a production system. Pay was minimal. Intended, after all, was maximum profit yield for the owner. Speed in food preparation involved repetitive tasks learned by rote. Customers were encouraged to "get about their business" by ordering, eating, paying, and leaving as quickly as possible. Customers as a group were not welcome to linger. A stool at a counter occupied after a customer finished eating was an additional business opportunity denied. Grillmen frequently doubled as waiters by turning to serve at the counter what they had just cooked on the grill, thus minimizing the number of employees and resultant labor costs (see fig. 4.1).[5]

Abhorrent, too, was the empty restaurant seat. Fewer customers meant fewer profits. In an economy of abundance for most, however, concern mounted to build a base of loyal, repeat customers, and to lure new ones into the market and from one's competitors. A visually oriented culture made it seem natural to fashion the restaurant's architecture like a sign. Messages, transmitted by sight to a society understanding their import implicitly, drew customers. For example, the Steak 'n Shake hamburger chain's slogan—"It's in Sight—It Must Be Right"—attempted to reassure wary customers with food prepared before their eyes. Emulated was a local bakery's slogan, which likewise reassured their customers of cleanliness (see fig.

4.2).[6] Sanitary food preparation was expected; only at "greasy spoons" was health threatened. They were presumed dirty and unkempt.[7] Hence, bright colors, most often white scrubbed to a gleaming finish, were part of a successful restaurant's ambiance (see fig. 4.3). In the restaurant, as if on a theater stage, uniformed personnel courteous to customers and obedient to the management set the pace and dictated the regimen for success. Standard food, but with some distinction to set the menu apart from the competition, and low prices enduring unchanged for what seemed a long time to cus-

FIG. 4.2 Steak 'n Shake's restaurant in Galesburg, Ill., about 1950, is a virtual billboard, several of whose slogans assert the chain's purity.

FIG. 4.3 The bright sheen of the building materials and counter equipment are evident in this view of Steak 'n Shake's grand opening in the late 1940s in Peoria, Ill.

tomers: these complemented the visual appeal. A package of integrated price, product, architecture, and personnel made a system of operations at one restaurant, and a systematic network of identical or similar restaurant units formed a chain. Nothing was more memorable than a seemingly distinctive place set amidst the modernizing world of sameness.[8] Thus grew places relied upon and desired for eating out, ones that varied little in real essence despite individualizing appeals.

FAST FOOD

Large institutions that tend to deny range for individual expression characterize much of modern society today. Chief among these are big government, big labor unions, big professional associations, and big business. Included in the latter are the large chain restaurants. People sensing a confining structure in modern life seek out restaurants, partly as an antidote, frequently along the roadside on vacation or to avoid the routine of making food at home. Restaurants also spring up partly because their founders seek empowerment—to control their own lives, to be their own bosses—and the establishment celebrates them for exemplifying the American dream and the vitality of American capitalism.[9] A tension between the standardized and the individualistic, where the standard tends to hold sway, is implicit. The market tyrannizes most, however, the economies of ever-larger scale allure through lower prices. Less heed is often paid to the degradations of cheapness.

The Food—Hamburgers, Fries, and Shakes

How did hamburgers come to be the primary food of convenience at roadside restaurants? How did the current linkage occur between hamburgers and french fries, the one usually stimulating thought of the other when either is mentioned? How did the milkshake gain access as a secondary complement? The long historical process began with the hamburger.

HAMBURGERS

Hamburgers, of course, are a beef product, a traditional staple of the American diet. Long rivaled by pork as a favorite American meat, beef asserted its primacy by structuring much of the nation's expansion in the nineteenth century. The British, fond of fatty beef in their diet, invested heavily in cattle-raising and meat-packing companies begun in the American West, and beef became the dietary symbol of the frontier experience hallowed in the American psyche. By the end of World War I, a beef trust controlled a large sector of the American economy, much as would an automobile trust, the hamburger's later ally along the roadside. American beef consumption increased 72 percent between 1910 and 1976. Beef consumption became concomitant with wealth and increased status and it should not be a surprise that hamburger became a food preferred among a people coveting upward social mobility. America's economy of abundance coupled with the culture of consumption was signaled by the end of the nineteenth century in no small measure by beef and its popular hamburger derivative.[10]

The hamburger's origins are uncertain, if not lost, like so many aspects of American life engendering rival claimants in the consumer culture about who created the first of a particular good or service, when they did it, and where. The earliest traceable evidence is to the "Hamburg steak" served at Delmonico's restaurant in New York City in 1836 or 1837. References multiply in the 1880s, and by the early twentieth century it can be reliably claimed that the hamburger had emerged as it is known now—a patty of cooked ground beef served, like a sandwich, between two bun halves. Here seemed to be a quickly and easily prepared food, an unambiguous dish incapable of bamboozling the customer with sauces, which one authority has claimed Americans feared restaurants applied to disguise undesirable food. The hamburger as it is known now was probably first served to large numbers at the Louisiana Purchase Exposition in St. Louis in 1904.[11]

Regardless of a possible alternative origin among mid-nineteenth-century German immigrants ("hamburg steak" served aboard the Hamburg-American steamship line), hamburgers became widely popular at the very time Americans were severely divided along geographic, social, and ethnic lines. Coming eventually to be regarded as the preeminent American food, the hamburger's function as a symbol of nationhood helped homogenize the American palate as well as the places where it was served.[12]

FRENCH FRIES

French fries are, of course, a potato derivative. As a cheap, nutritious, and easily grown food, the potato has a history that is long—dating from prehistoric times—and its preparations have been varied. Potatoes in America were for a long time served only after boiling, which was believed necessary to render eatable the otherwise poisonous vegetable. The french fry is a comparatively recent addition to restaurant bills of fare, gaining accompaniment with meat as another way of satisfying America's long-standing taste for meat *and* potatoes. The modifier "French" referred to the method of slicing transferred from the cutting of other vegetables in narrow strips and of cutting meat close to the bone. One reliable source dates the first printed reference to french-fried potatoes to 1908. There is no association with French culinary art, although the French do have their "pommes-frites." Americans should think of the deep-fat-fried, slender-cut potatoes that they prefer to call french fries as not French but quintessentially American.[13]

Beginning in the late 1940s, convenience structured how hamburgers and fries came to be thought of as the two halves of a main course distinctly road-side-oriented. The first restaurants to serve them emphasized other foods as well, the highway cafés giving more variety, the drive-ins less variety.[14] Nothing was natural about the association of hamburgers and fries except, perhaps, that both could be prepared quickly. People linked them as a fried food given in popular culture. As we will show, hamburger places at first offered many other accompaniments to the hamburger. With the growth of leisure time in the consumer culture after the mid-twentieth century and the popularity of its key facilitator, the automobile, a premium was placed on increased speed. Frying is a relatively easy and fast way of cooking. It is instructive of french fries' minor place among the early roadside foods that the best-known early arbiter of food for automobile travelers whose taste was decidedly middle class, Duncan Hines, does mention French frying—but strawberries, hardly potatoes—in a book published as late as 1955. When hamburger entrepreneurs hit upon french fries as a novelty accompaniment for the hamburger, both speedily served, they waited for someone to perfect the french fry taste, and link it through advertising to hamburgers. These steps the McDonald's chain took in carving its vast fast-food empire.[15]

MILKSHAKES

Milkshakes came to the roadside free of any association with other foods. Milk, ice, and flavored syrups in the right proportions shaken together yielded milkshakes available commercially beginning in the mid-nineteenth century. They were produced by a stationary blender on whose high-speed spindles were mounted various disks. Ice cream's appearance shortly thereafter on the popular food market made it an often preferred substitute for ice because the finished blend was thicker and cooler. The demand for shakes boomed during Prohibition as part of the general expansion of the ice cream and soft-drink industries. Soda fountains served milkshakes; their curb service literally first brought them to automobiles in the 1920s. Their profit potential was well appreciated by Ray Kroc in 1939 when he started in business selling an improved milkshake mixer far earlier than it occurred to him that shakes might be a desirable complement to hamburgers and fries. Hamburger places had begun to sell milkshakes in the 1930s, as the Steak 'n Shake chain disclosed in its very name.[16]

The Founder—White Castle

In the first half of the twentieth century, White Castle was the first company to create a distinctive "sense of place" widely accepted for selling hamburgers.[17] White Castle's success in formulating a place type for purveying hamburgers was widely copied and then elaborated. No less a hamburger mogul than Ray Kroc, McDonald's legendary founder, recalled vividly that it was at a White Castle, serving its distinctive, one-inch-square meat patties, that he first learned about hamburgers eaten outside the home.[18] In a culture valuing novelty and inducing constant change, White Castle's persistence today as a relatively small, family-owned enterprise adhering to its original marketing principles is unusual. White Castle's popularity today as a symbol of popular culture has much to do with its traditional business stance combined with its simple cuisine, an antidote to the perception of much of contemporary American life as needlessly complex and outgrown of human scale. Nor should the poor be forgotten who rely on White Castle's many inner-city restaurants as one of the few affordable hamburger places.

White Castle's formula of place-product-packaging was full blown almost

FIG. 4.4 A drawing of the first White Castle whose white-painted cement blocks were intended to signify purity and whose castle motif was intended to signify strength, permanence, and stability. (*Source:* Courtesy White Castle System, Inc.)

from the company's start, quite a remarkable feat. In 1916, in Wichita, Kansas, in beef-raising country, Walter Anderson, a cook, began frying low-priced hamburgers in a remodeled streetcar wherein so many "diner" operations were housed across the country. At the time, hamburgers were sold as a novelty food at fairs and amusement parks and were unusually poor-tasting concoctions of lumps of ground beef cooked to the dry and tasteless point and then served in cold buns. Anderson, however, innovated a frying technique to overcome the poor taste as well as counter hamburger meat's unsavory reputation as the residue of a meat-packing industry attacked by Progressive-era reformers.[19]

Edgar Waldo "Billy" Ingram, a real estate and insurance agent, became Anderson's partner in 1921. Anderson intended to profit from his invention; he had already opened three diners but had insufficient capital for further expansion until he met Ingram. The partners further benefited from Ingram's notion that a new name and architectural identity could add the luster required to capture the popular imagination augmenting success in a culture emphasizing visual appeals (see fig. 4.4). Heretofore, the use of white in restaurants to connote cleanliness had been restricted exclusively to interiors, but with White Castle's application of white to the exterior of its diners it took an important step in advertising.[20] Seemingly small features added up to innovating a stunning concept for a hamburger place.

Labor was utilized to further convince that White Castle was a reliable as well as respectable place. Employees were uniformed in white shirts and, at first, white linen caps. With these caps regularly shrinking in the washing necessary to retain their symbolic whiteness, Ingram hit on the idea of white caps of paper, which could be replaced at less expense. Uniformity of look was furthered by employing an all-male staff. Not until the scarcity of men on the homefront during World War II did White Castle start employing women.[21]

White Castle drove relentlessly in many ways for more and more sales despite operating an unprecedented 115 chain restaurants in 1931, a dismal Depression year. Before his partnership with Ingram, Anderson had begun the campaign to "Buy 'em by the sack," as a sales boost since there was little seating in his diners. In 1931, however, the partners began to promote the carryout trade, customers buying White Castle hamburgers and eating them away from the diner. Convenience of location was an imperative. In 1928, an all-metal building was designed for replication and relocation. Often only 30-day or other short-term property leases were available. When a lease was not renewed and White Castle was forced to relocate, the entire portable diner could be moved with relative ease to another location. Locations with room for parking lots were added, when possible, to tap the growing automobile-borne trade. Indeed, many White Castles appeared at the corners of downtown parking lots oriented to street intersections, a symbolic relationship with a distinctly automobile-convenient land use. Newspaper coupons for reduced prices were introduced in 1932. Griddles were the subject of regular experimentation to maintain the desired quality of hamburger while simultaneously accelerating the volume they could cook. By the early 1960s, Ingram boasted of a 2,000-hamburger-per-hour rate.[22]

In pursuit of maximum profit, White Castle set out after the female market at a time when many women still regarded diners as alien, male-dominated places. White Castle did so by naming an employee "Julia Joyce," who acted as a hostess on specific occasions, inviting women to inspect a White Castle diner and arrange functions at various women's clubs to serve White Castle foods. In having a female symbolize White Castle, the company was perhaps patterning itself after the likes of General Mills' "Betty Crocker." The company also pushed its sales of coffee as a special accent to the company's menu, which the company strived to make a coveted taste.[23]

White Castle was also reordered financially to make the most of its employees without exploiting them and yet cut costs. A cash bonus plan for all employees was based, beginning in 1924, on gross sales rather than profit. Ingram avowed an ethic of respect for his staff and he increased the number of restaurants, but slowly. A conservative investor, Ingram refused to operate on much credit. His loan for the first diner was paid off in 90 days from the diner's profit and his second one was not built until money was in hand. Franchising was not used to expand. And, finally, the company developed operating divisions to produce its buildings, paper supplies, and bakery goods as support for its food sales, all contributing to a highly systematized business.[24]

A series of individual yet interdependent activities aimed at efficiency—in this case measured in profits—had been designed under the direction of entrepreneurial vision. Ingram and Anderson, although the latter had sold his interests in 1933, truly had created the first type of successful hamburger place. A diner, specializing in low cost and dependable food of widely desired taste available throughout a chain, profited on a series of memorable reminders, cuing taste, smell, sound, and sight. Ingram was right in referring to White Castle as a system.[25]

A measure of White Castle's success is illustrated by the great depth of many people's commitment to its evocative sense of place embodied in its architecture. In the 1980s, a series of proposed demolitions threatened the company's few surviving buildings of the 1930s, the result of too few stools in the buildings and locations of too little sustained traffic for anticipated profit. One St. Louisan, in whose city the last 1930s-style store was taken out of service in 1983, remembered sadly: "My husband [deceased 10 years before] wooed me there, with hot chocolate and hotter kisses. There goes my love life, disappearing before my eyes."[26] Persuaded that White Castle's 1930s-style architecture was historic, a White Castle building of that vintage in Minneapolis was designated in the National Register of Historic Places, and several other examples were preserved elsewhere without any landmark designation.[27] Such conspicuous classification by arbiters of American culture synchronized with the emphasis on themed restaurants.

The heart of the White Castle system remained the point of contact with customers—its unique hamburgers and branded architecture (see fig. 4.5). Partial development of a vertical business structure behind the scenes supported the company's cozy public image. Lured by the obvious profit in the seemingly simple White Castle formula, other companies like White Tower in the Northeast and Rockybilt in Denver followed at various sites throughout the nation.

FIG. 4.5 White Castle's towering sign with "drive-thru" notice attracting business off the nearby interstate indicates the company's flexibility to the automobile's changeful roadside settings.

Snappy Service

From the 1920s through the 1930s, White Castle was the model for hamburger chains. How did White Castle impress the development of other early hamburger-place chains? What did those chains achieve? Where did they develop? What limits did they reach and when were those limits reached? In short, how did the White Castle "system" function when other companies implemented it? We turn to the instructive but now all-but-forgotten Snappy Service chain, perhaps White Castle's first mimic.

Paul C. Hill created Snappy Service. Hill was born in 1889, son to a general-store merchant in Denison, Kansas, a town of about 200 people approximately 110 miles northeast of Wichita where White Castle headquartered. With Kansas's agriculturally based economy and its dependent small towns declining in the 1920s, Paul realized he would have to provide for his family and fulfill his entrepreneurial talents elsewhere because working for his brother, who inherited the general store, would limit Paul's business opportunities. Paul decided on a restaurant business and chose to move to nearby Missouri, at the time more prosperous than his home area yet similar enough in lifestyle for him to understand its customers in a highly personal business. Hill inherited a meager $100 with which he started his restaurant business and admitted he set out to copy the impressive fledgling White Castle. The word "snappy" for his "Snappy Service" chain Hill took from the period's vernacular reference to an activity performed not merely quickly but well, reliably, and proudly. This strategy for popular appeal partly through popular language bound to a particular time would be repeated in the restaurant trade throughout the twentieth century.[28]

In October 1925 Hill opened his first Snappy Service at a prominent downtown location in Trenton, Missouri, a town of nearly 7,000 people about 80 miles northeast of Kansas City. The introductory newspaper advertisement revealed his formula's elements. These were economy (five-cent "hamburgs"), volume ("Buy 'em by the sack"), prominent location ("across from the Elks Club"), distinctive architecture ("little stucco building"), high-quality food ("Nothing but the Best Hamburger possible"), and egalitarian setting ("A good place for country people to eat while in town. Parents let your children eat their school lunches here").[29] Building and equipment cost a modest $1,367 and Hill hired Merle "Buck" Davis, a recent high-school graduate from Hill's hometown, to help staff the new business. Hill typically employed eager young men whose dependability, if proven, earned their promotion to store and eventually a city-wide chain management. Training on the job and promoting from within to eventual top-level management would become common in hamburger chains. Hill worked days and Davis nights to keep the restaurant open from 7 A.M. through midnight. Bess, Paul's wife, was pressed into service baking pies, an authentic homemade food laying another claim for Hill's quality.[30]

Expansion was rapid. By early 1929, two more Snappy Service Inns were open in Trenton, both in previously occupied buildings, and one in Chillicothe, about 20 miles to the south, in a free-standing building similar to the one with which he launched his chain. The Chillicothe operation continued the pattern of strong place identification established in Trenton. Restaurants were added in Bethany, Marysville, and St. Joseph in Missouri's northwestern corner, and Kirksville in Missouri's northeast corner, all within an easy driving radius for Hill's personal supervision. Memphis was Hill's lone foray outside the Midwest. After a cousin living in Memphis introduced Hill to the city, he added three restaurants there between 1927 and 1929. Numerous competitors, however, forced him to close in Memphis by 1940.[31]

Hill achieved his greatest success in the Industrial Midwest, a region that Jon Teaford explains developed in the early twentieth century when the smokestack industries multiplied and rose to their greatest productivity throughout the Midwest's small and medium-sized towns as well as its big cities.[32] Despite his profits in Missouri, Hill was lured eastward again, this time by Indiana's medium-sized industrial towns. "Find the highest smoke stack!" became Hill's simple self-directive for selecting an additional town to extend his chain.[33] In 1929 Hill moved to Terre Haute, Indiana, where he headquartered for the remaining 33 years of his life, eventually selling his Missouri stores. He bypassed prosperous Illinois with its own medium-sized industrial towns because that state had a sales tax, whereas Indiana had none. Notwithstanding Terre Haute's reputation for especially tumultuous labor-management relations and declining population in the 1920s due principally to the removal of the Pennsylvania Railroad repair shops and the mechanization of coal mining, Terre Haute proved a far better base of operations than Hill had experienced in Kansas or even Missouri. Light diversified industries imparted stability compared to Missouri's rural service centers. Terre Haute's Chamber of Commerce was very aggressive in attracting investors. Hungry employees on their way to or from work were among Hill's potential customers. As important for a restaurant specializing in a cheap menu of good quality, Terre Haute was a vibrant retail center drawing many people who wanted a quick and inexpensive bite to eat as they conducted business or shopped on their trip to the "big city." With a population of 62,000, Terre Haute offered a reasonable challenge to the would-be entrepreneur of a big hamburger chain of the 1920s.[34]

Eating out represented society's further democratization. The city's social elite as represented by the *Terre Haute Star* forcefully editorialized that "the proprietors of restaurants, cafes, shoppes and clubs are boasting how their cuisine rivals that of home, but they know they are only attempting to reach that elusive goal. Humanity is a cranky lot and no community institution will ever be able to cater to individual peculiarities," the newspaper contended in a conservative blow against standardized fare eaten out and for food catering exclusively to individualized tastes and prepared at home. Convenience was the chink in the armor of social custom, however. Spur-of-the-moment necessity did justify eating out, in the editor's mind.[35] Restaurants of every type also advertised for regular patronage in the same newspaper.[36]

Terre Haute's restaurants comprised an almost bewildering diversity of place types. They ran the gamut in personalized dining from individual rooms put aside in private residences where home-cooked full-course dinners were served to the advertised elegance of the dining room in the city's new Terre Haute House hotel.[37] Small storefront diners with a few seats and limited menus abounded and frequently used newspaper advertising. Chambers' Chile Shop at 710 Ohio Street "downtown" advertised almost daily during the late 1920s in the *Terre Haute Star*'s classified subsection "Good Places to Eat."[38]

Automobiles were influencing creation of an entirely new restaurant type, one combining the simple menus of the older storefront restaurants but with more convenience to its hurried customers. They were invited to "drive out."[39]

Downtown, with its predominately walk-in trade, still was a coveted location as contrasted with the city's outlying margins and their largely automobile-borne trade. June Brown's Lunch and Confectionery, for example, proudly advertised its relocation to 14 South Fifth early in 1929. In the traffic-congested downtown, free parking at restaurants became an advertised virtue. At such place types the distinctiveness of menu was less emphasized than it was at older-style restaurants where the name of the cook loomed larger than the restaurant's name.[40] Convenience was surging.

Another place-product-packaged restaurant emerged simultaneously with Hill's appearance in Terre Haute, the two-member chain of "Goodie Shops." Gender was helping to move decor toward themes. Originating as a cafeteria and delicatessen in the downtown area, "Goodie Shop No. 2" refined its ambiance by adding table service and set aside a balcony for a "ladies' restroom." Thus, women, who often avoided restaurants as exclusively male domains, were welcomed not only to profit from their purchases but as a service. Goodie's distinctive setting was further enhanced by extending the decor of the first to the second Goodie Shop.[41]

Hill broke into Terre Haute's stiff restaurant market by introducing the convenience and ambiance of the place type he perfected in Missouri. Counting heavily on the proven attraction of his combined food quality, simple menu, low prices, prominent location, and distinctive, yet inexpensive architecture, Hill launched his first Snappy Service in Terre Haute in 1929 without advertising in the *Terre Haute Star*, unlike competitors. Indeed, sufficiently effective was his system that Hill seldom advertised in newspapers except when special rates were occasionally offered. Downtown, at 25 North Fifth Street, Hill located a tiny, prefabricated, galvanized structure by the Butler Manufacturing Company of Kansas City, Missouri (see fig. 4.6). It housed a counter with six stools. By 1930, similar buildings were installed at two other downtown sites, first at 924 Wabash and last at 715 Ohio Street. Hill called them "stands," the English and American vernacular of the previous 200 years for a street vendor's small and impermanent structure. Although their small mass and starkly utilitarian semblance stood in sufficient contrast with the surrounding multistory and ornate commercial buildings to arrest the pedestrian's eye, once inside their stools, counter, and grill con-

FIG. 4.6 Hill's first Snappy Service in Terre Haute, Ind., in the early 1930s.

FIG. 4.7 The working-class ambiance of a diner resonates in this early view of one of Hill's Snappy Service interiors in Terre Haute.

versely projected the familiar ambiance of a diner (see fig. 4.7). Moreover, the help was all male, connoting Hill's modeling according to diners, habitually male hangouts, and the employees were uniformed in white pants and shirt set off by a black tie: all an effort for a serious image albeit in a humble galley kitchen in plain view to customers. Like White Castle, Hill employed no women until the shortage of manpower during World War II forced it. His stands and their personnel were his chief advertising.[42]

Menu complemented. Chili, coffee, and pie were served, but it was "nickel hamburgers," as Hill liked to call them, which distinguished his menu, the hamburger at any price being sufficiently innovative at the time in Terre Haute to attract.[43] High-volume sales of a few simple foods was Hill's aim rather than high-priced, elaborate dishes. "Buy 'em by the sack" remained Hill's slogan, taken from White Castle.[44]

Convenient location also was essential to Hill's formula. He chose sites downtown, near offices, stores, and schools, which tied his market almost entirely to a walk-in trade. Customers arriving in automobiles were secondary; little parking was provided for customers who drove up. All three Terre Haute locations were empty lots Hill leased but did not purchase, thus enabling him to throw up his easily assembled Butler stands and, if necessitated by changing traffic patterns, easily disassemble them for speedy relocation to a newly preferred location. In fact, however, he never found it necessary to move to new locations in Terre Haute. Illustrative of Hill's business acumen involving leases was his arrangement with Tony Hulman for the location on Wabash adjacent to Hulman's warehouse. Hulman promised never in his lifetime to rescind the lease, an arrangement making Hulman seem prescient as Hill's esteem grew in the city's business community. Hill thus achieved flexibility in his locational strategy and ignored permanence.[45]

Hill also continued recruitment of his managerial corps from promising young employees. Buck Davis, Hill's first manager, and Millard "Mid" Dean, a young man from Trenton, Missouri, who worked for no one else in his lifetime but Hill, were Hill's trusted managers in setting up the chain in Terre Haute. Everett Roberts, a 22-year-old farm boy who left Indiana State Normal at Terre Haute out of dissatisfaction with its curriculum, had his eye on making money when he started working for Hill in Terre Haute in 1929. By 1930, Roberts's personal neatness, reliability, and intelligence earned his promotion to the stand manager at 715 Ohio and eventually all three Terre Haute stands.[46]

Sales also depended heavily on the code of conduct Hill taught his employees. Serving full food portions, making honest change, staying sober, and, most important, treating children fairly, Hill insisted were keys to increased sales. Imagination, however, was an encouraged complement; regimentation was not the aim. Everett Roberts, for example, started flipping ice cream onto the ordered dishes of pie, and, with customers requesting the demonstration of dexterity, Hill permitted it to continue. Snappy Service was clearly a place of decency and even modest recreation, not to mention physical sustenance.[47]

Success came quickly. From his Terre Haute base, Hill expanded his Indiana chain in eight years, by 1937, to its widest extent: Anderson, Evansville, Kokomo, Indianapolis, Marion, South Bend, and Vincennes. Briefly, Owensboro, Kentucky, had two stands and Streator, Illinois, had one. Expansion to Michigan and Ohio was contemplated but appropriate sites were never found. Twenty-one stands comprised Hill's own Snappy Service chain at its height and he helped start three brothers-in-law in the hamburger business, two of whom used the Snappy Service name and operated in Illinois. A third brother-in-law operated McClarren's Silver Shanty chain in Indiana.[48]

Hill counted heavily on his young managerial corps for expansion. While Mid Dean was dispatched to Indianapolis to start and manage the branch there, Buck Davis went first to Evansville to start the chain and then to South Bend, the last town added to the chain. Grady Copeland, a 21-year-old with previous restaurant experience, was recruited by Davis in Evansville and af-

FIG. 4.8 Hill's
White Castle
mimic in
Evansville, Ind.

ter two years managed the Evansville stands. Relying on these stalwart managers, Hill himself never managed any stand after 1929. He instead spent his time traveling a circuit by automobile to talk with his managers and inspect each stand and its accounts.[49]

Architecture challenged Hill more than any other aspect of place in his chain. No stand's exterior seemed best in his mind. Terre Haute's portable and utilitarian Butler stands gave way in Evansville, the second Indiana city added to the chain, to stationary buildings of architectural pretense. While the first Evansville stand was another Butler stand, the second was stuccoed tile, the third was brick, and the fourth was ceramic block. Hill seemed to be groping for the right image until this fourth choice. Its white mass outlined in black, including a block with "H" for "Hill's" set in the gable end of a simulated pitched roof, was the creation of Jacob S. McCutchan, an Evansville architect. McCutchan had gone into practice for himself in 1929 after working and learning from a contractor and an architect and was doubtless eager for work, especially with the onset of the Depression. Hill likely became acquainted with McCutchan because of the architect's commissions for various other Evansville businessmen. Through McCutchan's professional expertise Hill was introduced to the latest architectural thinking; and, although McCutchan had probably designed the stuccoed tile stand of revivalist style for Evansville, both client and architect likely agreed its castellated roof line was too derivative of White Castle (see fig. 4.8). Probably to establish a distinctive and up-to-date place identity for the Snappy Service chain, McCutchan proposed the black-and-white ceramic block image with its 1930s' streamlining. The portable Butler stand lagged well behind in sophistication, although the shift from it to the chic black-and-white ceramic-block stand had occurred in the short span of only two years. McCutchan's black-and-white ceramic-block type did succeed in becoming Hill's architectural signature, at least for the early 1930s, as the chain was built to its greatest areal extent with these buildings (see fig. 4.9).[50]

FAST
FOOD

FIG. 4.9 The architectural style with which Hill's Snappy Service chain reached its greatest extent.

Business success continued to drive more architectural change. By the early 1940s, Hill ceased constructing the black-and-white ceramic-block stands because they simply could not serve enough customers simultaneously. To accommodate more diners, Hill started erecting porcelain enamel buildings supplied by various manufacturers. The fifth building type, and the last building opened in Evansville, in late 1941, seated about 35 customers. Another similar building in Indianapolis at Sixteenth and Meridian illustrates Hill's discarding of the diner image. The Indianapolis building's exterior was more streamlined than McCutchan's ceramic-block stands and housed a far larger counter with booths, seating about 35 customers in total (see fig. 4.10). The newer place also invited lingering for more casual eating than had the smaller, earlier places which seemed, by their size, to prod customers to move on. The 80 to 90 customers who could be served simultaneously at the Market Street Snappy Service in Indianapolis rendered it not only the largest but also the most leisurely place in which to eat in Hill's chain.[51]

Snappy Service peaked in profits during World War II. Diners queued outside Evansville's Main and Riverside stand were denied entrance by a locked door until enough customers exited. Hill could count 25 percent of his sales as profit after paying all other expenses.[52]

In the late 1940s the chain slowly declined. Paul Hill had earned enough by then to stop ceaselessly innovating. Although he never complained, he acknowledged quietly that the hamburger trade was grueling work even in his supervisory capacity. Hill turned toward other pursuits while nevertheless continuing to earn good money off the declining chain. With Forrest Sherer, head of a prosperous Terre Haute insurance agency, and Tony Hulman, heir to his family's fortunes, Paul enjoyed yearly fishing vacations near Grand Rapids, Minnesota, and, golf, long Hill's pastime, became a passion. Hill also purchased investment properties and helped finance several beginning businessmen. He clearly had no taste for building an ever larger restaurant operation. He contemplated neither franchising, practiced although not widely before the 1950s, nor partnerships, although he regularly promised to make partners of his key managers. Whereas Davis and Dean were content to continue working for a salary plus commissions, Copeland and Roberts quit to start their own restaurants in 1944 and 1950 respectively.[53]

In a chain dependent on place-product-packaging, lackadaisical treatment of any one of a system's standard elements spelled trouble. Such was the nature of integrated design. Not only did Hill's restaurants amount to a heterogeneous architectural collection of different building types by the late 1940s, but the employees' uniform dress was no longer enforced. Hill apparently never considered "updating" by rebuilding his stands in a single type or adopting more uniform work codes.[54] Hill's restaurants did not fully reinforce one another.

Hill failed to come fully to grips with the automobile. Cars brought increasing numbers of customers to eat in many of his restaurants while the walk-in trade diminished as inner cities decayed at midcentury. Although curb service was begun as early as 1939 in Terre Haute, Hill built only one drive-in and that shortly before his death in 1961. He neither searched for new locations to fully accommodate customers in automobiles nor tried to adapt his existing stands to them.[55]

FIG. 4.10 The streamlined motif of Hill's Snappy Service in Indianapolis featured a "double horseshoe" counter (in foreground and mid-ground) to seat more customers than earlier buildings of the chain.

FIG. 4.11 The Snappy Service appears in the center of this low-lying streetscape in downtown Marion, Ind., just before the stand was forced to close.

Dedicated to his business only to the extent that it was a livelihood supportive of his lifestyle and the wellspring of a goodly legacy for his family, Hill rejected Ray Kroc's offer for a business relationship at the start of the McDonald's chain. Hill was too independent in managing his own business to work with or for another entrepreneur. He always ran his business by himself, never even with an advisor, much less a board of directors. Following his death, his store managers became owners of the stores they managed. Their prospects dwindled with age and the changing financial interests of those from whom they leased the land on which the Snappy Service chain survived more as a relic than as a viable business (see fig. 4.11).[56]

Terre Haute's and Kokomo's stands closed in 1983, the last in the chain. Terre Haute's closing exemplified a struggle common to diners. Razed for a parking lot serving a neighboring Hulman and company warehouse, the Terre Haute stand's demise read like an obituary in the local newspaper. It marked the end of the era that introduced fast food to Terre Haute and the stand's habitués were genuinely doleful about the loss of a cherished place.[57]

Snappy Service went out of business locked to the end in White Castle's original formula: a small capital investment built into a considerable profit by high-volume sales, a relatively simple menu centering on the hamburger, food served in a clean restaurant whose architecture symbolized sanitation and modernity, management by family or close friends. Although sufficient proof of Hill's capacities are in his ability to attract a business offer from Ray Kroc at the start of his McDonald's chain, Snappy Service demonstrated none of the elements that would drive McDonald's to success: accommodation to automobile convenience and enforcement of an integrated system of service and product exuding a sense of memorable place.

By the early twentieth century, place-product-packaging and corporate territoriality worked in a society undergoing profound dislocations to determine how concomitant opportunities enabled hamburgers to define America's first roadside restaurants. Perceived as tasty, simple, cheap, and healthy, the hamburger appealed to white- and blue-collar workers' needs alike when easily available in places to and from their labors in the frenetic pace and specialized roles of an industrializing and urbanizing nation. Hamburgers were also compatible with the assembly-line production industrialism's entrepreneurs created. Employees came to work in hamburger places, largely unquestioning of the assembly line's specialization of labor, rapid execution of assignments, profits maximized for the owner, and profits hopefully shared in decent wages.

Hamburger Places—Part 1

Packaging the place where hamburgers were sold and eaten presented the most innovative entrepreneurs with cultural opportunities for society, not only financial earnings for themselves. Industrialization's and urbanization's diminution of the traditional home's food prepared routinely by women and eaten in a family setting left a void begging compensation. As the first food widely available outside the traditional home, entrepreneurs serving hamburgers created the setting to feed people, both literally and metaphorically. America's concurrent emergence as a society of people converging from different and sometimes antagonistic backgrounds also permitted the chance for the hamburger to provide a national food for a people still in the throes of nation-building. A simple series of additives to beef, a food widely popular both with the challenged older elite and the incoming ethnics alike, offered profit-making opportunities aplenty—but hinging on a compatible and satisfying place to serve customers. Hamburger places earned reputations as places where people from every walk of life ate side by side.

From the 1920s and 1930s, White Castle developed the first successful definition of a hamburger place extensively replicated in lookalike restaurants whose sameness helped assure wary customers traveling without reliance on home-cooked food. Many mimicked but could not or did not care to respond to a society changed, as Snappy Service exemplified. White Castle set the pace by adapting the common diner venue to the trolley and bus traffic. Another generation of entrepreneurs meanwhile raced ahead with newer automobile-convenient venues.

CHAPTER 5

Hamburger Places, Part 2

A mericans' cravings for hamburgers launched a number of chains at various locations throughout the nation beginning in the 1930s through the present, the strategies of place-product-packaging and corporate territoriality directing. Each chain expanded into a city or sometimes regional market, their menus enlarged variously beyond their hamburger specialization as a means of outdistancing their competitors.[1] It would not be until McDonald's appearance in the 1950s, however, that an entrepreneur would hit upon a system for hamburger sales surpassing White Castle's 30-year-long leadership in size and profit. The interval between the White Castle forerunner and the McDonald's giant merits attention to understand the various hamburger place themes tried along the American roadside.

Only a few of the numerous hamburger chains are treated here. It is not our intent to offer an encyclopedic treatment of every chain. The companies selected, however, do illustrate the variations developed for selling hamburgers. Emphasized are the successful chains that grew to great size, but some of the small and even defunct chains are outlined, too. What led to bigness is as instructive as what did not.

Jack in the Box

Jack in the Box started in San Diego in 1950, a typical hamburger place for Southern California, one of America's principal hamburger "hearths." Jack in the Box was a drive-through facility, thus automobile-bound, emphasizing hamburgers quickly served in visually arresting architecture. So committed to drive-throughs became Jack in the Box that it retained that venue exclusively at some of its sites as late as 1979, when competitors scrambled to develop alternative ways of serving. Jack in the Box was the first company after White Castle and its mimics to redefine memorably the hamburger restaurant, projecting a brash and gaudy image. A two-story sign, comprised of a stylized clown face seemingly to have sprung from a box like the child's jack-in-the-box, occupied the front of each chain's drive-through units, drawing the driver's attention from several blocks distance. As the driver approached, he or she saw a smaller version of the jack-in-the-box logo atop the drive-through and again at a smaller scale at the microphone where the order was finally placed. This technique of visual reiteration, so well illustrated by the early Jack in the Box venues, was seen as "reeling in" customers by offering positive reinforcement by stages. Pulled up momentarily in a special lane beside a window to receive their orders, motorists experienced a means of retailing that seemed natural in a culture unquestioning of automobility. Hamburgers, fries, and shakes, simple fare served rapidly (reputedly within 10 seconds of ordering), defined Jack in the Box's image. Good food fast and with a sense of humor set the chain apart.[2] Growth was rapid, first in California and then outward across adjacent states.

The 870-unit Jack in the Box chain, a subsidiary of Foodmaker, Inc. since 1951, was purchased by Ralston Purina in 1968, then a cereals and pet food company. Since 1900, Ralston Purina had contributed to the consumer culture through its easily identified checkerboard-square pattern on packaged goods in stores as well as on grain elevators and trucks. Jack in the Box in the 1970s began patterning itself after the hamburger sales leader, McDonald's. Television advertisements in 1975, amidst a so-called burger war, testified to McDonald's supremacy by ending with various taunts: "Watch out, McDonald's! Watch out, McDonald's!" Although Jack in the Box ended its exclusive dependence on the hamburger with the introduction of tacos, the hamburger remained its menu centerpiece. Trouble loomed. Operations, the term by which the fast-food trade comprehends all work at a restaurant, lost its competitive edge as measured in terms of output costs, profit margins, and customer satisfaction. Expansion to 1,100 units, including a network of stores on the East Coast, only multiplied problems.[3] The chain seemed to lack a clear identity. Was it price, convenience, quality of product, or good-humored promotion that set the chain apart?

In 1979, Jack in the Box sought to reinvent itself. First, it dropped 232 units along the East Coast and in the Midwest. Second, the nearly exclusive hamburger emphasis was replaced by a very diversified menu. Boxed dinners with steak (traditionally not associated with fast food), breakfasts, nonhamburger sandwiches, and salads, the first in the fast-food market, were added. The move was "away from a family, teens, and kids audience, and toward an adult market," explained one company executive. Concomitant with the diversified menu, speed of service was deemphasized with an extensive television advertising campaign in which an actual jack-in-the-box was exploded. Gone was the old, implanted was a new image, or so the company hoped. Architecture was also marshalled in the redefinition. The five different types of buildings that had accumulated in the chain from successive new designs were all abandoned for a single look. With the chain reorganized for another round of expansion, this time through franchising, Ralston Purina sold the chain back to Foodmaker in 1985. Reasons included a desire for "relatively stable earnings," elusive with Jack in the Box's remake. Also the chain's prod-

FIG. 5.1 Jack in the Box's sign on a tall pole, shown here in 1996, has been essential to the company's identity from its inception.

FAST FOOD

ucts proved incompatible with Ralston Purina's other food interests. The new building format, the broader menu, and a reduced number of units concentrated in its original western market did save the chain (see fig. 5.1).[4]

Jack in the Box remained identified in the public mind as a hamburger place—the fifth largest in 1988. The refashioned company continued growing until 1993 when four customers died and over 1,000 people got sick from undercooked hamburgers infected with a lethal bacteria. Demise threatened Jack in the Box once again. Various steps were taken to recover, including the sale (but retention of control) of the insufficiently profitable Mexican food chain, Chi-Chi's, purchased in 1988 to further diversify Foodmaker's investments. Through early 1994, 5 to 6 percent fewer customers patronized Jack in the Box and they spent 2 to 3 percent less. No restaurant rooted in hamburger lust can truly prosper without a reliable hamburger.[5] For Jack in the Box it has been back to basics.

Burger King

Burger King, the hamburger-place chain with the second largest number of units since the early 1980s, demonstrates how successive corporate managers can reinvent a hamburger place's relatively simple definition to profit amidst changing circumstances. Regardless of great size and profit, however, Burger King's potential has been limited by its sporadic attention to convenience and ambiance.

Burger King was born in the boom years of the 1950s. Matthew Burns of Long Beach, California, and Keith G. Cramer, Burns's stepson and owner of a Daytona, Florida, drive-in, founded Insta-Burger-King, Burger King's predecessor. In 1952, fully two years before Ray Kroc went to meet the McDonald brothers in California, Burns called Cramer to California to watch the McDonalds' business operate. Sharing the restaurant trade's fixation at the time for automated food production and the promise of wealth therefrom, Burns and Cramer were most impressed with an automatic broiler and milkshake maker named "Insta" which an inventor in Hollywood, California, was producing. Obtaining the rights to use both machines, Burns and Cramer returned to Florida, where in Jacksonville they opened a self-service drive-in in 1953. Food quickly made and sold through a chain of units rapidly opened via franchising: that was Insta-Burger-King's purpose. Twenty-three months after their start, Burns and Cramer were boasting that 41 units would soon be in operation. Machine and hamburger were inextricably identified in the Burns and Cramer venue; in April 1954 it was decided that all their franchising would include the Insta Company's machines.[6]

David R. Edgerton Jr., who bought Insta-Burger-King's franchise for Dade County, Florida, saw a chance for profit where Royal Castle, another White Castle clone, had operated about 100 hamburger places since 1938. Intrigued with mechanized food preparation, Edgerton improved on the newly developed Insta broiler and took a partner, James McLamore. Although McLamore had considerable experience owning and operating individual restaurants and drew on it for his Burger King venture to introduce a popular hamburger labeled "The Whopper" (for its quarter-pound size), it was the mechanized production and rapid expansion through franchising (under the name Burger King, begun 1957) that drove the partnership. Royal Castle eventually succumbed to Burger King's juggernaut of mechanized production—the Whopper's superiority as a product contributing—and Royal Castle went out of business in 1975.[7]

Burger King kept enlarging through various strategies. Numerous trade journal articles heralded Burger King's franchise system at a time when franchising was sweeping the nation's business communities as a kind of get-rich-quick novelty. Franchisees were carefully selected and taught Edgerton's and McLamore's methods at "Whopper College," opened in 1963, in Miami, two years after McDonald's started formal training. Burger King also led in television advertising. Although never a leader in architectural design, Burger King early catered to customers with a "patio" at a time when that architectural feature was a craze in new residential construction for backyard recreation. The focus of trade journal articles remained speed—speed in service, if not speed in adding new units. Surprisingly, however, only 274 units existed when Edgerton and McLamore sold their interests to Pillsbury in 1967.[8]

Burger King had a good product—its broiled hamburger was preferred by many to the fried variety. Unfortunately, Burger King neglected operational standards. Despite its early avowals to the contrary, Burger King had not regulated its franchisees, many of whom enjoyed territorial rights across large areas, the most notable examples being Chart House, which in the 1970s attempted to take control of the parent company, and Horn and Hardart, which in the 1970s also challenged the parent company's right to

FAST
FOOD

FIG. 5.3 A drive-through with menu board and speaker for ordering while seated in an automobile at one of Burger King's restaurants built in the mid-1990s expansion.

limit the number of units a franchisee could open. Great inconsistency also plagued Burger King from one franchise area to another. Very problematical was the wide array of architecture used across the sprawling chain. A truly uniform image had only been adopted in 1964.[9]

In 1977, Burger King's hiring of Donald N. Smith, McDonald's third highest-ranking executive, only underscored the extent to which real leadership had swung to McDonald's. Typical of the consumer culture's penchant for advertising slogans, Smith named his campaign of recovery "Operation Phoenix." Smith applied everything he had learned at McDonald's to Burger King. This included an appeal to the child's market. "Magic Burger King," a bearded, jolly figure long used as a Burger King logo but deemphasized by Pillsbury, was resuscitated in hopes of competing effectively against McDonald's "Ronald McDonald." More important, franchisees were more carefully regulated, and after 1979 no more territorial franchises were awarded. The restaurants owned by the company—where quality could be controlled directly—increased from 8 to 42 percent. Smith also reformed Burger King's executive leadership by replacing ten executives, eight with people hired away from McDonald's. To appeal to the growing adult market, "specialty sandwiches" were introduced, including fish, chicken, and ham with cheese.[10] But operations was Smith's expertise and it was operations that he stressed. He reasoned thus: "In a large franchise system, when you're weak in one store it has a detrimental effect on all stores."[11] Burger King's restaurants were to enforce the speed, cleanliness, and quality that were gospel at McDonald's. Frequent but unscheduled visits and two-day-long checks each year were required of all franchise locations.[12]

Operations' demands dogged the persistent effort to maximize a hamburger place's profit. In the late 1970s, Burger King's sales rebounded. With Smith's departure for PepsiCo in 1980, Burger King turned to television advertising, not to win new markets but to lure rivals' customers. In so doing it launched perhaps the most memorable advertising campaign in fast-food history, the "Battle of the Burgers" (see fig. 5.2). It began in September and lasted through November 1982. Burger King claimed its hamburgers were more popular than McDonald's or Wendy's, the latter chain really positioned in the market through emphasis on adult customers. Product seemed to have triumphed over place. Burger King settled out of court when McDonald's and Wendy's sued. This advertising campaign gained some momentary advantage for Burger King, which moved into second place among the hamburger chains with 4,701 units in 1987.[13]

As sales began to slump once again, another round of new executives was called upon to remedy Burger King's ailments. Again the new team focused attention on operations. A delicate balance was required between the distant central office and the franchisees' store managers struggling in the fast-food trenches. While many franchisees resisted the central management's directive to sell two hamburgers for the price of one in 1993, for example, other franchisees lamented the absence of field staff to help guide operations in the past. Commands downward through the hierarchy earned more attention than pleas up through the chain of command. Any attention at corporate headquarters was likely short-circuited with the satisfaction in counting further expansion, a jump to 6,620 units in early 1996 (see fig. 5.3). A corporate culture of ignoring smooth unit operations in favor of overall profit seems to have hampered Burger King from its inception.[14] Britain's Grand Metropolitan owns today's company.

Burger Chef

Burger Chef was founded in 1958, leaped to second rank among hamburger chains based on unit numbers in the 1960s, and died in the 1980s in circumstances peculiar to its time. Smitten like so many companies in the 1950s and 1960s with the promise for big profits won quickly through franchising, General Equipment Manufacturing Company, headquartered in Indianapolis, launched the Burger Chef chain in Kankakee, Illinois. McDonald's stunning assent from its headquarters in nearby Chicagoland likely caught General Equipment's eye and it copied McDonald's scheme for selling cheap hamburgers, fries, and milkshakes at a walk-up facility fashioned in modern pop architecture (see fig. 5.4).

Unlike Ralston Purina and Pillsbury, firms that sought to sell food products through their restaurant subsidiaries, General Equipment sought to sell its food-processing machines. But like Ralston Purina and Pillsbury, the restaurant business was rationalized as a means to an end and not an end itself. Inside, General Equipment's automatic conveyor broilers produced the chain's distinctive hamburgers—800 in an hour.[15] These broilers were patterned after a model manufactured for Burger King.[16] Automatic shake machines were manufactured and installed at Burger Chefs to produce a complementary supply of milkshakes. Burger Chef boasted about its food-production machines in a restaurant trade magazine soon after starting. Maximum profit through mass production was the aim within reach, Burger Chef announced: "This speed of service of quality items is not only enhancing customer satisfaction, it is also reducing critical payroll costs at the system's stores."[17] Here was a marvelous model of capitalist efficiency. The company's franchising earned a trade magazine's description as exemplifying the "bustling marketplace" of mid-1960s franchising (see fig. 5.5).[18]

FIG. 5.4 Burger Chef made a selling point of its cheap hamburgers, as shown on this page of printed advertising prescribed in a store operator's "ad kit." Also note Burger Chef's earliest architectural style in the upper left.

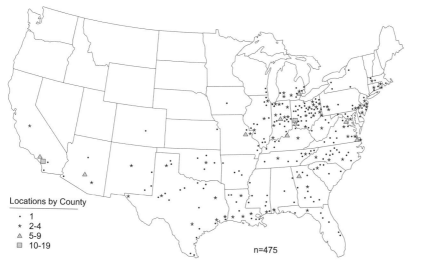

Locations by County

- ·   1
- ★   2-4
- △   5-9
- ▢   10-19

n=475

FIG. 5.5 By 1965, Burger Chef achieved strength throughout its base in the Midwest with fewer units in adjacent regions. Leading counties were: Montgomery (Dayton), Ohio (12 locations); Orange (Santa Ana), Calif. (11); Maricopa (Phoenix), Ariz. (9); Marion (Indianapolis), Ind. (8); and Fairfax (Falls Church), Va., Los Angeles (Los Angeles), and Wayne (Detroit), Mich. (7 each).

Burger Chef's eventual failure, however, illustrates important principles about hamburger places. Neither original products nor an original architectural package have been required for successful hamburger places. Mimicking McDonald's architecture and food, Burger Chef rose to within a few hundred units of McDonald's by the mid-1970s, a feat unimaginable to any rival since. But maintaining the total combination of product and architecture as a distinctive place whose service, price, location, and cleanliness enhance is imperative for success. Burger Chef's huge empire ballooned with poorly supervised franchisees. General Equipment's purpose had been to provide an outlet for its food-production machines (see fig. 5.6). It was satisfied with accomplishing that end when, in 1968, it sold Burger Chef to General Foods, a food processor equally unfamiliar with the fast-food industry. A poor foundation was laid which deteriorated from owner to owner.[19]

General Foods introduced experienced fast-food executives to run Burger Chef but their rally of a new architecture, diversified menu, and enforcement of high standards for customers in "total presentation and personal comforts" did not take hold before the concatenation of circumstances challenging the entire fast-food industry in the late 1970s: higher meat prices, increased minimum wages, and a saturated market. The vital role of place-product-packaging was not fully appreciated in the crisis. Burger Chef had already cut labor costs by firing its 54-man staff charged with recommending new locations; independent real estate agents would instead recommend sites. Realtors, however, would act more to enhance their own income through property sales rather than assess the long-term profit potential of the sites. New units were badly supervised. General Foods' investment in the

FIG. 5.6 Reflective of Burger Chef's modernist sensibilities, its 1966 store operator's manual depicts the operator winding up a store with a key as if it were a machine.

FIG. 5.7 In its attempt to remain competitive, Burger Chef adopted sit-down dining in the later 1970s and sent cards like the one shown above to neighborhood customers to boast its new homey image.

fast-food industry was already losing money a few years before the industry-wide crisis of the late 1970s.[20]

Burger Chef became a victim of the fast-food industry's periodic "shake-outs."[21] Brave talk at the company about resurgent profits by 1980 (see fig. 5.7) could not discount the more general public perception that Burger Chef was a loser, and in 1982 General Foods gladly sold its sagging chain of hamburger places to Hardee's. A rising hamburger-place chain comprising 1,395 units, Hardee's coveted the midwestern market where it had only a few units and Burger Chef had 679 units. Hardees converted Burger Chef's company-owned units into Hardee's operations format and most of the franchised units converted voluntarily. By the late 1980s, Burger Chef all but disappeared.[22]

Hardee's

Hardee's demonstrates how a succession of fairly anonymous entrepreneurs can build a competitive hamburger chain in increments. In 1990, Hardee's ranked as the fourth largest hamburger chain measured in restaurant numbers and seventh in sales among all businesses in the United States.[23]

The chain began in 1960 in Greenville, North Carolina, with Wilber Hardee, the owner and fry cook of his Hardee's restaurant, which needed capital to enlarge his trade, a beginning similar to White Castle's 40 years before. Hardee's claim to distinctive hamburgers was his charcoal grilling, but the rest of the format marked it as one of the increasingly common McDonald's mimics: self-service and inexpensive food featuring the hamburger (15 cents, identical to McDonald's) with soft drinks and milkshakes. From Rocky Mount, North Carolina, 40 miles to the east, came J. Leonard Rawls Jr. and James Carson Gardner, respectively a certified public accountant and executive officer of a dairy, to invest tentatively in Hardee's Drive-Ins. After they sold one million hamburgers by early 1961, they bought out Wilber Hardee later that same year. With their first restaurant, a walk-up having a flat roof canted upward toward the front and clad in red and white tiles, Rawls and Gardner carried dependence on McDonald's forward into architecture. In 1961, two companies became Hardee's first franchisees and Hardee's began its ceaseless push for big profits through rapid expansion from its small-town Piedmont base.[24]

By the end of its first decade, Hardee's had an ambitious program the elements of which competitors took up more gradually. Hardee's early advertised on television and entered the European market in Heidelberg, Germany. Developing limited vertical integration, Hardee's bought a bakery, a supplier of processed seafoods, and a supplier of frozen hamburger patties. Hardee's was the first fast-food company to sell its stock on the open market and to utilize modular buildings, which were suitable to rapid installation—six hours and thirteen minutes it was boasted—and relocation in the company's very problematic small-town market. Indicative of the itch at Hardee's for rapid development was the plan publicly disclosed in late 1968 for a $10 million leaseback fund with investment bankers. Hardee's heretofore had waited for acceptable franchisees to come forward before adding units, which the franchisee financed. With the leaseback fund, however, it was anticipated that a working unit could be established to attract prospective franchisees. The strategy was implemented by the early 1970s. Heraldry signaled Hardee's frenetic growth, red, white, and black being used from 1961 to 1964, green and orange to 1969, and orange and beige to 1976.[25]

In the 1970s, Hardee's focused on territorial expansion. In 1972, Hardee's opened restaurant number 300 and merged with Sandy's Systems, Inc., a hamburger chain begun in Peoria, Illinois, in 1958, and peaked at 225 units, one of the largest regional chains. Hardee's vaulted into midwestern prominence when Sandy's quickly converted their stores to Hardee's as one result of the merger. Also in the deal came Jack Laughery, Sandy's president and an entrepreneurial talent stepping rapidly to the top of the fast-food industry. Laughery was first involved with Sandy's as an insurance agent who sold the company a group policy. Attracted to Sandy's potential, he entered as a manager trainee with Sandy's and determined to head the company. With the 1972 merger, Laughery started as Hardee's officer in charge of operations while Gardner, one of Hardee's founders, resigned to take a congressional seat and Rawls, the other Hardee's founder, became chairman of the board. By 1975, Laughery was Hardee's chief executive and he directed the company's growth in the first strained fast-food decade. Laughery cut Hardee's losses by divesting the company of its diversified food companies. Operations management was then divided between four regional offices to assure quality at the store level. Then the search was undertaken for a new image because it was appreciated that a sense of place had gone undeveloped in the rush to extend the chain.[26]

Anxious for success, Hardee's hired an internationally renowned marketing and design consultant, Lippincott and Margulies. In 1976 their "retail communications audit" yielded a place-product-packaging prototype whose architectural component set the pace in the fast-food industry for a decade, thus ranking them as historical roadside designers along with such greats as C. A. Petersen in gasoline-station design for his "English cottage" and Rufus Nims and John Woodward for their motel-room design. Architectural historian and critic Philip Langdon proclaimed the appeal of Hardee's new buildings stemmed from their bold geometry. A restaurant trade periodical praised the design more pragmatically by summarizing that not only had it increased business by 124 percent at one restaurant but that it was more convenient for customers and staff alike. In addition, it was more adaptable to different materials and to the many different communities in which Hardee's entered as the chain grew. Cedar shakes, for example, were used to blend with the many small towns where Hardee's operated.[27]

Hardee's was well managed in the newly saturated market. It emerged in the 1970s sufficiently attractive for Imasco, a Canadian tobacco, food, and retail conglomerate, to begin buying Hardee's stock in 1977. In 1980, Imasco acquired the controlling interest but permitted Hardee's a very free rein as a subsidiary under Laughery's leadership. At the time, Hardee's comprised 2,141 units—839 company-owned and 1,302 franchised—throughout the United States, Central America, and the Middle East. Its diversified menu, including a breakfast line and roast beef, which was introduced in the late 1970s, grew so popular that it outshone the hamburger that was intended to be the company's main fare. In the 1980s, Hardee's again refocused on operations after absorbing the Burger Chef chain. William E. Prather, hired from Burger King, advised market segmentation. Aiming especially at working women, Hardee's added chicken and salads because their fewer calories were believed to be preferred by women over the standard fast foods. Along with the new thrust, Prather also insisted that high quality and consistency from unit to unit—the age-old fast-food strategy—would lead the resurgence. The 1988 annual report claimed success, the new menu items appealing especially to women between 18 and 35 and children under 12. It was also reported that Hardee's would continue its development strategy of expanding into contiguous geographic areas to lead in restaurant unit numbers. Most notable was Hardee's acquisition in 1990 of the Roy Rogers sandwich (primarily roast beef and secondarily hamburgers) chain whose 648 units were concentrated in the urban locations of Washington, D.C., Baltimore, Philadelphia, and New York; thus Hardee's attempted to penetrate the eastern megalopolis.[28]

Hardee's struggled along with its competitors. Headquarters continued pressing the point with franchisees that units remodeled according to the corporation's trend-setting architecture of 1976 would increase sales; hence the campaign entitled "Hardee's Light and Bright Remodels" arose (see fig. 5.8). Leadership changed. In 1990, Laughery retired as chief executive. While Hardee's insisted it was still a hamburger chain, its annual report underscored the strength of its diversified menu (annual 25 percent growth rate in chicken items and industry leadership in percent of total breakfast sales). The Roy Rogers chain's weakness, meanwhile, reduced Hardee's earnings and, in 1991, Hardee's began closing Roy Rogers's most unprofitable units. Although Hardee's also implemented new advertising (labeling theirs "real food") and reemphasized speedy and courteous service in clean restaurants, Imasco frankly reported the languid state of affairs to its stockholders.[29]

Between 1995 and 1996, Hardee's announced plans to decrease the number of units by 3 to 4 percent through sales including survivors of its Roy Rogers chain. Hardee's seemed best suited in the fast-food fray to serving its

FIG. 5.8 Hardee's developed a 21-page publication in 1989 to persuade franchisees to remodel. A page is shown here. (*Source:* Courtesy of Hardee's Food Systems, Inc.)

original small and medium-sized town base. National rivals yet bobbed and weaved for advantage wherever gain seemed possible. Wendy's bought the Roy Rogers units in New York and McDonald's bought them in Baltimore and Washington. By 1997, however, Hardee's too sold out, accepting the offer of the eastward-moving California giant, Carl's Jr.[30]

Hamburger Hamlet

Hamburger Hamlet, a small national chain of 16 restaurants by 1996, illustrates many of the traits of the hamburger's working-class origins and huge profit potential despite reliance on wealthier clientele and diminutive size. Husband and wife Harry and Marilyn Lewis, respectively a supporting actor in movies and a student of dress design when they were single in Hollywood in the 1950s, married in the desire to cook and manage a restaurant together.[31] Because of their Hollywood background, they saw a role for showmanship in making hamburger places successful. They emphasized low-cost food prepared and served with a personal touch. Although plebeian hamburgers were central, elite dishes such as lobster bisque highlighted them by contrast. Harry Lewis instructed the waitresses to be actresses, to "convey a feeling of being part of a show." Ambiance was a ploy, however. "You can't fall in love with location in business. You have to fall in love with money," pronounced Marilyn.[32] Behind the scenes, the Lewises worked tirelessly to increase their profits no less than any aggressive nouveau starting a hamburger stand. Labor and food prices were figured for maximum efficiency. A work routine was perfected for every employee. New managers took a special course in hiring on.[33]

Wendy's International

Wendy's, as it is most often called, achieved the rank of third largest hamburger chain based on the number of units, in 1978, 11 years after its founding. Earning the seemingly small market share of 9 percent testified to the difficulty of breaking into and maintaining a significant rank in a saturated market. Its meteoric rise is attributable to R. David Thomas, Wendy's founder, who exemplified many traits of the fast-food industry's earlier, first generation of entrepreneurs.

Typical of many self-made men, Dave, as he enjoys being known, has set forth his principles in two inspirational books and has been featured in many popular magazine and trade journal articles.[34] These have been distilled in Wendy's public relations packages widely distributed to all comers. Born in 1932 in Atlantic City, New Jersey, Thomas never knew his natural parents, and was adopted by a family who moved from state to state in pursuit of work. But he responded positively, as he said: "Work became my constant companion."[35] He worked at a succession of menial jobs through his teens, at 18 joined the Army, where he went to cook's and baker's school, and at 24, in Fort Wayne, Indiana, helped start a barbecue restaurant and run one of the first Kentucky Fried Chicken franchises. Thomas, who had risen to vice-president of the barbecue franchise chain by 1958, became frustrated with the long hours and the prospect that the firm's restaurants would never achieve his standards for cleanliness, product quality, and disciplined labor. His boss offered him a classic chance in 1962. If Thomas could make the failing fried chicken franchise profitable and pay off their $200,000 debt, his boss would give him 45 percent ownership. "I made up my mind that I was going to be in business for myself," Thomas asserted. Sensing his restaurants were failing because of their too broad menu, Dave reduced it to a few items and advertised extensively on the radio. He then bought four other franchise locations, prospered, and in 1968 sold them back to Kentucky Fried Chicken for $1.5 million.[36]

Thomas next learned from one of the fast-food industry's first-generation masters, Colonel Harland Sanders. Operations was one of Sanders's strengths, especially personnel management, and Thomas acknowledged that he learned much from Sanders. Becoming a regional operations director for 300 Kentucky Fried Chicken units, Thomas traveled with Sanders. Of equal importance, Thomas helped create Sanders's personal promotion style. Whereas General Mills and White Castle created fictional spokespersons to create personalized corporate images, Thomas helped create Sanders's persona as the master cook and guardian of secret recipes. Thomas was not especially fond of chicken or french fries and insists that he "remained 'drawn to hamburgers.'"[37] According to one account, Thomas has become "a business and media superstar, but he'd rather you know him as a sleeves-rolled-up hamburger cook."[38]

Throughout his time working for other restaurant chains, Thomas was restless, looking for his own opportunity to start a chain of hamburger places, convinced that the leaders lacked some indefinable quality. Thomas, therefore, jumped into the stiff fast-food competition of the 1960s and in 1969 opened his first unit in Columbus, Ohio, to which he had moved seven years earlier with Kentucky Fried Chicken. Might those seven years' exposure to White Castle, the hamburger-chain originator in Columbus, its headquarters, have solidified Thomas's conviction that it was with a hamburger chain that he should focus his entrepreneurship?

Charles Bernstein explains Thomas's operations success in opening Wendy's, as the chain was named. It offered a luxury hamburger, one cooked like all other Wendy's hamburgers, but served with special toppings that customers could order; 256 hamburger varieties were advertised. Wendy's hamburgers were also advertised as "old-fashioned" at a time of growing nostalgia for the American past, and the chain was named for Thomas's daughter, Wendy, always a deft marketing touch in a culture revering family and children. Wendy's hamburger patties were square, initially because more could be grilled at the same time and, with their edges overlapping the bun, were later advertised as proof of great size. It may be wondered too if White Castle's famous square patties, albeit far smaller, may have nudged Wendy's toward the square shape. Other Wendy's menu items were typical of hamburger places by the 1960s and lent themselves to mass production, too, including chili, fries, and a distinctive cross between a milkshake and ice cream called the Frosty. Wendy's introduced the "snake" line for ordering instead of the common multiple straight lines, the advantages being management control of a single line which required fewer employees. Seating was not especially comfortable, thus encouraging people to eat quickly and leave space for incoming customers. Wendy's installed a drive-through window because it increased sales without requiring space inside a unit.[39] Although not novel, Wendy's drive-through window nonetheless gained considerable attention from competitors after they witnessed the profits from Thomas's latest coup. Roadside industries operate so frenetically that they forget some of their own history. By the mid-1970s, Wendy's achieved lower labor costs relative to sales and higher profit margins per unit than any of the leading hamburger chains.[40]

Wendy's unique hamburger chain won a market niche no other hamburger entrepreneurs had foreseen—young adults. Americans born just after World War II reached their 20s and 30s with considerable discretionary income at the same time Wendy's launched. By the mid-1970s, 82 percent of the chain's customers were over 25 years old, contrasting markedly with all competitors. Anticipating that this postwar cohort, come to be called "baby boomers," would be the fastest growing group by the 1980s, Wendy's began deliberately pitching its concept of place to the group.[41]

At the same time, Thomas laid a firm foundation for the chain by inviting a personal acquaintance and experienced fast-food executive, Robert Barney, to be a partner. Barney convinced Thomas, already persuaded that he could start a successful chain, that Wendy's franchising was the key to expansion, as they had learned with Sanders. Rather than selling franchises unit by unit, as was most often done by competitors, Wendy's sold territorial franchises and these chiefly to people experienced with the fast-food industry. By 1976, Wendy's 407 units earned $26,000,000, a 90 percent increase over the previous year, and, due to America's saturated hamburger market, joined its competitors in opening in Europe and Asia.[42]

Wendy's meteoric rise, however, peaked in the mid-1980s, slipping from its high in 1985 at 12 percent of the market to 9 percent within two years. Several factors explain: a rise in beef prices in 1979 forcing a rise in menu prices and resulting in decreased purchases, and Thomas's retirement in 1982, leading to inexperienced successors diversifying the menu with a breakfast entree (served too slowly, it would prove) and too many expensive executives' salaries. Thomas persuaded a trusted and effective franchisee, Jim Near, to assume command. His father had worked for White Castle and Jim's own first job was as a drive-in cook. In the 1960s, he rose from the first manager of a Burger Boy Food-A-Rama to become vice-president of the 50-unit chain before its sale in 1969 to the Borden Dairy company. Near persuaded Thomas in turn to come back as a personal spokesman in Wendy's advertising (see fig. 5.9). These changes, coupled with new menu items to attract the baby boomers and, more recently, chil-

FIG. 5.9 Dave Thomas reifies Wendy's, here posing at the grand opening of one of his chain's restaurants. (*Source:* Copyright 1983 *The State Journal-Register.*)

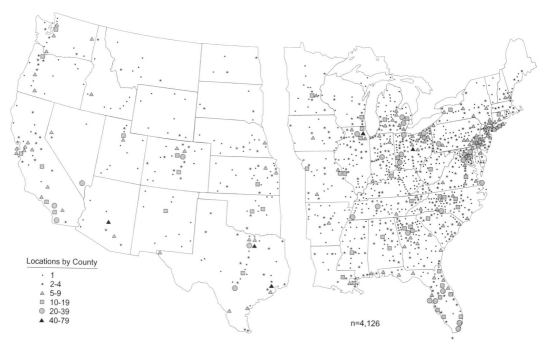

Locations by County
- ·   1
- ✶   2-4
- △   5-9
- ▫   10-19
- ◯   20-39
- ▲   40-79

n=4,126

FIG. 5.10 Wendy's maintained a nationwide presence in the United States, as shown in this map of its restaurants in 1995. Leading counties were: Cook (Chicago), Ill. (78 locations); Franklin (Columbus), Ohio (60); and Harris (Houston), Tex. (55). (*Source:* Wendy's International, Inc.)

dren, enabled Wendy's operations-oriented change to increase profits in the 1990s (see fig. 5.10).[43]

Other Chains

Chains preferring a regional market have long variegated the landscape with their distinctive place-product-packaging. White Castle's is the oldest but we take up here chains previously unmentioned.

Krystal was the first regional chain to profit greatly from mimicking White Castle. Begun in Chattanooga, Tennessee, in 1932, by Rody B. Davenport, a hosiery mill owner who had seen White Castle's busy operations in Columbus, Ohio, and J. Glenn Sherill, a banker, both looking for a Depression-proof business, Krystal expanded rapidly throughout the Southeast. There it precluded serious competition from competitors with cheap (five-cent) one-ounce hamburgers in diner settings located in big cities. "Clean as a whistle and clear as a crystal" was the vernacular adopted for the company's slogan, repeating every successful hamburger chain's insistence on purity. Throughout its life, Krystal has remained family-owned and struck a deep chord with many Southerners (see fig. 5.11).[44]

Krystal has revised its format according to the prevailing standards for hamburger chains since its original mooring to the White Castle format. Takeout was emphasized following Sherill's death in 1961 and red, ocher, and brown replaced the original black-and-white colors in 1972. To keep up with the national giants, Krystal introduced the quarter-pound "Krystal King" in 1974 and 1975. In the 1980s, seeking its niche in the saturated market, Krystal abandoned mimicry of the giants and developed a strategy combining its traditions with new approaches. The company's hamburgers and cheap prices were reemphasized. Most of the urban stores, however, were closed and Krystal started opening in suburban and highway locations. Franchising was begun and Krystal expanded northward into Indiana, Illinois, and Missouri. The original crystal-ball logo was returned, albeit with a red, yellow, and white motif. Krystal also acquired the Po Folks family restaurant chain and franchised Wendy's units in Baltimore, Washington, D.C., and St. Louis. In the 1990s, the "Krystal Kwik" was introduced to compete with the double drive-throughs. Resilient Krystal prospers.[45]

On the West Coast, Carl's Jr., another independently owned venture, has long been a major contender among the hamburger chains. In 1978 it was the region's largest independently owned restaurant business, and in 1984 it ranked second to McDonald's in market share.[46] Carl Karcher, a kind man who quit school in the eighth grade to help on the family farm in Ohio, came west in 1939 to find his fortune.[47] Running a series of hot-dog carts convinced him there was considerable money to be made in serving simple food and he and his wife started a family restaurant in Anaheim, California, in 1944.[48] Shortly thereafter he started a hamburger chain. His brother, Donald, joined the business in 1954 and together they ran the business like an extended family. As Carl noted, "I always remember people's names. And most

FIG. 5.11 In 1996, Krystal's grand openings in small towns—here La Grange, Ga.—are well-attended public events. (*Source:* Brooks Shows.)

of all I enjoy people. You have to love people—in our business and in all of life." Managers were promoted exclusively from within as a result.[49] Aggressive at the same time, the Karchers developed a vertically integrated company, purchasing its own food stuffs, processing them, and delivering them to its units. Committed from the outset to a niche between fast food and the California-style coffee shops especially common on the West Coast, Carl's Jr. introduced a host of innovations including salad bars in the late 1970s and a diversified menu.[50]

With expansion challenged amidst the industry-wide doldrums beginning in the 1970s, Carl's Jr. changed its program in the 1980s. It went on the stock market and began franchising, management by a team of nonfamily members, a new menu, more advertising, and territorial expansion.[51] Texas and Arizona were added. Problems, however, erupted in the 1980s and early 1990s. Incapable of penetrating the new state markets, Carl's Jr. left Texas, put franchisees only in Arizona, and concentrated on its core in Southern California. Brother Don, who had been in charge of the all-important operations, died unexpectedly, leaving Carl temporarily distracted from his overall leadership responsibilities. By 1992, it was decided Carl's Jr. would rebuild on its regional base (see fig. 5.12), the company's chief executive officer stating, "California is the sixth or seventh largest economic entity in the world. The saturation issue is theoretical. The area continues to grow, so you never stop having opportunities to grow."[52] This declaration notwithstanding, Carl's Jr. eagerly acquired the flagging Hardee's chain in 1997 with an eye to expanding eastward again.

Other notable examples attest to the viability of regional hamburger chains. Carrol's was the creation of a Tastee-Freez franchiser in the late 1950s who by 1963 made it a division of the ice cream company marketing throughout the Northeast, including Canada. Carrol's was franchised to Burger King shortly thereafter and disappeared as part of the giant's continuous expansion. Whataburger contrasted in stability. Founded in Corpus Christi, Texas, in 1950, it has entered the adjacent Southwest, West, and Mexico (see fig. 5.13).[53]

Characteristic of the hamburger's capacity to stimulate business opportunities through new formats is the latest version, the drive-throughs, especially the double drive-throughs. Drive-through windows are not new; Wendy's reintroduced them to the industry with the onset of the saturated market in the 1970s. But, beginning in the mid-1980s, the distinctive double drive-throughs began mushrooming at various locations nationally and inspired new entrants combining drive-throughs and seating. John Jay Hooker, founder of the failed Minnie Pearl chicken chain, was perhaps the first to build a double drive-through, although at this writing Hooker's Hamburgers remains one unit.[54]

The double drive-through has two traffic lanes, one on each side of the building, for customers to pull alongside of a window to receive their food. Some add minimal indoor and outdoor seating. The fastest promise hot food in 45 seconds. Kitchens housed in small buildings selling a "limited menu," cheap hamburgers, fries, and soft drinks: these characterized the replay of a previous venue but new to customers. Fast food's history is little remembered in the marketplace. For the ambitious businesspeople setting up the double drive-throughs, they were a stratagem to keep costs low and increase profits in a stiff market. Double drive-throughs were often modular, permitting rapid relocation in the highly volatile market, and proved cheap to build. Labor was cheap, too, because the format employed five to ten people at most whereas at least one hamburger chain's sit-down restaurants needed 50 to 60 employees per unit. The giant chains had diversified menus, raised prices, and slowed service, thereby losing the vaunted simplicity, speed, and low prices that enabled them to extend the market a generation earlier. Double drive-throughs were a return to origins.[55]

Symbolic descendants of the stands lining fair midways, the express burger strain generated places of titillation in brightly colored buildings and, where it existed, outdoor seating beneath dramatic canopies or jaunty umbrellas. The latter, however, remained a generally unaccepted invitation to pedestrian pause; most of the traffic coursed in the drive-through lanes. Despite their obvious appearance as members of a single genus, the individual companies have their own motifs worth noting in the rapidly changing landscape of fast-food places. Some follow. James A. Patterson, who originated the Long John Silver's seafood chain, began Rally's in 1985, rapidly building it into the first large double drive-through chain (see fig. 5.14). Rally's utilized architecture and landscaping in one of his most effective designs to arrest the passerby's attention with tinsel-lined signs and streamers reminis-

Locations by County

· 1
⋆ 2-4
△ 5-9
▢ 10-19
⬤ 20-39
▲ 40-79
■ 80-159

n=751

FIG. 5.12 Carl's Jr., 1996. Leading counties were: Los Angeles (Los Angeles) (138 locations); Orange (Santa Ana), Calif. (81); Riverside (Riverside), Calif. (40); San Bernardino (San Bernardino), Calif. (33); San Diego (San Diego), Calif. (15).

Locations by County

· 1
⋆ 2-4
△ 5-9
▢ 10-19
⬤ 20-39
▲ 40-79

n=513

FIG. 5.13 Whataburger, 1996. Leading counties were: Harris (Houston), Tex. (66 locations); Dallas (Dallas), Tex. (46); Tarrant (Ft. Worth), Tex. (31); Maricopa (Phoenix), Ariz. (29); and Bexar (San Antonio), Tex. (27).

Locations by County
· 1
★ 2-4
△ 5-9
▢ 10-19
◯ 20-39

n=501

FIG. 5.14 Based in Louisville, Ky., Rally's expanded considerably in its first decade as shown in this map of its locations in 1995. Leading counties were: Wayne (Detroit), Mich. (30 locations); Cuyahoga (Cleveland), Ohio (21); Hamilton (Cincinnati), Ohio (20); and Franklin (Columbus), Ohio, and Jefferson (Louisville), Ky. (18 each). (*Source:* Rally's Hamburgers.)

FIG. 5.15 Poles supporting a canopy topped with metal banners made to seem fluttering, the illusion of a park pavillion is Central Park's architecture. The motif is carried into the smallest detail such as the beverage cup, thus fully utilizing place-product-packaging.

cent of car dealerships (see fig. 16.17), no less spectacularly prepared to sell out to the Checker's double drive-through chain in 1999 for $29,300,000 in stocks.[56] Central Park occupied interstices between larger properties to squeeze in its distinctive double drive-throughs (see fig. 5.15). Elitists recoil at this type of retailing as tacky but its persistent reoccurrence in American life testifies to the common love of the sensational.

Old roadside demands—speedy service, cheap prices, more profit, and low-cost operations—seem to drive the latest burger mania. As some drive-throughs began bundling, that is, selling complementary fast-food brands to remain profitable, some franchisees grumbled about the parent company's dishonest finances and the expediency of menu expansion. The drive-through is contributing to a larger trend toward "food-to-go," as it is called in the trade, including carryout and delivery as well as drive-through, Americans having committed even more to automobility. A new niche may have opened for a time with the double drive-through; for the corporate giants seem unlikely to cut their prices although they have installed drive-throughs as yet another option in their market segmentation.[57]

More notable among the corporate giants' initiatives is the move abroad. Among those companies mentioned in this chapter, Burger King, Wendy's, and Hardee's led the way, in that order, in 1995 earnings mostly throughout Canada, Europe, and Asia.[58]

TABLE 5.1 Selected Prominent Hamburger Chains

Name	City of Origin or Headquarters	Year Started
Biff-Burger	Tampa, Fla.	c. 1963
Big Boy	Glendale, Calif.	1936
Bun N'Burger	New York, N.Y.	1939
Burger Chef	Kankakee, Ill.	1958
Burger King	Miami	1954
Burger Queen / Druthers	Louisville, Ky.	1963
Burgerville USA	Vancouver, Wash.	1964
Carl's Jr.	Anaheim, Calif.	1944
Carrol's	Gary, Ind.	1956
Central Park USA	Chattanooga, Tenn.	1982
Checker's	Clearwater, Fla.	1986
D'Lites	Atlanta	1981
Fatburger	Los Angeles	1952
Hamburger Hamlets	Beverly Hills, Calif.	1950
Hamburgers by Gourmet License	Houston, Tex.	1968
Hardee's	Greenville, N.C.	1960
Hot 'n Now	Irvine, Calif.	1984
Huddle	Los Angeles	c. 1956
Hull-Dobbs Houses	Memphis	1936
In-N-Out Burgers	Irvine, Calif.	1948
Johnny Rockets	Los Angeles	1986

(*continued*)

TABLE 5.1 (*Continued*)

Name	City of Origin or Headquarters	Year Started
Kewpee Hotel Hamburgs	Flint, Mich.	1926
Krystal	Chattanooga, Tenn.	1932
Little Canary Castle	Winston-Salem, N.C.	1931
Little Tavern	Louisville, Ky.	1927
Lordburger Restaurants	Cleveland	1972
McDonald's	Des Plaines, Ill.	1955
Minute-Man of America	Little Rock	1965
Mr. Burger	Amarillo, Tex.	1969
Mr. Fifteen	Muncie, Ind.	1960
Mr. Quick	Normal, Ill.	1959
O.K. Big Burger	Minneapolis	1967
Original Hamburger Stand	Newport Beach, Calif.	1982
Rally's	Jeffersonville, Ind.	1985
Rockybilt	Denver	1936
Royal Castle	Miami	1938
Sandy's	Peoria, Ill.	1958
Satellite Hamburger Systems	Indianapolis	1962
Silver Castle Lunch	Tulsa, Okla.	1937
Snappy Service	Trenton, Mo.	1925
Sonic Drive-Ins	Shawnee, Okla.	1953
Steak 'n Shake	Normal, Ill.	1934
Wendy's	Columbus, Ohio	1969
Whataburger	Corpus Christi, Tex.	1950
White Castle	Wichita, Kan.	1921
White Hut	Toledo, Ohio	1935
White Tavern	Shelbyville, Ky.	1929
White Tower	Milwaukee, Wis.	1926
Wimpy Grills	Bloomington, Ind.	1934

Source: Authors' survey.

Hamburger places have been Americans' favorite roadside restaurants since the automobile's advent, by 1979, for example, accounting for 13 percent of the nation's restaurant sales.[59] What an amazingly protean enterprise! Mom-and-pop places spring up ceaselessly without fear of the giant competitors. Some succeed. Some fail. And so the hamburger trade beckons (see Table 5.1), competitors sprinkled throughout the nation's ranks of top chain restaurants (see Table 5.2). Like life in a vast sea, established and new companies alike give birth in new locations, preparations, packaging, service, and menu companions to the common hamburger.

With Americans embracing the automobile unhesitatingly in the late 1930s through the 1960s, convenience loomed larger than before. Entrepreneurs flooded the hamburger market attuned to the fast-paced mobility that

TABLE 5.2 Leading Hamburger Chains, 1996

Chain	Headquarters	Units Worldwide	Sales (in millions)	Sales Rank Top 300
McDonald's	Oak Brook, Ill.	21,022	$31,812	1
Burger King	Miami	8,700	9,010	2
Wendy's	Dublin, Ohio	4,933	4,700	5
Hardee's	Rocky Mount, N.C.	3,538	4,085	7
Jack in the Box	San Diego	1,270	1,229	23
Sonic Drive-Ins	Oklahoma City	1,587	1,012	30
Carl's Jr.	Anaheim, Calif.	673	648	46
Whataburger	Corpus Christi	525	443	62
White Castle	Columbus, Ohio	306	351	67
Checker's Drive-in Restaurants	Clearwater, Fla.	478	328	70
Rally's Hamburgers	Louisville	467	316	74
Krystal	Chattanooga	338	297	75
Steak 'n Shake	Indianapolis	222	283	80
In-N-Out Burgers	Irvine, Calif.	116	130	150
Central Park USA	Chattanooga	77	50	272
Hamburger Hamlets	Sherman Oaks, Calif.	16	48	280
Hot 'n Now	Irvine, Calif.	75	45	296

Source: Restaurants and Institutions 107 (July 15, 1997): 66.

Hamburger Places—Part 2

automobiles facilitated en masse. The hamburger's primacy in appetites of heightened mobility thus was sustained because its suitability for rapid preparation synchronized with a society seeking maximum leisure in terms partly of routines reduced, such as making and eating meals.

Entrepreneurs rapidly improvised new variations on automobile-convenient hamburger places for eating out—the drive-through, the drive-in, and the walk-up. Jack in the Box was the first large chain to embolden place-product-packaging on their units' exterior with signs suited to the post–World War II rush. Inside each new hamburger-place type, entrepreneurs paralleled their impatient yet waiting customers by experimenting with many speedier ways to maximize profit, devising ever more efficient ways to use fewer workers and ending with largely automated production, such as Burger Chef did. Popular vocabulary eventually caught up by the 1960s, coining the word "fast food" for the complex of place-product-packaged food chains that the hamburger pioneered. Another round of emphasis on speed and low cost brought the double drive-through to the fore in the mid-1980s.

Places emphasized "operations," to use restaurant argot, even mercilessly enforced, and customer convenience continued ruling the hamburger market. Attempts to compensate for modern society's dislocations by extending courteous service in home-like cleanliness for reliable and tasty food all the while satisfying demands for speedy service ended disastrously for some hamburger places. Operations defeated Burger Chef ultimately, whereas an operations emphasis enabled Wendy's to break into a saturated market and re-emerge a second time after reemphasizing operations. Hamburger Hamlet proved the hamburger had crossed social class barriers to become popular with those of or aspiring to the upper-middle class outside the diner format. For all Hardee's efforts to expand nationally, its strength in small and medium-sized towns of the South and Midwest was akin to the regionals; it was compatible with people of a particular locale rather than a generalized national territory. Carl Jr.'s purchase of Hardee's would test the efficacy of a California-based regional succeeding in the South and Midwest. Burger King illustrates that success requires some originality but always requires persistent redefinition amid America's highly competitive consumer culture by the twentieth century's end. In that milieu, McDonald's nonetheless is the business that captured America's imagination as the preeminent hamburger and fast-food place. We move next to McDonald's.

CHAPTER 6

McDonald's

At every level of culture, McDonald's is an astounding American success, having captured much of the world's imagination. At the elite level, among financial analysts, for example, McDonald's is a marvel of profitability.[1] Academicians too, although some show disdain for eating there, generally praise its founder's business acumen.[2] At the folk level, that is, at the level of unwritten but spoken lore, McDonald's is a frequent answer to the question "Where to eat?," young mothers especially catching a bit of time together while supervising their children in a McDonald's playground or whole families escaping the usual eat-in routine. Coinage of the vernacular "fast food," risen to an accepted word in the American vocabulary, has been attributed to McDonald's own rise (see fig. 6.1).[3] Until the latest round of remodelings throughout the chain removed many, one could see a plaque beside all McDonald's order counters with Ray Kroc's likeness, a corporate homage to his having founded the company: "In 1955, Ray A. Kroc Established McDonald's System With The Highest Standards of Quality, Service, Cleanliness, and Value. His Vision, Persistence, and Leadership Have Guided McDonald's From One Location in Des Plaines, Illinois to the World's Community Restaurant." Why did his version of the hamburger restaurant triumph so completely in the American imagination?

Ray Kroc Originates McDonald's

Ray Kroc's ascension to living legend has been recounted often enough. The facts are simple but, as well, indisputably impressive. Any interpretation of the hamburger restaurants, indeed restaurants in general, must take them into account.

Raymond Albert Kroc was born on October 5, 1902, in Oak Park, Illinois, a Chicago suburb, the grandson of Bohemians who came in the swell of southern and central European immigrants to the United States at the turn of the nineteenth and early twentieth centuries. Characteristic was this group's rel-

FIG. 6.1 Recent promotion underscores McDonald's continued dedication to quality fast food.

FIG. 6.2 The opening-day advertisement in the local newspaper for Kroc's first McDonald's recited the appeals that the company would promote thereafter: speedy service, automobile access, cheap food, and volume—claiming the 15 million sales from Kroc's predecessors. (*Source: Des Plaines Journal,* April 14, 1955, 5.)

ish for upward mobility from what was for most families lower-middle-class status. Ray was an outgoing young man, a doer, but in school only a mediocre student. Underage for army enlistment, he successfully begged his parents to let him join the ambulance corps in World War I, and, after his service, alternated and sometimes worked two jobs, usually as a musician and as a salesman. In 1922, he married and gained access to the soda-fountain and restaurant trade when he became a Lily Cup salesman. Lured to Florida during its real estate boom in the 1920s, he returned to Chicago after only a few months. There he again applied himself to the sale of restaurant supplies and, during the Depression, his hard work yielded a good income. In 1938, he became the exclusive agent for a frozen confection blender, the Multimixer, as the result of his business with the founders of a chain of ice cream parlors in northern Illinois, Prince Castle. Seeking to be his own boss, Kroc borrowed capital from his employer. As a result he went $100,000 in debt, including $15,000 of his own money, and his marriage was badly strained because he had mortgaged his family's coveted suburban home. Kroc made no profit for the first few years, although he was able to buy Multimixer. He prospered in the post–World War II boom and in 1954 made a deal with the reluctant McDonald brothers of San Bernardino, California, to franchise a chain of restaurants patterned after their successful venue. Kroc was 52 years old, an age when most people have either achieved their dream or given it up.[4]

Kroc's restaurant empire grew because he worked hard on it. At the heart of McDonald's success was its chief food, a 1.6-ounce hamburger, 3.9 inches in diameter, on a 3.5-inch bun with .25 ounces of onion sold for 15 cents—a standardized product of high quality but also low price. Kroc opened his first restaurant in Des Plaines, Illinois, a Chicago suburb, on April 15, 1955 (see fig. 6.2). Attracting talented specialists to work under his aegis, the firm opened the two-hundredth McDonald's in 1960. In the 1960s, McDonald's emerged as the paradigm, epitomizing not only the hamburger chains, but fast food generally. Earning $37,000,000 in 1960 and $226,000,000 in 1967, McDonald's was featured in popular magazines including *Life* in 1966. Although by the late 1980s Burger King rivaled McDonald's in store numbers, McDonald's surged far ahead in sales per store. McDonald's swamped every other hamburger chain in volume and profitability.[5] McDonald's stayed dedicated exclusively to its fast-food business and resisted the temptation, seductive to many competitors, to diversify.

The Social Setting

Aspects of American social change in the post–World War II era conditioned McDonald's triumph, including the baby boom and the growth of the white middle class's expendable income.

A 200-year descent in Western society's fertility ended in the 1940s with a remarkable and unanticipated increase in the United States which sent baffled demographers scurrying for explanations. They found fewer women were birthing more children, one baby every seven seconds for the all-time high of 4.3 million children in 1957. As it turned out, all social groups contributed to the population surge. Increased expendable income contributed mightily. During the 1950s, per capita income rose 48 percent, the median family income rising to $5,657 from $3,083, and real wages increasing by nearly 30 percent. More free time from work converged with a general increase in income. The 40-hour week and the two-day weekend became standard in 1938 and three weeks' paid vacation became standard in the late 1940s, both exciting rise of a more leisure-oriented society.[6]

How these bounties effected was a matter of culture, an extension of the consumer values afoot since the late nineteenth century. Having babies and raising them became women's highest calling, so proclaimed culture's arbiters such as Dr. Benjamin Spock in his *Common Sense Book of Baby and Child Care,* first published in 1946. Fatherhood, or earning the income for one's family and providing an appropriate role model, became mature men's work.[7]

Motherhood, fatherhood, and family ties combined to sustain the traditional hegemonic value in American society for home ownership. The federal government injected new force into this ideal. Underwriting various lending institutions, the Federal Housing Administration and the Veterans Administration established low down payments and long-amortization loans to encourage single-family home ownership. Home in the Cold War, as the primary scene of family life, was further justified as a haven from public turmoil.[8]

Houses, the most expensive consumer goods, were built mostly in the most coveted neighborhoods, in suburbia. Land values in the mid-1950s jumped from 100 to 3,760 percent, depending on exact location. Levittown on Long Island symbolized national suburbanization. Levittown was first occupied in 1947 and comprised low-cost houses of several uniform variations, standard packages including appliances, lot size, and plantings. Numbering 82,000 people in 17,400 houses at its height, Levittown captivated Americans. Similar suburbs mushroomed throughout the nation, open countryside expropriated in a latter-day wave of American frontiering. Suburban population jumped 50 percent in the 1950s while central city areas trailed with 25 percent growth. For example, Detroit, St. Louis, San Francisco, and Washington, D.C., lost population, and New York City lost 1.5 million migrants to the suburbs. America began to look radically different, an estimated 80 percent of its built environment created since the 1950s.[9]

Mechanization took firm command by midcentury, as Siegfried Gideon wrote in 1948. Mass production was a concomitant. Automobiles rose in popularity. More than one truck or car could be counted for every American household by 1958, most operated in and from suburbia each day. Only 10 percent of the population walked to work and the automobile became the necessary means for annual vacations away from home. Household appliances grew more popular and houses themselves were the products of machined mass production. Ethics seemed to follow in the wake of mechanization as was pointed out in several popular books, most dramatically about corporate America's middle managers.[10]

A luxurious automobile within relatively easy financial reach symbolized fulfillment for many Americans immediately after World War II. Cheap food widely available and rendered automobile-convenient became further symbolic concomitant gratifying popular expectation.[11]

All of these circumstances sustained Kroc's vision for McDonald's. Hamburger chains serving customers in automobiles appeared throughout the nation. To guide possible investors, restaurant trade magazines regularly documented new franchise ideas as they appeared. White Hut, which originated in Toledo in 1935 and had grown to three units by 1956, for example, was the subject of an article that year in *Drive-In Restaurant and Highway Cafe Magazine*.[12] Drive-ins became the latest retailing mode serving hamburgers along with many other foods throughout urban centers of the American West in the late 1940s, but it was in Southern California that the drive-in flowered most impressively.[13] Kroc himself described this regional phenomenon.

> In the early 1930s in Southern California there developed a remarkable phenomenon in the food service business. It was the drive-in restaurant, a product of the Great Depression's crimp on the free-wheeling lifestyle that had grown up around movie-happy Hollywood. Drive-ins sprouted in city parking lots and spread along canyon drives. Barbecue beef, pork, and chicken were the typical menu mainstays, but there was an endless variety in approaches as feverish operators hustled to outdo one another.[14]

The drive-in's triumph required untiring promotion and advertising. Stiff competition also induced focus on efficiently designed restaurants to maximize the number of customers served. Volume became imperative. Fast food sprang as practice from this midcentury milieu—competition, the quest for volume, the mania for technological solutions, the sense of urgency about service, and the symbolic role of the pampered customer—before the word was coined in folklore. The ascent can be traced in a variety of restaurant trade as well as popular magazines.[15]

Utilizing technology developed for World War II, a drive-in in Milwaukee equipped its carhops with portable radio transmitters and receivers, colloquially known as "walkie-talkies," and advertised that novelty to attract business. Not only did it reduce the number of carhops from five to two while increasing the number of orders they could handle, but it became a way to distinguish itself from competitors.[16]

With the emphasis on more speed and more productivity, hamburger chains industrialized their workforce. Howard Kelley's experience with the Steak 'n Shake chain exemplifies. As a new hire in 1938, Kelley's incentive for profit led him quickly to the position of the chain's foremost store manager because Kelley improved various operations, for example, creating a work manual comprising long lists of step-by-step procedures, supported with photographic illustrations, for all workers.[17]

Americans ate out increasingly through the 1940s, but restaurant owners faced rising costs along with prosperity. They wrestled with ways to push the market, hence their profit. As explained in *Business Week*, "Since prices much higher than today can only bring lower volume, practical restaurant men see their sole hope in more efficient management, streamlining and standardized operations, new labor and time-saving equipment, and better trained employees."[18] Lily Tulip Cup Company, earlier Kroc's employer, especially pushed the "take home" trade among restauranteurs when it was not certain Americans would continue eating out in great numbers because, it was feared, faced with rising prices potential customers would save money by eating at home and justify it as a way to knit their families closer together. Restaurant advertising turned to picturing contented families eating out.[19]

Eating out did continue on the rise, and hamburgers were predisposed to outdistance the various other roadside foods as the most favorite in the twentieth century's last half. Not only were hamburgers already the most common of roadside foods by midcentury but their capacity for speedy preparation with uniformly satisfactory results continued meshing well with those demands of consumer and entrepreneur alike. Jeremy Rifkin points as well to the beef lobby's control of federal regulations in which beef put all other meats at a market disadvantage and defined the hamburger in the 1946 U.S. Department of Agriculture's code as a meat exclusively derived from beef and beef fat.[20]

Entrepreneurs acting on culture's predispositions transformed the way Americans ate out. Convenience to consumers and entrepreneurs alike spearheaded the latest formulation. In downtown San Bernardino, California, Maurice and Richard McDonald's version of a place for the mass production and sales provided several basic elements with which Kroc launched his grandiose operation. The walk-up was one element. Customers parked and walked to a window where they placed their order. The McDonald brothers having already proven that they could profit from customer-placed orders that not only speeded service but eliminated carhop salaries, Kroc was ready to use their format. It also meshed with social trends. Some critics still feel the walk-up's minimized service represents a step backward in civility. For many it was in fact a height of civility: food on demand widely available at low cost. The working and middle classes, nonetheless, continued patronizing the McDonald brothers' new restaurant. But McDonald's walk-up attracted, at first fortuitously, a new clientele on which the brothers and later Kroc were most eager to capitalize, namely, children. McDonald's walk-up had lost the teenage crowd, attracted to carhops, that loomed as an unruly and sometimes criminal age group, according to American thinking in the late 1940s and 1950s. McDonald's was glad to be relieved of a teenage hangout image. Into the market vacuum of dispatched teenagers flowed children with supervising parents in tow. Playful children in parental check have provided McDonald's a staple ever since (see fig. 6.3).[21]

The McDonald brothers' hamburger operation thus was among many drawing attention from both hungry customers and aggressive entrepre-

FIG. 6.3 Recent two-story "playplaces," one visible on the right, announce their prominence at McDonald's, bulking half the store's mass.

McDonald's

neurs. Two years before Kroc came to San Bernardino to observe—one of many who did—the McDonalds' operation was featured in the *American Restaurant Magazine* as a worthy model.[22] Mass production was sweeping the food trade just as it earlier had in other goods and services of the consumer culture.

French-frying lent itself to mass production, too, and the McDonald brothers applied it to the potato, in the process trying to perfect a crisp french fry to counter the usual soggy and none-too-delectable product served. Kroc would build on their efforts, working carefully with suppliers and experimenting with on-site storage facilities.[23]

Many challenges faced Kroc. The McDonald's phenomenon required fine-tuning a system, learning to replicate it widely, and instructing others to make it run smoothly. The broad patterns of American culture at midcentury, however, were right for McDonald's hamburger empire to emerge, just as a giant motel chain would evolve as predicted by Sinclair Lewis when Holiday Inn's founder, Kemmons Wilson, was but seven years old. Do not mistake Kroc's accomplishment. It demanded creativity, energy, dedication, nerve, teamwork, and luck to build a financial empire with hallowed status. Others tried and failed. But someone was probably going to do it in America's consumer culture booming after World War II.[24]

Kroc's Talents

From Kroc's own recollections, *Grinding It Out,* which Robert Anderson wrote, the habits of mind disposing Kroc to success are clear. There is every reason to accept *Grinding It Out* prima facie. Indeed there are painfully honest admissions, for example, discussion of his first marriage (which ended in divorce upon finding a more compatible marriage partner), his short temper, and in the admission that, after all, it had taken him a long time to find his life's work.[25] Kroc might surely have abridged his memoirs in short allusions to what he had learned about people and restaurants, waiting all the time for just the opportune moment to strike out on a triumphal procession to business success. Notably, however, Kroc entitled his memoirs *Grinding It Out,* "building my personal monument to capitalism," as he explained. No attempt is made to attribute to himself any genius leading easily to wealth and adulation. "But I was just like a lot of show business personalities who work away quietly at their craft for years, and then, suddenly, they get the right break and make it big" (57, 95).

Foremost among Ray Kroc's habits of mind was a keen sense for the importance of place. Not in all activities, but with those he enjoyed—playing music, watching baseball, and making money from a hamburger business— Kroc had a well-developed sense of the setting for each (115, 175, 177). Articulated to a degree was a hierarchical sense of place. Although dwelling on the dynamics and ambiance of the hamburger place he idealized, he was also aware that the environment outside a particular hamburger restaurant was essential to its success. Site and situation as geographical context figured highly in his expansion strategy.

Desired location was calculated partly from profit potential and partly from Kroc's preferred landscape. When Kroc opened his first hamburger place, he recognized its location was convenient to him, not an attraction to customers; "At most it was a mediocre site for a place that had no prior public exposure." For Kroc, the Des Plaines, Illinois, location was a short drive and a short walk from the commuter train he took daily to the city for his regular job. Echoes of the frontiering myth—empty ground seen as meaningless and wasted without manipulation for capital gain, both his and others—rang in Kroc's pride (see fig. 6.4) (69, 73–74, 167).

The sphere beyond the restaurant's specific real estate plot also came into play, for Kroc was partial to suburbs long before he started McDonald's.[26] Kroc associated the suburbs with the affluence he coveted and searched them for second-hand furniture he could afford before managing to live in one of them, Arlington Heights. Furthermore, as incubators for children, he liked the exercise of parental authority for which they were sacrosanct in American culture. Children controlled were fine in Kroc's worldview. Perhaps this unarticulated habit of his thought as well as his expressed desire to avoid underworld-owned vending machines in his restaurants were reasons why he banned vending machines. But telephones and jukeboxes, favorites of the adolescent crowds who patronized drive-ins, were also banned from his restaurants. He explained: "All of those things create unproductive traffic in a store and encourage loitering that can disrupt your customers." While Kemmons Wilson, Kroc's contemporary and legendary founder of the modern motel chain, used an airplane to find prospective sites for his businesses along interstates, Kroc used an airplane to locate communities with schools and churches. Although drawing on automobile-borne customers, it was not a transient trade but a youthful, growing, and home-bound trade that Kroc curried. Kroc valued discipline and wanted an ambiance of respectability at profit's base.[27]

On McDonald's "sense of place," Kroc lavished great attention. When, for example, his first manager failed to create the setting Kroc desired, he was

FIG. 6.4 March 1963, a McDonald's under construction at Binghamton, New York. (*Source:* Roberson Center and *Press and Sun Bulletin.*)

"furious," by his own admission. He grew angry with problems others would dismiss as, again in his own words, "little things." These could include an unlighted sign at night or a littered parking lot (75). No detail was too small.

Kroc's keen sense of place in developing McDonald's was clear from the outset. *Grinding It Out* gives a reliable account of his epiphany at the Mc-Donald brothers' walk-up. Surely it was money Kroc wanted to make that drew him to see their operation for himself. He was curious about the Mc-Donald brothers because his customers commanded that they wanted one of the mixers he was selling to the McDonald brothers. Once there, his entre-preneurial ambitions escalated. But it was after all to a specific place that he was drawn for first-hand observation. Might he not have stayed home and simply devised a marketing scheme for his milkshake mixer? Twice Kroc re-counts how he came inadvertently to launch the chain, in *Grinding It Out's* opening pages and again one-third of the way into the book. The second telling emphasizes his business negotiations with the McDonald brothers. However, Kroc's first telling reveals his highly developed sense of what a hamburger place should be, his excitement about it and the essence of it. And he begins his description of his fateful reconnaissance with it (6–11, 66–68).

On the day of his visit to San Bernardino in July 1954, he saw a "typical, ordinary-looking drive-in." It was male workers starting their routine for the lunch-hour rush that engaged Kroc. Comforting and familiar images of neat diners like White Castle's resonated. Activity's whir further excited Kroc. Observing the crew shunting various food supply carts into the restaurant it-self, Kroc concluded, "Something was definitely happening here. . . . The tempo of their work picked up until they were bustling like ants at a picnic." Productivity's promise was thus perceived in visual terms, not in monetary terms, according to Kroc's place-oriented sensibilities. Momentum rose. Only then did profit explicitly register in Kroc's memory of the first McDonald's sighting. "Eight Multimixers churning away at one time began to seem a lot less farfetched in light of the steady procession of customers lockstepping up to the windows." Kroc's excitable personality of high kinetic energy was stimulated by the roadside rush. His framework was certainly not contemplative repose or even the methodical man of action (6–7).

Much of Kroc's later strategy came to him as he watched the scene, abstracted later to become his mantra: "Quality, Service, Cleanliness, and Value." The element of cleanliness was lacking in the customer's explanation. It was in Kroc's recourse to his own observations after talking with the customer that he focused on the missing element of fastidious "housekeeping" as he referred to it. The McDonalds' control satisfied an essential need in Kroc's definition of place, especially for restaurants. The next interruption of his reconnaissance was a brief exchange with a construction worker who himself paused just long enough to describe the hamburger he was eating as better than "the old lady's cold meatloaf sandwiches."[28]

Kroc was clearly having a good time and, perhaps, fortuitously, his next pleasant reference was somewhat sexual. "In a bright yellow convertible sat a strawberry blonde who looked like she had lost her way to the Brown Derby or the Paramount cafeteria." She was upscale and attractive to Kroc who was keyed up: "It was not her sex appeal but the obvious relish with which she devoured the hamburger that made my pulse hammer with excitement." Kroc associated a successful hamburger place with fun, an activity McDonald's has since tried to kindle throughout its chain. Only after his initial observations did Kroc begin to home in on profit's possibilities.[29]

Notably, none of his exchanges with the customers at the McDonald brothers' store contradicted his predisposition and, in that sense, he really learned nothing he did not already know. No other hamburger entrepreneur, indeed no other early fast-food entrepreneur, has left so telling evidence that a sense of place was at the heart of their enterprise. Kroc's experiences at the McDonald brothers' operation fulfilled his preconceptions for a desirable hamburger place—busy, productive, controlled, yet joyful.[30]

After having seen and sensed in practice what he liked at McDonald's, Kroc looked into how to orchestrate such a setting. He scheduled a discussion with the brothers to learn what, for the first time, he labeled a "system." Rationalizations about place followed his titillations. Last, his profit motive reared.[31]

Ray Kroc was a quintessential entrepreneur, "driven by ambition," he admitted. Even by the mid-1960s, when McDonald's began earning millions each year, Kroc did not retire because he wanted to perfect his enterprise. Kroc never pursued wealth alone. "I was looking for work that offered something more than money, something I could really get involved in." A full-blown vision of the successful business, however, did not come to Kroc instantly. In his memoirs' characteristically honest fashion, Kroc acknowledged that he proceeded in increments from details. His only consistently held goal was a very vague one: make it big and quickly (17, 43, 95, 157).

Kroc had alternative work options. Given his musical and sales talent, he might have combined them to be a prominent and prosperous dance-band leader in an age when that was possible. It was in selling restaurant equipment, however, that he persisted. Doubtless because of his conservatism, he never treated music as more than an entertaining sideline, something done to augment his primary income through sales. Although he hit his stride as a salesman in Chicago by 1925, he still went to Florida with his wife that year in pursuit of greater opportunity, his failed real estate sales job leading to playing piano for an orchestra in a swanky nightclub. This job ended with his being jailed because the nightclub violated Prohibition. Before then Kroc was attracted to the nightclub as a place type. Kroc recalled that his first night of playing piano "made quite an impression on me. The place was fabulous—gorgeous, glamorous, and illegal." But not only was he put in jail because he played there, his automobile flight home to Chicago ended in disaster as he saw it when he avoided a traffic ticket because of a policeman's sympathy. Shortly thereafter, collapse of the Florida real estate boom that had drawn him initially seemed to punctuate his fling with getting rich quick. Until the late 1950s, for one-third of his life, Kroc turned to the mundane job of selling paper cups and milkshake mixers to restaurants (32, 34).

Food service became Kroc's business, most dramatically at McDonald's where he finally found the chance to combine his flair for showmanship with the restaurant trade he had watched so long from the audience as a salesman. The main attraction became the fast foods and on them Kroc spent considerable personal time to achieve the taste he wanted. He did not diversify his business interests as many competitors did, although he was unsuccessful with a chain of steakhouses and pie shops, and in his memoirs he recalled in detail his work to perfect the quality of hamburgers, milkshakes, but especially french fries.[32]

The latter became a signature item of the McDonald's menu, an item whose flavor set the standard for the industry. It may have been the novelty of a very tasty secondary food that struck the chord in Kroc's showmanship explaining his emphasis on french fries, rather than the hamburger heretofore considered the primary food at drive-ins. McDonald's made a selling point of its french fries long afterward. John Mariani has astutely emphasized the traditional promotional strategy of American food purveyors to utilize some gimmick.[33] Kroc's was a food. Of course, advertising was mobilized once Kroc had his tasty side dish.

Market Leadership Achieved

From its inception through the 1960s, McDonald's struggled to assert and maintain dominance in its corporate territory. Although John Love, McDonald's best historian, has cautioned that McDonald's emerged only tenuously in first place in the hamburger race by the late 1960s, in retrospect its leadership seems already to have been established in the 1960s.[34]

Franchising was the chief maneuver to rapid expansion as it was throughout the nascent fast-food industry. Kroc's version was matured by his long experience with food services. He had decided McDonald's would never supply its operators because that scheme had weakened other parent companies' franchisees and opened parent companies to federal antitrust charges. Furthermore, to maintain control over franchisees and ensure their execution of corporate standards, Kroc sold franchises individually and not for a region. With Harry Sonneborn's design of the Franchise Realty Corporation for McDonald's, the financing base was conceived and built with remarkable success, thus making Sonneborn McDonald's virtual cofounder. Hired in 1955, at 30 years of age and with considerable experience in franchising for Tastee-Freez, an ice cream chain, Sonneborn introduced a cool personality and financial expertise that complemented Kroc's excitable self and talents in purchasing and restaurant operations. In the first three years, one-half of McDonald's franchisees were people who had other livelihoods and they lacked Kroc's obsession, thereafter required of franchisees. Similar to the typical franchise arrangement, franchisees received a package deal including name, architecture, advertising, and training in return for their investment. McDonald's distinction was to work carefully thereafter with its franchisees to help assure their success by enforcing corporate standards. Kroc's eventual disagreement with Sonneborn, who resigned with a multimillion-dollar settlement in 1966, resulted from Sonneborn's goal to use McDonald's for managing real estate rather than franchising restaurants and to slow their addition in the face of a recession he anticipated in 1967. A year after Sonneborn's departure, McDonald's franchising empire was the subject of adulation in the business press.[35]

Business Week's article typified a McDonald's franchisee as "a man of substance" who had to put up more than half of the $97,000 franchise price before his McDonald's opened.[36] (The first franchises had sold for $950.)[37] On average he was between 35 and 50 years of age, and his business experience had left him "often disillusioned with corporate life."[38] Lending institutions, at first local banks, came to include large ones because McDonald's was counted a good risk. A McDonald's earned about five times the average of all other drive-ins, about $300,000 and a pretax profit of 12 to 15 percent. Franchisees agreed to pay from their gross earnings 2½ percent for counseling services and advertising, the latter including 1 percent in national advertising, most of it on television. Eight percent of the franchisee's gross was spent on the land rented from McDonald's, the parent company persisting in the original scheme of land ownership in order to best protect its investment in the restaurant without disadvantaging the franchisee.[39]

Corporate territoriality was carefully plotted. McDonald's picked the restaurant sites. Company policy remained consistently conservative from its inception on this issue, executive vice-president Fred L. Turner describing, "We want young families in the tricycle and bicycle neighborhoods—the station wagon set, or one car going on two." McDonald's sought "above-average-income residential areas, preferably near shopping centers," explained *Business Week*.[40]

Franchise agreements were signed for 20-year terms and McDonald's provided a very active staff of 25 to 30 specialized advisers in each of the five regional offices to help franchisees. Owner-operators were largely satisfied with this arrangement.[41]

McDonald's strengthened itself financially between 1967 and 1976 by *McDonald's* buying out many of its franchisees. Whereas in 1968 McDonald's owned only 15 percent of its restaurants, in 1976 it owned one-third of them. Buyout permitted firm control of operations in company-owned restaurants. Simultaneously it solidified its capital base, typical of its conservative orientation. McDonald's nonetheless remained committed to franchising. That strategy was rooted in Kroc's philosophy that a business's strength springs from the petit bourgeoisie, envisioning McDonald's as a mom-and-pop operation. McDonald's cut back to 25 percent restaurant ownership within a few years after the "big buyout era" ended in the 1970s, a percentage that has been maintained since.[42]

McDonald's dedication to franchisees and operations led to the creation of Hamburger University in 1961. Other chains trained personnel, most of them on the job in a store, but none so elaborately as McDonald's. The company's public relations manager attracted the widely circulated *Life* magazine to report on "Hamburger U," as it became known. It was viewed as Kroc's effort to change the public's perception of making hamburgers from that of a lowly pursuit to one of the respectable professions. Some journalists criticized Hamburger U, perhaps out of snobbery.[43] Some denied its high standards. Others saw it as a public relations ploy. Fred L. Turner, however, explained of the school, "It's a focal point for generating a family feeling. There's a sense of belonging."[44] Therein perhaps was an appeal to a lower-class recruitment base that could find self-esteem in work through professionalism's trappings. Hamburger University was also a mechanism for sustaining a corporate culture dedicated to business success.

Turner's climb at McDonald's tells something of the genuine opportunity Kroc offered, and what he was looking for. Turner, an ex–army typist pondering the possibility of college, began as a 23-year-old counterman in the Des Plaines restaurant the year after it opened and became, with several of his family members, one of Kroc's first franchisees.[45] "He had a natural feel for the rhythms and priorities that make a McDonald's restaurant click," Kroc appraised.[46] Sharing the same inchoate feeling for a fine hamburger place and the passion for making McDonald's excel, Turner perfected various aspects of kitchen operations and quickly became one of Kroc's most trusted early assistants. Turner never found a reason to go to college.

Kroc's blend of boosterish enthusiasm and absolute dedication to work informed the company's labor policies. By Kroc's lights, life meant work and work was to be viewed as a wonderful opportunity rewarded in exertion and creativity. White male would-be entrepreneurs and managers garnered the

FIG. 6.5 Golden arches, candy-striped building, and McDonald's slogan—"Your Kind of Place"—characterized the early McDonald's stands.

FIG. 6.6 Outside seating built into the stands also typified early McDonald's stands.

FIG. 6.7 "Speedee" preceded Ronald McDonald as corporate logo.

McDonald's

most attention. McDonald's, for example, experimented with various payment plans for the managers of its company-owned restaurants to find the one most equitable. Teenage girls were not hired, thereby avoiding loitering teenage boys, the milieu contradictory in Kroc's thinking of a high-class, family-oriented place. The policy against hiring women for staff positions was eventually dropped as a concession to male store operators who began hiring women in the mid-1960s. Labor unions, which drew on a long history of conflict and legislative remedy, were kept out of McDonald's after they tried and failed to organize McDonald's workers.[47]

Advertising, a key ingredient of the consumer culture, took hold slowly at McDonald's, historian Love explaining that despite Kroc's salesmanship he was unfamiliar with advertising. Eventually appreciating his deficiency in this regard, Kroc hired a public relations firm two years after launching his business. Although McDonald's entry into television marketing was slow by today's standards, by the end of the 1950s McDonald's was the fast-food leader in this new medium. Ronald McDonald, an image that helped clinch the children's market as well as identify McDonald's for many adults, was created in 1963 by McDonald's Washington, D.C., franchisees who immediately employed the persona on television. Beginning in 1966, franchisees were required to contribute to a national television advertising fund and a year later the company began its first advertising campaign on national television.[48]

Architecture was used as advertising, and McDonald's red and white candy-striped stands with golden arches springing from sloping roofs made quite an impression (see figs. 6.5, 6.6, and 6.7). Perhaps, it has been the architectural historian and critic Alan Hess's chief contribution to win for McDonald's early standard buildings appreciation as an important cultural icon. When McDonald's began, neither company nor the American public regarded those buildings as art.[49] Kroc never saw them as anything more than shelter for operations he was challenged to make more profitable by producing more volume. Some among the public were disgusted with them as garish. Although competitors began constructing McDonald's lookalikes for their chains in the early 1960s, McDonald's abandoned the small walk-up for the now common "mansard" style by decade's end, acceding to aesthetic objections against its gaudy pioneering, seeking to identify more with suburban domesticity, and needing indoor seating and more kitchen space.[50]

McDonald's remained a hamburger place throughout all the architectural changes. Although its menu was widened to include a fish sandwich in 1965, an extra large hamburger, the Big Mac, was added in 1968 in a direct faceoff to compete primarily with Burger King's Whopper. Kroc's initial resistance to the fish sandwich, and his introduction of the unpopular Hula Burger (a hamburger topped with cheese and a pineapple ring), proved his fallibility as well as adaptability.[51] In the hamburger's simplicity and essential sameness from place to place lies its popular appeal. Hula Burgers probably tasted, smelled, and looked too different to fall within the range of popular demand. We see therein an example of the homogenization of taste contributing to and resulting from the chains of which McDonald's was leader.

The 1960s witnessed essential corporate restructuring. In 1961, the McDonald brothers were bought out. In 1965, the company went onto the stock market. In 1967, the 15-cent hamburger was dropped. In 1968, Kroc stepped aside as chief executive officer and Turner replaced him.[52]

Market Domination Maintained

Since the 1970s McDonald's has led all hamburger chains. McDonald's outnumbers its nearest competitor, Burger King (see fig. 6.8), everywhere in the nation except Rhode Island. The Midwest ranks as McDonald's bulwark

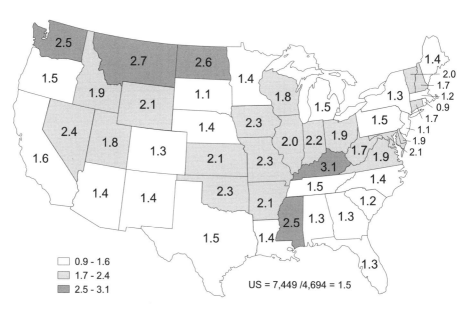

FIG. 6.8 The ratio of Burger Kings to McDonald's, 1988. (*Source:* Robert L. Emerson, *The New Economics of Fast Food* [New York: Van Nostrand Reinhold, 1990], table 5.6, p. 117.)

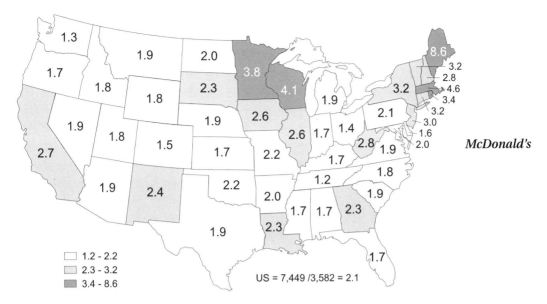

FIG. 6.9 The ratio of Wendy's to McDonald's, 1988. (*Source:* ibid.)

in its more than 40-year-old rivalry with Burger King, in some states achiev-ing ratios of 2 to 1 or nearly so. Kentucky has the highest ratio of McDonald's to Burger King, slightly more than three McDonald's for every one Burger King. Against Wendy's (see fig. 6.9), the major latecomer into the market, Mc-Donald's still outdistances it greatly in the Northeast. Ratios are generally lower throughout the South, Midwest, and West; yet in the huge California market, McDonald's holds an edge of more than 2½ to 1. Advancing outward methodically from its base in North Carolina (see fig. 6.10), Hardee's is the only competitor to have more units than McDonald's in several states, in-cluding Hardee's home state. Several northeastern states, however, have no Hardee's and several have astronomical ratios in McDonald's favor. With no presence in any western state except Washington, Hardee's has consider-able ground to cover before fulfilling its ambition to become a national com-petitor. Jack in the Box's competition with McDonald's (see fig. 6.11) reveals the former's retrenchment to states, mostly in the Southwest, California, and Washington, in which it originated. The strong but comparatively small White Castle company has engaged McDonald's in competition only where the older company had staked out its territory (see fig. 6.12). Together the maps vividly illustrate McDonald's powerful performance. Only the success-ful chains are mapped, not those that disappeared. In the rough and tumble fast-food market, McDonald's more surely than any other chain reinvented an attractively packaged place and product.

Was the fast-food market saturated? This was the foremost question in the fast-food market beginning in the late 1970s.[53] While analysts arrived at no consensus, the fast-food purveyors—McDonald's foremost among them—adopted new strategies beginning in the early 1970s thereby signal-ing the likelihood of full market maturation.

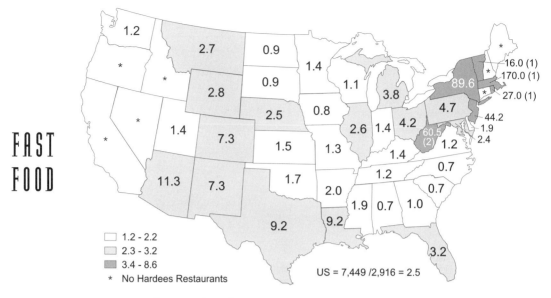

FIG. 6.10 The ratio of Hardees to McDonald's, 1988. (*Source:* ibid.)

What began was "nook and cranny expansion," the descriptor coined in-side McDonald's for opening in central-city neighborhood locations that had been previously ignored in favor of exclusive suburban orientation. Be-tween 1972 and early 1974, McDonald's opened almost 90 restaurants in shopping centers and malls, including major urban centers such as Manhat-tan and San Francisco. The publicly stated rationale was the habitual focus on efficiency and volume, for example, the downtown San Francisco loca-tions drew customers from within a few blocks, as opposed to suburban restaurants' standard two-mile radius, and frequently they earned more than their suburban counterparts. In truth, McDonald's was part of a fast-food tidal wave into the cities.[54]

In the inner city, McDonald's conceded to African-Americans' growing in-sistence on achieving equality in American society. The civil rights move-ment of the 1960s first affected McDonald's in Cleveland in 1968. Historian Love insists that McDonald's move toward a larger role for blacks was al-ready underway but was pushed into black recruitment in Cleveland, "a cat-alyst for one of the most dramatic breakthroughs ever made by minority groups into American business." Between 1969 and 1972, McDonald's num-ber of black franchisees jumped from four to almost fifty, nearly 10 percent of its franchisees. By 1974, the prestigious black periodical *Ebony* lauded the case of three black franchisees who opened a McDonald's in Detroit.[55]

Aggressive capitalism pursues ever-larger markets and McDonald's inter-national growth started as a consequence beginning in 1970. McDonald's domestic success engendered the classic dilemma of where to invest for the highest returns. Fast food's absence outside the United States represented opportunity, although the question became to what degree a uniquely American food and service could profit. McDonald's, nevertheless, jumped

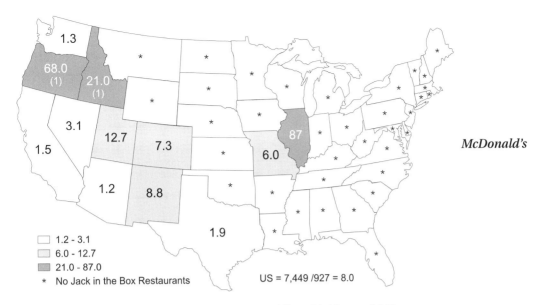

FIG. 6.11 The ratio of Jack in the Boxes to McDonald's, 1988. (*Source:* ibid.)

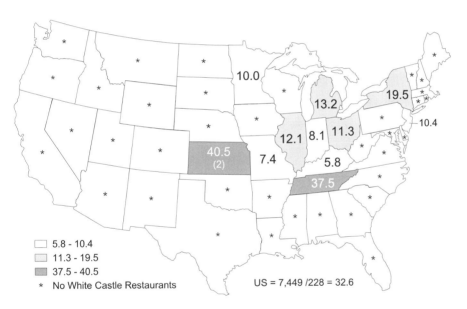

FIG. 6.12 The ratio of White Castles to McDonald's, 1988. (*Source:* ibid.)

into Canada, Australia, Japan, the United Kingdom, and Europe. Many foreign palates adapted quickly to McDonald's version of the American hamburger, the success indeed contributing to the general adoption abroad of American popular culture. At least among socially stratified French teenagers, indications are that McDonald's informality—for example, acceptance of customers in street clothes and loud talk—was a welcome antidote to France's often aristocratic restaurants. Problems, however, did arise with McDonald's exacting operations. Lacking reliable European suppliers, for example, McDonald's confronted lack of product consistency from restaurant to restaurant. It was hard too, at first, to find investors in Britain where capital was scarce. In Amsterdam, where the first restaurant opened in the suburbs, just as Kroc launched McDonald's in suburban Chicago, the company learned to move into the cities where affluent classes lived. These frustrations abroad reflected just how completely McDonald's had synchronized its product and delivery with America's social and geographical restructuring. The host cultures and McDonald's did accommodate each other ultimately, international expansion becoming not merely the fastest-growing but McDonald's "best hope of future growth," according to Love.[56]

The menu, too, was further diversified in hopes of new customers. Egg McMuffin, a middlebrow version of eggs Benedict, began as a franchisee's concoction in 1971. A succession of breakfast items to boost revenues accumulated in a full breakfast line by 1976. McDonald's thus became the first fast-food chain to offer a range of breakfast items greatly expanding business hours. Experiments with chicken were marketed at several restaurants beginning in the early 1970s but not added nationwide until the early 1980s. This development was instructive of McDonald's leadership, for the fried-chicken morsels that McDonald's introduced were not adequately duplicated for three years by the foremost chicken chain, Kentucky Fried Chicken. McDonald's identity, nonetheless, remained that of a hamburger place.[57]

Public opinion about McDonald's often crystallized not only around McDonald's food—many eating there heedless of the mounting charges against its high sodium and fat contents—but around McDonald's as a place.[58] One market analyst claimed that the baby boomer "used to be content with a clean place, reliable quality, and courteous service. But that's not enough these days. People are willing to pay more. . . . The best place to invest is in companies that are providing more of a dining experience and better food."[59]

With others, McDonald's labor practices infuriated. They were endemic to the industry, in fact. They included failure to incorporate improved wages and working conditions as incentives to increase productivity. The corporation's induced sense of belonging to a corporate family hardly compensated, critics charged. The de-skilled labor of assembly-line production was made even more discouraging by hiring a large number of part-time staff because it was not owed certain benefits required for full-time employees. Instead, it was assumed workers had other jobs while their fast-food employment did not constitute "real work." Students often worked under such terms to reach such short-term objectives as paying for an education that would enable them to avoid fast-food employment in the future. Turnover was rapid and chronic. People educated for restaurant careers seldom viewed the fast-food sector as a desirable opportunity. Such degraded circumstances bode ill for the financial and psychological life of a society increasingly given to the service industries. With the prediction that one of every fifteen Americans would work at some time for McDonald's alone and

FIG. 6.13 One of numerous similar signs along the road just inside Cape Cod, Mass., declaring the residents' aversion.

McDonald's

McDonald's claim to feed one-half of 1 percent of the world's population daily, some critics feared the fast-food industry was not investing its fair share in a nation hooked on their product and service. Industry leaders bristled when politicians categorized the employment of 14- and 15-year-olds as "child abuse" and fast-food restaurants as "sweatshops."[60]

It has been McDonald's specifically which has often drawn extensive charges against exploiting teenage labor. On the one hand, it is difficult to believe that cheap labor has not been a factor in McDonald's ascent, although its advocates' best analysis has not factored it in at length. Teenagers perhaps are more impressionable than older workers; therefore, they are well suited to the precisely defined routines that McDonald's demands. Teenagers may also be more manageable than older employees, therefore, willing to perform work their older counterparts refuse. McDonald's antagonists, Max Boas and Steve Chain, have achieved the qualities of an exposé in those passages of *Big Mac: The Unauthorized Story of McDonald's* (1976) chronicling the elders' defense of voiceless teenagers against McDonald's attempt to recruit them in San Francisco in 1972. On the other hand, it can as well be argued from Boas and Chain's own evidence that challenged restauranteurs and food handlers' labor unions attacked McDonald's in their own interests. And, while many young McDonald's workers expressed dissatisfaction to journalists, others spoke well of the company. Might the issue resolve itself into a question of whose aspirations are at the root of the answers, those of the respondents or those who interview?[61]

With still others, the very promise that McDonald's (most of all among the fast-food chains) would enter a neighborhood unleashed resistance (see fig. 6.13). The "town fathers" of upper-middle-class communities especially abhorred the perceived threat that their residential neighborhood communities would face from congested traffic, litter, transients drawn to inexpensive food, and—in Manhattan—loud mouths, loiterers, and drug addicts. Much of this resentment fermented against the entire fast-food industry but McDonald's was most often cited as the cause, perhaps not disproportionate to its size, however. The battle over place was joined, some seeking financial opportunities and increased tax base through McDonald's, others reviling the very sight of the golden arches. Building commissions fought in many towns to force adherence to their standards. The result was often a McDonald's restaurant, but not one of uniform design.[62]

In some towns, McDonald's and their fast-food kin were prohibited near schools, churches, and hospitals. Turner belittled many opponents. But there was no turning back to the time of McDonald's unchallenged sway in the marketplace if it was going to depend on new people and their places. McDonald's acceded in some cases and in others attempted to forestall opposition by adopting, in 1968, a more environmentally sympathetic architecture, hence, the mansard roof with its subsequent adaptations. The bright golden arches on red base were also made smaller. "Localization" of interior decor became a program. This included substantial elements of local history principally in the dining rooms such as photographs of the old Groton Company fishery's advertisements in Gloucester, Massachusetts.[63] Compromise worked in many cases but not all. A core group was persuaded that McDonald's represented a hostile world view: "Somehow the notion has arisen that everything should be quick and easy and in disposable packages."[64]

In the mid-1990s, as McDonald's moved in the matured market to small towns for expansion, resistance flared anew and often divided the targeted community. McDonald's in truth seemed to have become a victim of its own success, size, and style, notwithstanding its conciliatory modifications. Perhaps the surest symptom of McDonald's triumphal stature was opposition to the company as symbolic of what was wrong with America.[65]

Fast food's deaccelerating profits added strain in the 1990s. McDonald's menu, even with adjustments attempted for adult tastes, seemed unable to retain the aging baby boomers as customers although children and teenagers continued to enter the market as McDonald's core. Disgruntled with central headquarters' autocratic control while subtracting from their profit margins and lowering their real estate value, franchisees hesitatingly demanded fairer treatment.[66]

Expansion beyond the United States remained McDonald's growth horizon keeping alive the ethic of ever greater profit. By the mid-1990s, McDonald's led all American restaurant companies in growth overseas. More than 2,500 units earned slightly over $11 billion.[67]

With so many long-term antecedent forces and risk-taking businesspeople giving rise to the hamburger as Americans' roadside food of preference, Ray Kroc's and McDonald's contributions are comparatively latter-day and can be mistaken for nothing more than profit earned in historic proportions. As remarkable as Kroc's earnings were (he died in 1984) and McDonald's have continued to be, their remarkable essence is in the great depth to which the creator and the company understood the American consumer culture of the late twentieth century. Then it was possible to build a hamburger chain of vast extent and dominate the market through place-product-packaging.

Focusing on the aspects of personality relevant to Kroc's entrepreneurship illuminates the key individual in this epic. Kroc's well-defined sense of place was paramount. It attached to the narrow range of activities Kroc enjoyed but appears most strongly to have been felt and fully elaborated in his hamburger business. The dedication, discipline, and speed demonstrated in the teamwork generating a high-quality product evoked his joy from his first observation of the McDonald brothers' walk-up in action. All of these characteristics he strove to replicate in his chain. All of these characteristics he and Fred Turner loved individually and shared their excitement for. But unlike his comrade who stepped from choreographing a restaurant to directing an entire corporation, Kroc only started in the position he passed on to Turner. Kroc instinctively understood operations but spent no time running a restaurant, preferring others to do that. He was neither actor nor director but was producer. As such, no one else in the company paralleled his capacity to remove himself from the artistry of operations while at the same time propelling his fanatical dedication to them. It is instructive that stopping short of a career as a musician because of his sober side, Kroc years later likened his late-blooming entrepreneurship to the careers of show-business stars. McDonald's was the theater for Kroc's showmanship.

Focusing on American culture in the late twentieth century illuminates how well it meshed with Kroc's personality and vision to produce the McDonald's epic. White, upwardly mobile, middle-class families rushed to the suburbs, as Kroc had earlier, and became legendary for their disciplined children, who Kroc gladly hosted upon their arrival in cars under parental supervision at his restaurants. America moved from an industrial to a service economy and its preferred places for eating out reflected that, McDonald's customers differing from the workers and clericals who hurried a bite to eat at the earlier diners on their time off from work. A high point of America's enthusiasm for technologically assisted speed was sustained at the same time Kroc demonstrated examples in every McDonald's. The hamburger offered a reasonable focal point for these values in the roadside trade because its long-standing and vast appeal made possible its equation with fast food and McDonald's developed a system with the highest rate for it. McDonald's performed so spectacularly in an age of mass communications that the company ultimately eclipsed not only its rivals but its forerunners as well.

Focusing on American culture in the late twentieth century also illuminates significant disjunctures with Kroc's personality where various corporate concerns overcame his proclivities—his likes and dislikes—to yield yet another phase of the McDonald's epic. Women and blacks had little role initially at McDonald's, white male managers who shared Kroc's zeal being his favored cohort. From within, that cohort, however, started the reforms to which highest management acceded in quest for greater profits, encompassing different people and different cultures in the places. Urban and international expansion testifies. The hamburger's centrality despite menu diversification and the decision against offering a dining experience to its customers, however, raises questions about the extent to which McDonald's can continue to rely on its initial customers, now American suburbia's aging baby boomers. Does Ray Kroc's defining sense of a hamburger place haunt McDonald's?

FAST
FOOD

CHAPTER 7

Sandwich Places

We turn here to a food group with great diversity—the sandwich. Indeed, the various sandwich varieties might well have been treated in separate chapters, except that our overall focus on where the automobile traveler eats guides us to a relatively simplified synthesis. For all its deep satisfaction to many appetites, none of the other sandwiches save, perhaps, the hot dog has achieved wide popularity across social and regional lines. We picture here the sandwich types of both great and small demand regularly sold along America's roadside. Our emphasis remains the rise of automobile convenience as it played out in changing restaurant configurations asserting clear corporate identity throughout their market. As with our treatment of hamburger places, and in our subsequent chapters that focus largely on nonsandwich foods, we treat the biographies of only selected entrepreneurs and the histories of selected companies. Those, taken together, tell the important story in overview.

Hot Dogs

Hot dogs are the one food that might have rivaled the hamburger as America's roadside favorite. Early the hot dog held wide popular acceptance, an acceptance linked to recreation and entertainment. Like the hamburger and ice cream cone, other popular foods that came to the fore in leisure-time events at the end of the nineteenth century, the hot dog was first popularized at a fair. At Chicago's Columbian Exposition of 1893, Anton Ludwig Feuchtwanger, a Bavarian sausage seller, served hot dogs, giving customers white gloves to prevent them from burning their hands as they ate. When the gloves began to disappear as souvenirs, Feuchtwanger substituted bread rolls to hold the wieners.[1]

Hot dogs continued an association with mass entertainment through baseball. In 1901, Harry Maxely Stevens introduced hot dogs at the New York City's Polo Grounds. Under Stevens's instructions, vendors hawked,

"Get your dachshund sausages while they're red hot. They're red hot right now."[2] Cartoonist Thomas Aloysius "Tad" Dorgan witnessed the event and launched "hot dog" as a synonym for the previously popular term "frankfurter" or "wiener" with a drawing of a dachshund in a bun captioned "hot dog."[3]

Hot dogs, of course, predated these "introductions." Frankfurters or wieners arrived with German immigrants to America and were sold from pushcarts on New York City streets as early as the 1860s.[4] In the twentieth century their appeal, however, became widespread despite their reputation being, at first, not entirely positive. In keeping with his acerbic wit, H. L. Mencken defined the hot dog as "a cartridge filled with the sweepings of abbattoirs."[5] Nathan's, the first hot-dog chain, began in 1916 with men in surgeon's smocks eating hot dogs in front of the store to convince people of Nathan's reliability.[6] The hot dog's popularity waned in the 1920s, the victim of a lingering stigma at the very time hamburger entrepreneurs were sanitizing their product.

The hot dog did come early to the nation's roadside, but not in ways conducive to enhanced appeal. Evidence of its rank is reflected in the term "hot dog," which prefixed many references to roadside eateries through the 1920s. "Hot-dog stand," for example, was more often a generic reference to a business selling inexpensive meals beside the road than to a business specializing in hot dogs. Vernacular allusion emerged by the end of the 1920s to "hot-dog kennels" as a term of opprobrium. The implication grew among elitists that hot dogs were an often bad food, making problematic any place selling hot dogs or any road food for that matter. "Hot-dog kennel" passed out of use by the late 1920s, both as hot dogs lapsed in popularity and the architectural quality of roadside establishments improved.[7]

Hot dogs were limited to popularity in regional markets at the very time that hamburgers began to sell nationwide. Nathan and Ida Handwerker founded Nathan's simultaneously with Ingram and Andersen's White Castle, but the Handwerkers were satisfied with their single city market, albeit a huge one, New York City. (The chain was named for a popular song of the time—"Nat'an! Nat'an! Tell me for what are you waitin' Nat'an?"—rather than its founder.)[8] In 1995, after a period of rebirth, the chain numbered about 200 stores, 30 company-owned and some 170 franchised.[9]

Germans and other European immigrants may have sustained the hot dog as a food reminiscent of home. Yet even where Germans were numerous the issue of cleanliness could not be ignored. An editorial in the *Terre Haute Star* in 1929 reported that hot-dog consumption declined from 84,000,000 in 1926 to 62,000,000 in 1928 and reasoned that Americans of all stripes were demanding not only better food, but restaurants that at least appear clean. "The motorist cannot be certain of what he does not see, but he can exercise the privilege of refusing to buy from a stand whose appearance is anything but inviting."[10]

The hot dog was fostered in numerous regional variations, some rooted undoubtedly in ethnicity.[11] New York hot dogs were commonly garnished with steamed onions and yellow mustard. Sauerkraut and melted Swiss cheese topped hot dogs in Kansas City, coleslaw in the South, and yellow mustard, chopped raw onion, sweet relish, dill pickles, tomato, and celery salt on a poppyseed bun in Chicago.[12]

In the city, storefront restaurants and street vending predominated. Chicago, one of the hot dog's greatest centers of popularity, exemplified. Although a few restaurants of 100 or more seats specialized in hot dogs, most of the city hot-dog customers were catered to by roughly 3,000 street vendors as late as the 1980s.[13]

Nathan's chief executive officer verified the hot dog's "traditional role as a between-meal or after-meal snack."[14] Even an entrepreneurial self-help book encouraging entrance into the large hot-dog market of the 1970s implied that the hot dog was most profitable when linked to impulsive consumption. Hot-dog chains operating in shopping malls, for example, permitted customers to "eat their hot dogs as they continue to walk along and shop."[15] Children, often frivolous, were habitual hot-dog eaters; one fast-food chain specializing in fish successfully lured parents by diversifying its menu with hot dogs. It was common knowledge that children could veto their parents' eating preferences.[16]

Did the hot dog's association with impulsive consumption work against its becoming a successful competitor with hamburgers? Was the hot dog limited to being a novelty food, while the hamburger came to be viewed not only as healthful but filling? Could hot dogs constitute the basis for a real meal? Nathan's attempted to promote hot dogs as appropriate by publishing a series of hot-dog cookbooks.[17] Hampered by its reputation as homebound or a novelty when eaten out, hot dogs alone never engendered the drive to lasting corporate dominance mobilizing place-product-packaging. Where the hot dog was associated with root beer, however, the combination won wide acceptance along the emerging American roadside. To that end corporate territoriality was established with integrated design.

A&W

Root beer and hot dogs have been closely linked by the roadside. Although the combination has played a minor role compared with the hamburger, fries, and shake combination, it has been noteworthy. Root beer, a soft drink made from syrups, either synthetic or natural, took off in the mass-consumption market of the late nineteenth century along with other novelty foods.

Ever vigilant for business opportunities, Roy W. Allen, an Illinois native who went west accordingly, was buying, refurbishing, and selling old hotels when he met a chemist who claimed to have perfected a recipe for improving root beer's taste, a claim Allen verified at one of his hotels. Allen bought the rights to manufacture and market the new root-beer syrup, and opened a walk-up root-beer stand in Lodi, California, in 1919. In 1922, Frank Wright, one of Allen's employees, became a partner, and they blithely named it "A&W Root Beer." In 1923, in Sacramento, California, the company opened its first drive-in. Aficionados debate whether this was America's first drive-in. Beginning in 1925, Allen expanded the business—retaining the A&W name after Wright sold out in 1924—to build the nation's first system of franchise roadside restaurants. About 200 outlets displayed the chain's "bull's-eye and arrow" logo by the mid-1930s. Place-product-packaging and corporate territoriality went hand in hand again. However, operations varied considerably. Some were walk-ups. The signage, color schemes, and, of course, the root beer provided the rudiments of place-product-packaging.

J. Willard Marriott, who began his rise to prominence as a roadside restauranteur with an A&W franchise in Washington, D.C., in 1927, was attracted. Marriott quickly developed his own concept, the Hot Shoppes. Numerous mimics testified to A&W's leadership, many, like Marriott moving on to new food venues and store formats.[18] But A&W failed to innovate.

A&W did not develop a full-service restaurant for 50 years. The chain was content to focus on small-town markets, operating seasonal stands with little profit potential for the parent company. Many franchisees had bought their licenses for a pittance, $50 or $100, and complied simply by purchasing A&W's concentrate and equipment and maintaining standards of cleanliness. For a half century, Allen's simple system persisted, a manufactured syrup easily transported in bulk to a network of small outlets with appliqued logo. Throughout, the hot dog had been one of numerous adjunct foods, although a natural complement given its recreational origins in popular culture.[19]

A&W's contemporary era began in 1966 with acquisition by the United Fruit Company, later named United Brands. It planned to convert A&W from a rash of small root-beer stands with hot dogs into restaurants for family dining. A&W's chief executive, a former McDonald's vice-president, disclosed: "I think marketing should be the one to tell us where to go, and operations should make it happen. At McDonald's, operations runs the show. I don't think that's the best way."[20] Emphasis in restructuring market put the chain's top management at odds with franchisees. A battle ensued between the parent company and franchisees over control of the advertising budget.[21] While corporate civil war raged in the courts, the chain shrank by half to 1,200 units in the early 1980s. Beginning in 1993, under another new owner, a former Burger King executive, the ailing pioneer roadside restaurant chain once again attempted rejuvenation.[22] It was back to root beer, back to hot dogs, and, for many franchisees, back to seasonal operations. *Plus ça change, plus c'est la même chose.*

Root beer and hot dogs in automobile-convenient venues—simple food quickly served to motorists—did not attract the round of new hot-dog entrepreneurs who entered the market beginning in the 1980s. Most of the newcomers—Majors Hotdogs & Hamburgers in Atlanta, Georgia, Zab's Backyard Hots in Rochester, New York, Frankly Fries in Washington, D.C., and Callahan's in New Jersey—operated in shopping malls. Promoted were "gourmet toppings," customers selecting from a wide array of condiments according to personal taste. Mighty Casey's in Atlanta was dedicated to freestanding buildings convenient to customers arriving by automobile, but featuring indoor sit-down dining. In San Francisco, Ben Franks, launched in 1979, was dedicated to hot dogs, and to drive-through exclusively. Wendy's alone among the fast-food giants, beginning in 1986, diversified its menu with hot dogs.[23]

Hot dogs never became uniformly popular nationwide, being more popular perhaps in the Midwest and South. In markets where fast food thrived, hot dogs thrived, but always subsidiary to hamburgers. California, far less given to fast foods, had a disproportionately high percentage of hot-dog restaurants, Der Wienerschnitzel's success skewing the circumstance.[24]

DOG "N" SUDS

A chain launched in the Midwest, Dog "N" Suds might have established the hot dog as major roadside fare. Dog "N" Suds peaked at 650 franchised and company-owned units in 38 states in 1968. Started in 1953 by two high school teachers from Champaign, Illinois, Jim Griggs and Don Hamacher, to supplement their salaries during summers, their Dog "N" Suds tapped roadside demand well before other chains. So novel were such ventures at the time that Griggs and Hamacher were surprised when others asked about how they could replicate the partners' simple drive-in.[25]

Dedicated to hot dogs (and root beer as a subsidiary), although offering a variety of other soft drinks and fast-food sandwiches, the partners outlined a scheme for franchisees which earned attention in the restaurant trade magazines of the late 1950s and early 1960s. For $12,000, including equipment and a $500 fee, a person could go into the Dog "N" Suds business. Demographics and site selection were carefully prescribed: franchise area of 20,000 population, no town under 2,500, and an elaborate system of traffic classification. For example, a street drawing shoppers was considered best served with a drive-in on the side of the street facilitating access without crossing oncoming traffic. Pleasure trips drew customers where drive-ins

FIG. 7.1 A Dog "N" Suds drive-in in Quincy, Ill.

FIG. 7.2 Dog "N" Suds
logo.

were located near the recreational destination. Work trips yielded less profit than either shopping or pleasure trips. Lots next to traffic arteries were required to have a 100-foot frontage on corners and 140-foot frontage inside blocks. Architecture and landscape were carefully integrated. A long, low canopy shaded the drive-in anchored at one end by a small enclosure housing the kitchen and carhop facilities (see fig. 7.1). Picnic tables and semicircular benches awaited customers who wanted to eat outside their cars. A tall pole topped with the chain's logo—a chef-hatted dachshund hurrying to serve a hot dog and root beer—created an unmistakable company identity (see fig. 7.2). Numerous other details were elaborated in the company's instructions for franchisees.[26]

Dog "N" Suds' financial plan was carefully structured. Revealing its motives, however, the menu was mentioned less than was profit. Few franchisee services were provided. When Dog "N" Suds merged with the American Licensing Company of Chicago in 1969, various rationales were cited: better financing for improved building designs, management techniques, and franchisee services. But it was too late. Franchisees quit in droves. The chain—reduced to 15 units—was sold four more times before Don Van Dame of Lafayette, Indiana, bought it in 1991. Van Dame began to bottle and retail the company's root beer, its bottles sporting the distinctive dachshund logo.[27]

DER WIENERSCHNITZEL

Der Wienerschnitzel's founder, John Galardi, opened a hot-dog stand in Wilmington, California, in 1961, expanding through franchising to 200 units by 1968, largely through use of an A-frame building. The building's steeply pitched roof arrested the motorist's attention, but Galardi embraced the automobile even more fully by providing driveways through his buildings served by interior windows that were, quite literally, "drive-through" in purpose. There sacks of food were rapidly dispensed, the motorist's convenience amplified. Galardi gave his chain a multisyllabic, foreign (German)

Locations by County

· 1
★ 2-4
△ 5-9
□ 10-19
○ 20-39
▲ 40-79

n=283

FIG. 7.3 Der Wienerschnitzel remained a California-based chain, as shown in this 1996 map. Leading counties were: Los Angeles (Los Angeles) (67 locations); Orange (Santa Ana) (30); San Diego (San Diego) (20); San Bernardino (San Bernardino), and Santa Clara (San Jose) (17 each).

name to suggest European quality, thereby drawing attention. Never mind that *wiener schnitzel* meant Viennese-style veal, hardly hot dogs. Der Wienerschnitzel's name and architecture represented a bold attempt at redefining the hot dog as a roadside food apart from root beer.[28]

Galardi launched other food businesses in the 1980s, the Original Hamburger Stand (a cheap hamburger), Weldon's upscale dinners, and Chelsea's yogurt. They were bundled in the same locations with the intention of increasing total sales without each individual business losing its identity.[29] But throughout this reformation, the hot dog remained Galardi's galvanizing vision (see fig. 7.3).

Big Bun

"Big bun" sandwiches are as diverse in form and name as they have been divorced from automobile-convenience. The "hero" derived from the heroic undertaking of eating the large sandwich and by the 1920s the term stuck. A "grinder" was so named in New England because of the thick crust through which one had to chew. The more nationally current term "sub" was the creation of Benedetto Capaldo, a grocer in Groton, Connecticut, where submarines were built during World War II. Capaldo's sandwiches, with their elliptical buns, looked like miniature submarines. "Hoagies" were named by Italians who worked near Hog Island, Delaware, where they added "ie" to the island's name and applied it to their sandwiches. In 1929, the "poor boy" originated in New Orleans as a commercial product. Sandwiches by these names have been sold by various chains.[30]

From these designations, however, "sub" has emerged as the principal generic term, due principally to Subway, ranked at this writing as second only to McDonald's in number of units. Although begun in 1965, Subway did not start franchising until 1974. But Fred DeLuca, who started the business at 17 years of age in Milford, Connecticut, with a $1,000 loan from a family friend, was determined to make money. Graduating from college, he dropped his premed studies, explaining simply, "I thought a career in sandwiches was more promising."[31] Two years after franchising began, Subway jumped to 32 stores, by 1979 to 100 stores, and by 1984 to 400 stores.[32] Subway became the quintessential entrepreneur's dream in that start-up costs were low ($10,000 for the first store, $2,500 for the second), not only because DeLuca determined to keep franchise costs down but because the equipment required for a sandwich shop was lower than other food venues.[33] Most outlets occupied leased space in traditional commercial storefronts or in small neighborhood shopping centers.[34] In 1993, Subway began opening restaurants in convenience stores (C-stores) and truckstops, or bundling, operating at some 1,400 of these locations by 1996.[35] A mutually beneficial relationship yielded a new place type and so began the big-bun sandwich's transformation into an important road food, although it lagged far behind hamburgers both in percent of restaurant profits and numbers.[36] Subway's public relations package explained the new venue's advantages:

> With the small space requirement, low installation cost, no need for cooking and the ability to operate with a minimal staff, Subway fits into the c-store environment seamlessly. Add to that a portable product that is not time-sensitive because it is not hot, volume purchasing that keeps costs low and national brand-name recognition that brings more people in the door, and it's as if Subway and c-stores were made for each other.[37]

Blimpie's, the second-place sandwich chain in the early 1990s, followed Subway's lead by bundling with various gasoline station chains, most notably Texaco.[38]

Subway far surpassed all sandwich competitors (see fig. 7.4). Many of the stores were "satellites," as Subway defined them; that is, one franchisee operated several Subway stores. DeLuca structured the franchise royalties—10.5 percent of profits or roughly twice as much as competitors—to encourage his chain's expansion. Franchisees quickly reckoned that true profit quickly lay in opening multiple stores. The result has been somewhat problematic, however; without territorial exclusivity guaranteed for each franchise, many franchisees engage in heated competition. Subway faces self-saturation.[39] Geared to rapid growth, Subway had foregone rigorous place-product-packaging. As one franchise brochure declared, "Subway offers a great number of advantages including a bright modern decor package, a very low franchise fee, complete training and continual advertising, but, most of all,

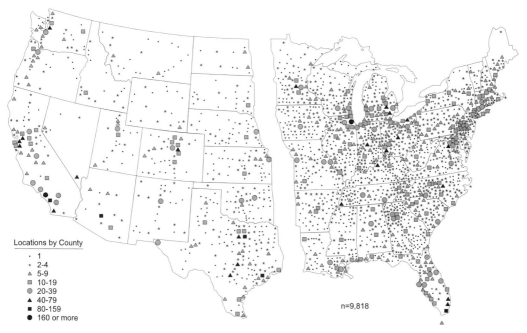

FIG. 7.4 Subway maintained a strong national market as shown in this map of its shops in 1996.

adaptability to a wide variety of building styles."[40] "Subway" in white letters superimposed on a brown and yellow logo widely applied and interiors wallpapered in a motif recalling the subway's construction in New York City achieved a modicum of integrated design. Exploring another dimension of its rapid growth strategy, Subway led the sandwich chains in expansion abroad by the mid-1990s.[41]

Barbecue

Barbecue's development as a roadside food provides a reverse image to that of the hamburger. Barbecue stands sprang up quickly for the first automobile travelers. Generic references to roadside eateries as "barbecue stands" were as common as "hot-dog stands" in the 1920s. Barbecue, like the hot dog, was what came readily to mind when Americans wanted a tasty food requiring little specialized service, especially as they traveled into the South and Southwest (see fig. 7.5). The Sunbelt was both a vacation destination for many automobile travelers and a hearth for an important regional food. Barbecue seemed preadapted to automobile-convenient eateries. The inexpensive roadside locations well beyond urban neighborhoods were ideal for the placing of barbecue pits, and the slow-cooking (16 hours for many recipes), smoke-inducing, highly personalized cuisine whose perfection, rooted in folk foodways, required constant attention. Barbecue appealed to automobile travelers seeking the "real" America of regional traditions and customs.

Some of barbecue's virtues, however, mitigated against its extended

FIG. 7.5 The Munger-Moss Sandwich Shop advertised regionally oriented barbecue, "old Kentucky style," in Missouri for those traveling southwest on Route 66 in the 1930s.

popularity in a culture generating national chains in service to hungry automobile travelers. For one, tastes varied substantially region to region, and even city to city. Texas, one of barbecue's hearths, cooked beef in a tomato-based sauce. This variety was not well received when the Luther's chain attempted to expand nationwide in the mid-1980s. In the Southwest, another variety featured pork and a vinegar-based sauce. Nashville was known for stringy meat with dry spices and Memphis for chopped pieces in sauce. Distinct flavors, textures, color, aroma, and setting yielded diversity even between cooks. Which regional variety would a chain entrepreneur dare to try extend across regions?[42]

In 1921, J. G. Kirby, a businessman with the financial backing of R. W. Jackson, a physician, founded the Pig Stands Company in Dallas, featuring barbecue but other sandwiches, too. By 1934, there were over 100 Pig Stands claiming to sell "America's Motor Lunch" throughout Texas, California, Louisiana, Mississippi, New York, Florida, Oklahoma, Arkansas, and Alabama. A rival thus to A&W's claim as the oldest roadside chain, Pig Stands also expanded through franchising and various automobile-convenient venues. Its barbecue, however, had not clinched sufficient claim on appetites to prevent the chain's decline during World War II, although a small chain headquarters in San Antonio to the time of this writing.[43]

Barbecue was not for those wishing to turn quick profits. Barbecue was labor intensive and did not lend itself to the assembly-line methods of "industrialized" hamburger production. In the South African-American males were the traditional master pit men as they could be hired at depressed wages. Although barbecue was perhaps the most popular short-order choice in the South before 1945, the emphasis on speed thereafter pushed barbecue to the background.[44] Barbecue did not lend itself to slick place-product-packaging. Geographer Richard Pillsbury emphasizes that Southern barbecue cannot properly be eaten in fancy places. Although barbecue pits have become more hygienic, as health laws force operations to screen the pits and move the tables indoors, the best barbecue restaurants are "still a bit frowzy, even by regional standards."[45] The format that attempted packaging "frowziness" usually failed.

Luther's chain operated a cafeteria lacking in distinctive decor.[46] Many patrons reacted against Luther's "big, empty hall."[47] The number of restaurants specializing in barbecue remained sufficiently small, too small to invite a reliable count until the mid-1980s: 5,228 or 1.7 percent of all American restaurants.[48] Most chain concepts failed. The International House of Pancakes and Butterfield Savings and Loan, both based in California, briefly tried to expand the barbecue market through the Love's chain. By 1979, it numbered 58 units. Beginning in 1985, Ronald C. Mesker planned Love's further expansion through several restaurant takeout formats, and packaging for supermarkets. Barbecue lends itself to takeout convenience because it tastes very good reheated, Mesker theorized. New Love's Express stores were established, the term "express" borrowed from the innovative hamburger drive-throughs.[49] Again, Luther's revealed barbecue's severe limitations in the roadside market. Headquartered in Houston, Luther's spread as far afield as Dover, Delaware, reaching its apex by the mid-1980s at 63 stores. By 1994, Luther's retrenched to 20 stores—14 in Texas, 4 in Louisiana, and 2 in Colorado—and was satisfied with 1 to 2 new stores per year.[50]

Roast Beef

In contrast to barbecue, roast-beef sandwiches did come to enjoy wide popularity and some degree of market penetration. Several chains enjoyed degrees of real success. Rax was one. Within five years of its founding in 1978, Rax numbered 221 units in 25 states, mostly in the Midwest, but especially Ohio and Pennsylvania. In declining industrial cities, Rax offered its limited menu of roast beef, fries, and soft drinks at low prices. When Americans began to shift to healthier food, however, Rax diversified its menu through introduction of an elaborate salad bar with some 50 items including uncommon items like garbanzo beans, Alfredo sauce, and Chinese food. Along with new products came a series of new bidding formats. Rax Roast Beef was renamed Rax Restaurants and its fast-food factory-like architecture of metal was replaced with motifs softened by wood and solariums out front, the whole symbolic of Rax's desire to be the "champagne of fast food." Rax's old image as a single-sandwich enterprise was blurred, and the low-profit salad bars lost their distinctive advantage when competitors followed suit with their own salad venues. Rax's upscale image became a liability with working-class customers who equated upscale decor with high prices. Women were attracted to the "light" menu, but men, on whom Rax initially depended, were not. In 1990, Rax abandoned the salad bars and returned to sandwiches, again principally roast beef. Rax momentarily stabilized at 504 units through the new initiative but fell to 77 units by 1996.[51]

The Roy Rogers chain was started in 1968, its first store in Falls Church,

Virginia, a suburb of Washington, D.C. With roast beef leading the way and hamburgers, chicken, and salad bar as subsidiaries, Roy Rogers successfully appealed to an older clientele. In 1979, the Marriott Corporation, which owned Roy Rogers, accelerated the roast-beef chain's growth, purchasing a number of small competitors in the Washington, D.C., and New York City areas, and, in 1983, acquired the large Gino's chain centered on Philadelphia. The chain was sold in 1990 to Hardee's, which intended to rebrand its locations.[52]

Arby's was the biggest roast-beef success. An acronym from the first letters of the Raffel brothers, Arby's had among the oldest roots in the roadside restaurant trade. The Raffel family owned a 16-unit hotel and restaurant chain begun in New Castle, Pennsylvania, in 1919. Brother Leroy Raffel, who later emerged as Arby's director, received executive training at the University of Pennsylvania's honored Wharton School of Finance and Commerce while brother Forrest Raffel attended the equally renown School of Hotel and Restaurant Management at Cornell University. Leroy and Forrest purchased a restaurant equipment company in 1949 and became one of the nation's foremost consulting firms in contract food service.[53]

Seeking alternatives to hamburgers and pancakes, the Raffel brothers opened their roast-beef chain in Boardman, Ohio, in 1964. The venue was the decade's popular drive-in and simplified fast-food menu—three-ounce sandwiches with potato chips and soft drinks. Yet the Raffels were able to change more than the standard hamburger price—69 cents versus 15 cents—and succeed. Roast beef offered a refined taste which, enhanced by special sauces, appealed to more discriminating customers. Here was a selling alternative to ordinary hamburgers.[54]

Arby's took over the roast-beef roadside segment, driving out 20 competitor chains by the late 1960s and operating over 400 units, 90 percent of them franchised by the end of the 1970s. The Raffels overcame debt in the early 1970s to lay the basis for an attractive investment bought in turn by Royal Crown in 1976, DWG in 1984, and Triarc in 1993. With financial tycoons rather than restauranteurs in charge through the 1980s, Arby's faltered, unable to reach its full potential. Arby's grew nonetheless to 2,500 units by 1990 and Triarc contemplated expansion through a merger with Long John Silver's Restaurants in 1994. Arby's chuckwagon building was long a distinctive logo until its stores were more recently packaged in red-trimmed beige walls pierced with extensive glazing, the high cowboy hat sign, however, surviving throughout Arby's history. In the latest entrepreneurial move of bundling, Arby's became one of the most desirable companions in a store. By the mid-1990s, Arby's also led in the internationalization of roast beef, placing the chain among the top 14 restaurant companies in earnings abroad.[55]

Specialty Sandwiches

Discussion would not be complete without mention of the at least several specialty sandwiches confined regionally in the United States. Maid-Rite, for

FIG. 7.6 An early Maid-Rite sidewalk stand in Canton, Ill.

Sandwich Places

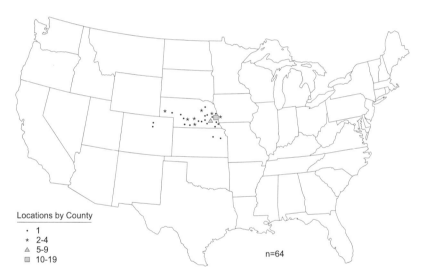

Locations by County
·   1
★   2-4
△   5-9
▢   10-19

n=64

FIG. 7.7 Runza's restaurants in 1996. Counties with the most restaurants in the chain were all in Nebraska: Douglas (Omaha) (15 locations); Lancaster (Lincoln) (11); and Adams (Hastings) (4).

example, evolved to serve the small towns of Iowa and western Illinois (see fig. 7.6). The Angell family began Maid-Rite in Muscatine, Iowa, in 1926, their product a distinctively seasoned, crumbled hamburger sold in buns. Eschewing full place-product-packaging, Maid-Rite nonetheless consistently relied on a hexagonal red-and-white logo. The Maid-Rite sign hung in front of a wide variety of restaurant types from traditional storefronts to drive-ins.[56]

The Runza chain, headquartered since its founding in 1950 in Lincoln,

Nebraska, has steadily modernized, today operating indoor walk-ups with drive-through windows. Three relatives, Sarah "Sally" Everett, her brother Alex Brening, and Milan Everett, brother-in-law to both, founded Runza. Sally Everett named it for the sandwich she adapted from her mother's German-Russian recipe on the family farm in Sutton, Nebraska. German-Russians have called their sandwich *bierock,* too strange-sounding for a popular market. The unique sandwich comprised seasoned ground beef and cooked cabbage inside bread. The family-owned company's initial venue was the drive-in but by 1996 the company was renamed Runza Restaurant to convey the sense of fuller service. More widely recognized sandwiches than the signature-entree Runza and onion rings diversified the menu. The Runza sandwich is, perhaps, too distinctive to warrant the chain's expansion much beyond its Nebraska base (see fig. 7.7). Such assessment may underestimate the force of advertising.[57]

TABLE 7.1 Leading Sandwich Chains, 1996

Chain	Headquarters	Units Worldwide	Sales (in millions)	Sales Rank Top 300
Subway Sandwiches and Salads	Milford, Conn.	12,516	$3,200	8
Arby's	Ft. Lauderdale	3,025	1,979	12
Blimpie Subs and Salads	New York, N.Y.	1,786	275	82
A&W Restaurants	Livonia, Mich.	778	266	84
Schlotzsky's Deli	Austin, Tex.	573	202	112
Roy Rogers	Rocky Mount, N.C.	300	200	113
Au Bon Pain	Boston	296	182	119
Miami Subs Grill	Ft. Lauderdale	185	150	136
Wienerschnitzel	Newport Beach, Calif.	312	132	148
Togo's Eatery	Campbell, Calif.	195	109	163
La Madeleine	Dallas	46	101	169
D'Angelo Sandwich Shops	West Bridgewater, Mass.	86	203	191
Nathan's Famous	Westbury, N.Y.	175	85	192
The Great Steak & Potato Co.	Hamilton, Ohio	165	74	213
Wall Street Deli	Birmingham, Ala.	117	70	223
Saint Louis Bread Co.	St. Louis	58	58	248
The Steak Escape	Columbus, Ohio	125	56	253
Rax	Dublin, Ohio	70	55	261
Jerry's Subs & Pizza	Gaithersburg, Md.	94	50	271
Souper Salad	San Antonio, Tex.	66	49	275
Cousins Submarines	Menomonee Falls, Wis.	111	46	283

Source: Restaurants and Institutions 107 (July 15, 1997): 66.
Note: This table does not include bagel shops.

FIG. 7.8 Schlotzsky's formats adapted to the circumstances of each location, here a walk-up and drive-through in Hillsboro, Tex., in 1996.

Sandwich chains are not nearly as numerous as their hamburger counterparts (see Table 7.1). Only two companies exceeded 1,000 units. The philosophy of one of the aggressive new entries into this market segment may explain the lack of large chains (see fig. 7.8); Schlotzsky's, based in Austin, Texas, disclosed: "Our goal is to add incremental sales in the evening. . . . People don't buy sandwiches after 4 p.m.; 65% of our business comes between 11 a.m. and 2 p.m." We reiterate that Americans may not perceive sandwiches as full meals. Schlotzsky's answer to investors seeking more profit was to add pizza to the evening menu.[58] Sandwiches might remain a company's hallmark but not the portal to large roadside food empires.

Nonetheless the sandwich market niche is not inconsequential. From the traditional hot dog through the "sub," which the Subway Corporation more recently popularized, sandwiches have satisfied lighter hunger pangs, either a sudden stimulus for a "bite to eat" or a craving for fast, unpretentious midday fare. In their satisfaction of impulsive and quick consumption, sandwiches have been welcome road food. Here is a characteristic expression of the consumer culture, spur-of-the-moment gratification bought with discretionary income at various speedy service venues. With some Americans' recent search for healthy food and the gendered palate—women more often seeking lighter fare than men—vigilant entrepreneurs may prove other kinds of sandwiches more popular than hamburgers. Several of the bigger chains probe markets abroad, perhaps indicative of the American market's approaching maturation.

CHAPTER 8

Ice Cream Places

Whereas the hamburger and other kinds of sandwiches sustained the roadside restaurant as an institution, the role that other foods played cannot be overlooked. In this chapter we turn to ice cream which, along with the hamburger and hot dog, entered the American consciousness as an exotic specialty food in the late nineteenth century. Widely popularized at world's fairs, first in sodas and then in cones, ice cream's popularity was initially that of a between-meal and after-meal treat. Nonetheless, ice cream provided entrepreneurs a new focus around which to configure restaurants, from soda fountains to roadside stands to frozen yogurt shops. Ice cream evolved as a distinctive market segment in the restaurant industry, especially with the coming of the automobile, the story we tell here. In the 1990s, the typical American consumed some 13 quarts of ice cream a year, in the aggregate spending some $3 billion annually on the product.[1]

Ice cream desserts first appeared in late colonial America as ices frozen out of wine and fruit juice, and then later out of flavored cream and egg mixtures initially called butter ice and then cream ice.[2] A summer dessert concoction, such sweets were early associated with society's elites who could afford the ice required for chilling. Ice was cut from northern lakes and stored in icehouses, entrepreneurs like Frederic Tudor of Charlestown, Massachusetts, establishing the early nineteenth-century commerce in ice along the Atlantic and Gulf coasts, and as far away as the Indian subcontinent of Asia. The first commercial ice cream was obtained from recipes brought from Europe, especially from France. Indeed, French nationals were the first to retail ice cream in New York City, especially in the fashionable pleasure gardens or summer retreats for the city's elites. Augustus Jackson, a cook in the White House who went on to become one of the nation's wealthiest African-Americans, introduced ice cream to Philadelphia when he established his successful catering business there in the 1820s. Both Thomas Jefferson and James Madison had popularized the food at formal functions, Dolley Madison serving both presidents as official White House hostess.[3]

Nancy Johnson's 1846 invention of the hand-cranked ice cream freezer, which utilized salt brine to chill, quickly changed ice cream from a rich man's delicacy to a commonplace treat. *Godey's Lady's Book,* which served as a kind of Bible for upper-middle-class housewives, pronounced ice cream to be a necessity for home entertainment. "A party without it," it asserted, "would be like a breakfast without bread or a dinner without a roast."[4] Joseph Fussell, a Baltimore merchant, is credited as the first wholesaler of ice cream, and thus the founder of the ice cream industry. In 1851, Fussell launched a dairy in Baltimore, obtaining fluid milk by railroad from farmers as far away as York County, Pennsylvania. In confronting frequent milk surpluses, he entered the ice cream business, supplying retailers in Philadelphia and Washington as well as Baltimore.[5] In New York City he partnered with J. M. Horton, who applied steam power to turning enlarged ice cream freezers. The Horton Ice Cream Company eventually became part of the Borden Company.

Ice cream's popularity soared between 1910 and 1950, annual per capita consumption rising from 1.9 pounds to 17.2 pounds.[6] The coming of Prohibition accounted for much of the increase as soda fountains thrived in the 1920s, in part as an alternative to the nation's closed saloons. In 1925, 30 percent of the country's ice cream was sold through confectionery stores; 16 percent through drugstores (again mostly through soda fountains); 10 percent through "wayside stands"; and 8 percent through other restaurants, including those in hotels. Grocery stores sold some 19 percent.[7] By 1965, food stores were marketing some 55 percent of the nation's ice cream, a reflection of quick-freezing technologies, the development of self-serve freezer chests in stores, and the development of home freezers or freezer compartments in refrigerators. Restaurants accounted for 13 percent of the ice cream sold, drugstores 5 percent, and confectionery stores only 1.5 percent. Street vending and vending machines accounted for 1 percent each.[8]

The origins of the ice cream cone and ice cream sundae are clouded by claims and counterclaims. Ernest Hamwi, a Syrian immigrant to the United States, was credited by historians as the originator of the ice cream cone, an event associated with the St. Louis 1904 Louisiana Purchase Exposition. Seller of a crisp, sugared, wafer-like Persian pastry baked on a waffle iron, Hamwi came to the rescue of an ice cream vendor who had exhausted his supply of serving dishes, the ice cream served in waffle cones. However, Italo Marchiony, an Italian immigrant in New York City, actually patented a cone mold earlier in 1904. David Avayou, a Turkish immigrant, and Abe Doumar, a Jewish immigrant, also claimed to have invented and sold ice cream cones at the St. Louis fair, the latter calling his innovation the "cornucopia." It is apparent that by the close of the Louisiana Purchase Exposition numerous vendors on the grounds were selling cones—ice cream placed in folded or wrapped waffles. Many continued selling them after the fair closed, Doumar in a chain of ice cream stands at Coney Island and Avayou in a chain at Atlantic City. Hamwi went on to found the Missouri Cone Company.[9] An automatic cone-rolling machine was patented in 1914, and a completely automated rolling and baking machine in 1938.[10]

So also are there conflicting claims regarding the ice cream sundae. Ed Berner, operator of a soda fountain in Two Rivers, Wisconsin, poured chocolate syrup on a dish of ice cream at a customer's request, the concoction becoming an overnight sensation locally. Another fountain operator in nearby Manitowoc, forced by customer demand to offer the concoction also, did so only as a Sunday loss-leader. In the Chicago suburb of Evanston, where temperance enthusiasm ran high in the 1890s, a "Sunday Soda Menace" was recognized and legislated against. The term "Sundae" may have evolved there to designate the new dessert introduced in lieu of sodas. Ironically, ice cream sodas were later given strong endorsement as an alternative to alcoholic drinks by the Evanston-based Women's Christian Temperance Union (WCTU).[11] Sundaes came to complement soda drinks as a mainstay of the soda-fountain trade.

Dairy Stores

Ice cream was sold in dairy stores operated by creameries. In small towns, such retailing usually was located at the dairy itself, often at the edge of town. In cities, large dairies maintained small chains of outlets oriented to neighborhood business districts strung out along streetcar lines, and, with the coming of the automobile, in peripheral commercial strips as well. Ice cream was sold in pint, gallon, and half-gallon containers hand-packed from freezer chests. Many stores provided soda fountains where sodas, sundaes, and cones could be consumed on the premises as well. Nonetheless, dairy stores were fundamentally places where milk products were sold, most especially bottled milk and cream, packaged butter and cheese, and sometimes a complementary assortment of baked goods and other convenience groceries.

William Breyers established a dairy store in Philadelphia in 1866, expanding quickly to three locations. In 1905 he opened a new manufacturing plant to distribute bulk ice cream to retailers across the New York City, Newark, Washington, and Philadelphia metropolitan areas. In 1951, Breyers was the world's largest producer of ice cream with stores and packaged ice cream available in supermarkets across eight northeastern states and the District of Columbia.

In the 1890s, William Isaly bought dairies in the Ohio cities of Mansfield, Marion, and Youngstown, and established chains of neighborhood dairy stores first in Pittsburgh and then in Columbus. By 1953, 400 retail outlets stretched from western Pennsylvania across northern and central Ohio with stores in northern West Virginia also.[12] Most Isaly outlets were located in standard storefronts, but with facades covered in porcelain enamel featuring the chain's green, red, and white color scheme with the word "Dairy-Dell" stenciled in black.

Roadside Stands and Drive-Ins

Other dairy companies experimented with restaurant formats divorced from standard storefront architecture. Wolles Bungalow Ice Cream Company of Sioux City, Iowa, operated seven "bungalow stands." Only large enough to contain a freezer, a storage cabinet, a sink, and limited counter space, these little rectangular, gable-roofed boxes, house-like in silhouette, were appropriate to locations at the residential edges of neighborhood business districts. Immediately after World War II, M. J. Muldoon of Mishawaka, Indiana, converted a vacant storefront adjacent to his dairy store, literally creating a "drive-through" addition. But at nearby South Bend in 1950, he built the Bonnie Doon Drive-In, featuring indoor soda-fountain service as well as outdoor carhop service. The building with canopy extension sat in a large parking lot topped by an oversized imitation of an ice cream carton.[13] The Milk Maid Ice Cream Company of White Plains, New York, developed a prototype "self-service" dairy store for roadside franchising, and 18 outlets in suburban New York City were operating in 1956.[14]

The Dutchland Farm Stores, with their distinctive orange roofs, white walls, and blue-green trim, became roadside landmarks across southeastern Massachusetts and parts of Rhode Island, Connecticut, and New Hampshire in the late 1920s (see fig. 8.1). The chain was founded by D. W. Field who, raised on a dairy farm, bought a dairy in Brockton, Massachusetts, after accumulating a small fortune as a shoe manufacturer in that city. Field moved aggressively to retail milk products, especially ice cream, at highway locations. Dutchland Farms was the actual inspiration for Howard Johnson's roadside marketing. Johnson even adopted Dutchland Farms' orange roof and blue-green trim for his own buildings. In 1940, Johnson and the Hillcrest Farms Dairy jointly purchased the Dutchland Farms chain, Johnson taking the roadside properties as locations for his own restaurants, and Hillcrest the home-delivery business. Field was by no means the only entrepreneur to envision a chain of roadside ice cream restaurants along New England highways. James McManus launched in 1927 his "roadside fountains," 18 of

FIG. 8.1 Dutchland Farms restaurant at Scituate, Mass., 1935.

which were operating in 1935.[15] But McManus bought his ice cream from suppliers. He was not a milk producer or processor extending forward into retailing. He was a restauranteur developing an idea innovated by dairy interests.

Many chains used programmatic architecture. In Texas, the makers of Sherry's Elite ice cream opened a chain of "drive-in stations," each housed in a "Dutch windmill," as some of the Dutchland Farms stores were also housed. The Los Angeles–based Big Freezer chain featured stands shaped like hand-cranked ice cream freezers. The Mowrer's Ice Cream Company of Bethlehem, Pennsylvania, established stands housed in giant ice cream "cups," each built to look like a giant 28-ounce Lily Tulip cup, a standard ice cream container of the 1930s.[16] Several Big Cone stands were opened by the Pure Ice Cream Company of Parkersburg, West Virginia. Each building was styled to appear like a giant inverted ice cream cone waffle.

Street Vending

Americans also obtained ice cream from street vendors who sold from freezer chests on push carts, cycle-mounted freezers, and, of course, truck-mounted freezer compartments. This sort of selling characterized the nation's fairgrounds, its parks, and its resorts, especially its beach resorts. In the 1920s, vendors took increasingly to city streets and, using motorized vehicles, to suburban business and residential streets as well. Street vending became for many ambitious entrepreneurs a preliminary step toward restaurant ownership, not unlike the many peddlers who opened grocery and clothing stores with their accumulated savings.

Street vending thrived on standardized ice cream novelties registered under trademark law. In 1919 a confectionery store operator in Onawa, Iowa, Christian Nelson, a Danish immigrant, coated ice cream with chocolate, refreezing it as the "I-Scream Bar." Taking his idea to nearby Omaha, he met ice cream manufacturer Russell Stover who established an office in Chicago from which to popularize the new product nationwide, changing its name to "Eskimo Pie." By 1922 over 1,500 Eskimo Pie franchises had been granted for the making and selling of the bar, with Nelson collecting upwards of $30,000 weekly in royalties.[17] Imitators freely infringed on the patent, however, frustrating Stover, who withdrew from the business to launch his successful candy enterprise at Denver.

Harry Burt Sr., a Youngstown, Ohio, confectioner, sought to replicate Nelson's success. Already marketing a novelty he called the Good Humor sucker, Burt struck on the idea of putting ice cream bars on sticks. Burt took another step when he outfitted a truck with a set of bells, dressed its driver in a white uniform, and sent it jingling out onto Youngstown's streets. On Burt's death the Good Humor trademark was bought by a Cleveland investor group who turned, like Nelson and Stover, to franchising. Thomas Brimer bought territorial rights to Detroit and Chicago. Harry Burt Jr. retained the Miami territory given to him by his father, and later purchased rights to the Tulsa area. Paul

FIG. 8.2 Good Humor truck, Chicago, 1977.

Hawkins obtained rights to California, to thrive initially in the Los Angeles area, especially after Columbia Pictures released the *The Good Humor Man* starring Jack Carson.

In Chicago, Brimer quickly learned that the best "roaming grounds" for his trucks included factory gates at noon, schools at midafternoon, neighborhood business corners in the early evening, and wherever crowds were gathered as at the city's lakefront beaches. He learned the value of highway locations. "Ride out of the city 10, 15 or even 20 miles," reported the *Ice Cream Review* in 1930, "and at every important highway intersection one will see these neat appearing white painted Good Humor trucks with the ever ready immaculate, white uniformed ice cream salesman in attendance."[18] Of course, Good Humor trucks operated only in the warm months in the North, going into storage during the winter. The trucks themselves, although always painted white with the shared Good Humor logo, actually varied in configuration from city to city. For Chicago, truck freezers, chilled with dry ice, held upwards of half a ton of ice cream accessed by side and rear doors (see fig. 8.2). The driver's compartment was open on the right side, placing the attendant always in view and giving him ready access to the freezer compartments.[19] Cultivated was a paramilitary tone through the white uniforms accented by shiny Sam Browne belts. In the 1930s, many Good Humor franchisees required their drivers to raise their caps to women customers and greet men customers with snappy salutes.[20] A manual, distributed nationwide, *Making Good with Good Humor,* outlined the rules for courteous, prompt service and traffic safety. In the 1980s, Good Humor trucks disappeared from America's streets, only the brand name remaining, attached to ice cream novelties available to customers from supermarket freezer chests.[21]

In 1924 Frank Epperson, a lemonade vendor at an Oakland, California, amusement park, perfected a frozen lemonade bar which he first termed "Epsicles," and then "Popsicles." "Frozen suckers" were not new, bars of frozen fruit juices called "Hokey-Pokies" having been sold in New York City as early as the 1870s.[22] Like Eskimo Pies and Good Humor bars, Popsicles found a national market as a branded product. Thousands of entrepreneurs across the U.S. established street-vending businesses, but few grew beyond local markets. For example, the Best Ice Cream Company of New Orleans operated a fleet of "musical trucks," as well as a chain of dairy stores, but never expanded outside the New Orleans area. Even when the names of nationally prominent celebrities were adopted, local enterprises usually stayed local. In the 1950s, a fleet of Howdy Doody ice cream trucks ventured forth in New York City, especially in Queens, riding on the popularity of television's "Buffalo" Bob Smith, Clarabelle the Clown, and, of course, the puppet Howdy Doody.

Street vending was reenergized with the introduction of soft ice cream. A softer ice cream product, concocted of milk, sugar, vanilla and other extracts, cornstarch, and gelatin, could be drawn from machines, eliminating "hand-dipping." Coolers were equipped with pressure valves to release in steady-flow custard-like ice cream into cones or other containers. Thus was service vastly accelerated. And, as important, an ice cream with novel texture, flavored for novel taste, could be produced. A number of companies organized to market nationally several new soft ice cream brands, prime among them Mister Softee. The firm was founded by James Conway, owner of the Boyertown Auto Body Works of Boyertown, Pennsylvania. Conway was not a dairy operator or a restauranteur, but a mechanic. Patented was a specially designed truck body derived from the standard one-ton delivery van suitable to either a Ford or General Motors truck chassis. Mister Softee ice cream was also vended off the right side of the truck, panels opening to disclose ice cream spigots, cone dispensers, and other sales paraphernalia. In 1958 there were some 150 Mister Softee trucks operating across 12 states.[23] Trucks were sold to franchisees licensed for specific territories who, in addition, were required to purchase a special ice cream mix. There were imitators, including the makers of Ding Dong Cart, Dairy Dan, Freddie Freeze, and Sani-Serve truck bodies.[24] All across America the jingling of ice cream truck bells was complemented by the blaring of "Old McDonald Had a Farm" and "Little Brown Jug" from truck loudspeakers.

Prince Castle

Earl S. Prince and Walter S. Fredenhagen opened their first Prince Castle ice cream restaurant in Naperville, Illinois, in 1931. A small cement-block building with counter and stools inside, it was faced with precast stone and otherwise ornamented to appear castle-like, especially in the castellated roofline. Later units followed this design motif even when prefabricated metal structures were built. Prince Castle introduced "One in a Million" malted milkshakes in 1937 using the single-spindle mixers then on the market. Peak hour demand soon outstripped capacity at most stores, leading Prince to develop new multispindle machines patented as Multimixers,

Prince developing a company to manufacture the machines while Fredenhagen tended to the stores. Ray Kroc, a salesman with the Lily Tulip Cup and Specialty Company of Chicago, undertook to coordinate Multimixer sales, his employer becoming the exclusive distributor of the machine. Kroc saw Multimixer and paper-cup sales as integrally linked, his firm even designing a new disposable container to be used with a metal collar to fit the new mixers, thus eliminating much of the cleanup problem associated with milkshakes.[25] Another Prince Castle innovation was the firm's hiring of women to manage its stores. By 1948 there were 39 outlets across northern Illinois and in adjacent sections of Indiana and Iowa.[26]

Henry's

Seventeen-year-old David Bresler spent 1930 traveling among county fairs selling automobile flags and other novelties. In Louisiana he befriended an ice cream vendor whose business hinged on cutting packaged ice cream "bricks" into bars and coating each slice with chocolate before refreezing—a variation of the ice cream bar formula. Bresler brought the idea home to Chicago and set to work making ice cream bars in his parents' garage. Soon he had his brothers hawking ice cream from insulated shoulder boxes in Chicago parks. The Bresler Ice Cream Company expanded quickly, leasing an ice cream factory and introducing a broad range of ice cream products into grocery stores, tobacco shops, movie houses, and other retail outlets, first in Chicago and then in Los Angeles. In 1954, the company launched a chain of self-service drive-in restaurants named Henry's, the name honoring one of the brothers, who had died.

Henry's entered the Chicago market at the same time as Ray Kroc's McDonald's, and, like McDonald's, used the new outdoor walk-up format. Customers arrived by car, parked, and walked up to windows to order. Although the Bresler company created Henry's as a vehicle to market ice cream, the new drive-ins also offered hamburgers, hot dogs, and fish and chips. The chain's logo was a milkshake cup and a hamburger side by side, the hamburger given a human face as a cartoon character. By 1956 there were 35 Henry's in the Chicago area, most of them franchised. Franchisees bought a turnkey setup ready to operate with a guaranteed sales territory. Uniformity in the Henry's system, reported the *Ice Cream Review,* was all-inclusive. "It covers everything—construction plans, plans for operation, financing, insurance, equipment, packaging, utensils—just everything."[27] By 1965, 138 Henry's restaurants were operating in 35 states.[28] Henry's was not only a McDonald's competitor, but substantially a McDonald's clone. The Henry's prototype was patterned after the Hamburger Handout restaurant in Los Angeles, a direct copy of the McDonald brothers' drive-in in San Bernardino. On the other hand, Henry's also influenced McDonald's. The kitchen designer for the Henry's prototype was hired away from Bresler's to join McDonald's design group.

Dairy Queen

Of all the ice cream chains to emerge in the Chicago area in the 1930s, none proved as expansive and as durable as Dairy Queen. J. F. and H. A. McCullough, father and son proprietors of the Homemade Ice Cream Company of Green River, Illinois, began to experiment with soft ice cream. Traditionally, ice cream was served hard at about 5 degrees Fahrenheit, but the two McCulloughs preferred its taste as it first emerged from the mixer before hard-freezing. Optimum, they thought, would be a semifrozen, custard-like dessert served at about 20 degrees.[29] The immediate problem was perfecting a machine to dispense the product. By chance they learned of a device developed by Hammond, Indiana, hamburger stand operator Harry M. Oltz. An agreement was struck, the McCulloughs gaining manufacturing rights for the machine, and its use in Illinois, Wisconsin, and the states west of the Mississippi River. Oltz retained use rights to the remaining states plus percentage royalties on all the ice cream mix sales throughout the country.[30] The McCulloughs took responsibility for perfecting the mix and for finding an equipment manufacturer to make the machines. They also chose the Dairy Queen name.

The first Dairy Queen restaurant opened in 1940 in Joliet, Illinois, under license to Sherb Noble, a restauranteur. The McCulloughs started their first store a year later at Moline, Illinois. Before World War II intervened, Noble opened additional stores, patterned after confectionery shops, in Kankakee, Elgin, and Aurora, cities that, like Joliet, were all industrial satellites of Chicago. The Moline store, however, was the prototype for postwar expansion— a highway-oriented, rectangular box with glass front, its flat roof slightly extended out over the service windows, a large sign featuring a "cone with a curl" topping the building (see figs. 8.3 and 8.4). Tiring of the ice cream business, the two McCulloughs sold out to Harry Axene, regional sales manager for a large farm implement manufacturer, who on several of his sales trips

FIG. 8.3 Dairy Queen, Council Bluffs, Iowa, 1994. A 1950s store little changed.

FIG. 8.4 Dairy Queen, Austinburg, Ind., 1996. An early Dairy Queen logo.

had come across Dairy Queens with long lines of customers queued. Axene aggressively pushed the franchising program the McCulloughs had begun, a Chicago cone manufacturer having helped recruit early franchisees. Sold were territorial licenses varying from single towns to whole states. The number of Dairy Queens soared from 17 locations in 1947 to some 400 in 1949, to over 800 in 1950, and to some 2,100 in 1952.[31] Most were seasonal operations closed in the winter months.

Neither the McCulloughs nor Axene sought to set strict operating standards or to offer business support to franchisees. Display of the Dairy Queen sign and purchase of the mix were all that was expected once license fees had been paid. Thus in 1948 a group of franchisees formed the nonprofit Dairy Queen National Trade Association to encourage chain uniformity. It was an act of group self-protection. In the mid-1950s, the organization became the for-profit Dairy Queen National Development Company which in the early 1960s was renamed International Dairy Queen. The corporation bought many territories back from franchisees, established clear ownership of the Dairy Queen name, launched the chain's first national advertising program, and broadened the chain's menu, introducing, most important, the Brazier food line.[32]

The 1960s also saw introduction of a new Dairy Queen building prototype, the "Country Fresh" design. Franchisees were encouraged to upgrade old buildings or build new ones with prominent red, all-aluminum, front-facing gambrel roofs, roofs reminiscent of the classic red barn of America's heartland (see fig. 8.5).[33] However, what the company pretended in its advertising was a Pennsylvania Dutch motif. Introduced was the "Miss Dairy

FIG. 8.5 Dairy Queen, Paris, Ill., 1996. The "Country Fresh" look in the Dairy Queen red barn motif.

Queen" logo, a little Dutch maid holding a tray of Dairy Queen products. The building format survived, but the logo did not, being replaced by the modernistic "red kiss" more readily seen along the roadside from rapidly moving automobiles.

Dairy Queen seemed to thrive in spite of itself. The chain contains a wide variety of store venues from seasonal roadside ice cream stands little changed from the late 1940s to large, contemporary, full-menu, indoor-walk-up and drive-through stores. Of the 5,209 locations operating in 1991, 3,442 offered burgers, hot dogs, fries, and other food, but 1,128 were still "soft-serve only." Fifty-two locations were "Treat Centers," combining the Dairy Queen, Karmelkorn, and Orange Julius brands in shopping malls.[34] Thus customers never really know just which Dairy Queen menu items are available from one location to another. Even more problematical than lack of uniformity is the company's lack of quality control store to store, a function of the convoluted array of franchising agreements in force, many since the 1940s. Regularly, International Dairy Queen extends incentives to franchisees, encouraging them to improve store cleanliness and appearance and broaden menus. "Many Dairy Queen owners became complacent and let their restaurants become dirty, unattractive and inconsistent, experts say," the *New York Times* reported in 1990.[35]

Dairy Queen success may be laid to several factors. First, the basic ice cream product has remained of high quality, a very strong base, indeed, around which to build a restaurant idea. The chain's soft ice cream has a special taste easily remembered. The very name "Dairy Queen" resonates positively and has become something of a generic term for soft ice cream generally. The chain successfully targeted America's small towns, the only national chain to do so save for A&W. Only when McDonald's began to compete for small-town markets through scaled-down stores in the late 1980s did Dairy Queen start experimenting with new venues and formats. Its purchase of the Karmelkorn and Orange Julius brands (220 and 774 mall locations respectively in 1986) brought the corporation more firmly into large urban markets. In addition, the company bought the 99-outlet Golden Skillet chain which facilitated introduction of fried chicken into Dairy Queen's Brazier line.

Tastee-Freez

In 1948, Dairy Queen's Harry Axene partnered with Leo Moranz, a mechanical engineer and developer of a new, smaller automatic freezer, to form a new also-Chicago-based chain, Tastee-Freez. The chain grew rapidly to over 600 locations in 1953.[36] Tastee-Freez sold its freezers at cost to franchisees, making its profit on the sale of ice cream mix. A 1967 advertisement depicts one of the chain's later prototype buildings and emphasizes the services extended to Tastee-Freez franchisees (see fig. 8.6). Like Dairy Queen, Tastee-Freez introduced a food line highlighted by "Big Tee Burgers." Earlier, Moranz had launched the Carrol's hamburger restaurants named for his daughter.[37] In 1982, the DeNovo Corporation of Utica, Michigan, bought the Tastee-Freez brand and launched a program of store modernization. In 1992, there were 340 locations, about 20 percent of the original outdoor-walk-up style.[38] The Tastee-Freez logo remains a readily recognized roadside symbol.

Carvel Dari-Freez

Thomas Carvel entered the ice cream business vending off the back of a truck at county fairs and beach resorts. A tire blowout at Hartsdale near

FIG. 8.6 Tastee-Freez Advertisement. (*Source: Modern Franchising* 9 [February/March 1967]: 32.)

FAST FOOD

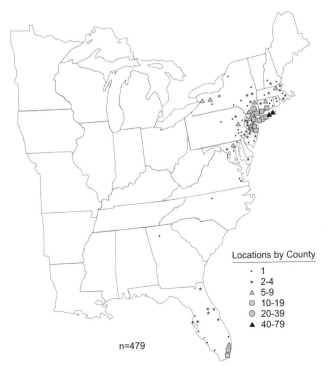

FIG. 8.7 Carvel Ice Cream Bakeries, 1995. Leading counties (all New York) were: Nassau (46 locations), Suffolk (41), Westchester (31), Queens (26), and Kings (20). (*Source:* Carvel Ice Cream Bakery, Inc., Farmington, Conn.)

Locations by County
- · 1
- ⋆ 2-4
- △ 5-9
- ▣ 10-19
- ◉ 20-39
- ▲ 40-79

n=479

Yonkers, New York, in 1934 changed his fortunes as he stayed to do business at what proved to be a lucrative roadside location. There he opened his first soft-serve ice cream stand in 1947. In five years, some 125 franchised stores were operating, spread from Maine to Florida.[39] Carvel's franchise package included blueprints for a metal 20- by 30-foot building with glass front, and a facade that "leaned" forward under an extended flat roof pitched slightly upward. Carvel introduced an ice cream novelty comprised of two large chocolate chip cookies sandwiching a slab of ice cream. In 1995, the chain, owned by a Bahrain-based investment firm, operated some 600 Carvel Ice Cream Bakeries, most of them in the northeastern United States (see fig. 8.7). Emphasized were ice cream desserts fashioned after bakery goods, including so-called character cakes with names like "Cookie Puss" and "Fudgie the Whale." The firm also marketed dessert specialties through supermarkets, and its ice cream was available through the stores of the Krystal chain in the Southeast.

Soft Ice Cream Small Operators

Numerous were the ice cream stands along America's highways, not only those of the large corporations, but the small chains and single-store mom-and-pop operators. We would be remiss not to mention at least a few of the smaller chains. Foster Freeze of Sacramento opened its first stand in 1945, growing to 182 outlets in 1984, most of them franchised.[40] Dairy Isle was started in 1951 at Wooster, Ohio, and grew to over 160 locations. The

Mister Swiss chain of Oklahoma City grew to 186 outlets in 25 states in the mid-1960s.[41] The vast majority of the soft-serve ice cream stores were independently owned and operated. Outdoor walk-ups were relatively cheap to build and equip. Recipes for soft ice cream were relatively easy to concoct. In small towns and in cities alike one could encounter independents doing business under such signs as Dairy Princess, Dari Twirl, or King Kone. There was not a locality that did not have its one-of-a-kind Dairy King, Dairy Delight, Dairy Whip, or Custard Cup. By 1956, there were an estimated 12,000 soft ice cream stands in the United States.[42]

Friendly's

Curtis L. and S. Prestley Blake opened their first dairy store and soda fountain in 1938 on Boston Road just east of Springfield, Massachusetts, followed quickly by a second store on the opposite side of the city. Forced to close during World War II when gas rationing cut highway travel, the brothers expanded anew at the war's close. Developed was a chain of highway soda fountains contained in Georgian Revival "colonial" buildings, many located in conjunction with the Atlantic Refining Company's placement of new gasoline stations.[43] Hard and not soft ice cream remained the brothers' mainstay. Accordingly, the Blakes modeled their restaurants not after the newly emergent Dairy Queens, but more along the lines of Dutchland Farms and Howard Johnson's. Friendly's restaurants differed from Howard Johnson's in that they did not contain dining rooms, but only soda-fountain counters and booths. In 1954 there were 12 stores in Massachusetts, 3 in Connecticut, and 1 in Florida, the latter reflecting the Blake brothers' winter vacation habits.[44] Tourists and other highway travelers were targeted in all of their stores along with local customers.

The firm expanded in the 1950s across southern New England and then in the 1960s southward into suburban New York City, Philadelphia, Baltimore, and Washington, D.C. Friendly's also spread westward across upstate New York from Albany to Buffalo. The company spent little on advertising beyond point-of-purchase displays, depending substantially on the word-of-mouth recommendations of satisfied customers, a strategy that worked especially well in New England where new stores were always relatively close to previously established locations. In New England, the chain grew incrementally, diffusing through what geographers call a neighboring effect.[45] However, in upstate New York, and in northern Ohio, northern Indiana, and southern Michigan, where the company sought to expand in the 1970s, the company was not well known. Its new stores were established at widely separated locations and yet, as before, little advertising money was spent. The restaurants did not sell themselves and the firm was forced to retrench, collapsing back on established markets (see fig. 8.8). Geographical concentration was initially enforced by company reliance on a central commissary located at West Springfield. From there trucks transported prepackaged and/or partially cooked foods to restaurant locations limited to a 500-mile radius.

FIG. 8.8 Friendly's Ice Cream Shops, 1994. Leading counties were: Hartford, Conn. (39 locations), Middlesex, Mass. (30), Hampden (Springfield), Mass. (27), Nassau, N.Y. (27), and Suffolk, N.Y. (25). (*Source:* Friendly Ice Cream Corporation, Wilbraham, Mass.)

Locations by County

· 1
★ 2-4
△ 5-9
▢ 10-19
● 20-39

n=762

FIG. 8.9 Friendly's Ice Cream Shop, Plymouth, Mass., 1995.

Friendly's architecture proved problematical in the Middle West. Midwest customers not previously familiar with the Friendly's format misread the Georgian Revival architecture, expecting to find full-service family restaurants rather than ice cream shops when entering. Many customers never went back. Accordingly, the company enlarged its menu in the 1980s, doing as Dairy Queen had done—enticing dessert-conscious patrons into buying full meals. At the same time, Friendly's simplified its stores; new design motifs merely echoed Georgian style through roof profile (including cupola) and use of brick (see fig. 8.9). Outdoor walk-up windows and drive-through windows were also added. The firm operated 440 company-owned restaurants in 1975, 762 in 1995.[46] During the 1970s, Hershey Foods owned the Friendly's chain. Like most other food manufacturers experimenting with restaurant subsidiaries, however, Hershey withdrew, selling the chain to the Chicago-based Tennessee Restaurant Company, developer of the Perkins Family Restaurants.

Ice Cream and Yogurt Shops

Hard ice cream made a substantial comeback in the 1960s, bringing to the fore a new kind of ice cream store. These were not dairy stores reincarnate. Contrived were "Gay Nineties" ice cream "parlors" where cones and hand-packed cartons were sold. Stores were located in traditional storefronts, but also in shopping centers and in outdoor walk-up locations. For example, the Bresler Ice Cream Company launched a second chain, Bresler's 33 Flavor Ice Cream Shops. In 1991 there were some 250 franchised outlets and 10 company-owned stores nationwide. Also owned by Bresler's was the 40-unit Larry's Ice Cream and Yogurt chain in Florida. With the phasing out of its Henry's chain, it was back to ice cream basics for Bresler's, one of the more persistent names in ice cream retailing.

Earle Swensen opened his ice cream parlor in San Francisco in 1948, building up a 30-outlet chain within a year. Swensen had learned to make ice cream while a cook on a troop transport during World War II. In 1980 there were some 260 franchised stores.[47] Also in 1948, brothers-in-law Burton Baskin and Irvine Robbins opened their first location, the Snowbird Ice Cream Store in the Los Angeles suburb of Glendale where the Big Boy was born. Robbins's father was in the dairy business. In 1990 there were 3,318 Baskin-Robbins stores in the United States, most of them franchised.[48] In 1978, Vermonters Ben Cohen and Jerry Greenfield launched their Ben and Jerry's chain in a converted Burlington gas station (see fig. 8.10). By 1990 there were 5 owned and 80 franchised outlets in 18 states.[49] Company mythology has the partners starting with a $5.00 mail-order course in ice cream making from Pennsylvania State University and a rock-salt ice cream machine.

Several large food manufacturers either started or bought ice cream store chains. Pillsbury's Häagen-Dazs chain was launched at Buffalo in 1970 and, at first, featured only soft ice cream. By 1984 it had grown to over 300 outlets featuring hard ice cream.[50] Sold to Grand Metropolitan, Burger King's parent, the chain was pared down to 260 shops in 20 states in 1990.[51] Swift and Company's Dipper Dan Ice Cream Shoppes and Carnation's Icecreamland stores were launched in 1964, with scores of outlets opened by both companies within a very few years. Big companies could bring large-scale financing to drive rapid expansion. But again, none of the large food manufacturers did well in the ice cream restaurant business. The manufacture and distribution of packaged food mainly through impersonal supermarket selling differed substantially from highly personalized, service-based restaurant selling.

Americans concerned with health turned increasingly to frozen yogurt with its lower butterfat content. New chains appeared. TCBY (The Country's Best Yogurt) was started at Little Rock in 1985 and grew very rapidly to 1,175 stores in only four years.[52] The firm also owned the Mrs. Fields Cookies brand. Success brought imitators, among them Penguin Place (Thousand Oaks, California), I Can't Believe It's Yogurt (Dallas), and Zack's Famous Frozen Yogurt (Metairie, Louisiana). General Mills entered the fray with Columbo Frozen Yogurt distributed not through its own stores but vended in a wide variety of different retail outlets. Like ice cream parlors, many yogurt shops tended to shopping centers, and many, at least initially, were decorated to simulate turn-of-the-century soda fountains. Yogurt chains grew quickly to compete with both soft ice cream and hard ice cream chains (see Table 8.1).

TABLE 8.1 Leading Ice Cream Chains, 1996

Chain	Headquarters	Units Worldwide	Sales (in millions)	Sales Rank Top 300
Dairy Queen	Minneapolis	5,717	$2,508	10
Baskin-Robbins	Glendale, Calif.	4,244	800	35
Friendly's	Wilbraham, Mass.	707	650	45
TCBY	Little Rock	2,696	291	78
Braums	Oklahoma City	56	222	102
I Can't Believe It's Yogurt	Carrollton, Tex.	1,966	173	124
Carvel	Farmington, Conn.	452	150	134
Tastee-Freez	Utica, Mich.	252	115	159
Häagen-Dazs	Minneapolis	270	87	188
Swensen's	Ronkonkoma, N.Y.	280	85	195
Bressler's	Carrollton, Tex.	466	62	240
Foster Freeze	San Luis Obispo, Calif.	135	60	243
Freshens	Atlanta	550	55	258
Ben and Jerry's	Waterbury, Vt.	151	52	266
Everything Yogurt	Staten Island, N.Y.	17	45	294
Culvers	Sauk City, Wis.	50	44	297

Source: Restaurants and Institutions 107 (July 15, 1997): 66.

FIG. 8.10 Ben & Jerry's Homemade Ice Cream Store, Burlington, Vt., ca. 1980.

Dairy stores and then ice cream restaurants, some dairy-sponsored and others founded by restauranteurs, popularized ice cream on the roadside first at stands, then at drive-ins, sometimes in coffee shops or family restaurants, and finally at outdoor and indoor walk-ups. Soft ice cream, for its part, not only reenergized street vending but sustained, perhaps more than any other kind of food, the outdoor walk-up as a viable restaurant venue. Ice cream parlors and yogurt shops, on the other hand, traded on the idea of the dairy store, but without the milk and other dairy products. They resuscitated something of the soda fountain, but without the fountain itself. The selling of ice cream by the roadside has turned in cycles, variously embracing and discarding restaurant formats.

Successful roadside ice cream restauranteurs have tended to one of two tracks. Most operators, especially those going it alone as independents, have settled for the roadside stand and outdoor walk-up arrangements. There ice cream is sold as a between-meal and after-meal treat, other foods, if available, remaining fully subsidiary. Other operators have used ice cream desserts, augmented by hamburgers, as a base around which to configure broader menus, using drive-in, indoor walk-up, and even modified soda fountain and dining-room formats.

This split in ice cream restaurant orientation is found within the largest chain, Dairy Queen. Lingering within the system are hundreds of roadside stands and small outdoor walk-ups, holdovers from the early years of territorial franchising. Yet the parent Dairy Queen International has persisted in upgrading the chain by promoting a complementary food line based on hamburgers and by introducing upscale, sit-down restaurants styled and arranged for customer comfort as well as convenience. The hamburger is basic to the enlarged Dairy Queen menu, and thus to the success of its upscale stores. The chain's advantage is having a range of ice cream desserts for indulgence after one's hamburger has been eaten, desserts that go well beyond the usual milkshakes or cones. At Dairy Queen, it is what comes after the hamburger that counts. Ice cream places, like the local Dairy Queen, do offer an alternative food, but not altogether totally divorced from America's roadside hamburger lust.

FAST
FOOD

CHAPTER 9

Breakfast Places

R estaurants developed around breakfast foods—donuts, pancakes, waffles, and even sausage. Donuts were linked with coffee not only as breakfast fare, but to attract customers to midmorning and midafternoon coffee breaks. At pancake and waffle shops the standard breakfast of coffee, bacon, and eggs was augmented by assortments of grilled pancakes and waffles. Menus featuring "breakfast anytime" meant that breakfast food was served throughout the day, in part to accommodate workers with "inverted" night-time work schedules. Breakfast food was easily complemented by sandwiches (especially hamburgers), salads, and soups. Such was the menu array at most roadside coffee shops or family restaurants. In recent years, bagel bakeries, and the new coffee cafés, have added to the variety of breakfast venues found in the United States. Like ice cream, breakfast food offered relief from the ubiquitous hamburger, but was not totally divorced from its influences.

Donuts

"Doughnuts," or Dutch crullers, were brought to colonial New England by the Pilgrims. Originally round dumplings made from wheat flour or cornmeal, they were called "fat-cakes," "fried cakes," and even "cookies" in other colonies.[1] The ring-shaped donut was popularized during World War I, the Red Cross and other relief agencies making coffee and donuts available to "doughboys" removed from the trenches of northeastern France. The Salvation Army similarly used coffee and donuts in disaster-relief work after the war. First bakeries, and then restaurants, especially the specialized donut shops, made them readily available both for sit-down and take-home trade. The sale of donuts nationwide grew from a $20-million business in 1920 to a $300-million business in 1961.[2]

The stereotypic consumer of restaurant donuts is the commuter who either sips coffee over donuts (while smoking a cigarette) perched on a stool at a counter or grabs a sack to take home or to factory floor or office. Police officers almost everywhere across the United States frequent donut shops on extended coffee breaks, creating still other stereotypes, not the least of which are the boxes of donuts consumed on stakeouts.[3] Not generally appreciated is the extent to which donut consumption in America is associated with children. In 1962, 59 percent of all households had children under 18 years of age. According to industry statistics, 91 percent of those families bought donuts on a regular basis, as compared to only 74 percent of those families without children. "Children are unquestionably the motivating force behind the purchase of donuts," concluded one industry report.[4]

Donut retailing lends itself to franchising. The equipment is highly specialized but not too expensive, therefore appropriate to sell as part of a franchise package. The typical restaurant is small, requiring relatively little startup capital compared to other restaurant ventures. Needed as much as anything is a clear business image—an identity that links the individual shop into a marketing system—which franchising provides. One of the earliest chains was Spudnut, with its unusual product made of dehydrated potatoes. Yeast-raised "spudnuts" are soft and fluffy, unlike the usual grease-soaked, heavy donuts often found in restaurants. The chain was launched in Salt Lake City by Albert Pelton, a vacuum-cleaner salesman, and his brother Robert. In 1960, there were some 400 franchisees in the United States and Canada, the cost of a new franchise pegged at only $4,175. The company trained each new dealer in his own shop, and supplied operating manuals and point-of-purchase advertising. Dealers were required to purchase the special donut mix.[5] Introduced in the 1980s was a self-standing prototype building for highway locations, developed in hopes of combating the chain's decline to only 40 stores.[6]

WINCHELL'S

The Winchell's Donut House chain was founded in Los Angeles in 1948 by Verne H. Winchell (see fig. 9.1). The company was merged with Denny's 20 years later, the two chains, however, remaining separate. Winchell's merger with Denny's, the nation's leading coffee-shop chain, promised greater penetration of the breakfast food market, and cost savings accrued through integration of purchasing and commissary functions. Winchell had preferred to expand his donut chain through company-owned stores, and the last of the franchisees were bought out in 1971. From Los Angeles Winchell's expanded northward into the San Francisco, Portland, and Seattle areas and eastward into metropolitan Phoenix and Denver.[7] Then came the Texas cities and selected cities of the Middle West. There were 870 Winchell's locations in 1982 compared to 900 Denny's locations.[8] Standard Winchell stores were 20-seat counter-and-stool restaurants. However, some 80 percent of the business was takeout, restaurants actually functioning more like bakery shops. Eighty percent of sales occurred before noon.[9]

With the trend toward lighter, healthier foods in the 1980s, donut sales across most of the United States began to falter, and Winchell's was sold to TW Services, which passed it along to a Canadian investment group.[10] Fran-

FIG. 9.1 Advertisement for Winchell's Donuts. (*Source: Franchise Journal* 1 [November / December 1968]: 38.)

FIG. 9.2 Mister Donut, Peoria, Ill., 1989. A "prebuilt" store delivered to the site in pieces and erected.

chising was reintroduced. Donut sales did not falter in Canada, nor in the colder regions of the United States like New England. Perhaps there was something about hot coffee and warm donuts on cold winter mornings not fully appreciated in places like Southern California? Rapidly growing Canadian chains, like the Tim Horton's system, complemented donuts with sandwiches and other light fare to capture much of Canada's fast-food trade. In 1994, Canada had roughly five times the number of donut shops per capita (one shop for every 68,000 people) than the United States.[11] In 1990, Tim Horton's was bought by Wendy's, giving the American hamburger chain a Canadian presence. Immediately, Wendy's began in the United States to co-brand its own brand with that of Tim Horton's, a move pointed at McDonald's dominance of the American fast-food breakfast market. As for Winchell's, many of its California stores were sold to Cambodian immigrants, the Cambodians establishing a special economic niche for themselves through donut shops, not unlike other Asians, especially Indians, in the nation's motel industry. In 1995, 80 percent of California's approximately 2,000 donut shops were Cambodian-owned. "Where we had one Winchell's shop, they now have three or four Cambodian shops," observed an ex-Winchell's executive.[12]

DUNKIN' DONUTS

William Rosenberg opened a donut shop in Quincy, Massachusetts, in 1950. Immediately after World War II, he and his brother Leon had started selling coffee and sandwiches to factory workers off the back of a truck. In three years they built up a fleet of 140 trucks and were operating 25 in-plant

Locations by County
- · 1
- ∗ 2-4
- △ 5-9
- ▫ 10-19
- ● 20-39
- ▲ 40-79
- ■ 80-159
- ⬤ 160 or more

n=3,009

FIG. 9.3 Dunkin' Donuts, 1995. Leading counties were: Cook (Chicago), Ill. (176 locations); Middlesex, Mass. (130); Essex, Mass. (75); Norfolk, Mass. (68); and New Haven, Conn. (64).

cafeterias as well, donuts comprising a large proportion of their total sales. At their restaurant William developed the distinctive Dunkin' Donuts logo, initially for takeout packaging. Then he began to license friends to open additional shops using the logo.[13] Like another local entrepreneur, Howard Johnson, Rosenberg launched into restaurant franchising. In 1968, there were 334 stores, and in 1971 nearly 700.[14] In the late 1970s, four out of five Dunkin' Donut restaurants also served sandwiches, including hamburgers. The firm, having sold its cafeteria and vending operations, experimented briefly with Chas. Goodlight and Sons Ltd., a fish and chips chain. In 1986 there were some 6,900 donut shops in the United States, with Dunkin' Donuts accounting for some 20 percent.[15] Dunkin' Donuts bought the Mister Donut chain in 1990, the nation's second largest donut chain (see Table 9.1). Mister Donut originated at Revere, Massachusetts, in 1955.[16] The firm pioneered the use of prefabricated metal buildings, many of which were located on corner city lots vacated by gas stations (see fig. 9.2). In 1991, Allied-Lyons PLC, owners of Baskin-Robbins, bought Dunkin' Donuts. In 1995, there were over 3,000 Dunkin' Donut locations, the largest concentration still in the Northeast, a reflection of the chain's roots (see fig. 9.3).

Pancakes and Waffles

While they are called "griddle cakes" (across the Northeast and Middle West), "hot cakes" (across the South and West), and "flapjacks" (nearly everywhere in the United States), other designations for pancakes include "wheat cakes" (upstate New York), "batter cakes" (in the Deep South), "flannel cakes" (in Appalachia), and "fritters" (in Kentucky).[17] The word "pancake," however, is the commercial referent by which Americans seek thin, pan- or grill-fried batter cakes as restaurant food. Readily prepared on the same grill with fried eggs and bacon, and, more important, with hamburger patties, pancakes became a breakfast mainstay at lunch counters, main-street cafés, and, of course, the latter-day roadside-oriented eateries with sit-down service, especially at coffee shops or family restaurants. Not surprisingly, some restauranteurs in the 1950s began to emphasize pancakes, creating the pancake house as a new restaurant alternative. Les Hight opened in 1953 the first Original Pancake House in Portland, Oregon. John Dahl, former Portland dinnerhouse operator, launched the Uncle John's Pancake House chain in Santa Barbara, California, in 1956. Both Hight and Dahl experimented with lighter pancake batters as well as with new fruit, nut, and other flavorings. As Dahl put it, pancakes had a profound shortcoming. They were "heavy" and "too often left the eater with that 'full up' feeling."[18] The secret was to lessen the starch concentration, converting most of the batter's starches to sugar, thus making the finished pancake partially "predigested." Also, the gluten of the flour could be manipulated toward making pancakes less fibrous. Special toppings, including whipped butter and flavored syrups, were also introduced.

Two chains were started by the Quaker Oats Company of Chicago. Aunt Jemima's Kitchen first opened at Disneyland in 1955 and quickly evolved into a highway-oriented chain. A cooperative partnership with Chicago's Pure Oil Company and San Diego's TraveLodge spawned a number of gas station, motel, and restaurant complexes at new interstate highway interchanges across the Midwest.[19] Featuring the Aunt Jemima logo, long used to identify Quaker Oats pancake mixes, restaurants were configured in "Early American" decor with something of the plantation South implied. More upscale, using Parisian French motifs, were the company's Magic Pan Creperies. From two restaurants bought in 1969, the chain expanded in two years into a 55-unit system. Magic Pans were located in upscale specialty shopping areas in downtown and suburban mall locations.

PERKINS

Two brothers, Matt and Ivan Perkins, opened their first Perkins Pancake House in Cincinnati in 1958, featuring recipes obtained from a Seattle restauranteur. After some experimenting, menus were expanded with a selection of inexpensive steaks. In 1969, franchising rights passed to Wyman Nelson, originally the chain's Minnesota franchisee. It was Nelson who actually unified what was a loose collection of territorial licenses into a nationally promoted restaurant brand. Emphasized was a new prototype building for highway locations (see fig. 9.4). Ownership passed in 1979 to the Holiday Corporation, the motel company viewing the Perkins format as appropriate to certain kinds of Holiday Inn locations as well as capable of standing alone as a coffee-shop chain.

In 1985, Perkins was bought by Chicago's Tennessee Restaurant Company,

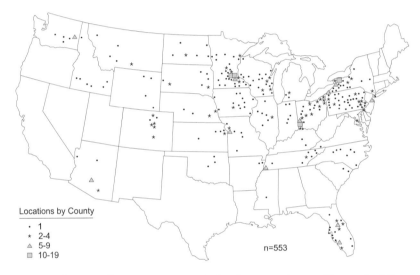

FAST FOOD

FIG. 9.4 Prototype building for Perkins Pancake and Steak House, ca. 1970.

FIG. 9.5 Perkins Family Restaurants, 1996. Leading counties are: Hennepin, Minn. (15 locations); Hamilton, Ohio (13); Monroe, N.Y. (10); and Ramsey, Minn. (10).

originally a limited partnership comprised of Holiday Inns, Investment Limited Partnership (the Bass Brothers' financial group), and restauranteur Donald N. Smith.[20] Menus were expanded once again and the chain renamed the Perkins Family Restaurants. The route from pancake house to family restaurant was a familiar one, having been taken earlier by Sambo's. Although Sambo's did not survive as a chain, Perkins did. In 1996, there were 553 restaurants in the chain with the largest concentrations around Minneapolis–St. Paul, Cincinnati, and Rochester, areas where strong franchisees had established themselves early (see fig. 9.5).

IHOP

Like the Rosenberg brothers and their donuts, Al Lapin Jr., founder of the International House of Pancakes chain, started with a mobile snackbar operation. His first pancake house was opened in 1958 in North Hollywood, a Los Angeles suburb. In six years there were 74 IHOPs operating. It was the "international" menu that was presumed to make the chain distinctive— the Tahitian orange-pineapple pancakes, the Brazilian banana pancakes, and the Danish Aebleskivers pancakes, for example. For an initial investment as small as $15,000, franchisees could insert themselves into a selling system, a system forcefully symbolized by one of the most readily identifiable building prototypes ever devised for America's roadsides, a large A-frame structure painted turquoise (see fig. 9.6).

Lapin also franchised a number of other restaurant ideas: Woody's SmorgasBurgers, the Dog House hot-dog stands, the Copper Penny coffee shops, the Orange Julius orange juice kiosks (later sold to Dairy Queen), the Wil Wright's Ice Cream Shoppes, and the Original House of Pies. Lapin was really in the franchising business for, in addition, he promoted the House of Nine, a women's apparel chain, United Rent-All, Sawyer Business College, and United Colleges, the latter for training medical and dental assistants. Spread so far afield, the parent, International Industries, faltered. In 1979, the German firm Wienerwald, owner of some 750 restaurants in Europe

FIG. 9.6 Advertisement for the International House of Pancakes. (*Source: Franchise Journal* 1 [May/June 1968]: 27.)

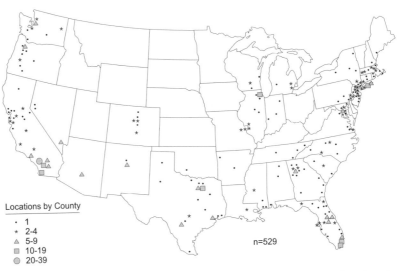

Locations by County

- ·   1
- ★   2-4
- △   5-9
- ▢   10-19
- ◉   20-39

n=529

FIG. 9.7 International House of Pancakes, 1992. Leading counties are: Los Angeles, Calif. (37 locations), Orange, Calif. (17), Broward (Fort Lauderdale), Fla. (16), and Cook (Chicago), Ill. (15).

FIG. 9.8 Waffle House, Kissimmee, Fla., 1996.

as well as the 275-unit Lum's chain in the United States, bought IHOP, only it-self to move into receivership several years later. But the IHOP chain persist-ed, operating in 1992 at 529 locations (see fig. 9.7). The company has proven most successful in Southern California, its place of origin, and in the greater New York City area and in Florida.

WAFFLE HOUSE

Batter-poured but grilled in molds, waffles are closely related to pancakes as a breakfast food. One major chain, Waffle House, successfully promoted

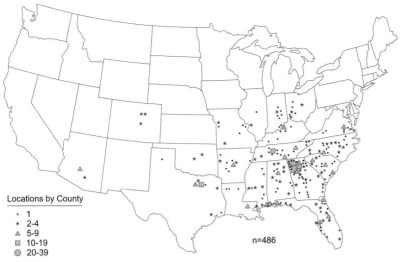

Locations by County

- · 1
- ⋆ 2-4
- △ 5-9
- ▥ 10-19
- ◉ 20-39

n=486

*Includes Waffle and Steak Restaurants in Indiana

FIG. 9.9 Waffle House, 1984. Leading counties were: Fulton (Atlanta), Ga. (26 locations), Dekalb, Ga. (19), Cobb, Ga. (16), and Davidson (Nashville), Tenn., and Dallas, Tex. (each with 11).

TABLE 9.1 Leading Breakfast-Oriented Chains, 1996

Chain	Headquarters	Units Worldwide	Sales (in millions)	Sales Rank Top 300
Dunkin' Donuts	Randolph, Mass.	4,446	$1,848	16
IHOP	Glendale, Calif.	429	796	36
Cracker Barrel	Lebanon, Tenn.	257	734	39
Perkins	Memphis	465	667	44
Bob Evans	Columbus, Ohio	394	594	50
Waffle House	Norcross, Ga.	1,100	585	51
Cinnabon	Seattle	368	127	153
Huddle House	Decatur, Ga.	305	118	156
Winchell's Donuts	Santa Ana, Calif.	300	70	224

Source: Restaurants and Institutions 107 (July 15, 1997): 66.

itself around this breakfast specialty (see fig. 9.8). With 13 outlets in 1964, the company, headquartered in suburban Atlanta, grew to 486 outlets in 1984 (see fig. 9.9).[21] Founded by former employees of Huddle House, a southern White Castle "clone," the company has developed a series of diner-like building prototypes for use primarily at interstate highway interchange locations. Waffle House became the largest of breakfast food chains (see Table 9.1 above). In recent years, the chain has sought, following from the earlier Perkins example perhaps, to introduce inexpensive steaks as a waffle complement.

Other Breakfast Foods

Few of the breakfast-food chains were content to serve only traditional breakfast foods. Most right from the beginning experimented with complementary foods, searching for successful novelties, especially from the nation's regional cuisines. Perhaps the American South (including much of the southern Midwest) has contributed the most; biscuits and gravy, grits, and "country" ham, for example, have always been available at mom-and-pop eateries along Southern roadsides. From the nation's cities with large Jewish populations came the bagel, always available in delicatessens. And from the Pacific Northwest came a penchant for gourmet coffees.

BOB EVANS

Bob Evans Farms combines the manufacture of sausage, and its distribution through supermarkets, with the running of company-owned restaurants. Evans started in the restaurant business in 1944 in his native Gallipolis, Ohio, an Ohio River town. To attract customers he began making his own sausage. Off to war, it was to sausage-making that he returned, purchasing a farm at nearby Rio Grande, Ohio, where he raised cattle and built a meatpacking plant. There he also opened a restaurant. Chain development, seen as a means of enhancing sausage sales, began in 1968 at Chillicothe, Ohio. A distinctive "steamboat gothic" building was designed, a modified version of which is still in use today (see fig. 9.10).

Evans saw himself catering to travelers, working people on their way to and from work, business people at lunchtime, and family groups, especially in the evening and during weekends.[22] Promoted was a "just-plain-folks," "homespun," "down on the farm" appeal not so much for rural or small-

FIG. 9.10 Prototype building for the Bob Evans Farms chain, 1981. (*Source:* Courtesy of Bob Evans Farms, Columbus, Ohio.)

town people as for city people removed from their country roots.[23] The chain, like Friendly's, expanded incrementally outward from its initial commissary—for Bob Evans a commissary located in Columbus (see figs. 9.11 and 9.12). With purchase of the Owens Country Sausage Company of Richardson, Texas, the firm opened stores in Texas, using the same prototype building, but the Owens name.

FIG. 9.11 Bob Evans Farms Restaurants, 1981. Leading counties were: Franklin (Columbus), Ohio (6 locations); Cuyahoga (Cleveland), Ohio; and Hamilton (Cincinnati), Ohio (5 each).

FIG. 9.12 Bob Evans Farms Restaurants, 1995. Leading counties were: Franklin (Columbus), Ohio (19 locations); Hamilton (Cincinnati), Ohio, and Marion (Indianapolis), Ind. (9 each); and Cuyahoga (Cleveland), Ohio, and Montgomery (Dayton), Ohio (8 each).

CRACKER BARREL

The Cracker Barrel Old Country Stores of Lebanon, Tennessee, have pursued a market niche similar to that of Bob Evans, although Cracker Barrel is even more dependent on long-distance travelers. The majority of the chain's restaurants are located at or near interstate highway interchanges. It is not the farm motif that dominates so much as the ambiance of the traditional country general store. Besides sit-down dining, each outlet contains a large gift shop specializing in reproductions of "early American" glassware, wrought iron, and woodcrafts as well as candies, bakery goods, and other foods. Here is the Stuckey's idea reborn, but given a strong "country" spin. The first Cracker Barrel store opened in 1969 and by 1995 the chain had 146 outlets, all company-owned (see fig. 9.13). Stuckey's, by comparison, operated at 127 locations.[24] Featured at Cracker Barrel was "Southern-style" cooking—for example, biscuits and gravy, grits, and country ham for breakfast, complemented by pork chops, fried chicken, and fried catfish at other meals.

BAGELS AND COFFEE

In the recent decade, health-conscious Americans have turned to bagels (from the German *beugel*) as a breakfast and snack food. With their low-fat appeal and fresh-baked availability, bagels have encouraged chain development, some of it through indoor walk-up and/or drive-through restaurant formats, both, of course, automobile-convenient (see Table 9.2). Among the more aggressive franchisors is Bruegger's, founded in Burlington, Vermont, with 152 outlets in 1994 and 435 in 1996.[25] The company's growth strategy required franchisees to develop a minimum of 10 stores. The idea was

FIG. 9.13 Cracker Barrel Country Stores, 1995. Leading counties are: Davidson (Nashville), Tenn. (6 locations), and Knox (Knoxville), Tenn. and Marion (Indianapolis), Ind. (4 each).

TABLE 9.2 Leading Bagel and Coffee Chains, 1996

Chain	Headquarters	Units Worldwide	Sales (in millions)	Sales Rank Top 300
Starbucks Coffee	Seattle	990	$501	56
Bruegger's Bagels	South Bend, Ind.	425	220	103
Manhattan Bagels	Eatontown, N.J.	293	86	189
Chesapeake Bagels	McLean, Va.	164	80	205
Noah's New York Bagels	Alameda, Calif.	90	45	290
Barnies Coffee	Orlando	112	45	295

Source: Restaurants and Institutions 107 (July 15, 1997): 66.

to quickly access the 60 top metropolitan markets. In lieu of the usual franchise fee, operators purchased $35,000 in stock options per store. Charged annually were sales and advertising fees. Attracted were several large management companies. When sold in 1996 to Quality Dining of Mishawaka, Indiana (operators of 62 Burger Kings, 42 Grady's American Grills, and 18 Chili's, as well 18 Bruegger's), the chain had 40 owned and 235 franchised outlets spread across 26 states.[26] Bruegger's menu included 10 varieties of bagel and 14 toppings, the latter including the expected cream cheese, olive pimento, and jalapeno spreads as well as specialty concoctions such as Vermont maple honey.

The enthusiasm for bagel shops was part of the larger enthusiasm for restaurant "bakeries," eateries that under the bakery label offered freshly baked breads, sandwich condiments, salads, and soups. By the mid-1990s, several regional chains were prospering, including the St. Louis Bread Company (with 59 outlets in 1995 in Missouri and Illinois), the Zaro Bread Basket, and the Hot and Crust stores both of New York City, and Big Sky Bread in the Cincinnati area.[27] From the 1950s through the 1980s, the nation's mom-and-pop neighborhood bakeries were made obsolete, victims first of wholesale bakeries and then of supermarket bake shops. The new bakery/restaurants were intended to fill the vacuum left, to provide places where freshly baked bakery products could be obtained and where, in addition, sit-down comfort could be had. Highly specialized bakery venues also appeared as franchise ideas, some as early as the 1970s. Most, however, quickly disappeared, for example, the B. J. Bull chain of Los Gatos, California, with its Cornish pasties, and the House of Kolaches chain of New Orleans with its sweet rolls (of Slavic origin) filled with fruits, cheeses, or meats. Few bakery venues, by whatever focus, have ever impacted substantially roadside eating save in shopping centers.

The same might be said for the new coffee cafés or coffee bars which, following the lead of such companies as Seattle's Starbucks (970 outlets in mid-1996 up from 116 in 1991), came mainly to traditional business locations and shopping centers as well as to chain bookstore and department store "in-house" cafés.[28] Nonetheless, several chains targeted the roadside, some with double drive-through buildings. In 1996, Chock Full O' Nuts, an old

FIG. 9.14 The Morning Call, New Orleans, ca. 1940.

confectionery store chain, operated the 12-unit Quikava chain.[29] Although specialty coffees remain the stock-in-trade of the new coffee cafés, available also are selections of bagels and other pastries. The "bottomless cup" syndrome, introduced a century ago in lunchrooms and continued in both quick-service and upscale restaurants since, and the rise of but a few coffee manufacturers with highly standardized products, directed Americans away from the great diversity of coffee tastes available worldwide. Only in a few locales did Americans enjoy special coffees outside the standardized mainstream. New Orleans was one such place with institutions like the Morning Call in the Vieux Carré. Here coffee and the distinctive donut-like "beignets" attracted tourists, but also locals, many of whom, as the postcard view shows, arrived by automobile in the decades before World War II, making the French Market a kind of morning drive-in (see fig. 9.14).

Restauranteurs worked to complement breakfast menus, making donut shops but, more especially, pancake houses, waffle houses, and coffee shops more competitive at other times of the day. They also worked to extend demand for breakfast food to other meals. Success prompted the operators of other kinds of restaurants to embrace breakfast menus themselves. Chains like White Castle always relied on a breakfast trade built around bacon and eggs, with diner clones like Toddle House and Krystal more fully emphasizing the same. But when latter-day McDonald's made entree into the breakfast market, eating out for breakfast came fully of age—no longer the focus of the specialist, but now the entree of the generalist as well. McDonald's Egg McMuffin was joined by the likes of Hardee's Frisco Breakfast Sandwich (on sourdough bread) and, of course, Wendy's embrace of donuts through Tim Horton's. In the 1990s, chicken chains like Grandy's, Bojangles, Chick-fil-A, and Church's also launched breakfast menus, as did sandwich chains like Subway and Blimpie. Taco Bell introduced its breakfast quesadilla and, not to be outdone, McDonald's introduced its breakfast burrito. In addition, foods once associated only with breakfast came to typify other meals. Some 55 percent of all bacon consumed in the United States is consumed through fast-food restaurants, with most of it used as garnish on hamburgers.[30]

Like ice cream restaurants, breakfast places have evolved along one of two tracks—retention of a narrow breakfast focus in a quick-service restaurant (the route followed by most donut shops) and, conversely, broader menus in a more upscale sit-down format (the route followed by pancake houses repositioning themselves as family restaurants). What the breakfast sandwich pretends across a wide variety of restaurant venues is simply the "quick-service" breakfast firmly tied to automobility, for example, a breakfast handed out of a drive-through window to a harried commuter headed to work.

In traditional donut shops, pancake houses, and family restaurants, and in the new bagel bakeries and coffee cafés as well, customers are invited to sit and linger over morning newspapers or engage in idle conversation. Such breakfast places epitomize the "third great place," the alternative place to home and work where people eat, but, more important, where they go to see and be seen. Whether arriving by automobile or not, customers in such places eat but also engage, if only vicariously, in socializing—what is for any locality an important building block to community. That may be the special value of breakfast places, and the explanation as to why they survive in the face of so many aggressively promoted restaurant options built around speed and convenience, especially of the automobile kind.

CHAPTER 10

Chicken Places

hicken has long been a core staple in the American diet. Indeed, nothing may seem more quintessentially American than a Sunday dinner of fried chicken, mashed potatoes, and apple pie. "A chicken in every pot," one remembers, became a political rallying cry during the depths of the Great Depression. Never the prestigious meat that steak represented, chicken was, for special meals like Sunday dinner, the "fallback" for less-affluent families. And for many Americans it remained an entree of choice even after family fortunes rose. Chicken is also popular in ethnic and gourmet cuisines as a meat amenable to almost any flavoring and almost any cooking technique. In recent years, health-conscious Americans have turned increasingly to chicken, as well as to seafood, seeking to avoid the higher-fat implications of red meat. Between 1960 and 1976, beef consumption per person increased from 64.3 pounds to 95.4 pounds, and for chicken from 27.8 to 43.3 pounds.[1] But between 1965 and 1991, among wealthier white Americans, red-meat consumption dropped an estimated 89 percent while poultry increased an estimated 25 percent.[2] Americans ate some 70.5 pounds of chicken per person in 1995.[3]

Chicken may be all things to all cooks, but throughout much of the United States it has been fried chicken that has truly counted. Especially in the American South is fried chicken a staple, 46 percent of Southerners, by one estimate, consuming fried chicken on a regular basis, compared to about 30 percent for other regions.[4] Those in the Northeast, on the other hand, have preferred baked or roast chicken, eating little fried chicken at least at home. Nonetheless, it was frying that guaranteed chicken's popularity as a restaurant food. Roasting and baking were too time-consuming, and servings could not be prepared to order. Frying in pans or deep frying in vats or pressure cookers was faster.

Mom and Pop

Independent mom-and-pop restaurants led the way, some to grow into very large operations, and some into chains. Most chicken places, however, remained small, built around a wide variety of restaurant formats from counter and booth arrangements to dining rooms. Also, small takeout stores evolved in many urban neighborhoods. The Chicken Box in suburban Chicago did an early takeout business, the building oriented to sidewalk and street, but most of its customers parking in an adjacent parking lot (see fig. 10.1). Chicken lent itself to takeout sales, retaining, when carefully wrapped, its heat and its flavor. But it was the upscale, sit-down dinner restaurant that truly thrived early.

The automobile was central to the success of most chicken dinner places. The Golden Drumstick in Long Beach, California, accommodated large crowds, customers arriving by car to park in large adjacent lots. The building sat close to the highway. Its front entrance pretended sidewalk orientation, but was actually a porte-cochere where drivers could drop off passengers (see fig. 10.2). Inside, both counter service and table service was available, the latter filling several large rooms and capable of accommodating hundreds of customers, especially on Sunday (see fig. 10.3). Chicken restaurants, like cafeterias, were especially popular with retired people living on limited incomes who, after Sunday church, came not only seeking food but an "outing." Chicken kept prices down, chicken being cheaper than beef. Nonetheless, a dinner-house ambiance suggested, despite the low cost of the food, a dining experience beyond the ordinary. The Golden Drumstick also promoted a carryout trade at a counter just inside the front entrance (see fig. 10.4).

FIG. 10.1 The Chicken Box, Irving Park, Ill., ca. 1958.

FIG. 10.2 The Golden Drumstick, Long Beach, Calif., 1952.

FIG. 10.3 The Golden
Drumstick, Long
Beach, Calif., 1952.

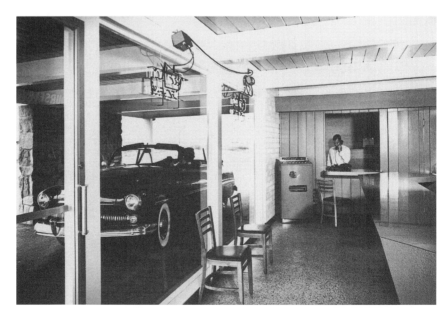

FIG. 10.4 The Golden Drumstick, Long Beach, Calif., 1952.

Chicken places easily developed into destination restaurants, catering most particularly to weekend motorists combining eating out with recreational driving. Examples included Zehnder's in Frankenmuth, Michigan, and Knott's Berry Farm and Ghost Town in Buena Park, California. In 1928 the Zehnder family traded their farm for an old hotel building, opening a restaurant specializing in chicken dinners. Customers came from nearby Flint and, as roads improved, from as far away as Detroit and Toledo (see fig. 10.5). By 1980 the restaurant (not including the separate Bavarian-style eatery built across the highway) had grown to the nation's sixth largest independent restaurant. Fried chicken with "mother's dressing," chicken noodle soup, cabbage salad, mashed potatoes, vegetables, and ice cream sold as a package. In 1980, the restaurant served some 19,000 customers per week, using over 11 tons of chicken.[5]

FIG. 10.5 Zehnder's, Frankenmuth, Mich., ca. 1948.

FIG. 10.6 Walter and Cordelia Knott in front of their Original Berry Stand, Buena Park, Calif., ca. 1955.

FAST
FOOD

FIG. 10.7 Chicken Dinner Restaurant, Knott's Berry Farm and Ghost Town, Buena Park, Calif., ca. 1955.

FIG. 10.8 Menu, Chicken Dinner Restaurant, Knott's Berry Farm and Ghost Town, 1963.

Walter and Cordelia Knott moved to Southern California, rented a farm, and in 1921 opened a wayside stand from which to sell homegrown berries (see fig. 10.6). Buying the property, they expanded into selling jams and berry pies, and in 1934 launched a chicken-dinner restaurant. The restaurant was enlarged to seat some 880 customers in 1946, and accommodated 1,750 customers in 1962 when the Knott family served some 1,808,000 meals (see figs. 10.7 and 10.8).[6] Behind the restaurant, the Knotts developed a theme park, the "ghost town," with its "Wild West" main street, rides, and other attractions, a precursor to nearby Disneyland. Here was a destination for motorists, and it remains one of California's leading tourist attractions.

Early Chains

Restaurant chains specializing in chicken evolved as early as the 1920s. For example, the roadside-oriented Coon-Chicken chain launched in Salt Lake City, and spread to Spokane, Seattle, and Portland.[7] Buildings all carried a large cartoon-like face of an African-American male, which Americans today would find most distasteful, but which did characterize the nation's insensitivity to blacks at that time. The idea, presumably, was to suggest authenticity of the Southern kind, what later generations might term "soul food." What came across, of course, was a belittling of blacks as caricature. Another chain more tasteful in its packaging was Leslie Fried Chicken's "Chicken Shacks" which featured "California-style" chicken in a variety of Texas cities (see fig. 10.9). The personal message on the back of the postcard reads: "Chicken. No knives or forks. This is where we ate Feb. 25, 1947—Our 25th Wedding Anniversary. Love Gladys." The chain's logo was a chicken carrying an umbrella.

More widely adopted was the Chicken in the Rough, its logo a chicken carrying a golf club (see fig. 10.10). Chicken in the Rough was not a restaurant chain so much as a brand name that identified those independent restaurants that served a distinctive kind of chicken, a product prepared on a unique grill that fried and steamed simultaneously. In 1936, Beverley Osborne, a former "soda jerk" and confectionery store operator, took over a six-stool lunch counter serving pancakes and waffles. Osborne introduced chicken. The name "Chicken in the Rough" was coined on a family picnic where silverware had been forgotten. Born was the idea of serving fried chicken, shoestring potatoes, and hot biscuits in a basket to be eaten in the "rough," that is, with the hands. There followed in 1949 development of the special grill, and then franchising. Among those buying licenses was Glenn Amundson, developer of the modernistic Carpenter's and Henry's Drive-Ins in the Los Angeles area (see fig. 2.17). Beverley reserved the Oklahoma City market for himself, operating eventually some eight Beverley's Drive-Ins. When sold in the 1960s to an investor group headed by a former McDonald's executive, there were 68 franchisees still operating out of the nearly 300 once spread across 38 states.[8]

The Chicken Delight idea, created in 1952 by A. L. Tunick, a scrap dealer in

FIG. 10.9 Advertising postcard for Leslie's Chicken Shack.

FIG. 10.10 Advertising postcard for Chicken in the Rough.

Rock Island, Illinois, proved even more successful. In 1964, there were some 550 franchised outlets operating in 48 states.[9] The chicken, fries, cranberry sauce, and muffins were boxed, largely for the takeout market. Franchisees obtained the right to use the chain's logo and its specially designed fryer, but assumed an obligation to purchase all paper products and takeout packaging from the company as well.[10] The chain's unique chicken fryer used "conduction cooking" to seal in the meat's juices. Tunick started his restaurant business when his wrecking company, dismantling a factory building, came into the possession of a large inventory of abandoned cookers. The best way to sell them proved to be the restaurant chain idea.[11] Tunick sold out to Consolidated Foods in 1965. Six years later Chicken Delight franchisees successfully sued to void the chain's obligatory purchase requirements, the Supreme Court ruling that such obligations constituted an illegal tying arrangement. By 1984, Chicken Delight was Canadian-owned with 86 outlets in the United States and 34 in Canada.[12]

Kentucky Fried Chicken

Harland Sanders, like Ray Kroc, has become the subject of almost mythic adoration. Sanders's story reads as an American success story, the self-made man striving ultimately to succeed. Sanders left home as a teenager, quitting school in the seventh grade to work as a farmhand, streetcar conductor, and railroad locomotive fireman. He studied law by correspondence and served as a justice of the peace in Little Rock, sold insurance, operated a ferry at Louisville, was director of a small-town chamber of commerce, manufactured and sold portable acetylene lighting systems, sold tires, and managed several gas stations.[13] At Corbin, Kentucky, he opened his own service station, adding a small lunch counter and cabin court, the complex completely rebuilt in 1939 following a fire (see fig. 10.11).

As a restauranteur, Sanders promoted "Kentucky Fried Chicken" to set it apart from that of competitors. With its special flavoring, the product won the acclaim of even Duncan Hines. Sanders was rewarded with the title of "Kentucky Colonel" for presumably adding to the state's visibility through his distinctive chicken recipe. He remained frustrated, however, both by the time required to fry chicken and by the often dry, unevenly cooked meat that resulted. It was then that he hit on using pressure cookers, the chicken deep fried in his special mixture of herbs and spices. Sanders's experimentation took him to a food-service seminar in Chicago where he met Pete Harmon, a hamburger restaurant operator from Salt Lake City. Harmon's business boomed when he introduced Sanders's recipe and new frying process and thus Harmon urged him to take up franchising. Sanders was aware of the successes scored by Chicken in the Rough, so Harmon became Sanders's first franchisee.[14]

In 1955, plans were announced for a new interstate highway to bypass Corbin, and a year later Sanders liquidated his roadside holdings, turning at age 66 to selling franchises full-time. The Colonel traveled by car (where he sometimes slept) to interest restaurant operators in his cooking system. As often as not he would prepare a meal in the kitchen of a prospective franchisee's restaurant as a sales demonstration. By 1960 Sanders had some 200

FIG. 10.11 Sanders Courts, Corbin, Ky., ca. 1940.

FIG. 10.12 Kentucky Fried Chicken Store, Colorado Springs, Colo., 1971.

FAST FOOD

restaurants under license, and some 600 by 1963.[15] His company, having outgrown his briefcase, was headquartered in a small office building behind his house near Shelbyville, Kentucky. The firm employed 17 people. There was no franchise fee charged. Rather, franchisees paid four to five cents per chicken cooked, and agreed to buy the Colonel's special seasoning. Sanders also began to push a second franchising idea, one for new freestanding take-out stores highway-oriented (see fig. 10.12). Granted were territorial franchises, Sanders reserving for his daughter "take-home" rights to the state of Florida.

John Y. Brown Jr. joined Sanders as an employee, and then, with Jack Massey, a wealthy Nashville businessman, convinced Sanders to sell out. Under the agreement, Sanders retained territorial rights to Canada, agreed to serve with salary as a corporate advisor and "goodwill ambassador," and walked away with $2 million. Under Brown and Massey, the chain stopped licensing already existing restaurants. In another change, takeout-store franchisees paid royalties as a percentage of sales, an annual advertising fee, and were committed to purchasing paper goods as well as seasonings from the parent firm. The chain quickly expanded with 2,942 outlets open in 1970, but with over 6,000 franchise agreements actually sold. The easily identifiable red-and-white-striped pyramidal-roofed stores appeared literally everywhere in the United States. The Kentucky Fried Chicken Company became the nation's largest commercial food-service organization, exceeded in size only by the Army, the Navy, and the Department of Agriculture's school-lunch program.[16] By 1975, 2 million containers of chicken were being sold every day.[17] In his semiretirement, Harland Sanders became a celebrity with his white suit, goatee, and string tie, appearing frequently in television, billboard, and newspaper advertising.

In 1971, Brown and Massey sold Kentucky Fried Chicken to Heublein for a reputed $280 million of Heublein stock. With some 90 percent of the restaurant chicken market, Heublein, a distiller and maker of a wide variety of food products, saw the chain as a logical adjunct to its business. Sales, however, began to falter as competitors moved into the chicken restaurant market, substantially redefining it with different restaurant formats. Complacency emerged. The chain was no longer growing rapidly and opportunities for advancement in management were declining. As experienced store managers left, stores became run down, and the food declined in quality.[18] Even Harland Sanders criticized. As customers left and sales fell, a downward spiral set in.

For Heublein, managing a service-oriented venue was quite different from manufacturing and distributing packaged food, the lesson that Hershey, Pillsbury, and other large manufacturers were discovering with their own restaurant chains. Managing a brand and managing a restaurant were two different things. "If a customer goes into a liquor store to buy a bottle of Smirnoff and the clerk is rude, or the store isn't as clean as it should be, he doesn't get mad at Smirnoff. But the same customer who goes into a KFC and is met by a rude clerk, or a dirty store, gets mad at KFC," commented the company's chairman.[19]

Heublein sought to reverse the chain's fortunes by offering inducements to franchisees, encouraging them to enlarge stores with booths and tables, converting them thus to indoor walk-ups. Introduced were a variety of new building prototypes: the "Southwest" (a stucco-walled building in "desert" colors), the "Country Station" (with a front porch of railroad station implication), the "Spectrum" (streamlined and high-tech in look with lots of glass and neon), and the "Lexington" (veneered with brick with a mansard roof).[20] More important, the chain introduced new chicken products, for example, Kentucky Nuggets, deboned chicken pieces lightly breaded and fried.

Heublein itself was purchased by R. J. Reynolds in 1982, which passed Kentucky Fried Chicken on to PepsiCo in 1986. PepsiCo launched another round of store remodelings, and again broadened store menus around complementary cooking methods: oven roasting, oven baking, and open frying in addition to deep frying. Menus reflected growing consumer demand for low-fat food. Indeed, the name of the chain was changed to KFC, the increasingly offensive word "fried" dropped from store signage. PepsiCo, staunch competitor with Coca-Cola for the worldwide soft-drink market, entered fast-food franchising with Pizza Hut and Taco Bell in the 1970s. The company also diversified by acquiring Frito-Lay, maker of snack foods and other food products, North American Van Lines, and Wilson Sporting Goods.

In 1994, the KFC chain comprised 5,149 outlets in the United States (2,039 company-owned), and 9,407 worldwide. Domestic sales stood at $3.5 billion, representing some 1.1 billion meals or some 274 million chickens consumed. Thus the chain sold the equivalent of 11 pieces of chicken for every man, woman, and child in the country. The number of employees stood at 102,980.[21] PepsiCo saw its fast-food chains as important outlets for its soft drinks, Pizza Hut, Taco Bell, and KFC outlets carrying nothing but PepsiCo beverages. The connection, however, was not without its negative repercussions. Most of the larger fast-food chains refused to handle PepsiCo's products, considering the company not a supplier but a competitor. Thus in 1997 PepsiCo moved to divest itself of its restaurant subsidiaries, creating a separate corporate entity, Tricon Global Restaurants, as a mechanism for divestiture.

With Kentucky Fried Chicken's phenomenal success, imitators were drawn to the market. Some sought only to replicate the Sanders approach through takeout stores. Chains enjoying some success included All-Pro Chicken (Pittsburgh), Chicken Hut (Fayetteville, Arkansas), Maryland Fried Chicken (Macon, Georgia), Ozark Fried Chicken with "Miss Alma's recipe" (Dallas), and Pioneer Chicken Kitchen (Los Angeles). Among the more original names were Cock-a-Doodle of America, Pail-O-Chicken, and Wife-Saver Chicken. Some chains adopted celebrity names. From the world of country-western music came Eddy Arnold's Chicken and, of course, Minnie Pearl's Chicken.

Kentucky Fried Chicken's market dominance was challenged most directly by chains using formats other than takeout. Ron's Krispy Fried Chicken introduced indoor-walk-up stores, and provided drive-through windows as well. By 1981, Ron's operated at 76 locations in the Houston, Dallas, Memphis, and Mobile areas. As insurance, however, the company was also the franchisee for 25 Kentucky Fried Chicken stores in Houston.[22] Chicago-based Chicken Unlimited's indoor-walk-ups included upscale "dining rooms" with booths and tables with coffee-shop ambiance, but no waitresses (see fig. 10.13). In 1971, the chain operated 121 stores mostly in the Chicago area.[23] The Giragosian brothers, Charles and Kegham, entered the restaurant business from real estate and construction, although during their college years they had vended hot dogs from the back of a truck, owning a drive-in for a short time after graduation. For Chicken Unlimited,

FIG. 10.13 Advertisement for Chicken Unlimited. (*Source: Modern Franchising* 11 [Aug./Sept. 1969]: 38.)

land and restaurant buildings were either owned or leased by the Giragosians and then rented to franchisees at 7 percent of gross sales. Another chain successful with the indoor-walk-up format was Lee's Famous Recipe Chicken, a subsidiary of Shoney's based in Nashville. By 1985 there were 274 restaurants in the Lee's chain spread across Kentucky, Indiana, and Ohio, 32 of them company-owned.[24]

Popeye's and Church's

America's Favorite Chicken is today the holding company for the nation's second and third largest chicken chains, Church's and Popeye's. Popeye's was the succeeding corporation following merger of the two chains in 1989 (see fig. 10.14). Popeye's was started in 1972 in response to Kentucky Fried Chicken's entry into the New Orleans market. Al Copeland, a franchisee in his brother's Tastee Donut chain, saw an opportunity to branch off on his own. In four years he opened 25 company stores and had begun to franchise. In 1981, over 1,000 franchises had been sold, 230 of the approximately 300 stores actually in operation owned by franchisees.[25] The chain's name came not from Popeye, the cartoon character (although the company uses that image on license from the King Features Syndicate), but from the character Popeye Doyle in the film *The French Connection*. Initial expansion was outward from New Orleans across Louisiana, Mississippi, Alabama, and Florida. The chain entered the Midwest at Chicago to spread into the Northeast, orienting primarily to the African-American market.[26] Among the largest franchisees was the Marriott Corporation with stores in Pennsylvania and New Jersey.

Church's was an even older firm. George Church Sr. quit his job selling chicken incubators in 1952 to open his first chicken restaurant in a downtown San Antonio storefront. A small chain emerged. George Jr. took over in 1963, expanding across Texas with 44 stores. Franchising at first, the company then expanded through joint-venture agreements, Church's maintaining 25 percent ownership in stores developed by "affiliates."[27] Ownership, even part ownership, enabled better quality control. In 1977, the chain operated some 740 stores in 22 states, and was considered a leader among all U.S. companies in profit growth.[28] The firm placed great emphasis on streamlining store operations and exerting tight controls on meal quality—the company's objective being to offer higher quality food at lower prices. The chain used larger chickens than most other chicken restaurants, and delivered them to its stores fresh rather than frozen. The chain invested heavily in sales contests and other manager-incentive programs.

Church's emphasized strict place-product-packaging. "The philosophy behind establishing a chain is brand identification," emphasized George Church Jr. "People recognize a brand and know what to expect. We want our customers to recognize Church's with quality food and efficient service no matter where they might be."[29] Central was development of building prototypes and use of prefabrication. Modular construction enabled stores

FIG. 10.14 Popeye's, Winter Haven, Fla., 1997.

FAST FOOD

to be constructed and placed in operation in as little as four weeks.[30] In 1989, the church's chain of some 1,300 stores was bought by Copeland's 729-unit Popeye's. Church's restricted menu, and its substantial black inner-city orientation, especially in the Midwest and Northeast, had depressed profits, as inner-city neighborhoods declined in affluence. Copeland maintained the chain's integrity as a separate brand, but nonetheless closed hundreds of under-performing restaurants and franchised most of the remaining company-owned stores. America's Favorite Chicken took control in 1992, itself bought out in 1996 by a Los Angeles investment firm.

Later Chains

Bojangles started in 1977 in Charlotte, its prototype building introduced a year later. By 1981 there were 32 restaurants, 11 company-owned.[31] Emphasized was a "Cajun-spiced" chicken with rice and biscuits. "New Orleans style" dominated restaurant decor with bright yellow and orange colors and special accents such as ceiling fans. Bought by Horn and Hardart (the old automat chain and latter-day franchisee for Burger King), the chain prospered in a limited region centered on Charlotte, operating in 1996 at 214 locations (see fig. 10.15).[32] Chicken George Chicken and Biscuits, a black-owned chain, started in 1971 in Baltimore, growing to 32 outlets in 1984.[33] The chain targeted African-Americans in inner-city Baltimore, Washington, D.C., Philadelphia, and Norfolk. Offered, as at Bojangles, was a highly spiced chicken, complemented with rice, greens, chicken gumbo soup, and buttermilk biscuits. According to chain research, African-Americans consumed 38 percent of the chicken sold nationwide, eating 50 percent more chicken than whites.[34] Bojangles adopted the black personae of a popular song. Chicken George followed from the slave name used in Alex Haley's blockbuster book, *Roots*.

Several chains developed indoor shopping mall locations, diversifying later into freestanding stores, especially double drive-throughs. Atlantan S. Truett Cathy launched Chick-fil-A in 1967. Developed was a boneless chicken fillet sandwich served on a bun rather like a hamburger. By 1980 there were 152 Chick-fil-A stores in 23 states.[35] Reflecting Cathy's deeply held Christian beliefs, the company placed great emphasis on mentoring its employees through generous pension, health insurance, training, and other benefits. Manager turnover rates remained very low—5 to 6 percent per year versus an average of 35 percent in the fast-food industry as a whole. In 1996, there were some 600 outlets in the chain, none of them open on Sundays.[36]

Grandy's originated in 1973 in Lewisville, Texas, a Dallas suburb, growing to 46 outlets by 1981.[37] Its founders, Rex E. Sanders and Walter E. Johnson, both had backgrounds in cafeteria management, and had together started an earlier fast-food chicken chain sold to the Jim Dandy organization. Sanders and Johnson envisioned a market niche for chicken between fast food and that of the upscale dinner house. The chain specialized not only in fried chicken, but in country fried steak (called chicken fried steak across the South) and, in addition, biscuits and gravy, with restaurants operating at breakfast as well as at other meals. Sold to the Saga Corporation in 1983, Grandy's became part of a stable of brands including Stuart Anderson's Black Angus Cattle Company steakhouses, Spoons gourmet hamburger cafés, and Straw Hat Pizza. Saga, started in 1948 as a contract feeder, was sold to Marriott in 1986, and then was almost immediately sold again to restauranteur Anwar Soliman.[38] In 1996, the Grandy's chain comprised 160 locations, most of them concentrated in Texas and Oklahoma (see fig. 10.16).

Similar to Grandy's in menu and decor was Winner's Fried Chicken launched in 1979 in Nashville by Volunteer Capital Corporation, the largest Wendy's franchisee. Volunteer was John Massey's company, Massey having partnered with John Y. Brown Jr. in purchasing Kentucky Fried Chicken

Chicken Places

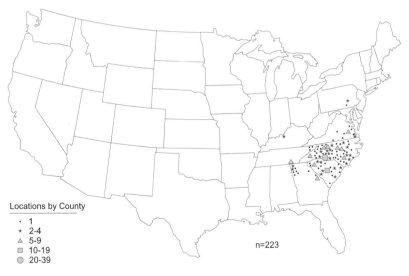

Locations by County

· 1
★ 2-4
△ 5-9
▢ 10-19
◉ 20-39

n=223

FIG. 10.15 Bojangles, 1996. Leading counties were: Mecklenberg (Charlotte), N.C. (20 locations), Richland, S.C. (10), and Greenville, S.C., Gilford, N.C., and Henrico (Richmond), Va. (8 each).

from Harland Sanders. Winner's spread quickly across Tennessee and into parts of Kentucky, Arkansas, and Georgia with stores as far afield as southern Indiana and southern Ohio. Expansion was accelerated through purchase of the Granny's Fried Chicken chain.[39]

El Pollo Loco ("The Crazy Chicken") began in 1975 as a roadside stand in Guasave, Mexico, the first U.S. El Pollo Loco opening in 1980 in Los Angeles. The American chain grew to 19 outlets in three years when it was purchased by Denny's, itself soon bought out by Flagstar.[40] Featured was the "pollo" style of marinated chicken grilled on an open flame, popular across much of Latin America. Built were freestanding white-stucco buildings with tile roofs incorporating large expanses of window glass. All of the chain's restaurants featured drive-through windows and indoor seating for about 50 customers. Emphasized was the low-cholesterol aspects of both the chicken and its preparation. Although "ethnic" in implication, the chain's real market was the nation's health-conscious, educated middle class. Imitators followed, including Phoenix-based El Pollo Asado and Cincinnati-based Marco Pollo. But El Loco Pollo proved the most successful, growing to 216 outlets in 1996.[41]

Roasted chicken prepared on rotisseries, irrespective of the spices used, was so successful that KFC, still the chicken giant, moved to add it to its stores, as did most other chains. Several new chains emphasized roasted chicken as part of a complete meal, everything available for carryout. Boston Chicken (renamed Boston Market) was prime among them. Boston Chicken's growth involved a network of area partners rather than traditional single-unit franchisees. Reported one trade journal:

> Under this system, the company provides 75 percent financing for a limited number of area partners, who commit to invest $2 million to $5

FIG. 10.16 Grandy's, 1996. Leading counties were: Dallas, Tex. (20 locations) and Harris (Houston), Tex., and Tarrant (Fort Worth), Tex. (13 each).

TABLE 10.1 Leading Chicken Chains, 1996

Chain	Headquarters	Units Worldwide	Sales (in millions)	Sales Rank Top 300
KFC	Louisville, Ky.	9,863	$8,200	3
Boston Market	Golden, Colo.	1,087	1,160	25
Popeye's	Atlanta	1,025	755	37
Church's	Atlanta	1,282	667	44
Chick-fil-A	Atlanta	717	570	52
Kenny Rogers	Ft. Lauderdale	269	265	86
El Pollo Loco	Irvine, Calif.	240	225	100
Bojangles	Charlotte, N.C.	242	214	108
Grandy's	Lewisville, Tex.	159	144	139
Lee's Famous Recipe	Nashville	225	136	144
Mrs. Winner's	Atlanta	131	96	174
Pollo Tropical	Miami	45	73	215
Buffalo Wild Wings and Weck	Minneapolis	71	71	218
Goldens Fried	Dallas	95	46	285
Browns	Oak Brook, Ill.	68	45	292

Source: Restaurants and Institutions 107 (July 15, 1997): 66.

million to build anywhere from 35 to 100 units in a market over a three- to five-year period. These regional partners pay approximately 10 per- cent of revenues to the company, including a 5 percent advertising and marketing fee.[42]

An agreement, for example, was struck with Carl Karcher Enterprises to es- tablish 300 outlets in Southern California. The "partnering" scheme already had been proven successful in building the Blockbuster video-store chain, Boston Chicken's mentors, Scott Beck, Saad Nadhir, and Jeffrey Shearer, be- ing former Blockbuster executives.[43]

Rooster Corporation's Kenny Rogers chain grew to 250 outlets in just three years, building on the country-western singer's persona, but also fea- turing "nonfried" chicken.[44] The company also introduced roast turkey in its South Florida stores. The chain made extensive use of neon lighting to titil- late the eyes, vented rotisserie smells indoors to stimulate the nose, and, at the same time, featured a background of Kenny Rogers's songs to excite the ears. Here was a total environmental surround, an encompassing environ- ment of sight, smell, and sound to be linked with distinctive food tastes. Here was place-product-packaging amplified for the senses. Despite such new innovations, however, chains established around fried chicken using in- door walk-up and drive-through formats still dominated in the early 1990s (Table 10.1).

Chicken did not remain the province of chicken restaurants only. To McDon- ald's came McChicken sandwiches and Chicken McNuggets. To Burger King came Chicken Tenders. To Hardee's came Chicken Biscuit. To Jack in the Box came Chicken Fajita Pita. To Arby's came Chicken Cordon Bleu. Not only did Wendy's add chicken sandwiches to its stores, but it launched its Sisters subsidiary dedicated to chicken. Although beef remained "king," chicken made substantial inroads as, perhaps, the industry's crown prince in waiting. Chicken benefited from its health implications as being a lean meat with less fat. And it was lower priced, attracting the budget-conscious as well as the health-conscious.

Chicken did not come late to the American roadside. Chicken was sold right along with steak, fish, and other foods in roadside eateries, especially the more upscale dinner houses. Destination restaurants thrived with Sunday chicken dinners made available throughout the week. But chicken did come late as a fast food. In that regard, hamburger proved the true roadside pioneer. Chicken, even fried chicken, was slow to prepare to order. It had not lent itself well to the quick-service restaurants of the pre-automobile era. And it did not lend itself to quick service when impatient automobilists waited at the curbside. Yet chicken had always been a staple in the American diet, symbolizing much to the middling and lower classes. It was only a matter of time before new technologies—deep frying in pressurized cookers most especially—would make chicken a true hamburger competitor.

CHAPTER 11

Seafood Places

There was a time not too long ago when Americans considered the world's oceans to be an infinite food source. If there was a problem, it was a problem of transportation, of moving highly perishable seafood quickly long distances. With the coming of the railroads, oysters preserved in salt brine could be shipped far inland and, accordingly, oyster houses appeared even in frontier boom towns. The coming of quick-freezing techniques and refrigerator trucks made frozen fish available everywhere, and the rise of air freight enabled fresh fish, in limited quantities at least, to be delivered to supermarkets and restaurants across the United States as well. Fish canned for home consumption was especially important during the world wars, but never significant in restaurants. Per capita consumption of commercial seafood steadily increased from an estimated 10 pounds in 1900 to some 16 pounds in 1989 when seafood supplies began to decline.[1] Seafood consumption, of course, has varied regionally, the highest levels being consistently recorded for the coastal South with New England close behind.[2]

By the mid-1990s four of the world's major fisheries were depleted, and nine others in serious decline.[3] Overfishing and the effects of industrial and other pollutants, tied to a burgeoning world population risen to 5.7 billion people, had brought some fish species to the brink of extinction. Fish catches worldwide peaked at 86 million tons in 1989 up from an estimated 3 million tons at the turn of the century. Fish catches had increased fivefold since 1950 alone.[4] In the Atlantic, haddock stocks were classified as "collapsed" and cod as "nearly collapsed." Red snapper had all but disappeared from the Gulf of Mexico. Seafood restaurants were plagued by rapidly rising seafood prices and uncertain supplies. Aquaculture helped stabilize the market for some species, especially shrimp and salmon, but in general a scarcity of product became increasingly problematical.

At the same time, demand for healthy foods grew, placing seafood in a new light. Dieticians became alarmed at the nation's growing fat intake. In 1976, Americans consumed 27 percent more dietary fat than in 1910, 159 versus 125 grams per person per day. Much of it came from separated fats and oils, but a significant amount came also from meat, especially beef and pork.[5] Low-cholesterol diets called for cutting back whole milk and eggs as well as red meat, and boosting low-fat milk and fish consumption. Fish provided a means of "lightening" meals and represented, as well, a source of vitamins and minerals.[6] Seafood also afforded variety, a change of pace from usual fare. Of course, much of the fish consumed, especially in restaurants, was fried, contributing not a little to the nation's fat-induced health problems. It is ironic that just when other kinds of cooking came into popularity—baking and grilling, for example—the nation's fish supplies began to falter.

Dinner Houses

As with chicken, the dinner house or upscale destination restaurant developed early along the nation's highways to serve seafood tastes. For example, the Phillips Seafood House became a roadside landmark outside Ocean City, Maryland, developing branches in recent decades in Baltimore, Washington, D.C., and Norfolk. Started by Brice and Shirley Phillips in 1956, the restaurant was at first primarily an outlet for surplus crabs and crabmeat from the family's nearby processing plant. Originally the Crab Shack, a roadside stand, the business emerged quickly into a 1,200-seat dining facility.[7]

Resort seafood restaurants often had a water view, but some restauranteurs did settle for highway locations, content to intercept customers coming and going to beach or harbor attractions. Some businesses developed both locations, as in the case of Kimball's and Hugo's located at Cohasset

FIG. 11.1 Hugo's and Kimball's, Cohasset Harbor, Mass., ca. 1950.

FIG. 11.2 The Kingfish Over the Water, Treasure Island, Fla., ca. 1950.

FIG. 11.3 Smith Brothers
Fish Shanty, Port Washington, Wis., ca. 1940.

FAST FOOD

FIG. 11.4 New Meadows Lobster Pound, Boothbay Harbor, Maine, 1948.

Harbor, Massachusetts (see fig. 11.1). Kimball's clung to the harbor with its water view. Hugo's clung to the highway, its mock lighthouse and contrived seashore rusticity implying water orientation. Inside, maritime themes predominated as at the Kingfish Over the Water at Treasure Island near St. Petersburg, or at the Smith Brothers Fish Shanty at Port Washington, Wisconsin, north of Milwaukee on Lake Michigan (see figs. 11.2 and 11.3). At the Kingfish, mounted fish trophies and murals of coastal scenes stood suggestive. Smith Brothers advertised on its postcards the following: "This unique restaurant . . . reproduces the interior of a Great Lakes fisherman's shanty. . . . Dining rooms, with nautical furniture and knotty pine walls, hung with relics of the sea, lend a distinctive marine atmosphere." As a destination restaurant this "shanty" could seat hundreds.

In coastal resorts, restaurants usually specialized in the prime or "status" seafood at hand. "Downeast" the lobster pound thrived, many as an outdoor stand at wharfside surrounded by symbolic if not real lobster pots, and others, like the New Meadows at Boothbay Harbor, Maine, out on the highway (see fig. 11.4). Around the Chesapeake Bay oysters or crabcakes might be featured. In the Great Lakes it might be whitefish. In the Pacific Northwest it might be salmon. Whole towns came to specialize in seafood dinners. For example, Calabash, North Carolina, once a small fishing village, had by the 1970s evolved into a complex of parking lots serving several very large restaurants, all reinforcing one another as a major regional tourist draw.

In coastal cities like Boston, seafood always has been important. Boston, indeed, is the center of New England's fishing industry, the place from which seafood is wholesaled back across New England including its fishing ports. Located in Boston are such institutions as the Union Oyster House, one of the nation's oldest, if not its oldest, continuously operating eatery (see fig. 11.5). The back of the postcard, postmarked in 1947, reads in part: "We had dinner here tonight—upstairs. Delightful place and such a good dinner. Have driven out to Lexington and Concord. . . . Leave for Portland to-

FIG. 11.5 Union Oyster House, Boston, 1948.

FIG. 11.6 Langley's Marine Grill, Portland, Maine, ca. 1940.

morrow. Eleanor." In downtown Portland, Eleanor and her husband might have eaten at Langley's Marine Grill, which featured "shore dinners." Langley's interior was contrived as the deck of a sailing ship with wall murals depicting the sea (see fig. 11.6). In both of these places, decor reinforced the choice of fish as an alternative to steak, chicken, or other entrees. Customers were invited to purchase a sense of place as well as food. Restaurants were organized around an integrating theme—the sea.

The "fish house" idea was ideal for chain development, not just expansion to a handful of locations, but expansion pointed nationwide. The Brighton Fish Pier chain was one of the first to try. Founded by an investment group in the late 1960s, the chain developed "medium-priced, table-cloth restaurants with a nautical theme, featuring seafood."[8] Each restaurant displayed a collection of memorabilia from sailing ships and early steamships once of British registry. Waiters were dressed like stewards on former Cunard or White Star oceanliners. Growth strategy was to expand city by city across the country rather than to develop regional strengths. By 1977 there were 45 restaurants in the chain spread from coast to coast. The novelty of its restaurant decor, however, was not enough to keep the chain alive.

RED LOBSTER

No upscale seafood chain has been as successful as Red Lobster. William B. Darden began his restaurant career at age 19 in 1938 when he opened the Green Frog in Waycross, Georgia, a drive-in featuring "Service with a Hop." After World War II he developed nine Howard Johnson's restaurants and then 12 Bonanza Steak Houses. In 1963, he bought Gary's Duck Inn in Orlando and it was from there that a five-unit Red Lobster chain evolved. Joe R. Lee, who went to work for Darden at the Green Frog, became co-manager of the first Red Lobster at Lakeland, Florida, and then president of the chain. In 1970, General Mills acquired Red Lobster, hiring Lee who ultimately came to head all of the company's restaurant operations including the Good Earth, Darryl's, York, Casa Gallardo, and Olive Garden chains. General Mills' successes in the restaurant business related to its decentralizing management such that restaurants could be run as service-oriented businesses, fully responsive to customer likes and dislikes.

Initially, Red Lobster offered a no-frills restaurant package—open rooms with battleship gray walls, plastic nautical wall accessories, and tile floors. Seafood was fried. Lee began to upgrade with new color schemes, booth-high room dividers, and wall treatments themed to different coastal regions. More important, he introduced more baked and steamed food such as crab legs and shrimp.[9] By 1979, 244 restaurants were operating and by 1985

FIG. 11.7 Red Lobster, Springfield, Ill., 1996.

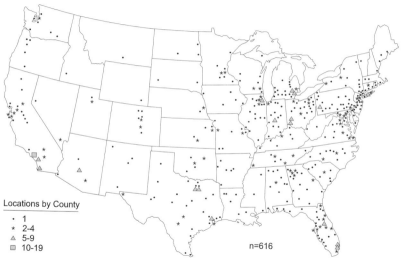

FIG. 11.8 Red Lobster, 1993. Leading counties were: Los Angeles, Calif. (12 locations), Cook, Ill. (9), Dallas, Tex. (8), Harris (Houston), Tex. (8), and Maricopa (Phoenix), Ariz. (8).

370—all company-owned.[10] By 1996, 729 restaurants were operating, the chain both adding new and closing under-performing locations at the rate of some 30 a year (see figs. 11.7 and 11.8).[11]

Red Lobster's success followed not only from periodical upgrading of menu and decor, but from an ability to maintain seafood supplies. George Goss, a former State Department fisheries attaché, and William Hathaway, who succeeded Lee as chain president, established a worldwide supply system, organized eventually as the Pinellas Seafood Company subsidiary.[12] Seafood came from Iceland, Mexico, Brazil, and Canada, as well as from Alaska and the West Coast. The chain also turned to aquaculture with farm-raised rainbow trout, catfish, halibut, and salmon critical to sustained operations. Menus were enlarged with chicken, pasta, and salad plates.

Fish and Chips

The apparent infinite supply of fish, especially North Atlantic cod, the perfection of deep-frying techniques, and the example of the burgeoning roadside hamburger and chicken chains inspired a host of fish chains in the late 1950s and early 1960s. Most were oriented to takeout business much like the early Kentucky Fried Chicken stores. Barnacle Bill's, headquartered in Irwin, Pennsylvania, included comedian Stan Freberg on its board of directors; Freberg's job was to create imaginative radio promotions. Restaurants featured "authentic touches" like captain's chairs, treasure maps, ship rigging, fish netting, and pennant flags—all calculated to the creation of a "nautical atmosphere."[13] Captain Kidd's Fish n' Chips of Phoenix emphasized interior play areas for kids, including a Captain Kidd's Cave and an 86-foot replica of a pirate ship.[14] In the Yankee Clipper Seafood Galley, a chain launched at Wichita by several ex–Pizza Hut executives, walls were hung with artifacts "actually recovered from sailing ships."[15]

The English idea of fish and chips was what energized most of these chains. And so it was that many chains took on English pretensions— Cedric's Fish and Chips, Friar's Fish, British Fish and Chips Ltd. H. Salt Esq. Fish and Chips was created by Haddon and Grace Salt, husband and wife immigrants from England, in Sausalito, California, in 1965. Built to 91 franchised locations in California by 1969, the chain was sold to Kentucky Fried Chicken, which immediately opened 10 stores in Louisville. A year later there were 226 locations nationwide.[16]

ARTHUR TREACHER'S

Among the fish-and-chips chains featuring Atlantic cod and french fries was Arthur Treacher's. Treacher, a veteran show-business personality whose career began in English music halls, won a large late-in-life following on Merv Griffin's syndicated television show. Launched by Orange-co, Inc., a maker of juice concentrate in Florida, the chain grew to 15 locations in 1970 before franchising began. By 1982 there were over 780 restaurants operating. From the beginning the chain was primarily a real-estate venture. "Treacher's went in thinking they could be like McDonald's, building restaurants and profiting through lease arrangements. But they didn't have the depth of knowledge required for cooking and selling fish," concluded James Cataland, Treacher's general counsel and eventual owner of the company.[17] The troubled chain changed hands repeatedly. In 1979 it was sold by Mrs. Paul's Kitchens of Philadelphia to Lumara Foods of Youngstown, Ohio. Mrs. Paul's had cut off the supply of expensive Icelandic cod, replacing it with its own precooked fishcakes, precipitating a revolt by franchisees and disastrous court litigation. Quickly, the chain declined to fewer than 400 units, taking Lumara into bankruptcy and forcing the selloff of all but 21 of its remaining 110 company-owned stores.[18] A reorganized Arthur Treacher's, Inc. emerged, operating primarily in Ohio.

LONG JOHN SILVER'S

The most successful of the indoor-walk-up fish chains remains Long John Silver's, launched in 1969 by Jerrico, Inc. of Lexington, Kentucky, under the guidance of Warren Rosenthal and James Patterson. The name Long John Silver was adopted from Robert Louis Stevenson's classic *Treasure Island*. A distinctive gray and blue building with gable roof and cupola was introduced, pretending association with "early American fishing villages"—a design, it was claimed, that would "appear as acceptable in 2090 as it was in 1790" (see fig. 11.9). By 1975 the chain had grown to 286 locations in 23 states, expanding outward from early concentrations in Kentucky, Iowa, and Texas.[19] Franchisees had to meet two requirements: the capability to open at least five stores within a given territory and the ability to provide experienced store managers. Encouraged from the beginning were management companies. Like many of the chicken chains, Jerrico introduced a unique

FIG. 11.9 Long John Silver's, Indianapolis, 1996.

frying system for its batter-fried fish. At each restaurant, cod fillets were cut to size, held in cold storage, and fried as a batch in anticipation of customer demand. In 1976, there were 600 outlets, 144 of them company-owned.[20]

The rising price of fish, occasioned by an increasing fish shortage, caused the company to reassess. Its supply system was strengthened, its products altered, and its stores upgraded in an aggressive reaction to rising costs of operation. To offset a 13 percent increase in the price of cod in 1976 alone, the chain changed its method of cutting fish fillet to get smaller individual pieces. Offered was a new plate combination, "Fish and More," with less fish and more french fries, coleslaw, and hushpuppies. The chain also began to test new sandwiches made with pollack and ocean scallops.[21] By the end of 1977, the cost of cod had increased some 70 percent over its 1969 price. The chain began to extend to franchisees incentives to upgrade stores, reducing royalty and other fees. Thus while other chains faltered in the changing market, Long John Silver's continued to grow, reaching 1,183 outlets in 1982. In 1989, the chain had some 70 participating franchise groups ranging in size of operation from one outlet to 89 outlets. Of its 1,444 locations in 1994, 994 were company-owned.[22]

Midscale Chains

Between the upscale seafood houses, including the Red Lobster chain, and the chains that were essentially fish and chips derivatives, clustered a small group of companies targeting a middle market segment. Skipper's Chowder 'n Seafood Restaurants, based in Bellevue, Washington, operated with precooked seafood kept hot under warming lights until served. Thus the chain could offer upscale food, but also quick service. Customers entered, placed their orders, sat down, and were served at their tables in a "semi-service" operation.[23] Featured was fresh Alaska cod cut trimmed at each restaurant and then deep-fried in a light breading. Available also were fried shrimp, clams, and bite-size salmon fillets as well as chicken fillets. Meals were served with French fries and coleslaw.

Captain D's began in 1969 when Ray Danner, a Shoney's Big Boy franchisee, grew frustrated at not being able to expand his Big Boy chain beyond his franchise territory. Launched was Mr. D's, the name changed in 1975 when Danner took control of Shoney's. In 1980, Captain D's boasted 330 outlets as compared to Shoney's 320.[24] By 1985, the chain had grown to 266 company-owned and 211 franchised outlets. A nautical "Cape Cod" theme dominated the chain's indoor-walk-up buildings. "A Great Little Seafood Place" was the chain's slogan. Also offered were hamburgers and chicken fillet sandwiches in part to hedge against rising fish prices. "While seafood continues to grow in popularity, some people just don't like it," Danner argued. "This way, if a group of four people is looking for a place to eat, they can all find something to enjoy at Captain D's."[25] The chain practiced "upselling." Featured at the entrance to each restaurant were backlit advertising panels to encourage impulse buying of higher-ticket items. Some 40 percent of the chain's business was take-out.

Few seafood chains grew to any size, the increasing cost of fish and the uncertainties of its supply the principal retarding factors (see Table 11.1). In addition, hamburger, chicken, and other chains began to add seafood to their menus, increasing pressure on supplies. Fish, like chicken, came to represent an important "change of pace" food, a significant complement to hamburger and beef. Important also, of course, was the rising concern for low-fat foods. Today, McDonald's offers crabcakes in the Chesapeake Bay area and lobster rolls in New England in addition to its Filet-O-Fish sandwiches nationwide. "Meatless" Fridays, long observed by Roman Catholics, reverberate still in quick-service menus everywhere, but especially in heavily Roman Catholic areas. With the giant chains all clamoring for seafood supplies, small operators, lacking economies of scale, have been disadvantaged.

TABLE 11.1 Leading Seafood Chains, 1996

Chain	Headquarters	Units Worldwide	Sales (in millions)	Sales Rank Top 300
Red Lobster	Orlando	729	$1,900	15
Long John Silver's	Lexington	1,461	885	33
Captain D's	Nashville	598	468	59
Landry's	Houston	44	146	137
Legal Sea Foods	Boston	14	75	212
C. A. Muer	Detroit	18	67	229
Arthur Treacher's	Jacksonville	131	65	235
Shells	Tampa	32	49	276

Source: Restaurants and Institutions 107 (July 15, 1997): 66.

Seafood, therefore, has not sustained many mom-and-pop operators in the restaurant business.

Seafood made its way to the roadside in stages. In coastal areas, where fresh fish was available, the dinner house made its appearance not only as a steak or chicken place, but as a seafood place. Not surprisingly, upscale seafood chains were launched once the nation's interstate highways evolved to speed refrigerated trucks in their seafood deliveries and once, of course, air freight service matured. Florida and West Coast entrepreneurs led the way. Away from the coasts, seafood chains evolved primarily with fish and chip venues. Fish, as a fast food, drove chain development from such places as Lexington, Louisville, and Nashville. Fried fish, not only Atlantic cod but catfish also, combined with french fries to produce quick-service entrees potentially competitive with even hamburgers. But the inconsistency of supply and the rapid rise in price precluded seafood chains from fully realizing that potential. Americans, looking for alternative fast foods along the nation's highways, turned instead to exotics such as pizza and tacos.

Not only did place-product-packaging play out forcefully among the relatively few seafood chains to thrive, but it did so around distinctive "nautical" or "maritime" designs. The seafood restaurant, like the nation's Italian and Mexican restaurants, and certainly its Chinese restaurants, invited theme development, the forceful linking of food with exterior design and interior decor. Indeed, highly stereotypic design vocabularies evolved. Hamburgers might sell themselves, but fish seemed to require special effort, the seafood restaurant made out to be an alternative kind of place somehow "maritime" in context. In upscale fish houses the pretense could be quite elaborate. In downscale fish-and-chip takeout stands, it might be only suggestive. Nonetheless, it was always there—in colors selected, in wall decorations, in logos. And, of course, nautical ideas were almost always incorporated into restaurant names. Despite the heavy theme orientation, however, architecture remained derivative, seafood chains copying formats used elsewhere. Seafood places needed to look like seafood places, but they also needed to look like restaurants.

CHAPTER 12

Pizza Places

Pizza and other Italian-derived foods came late to the American roadside. As the most popular ethnic cuisine in a nation with a large population from Italy, it should perhaps be expected that Italian food was eventually taken up by the vigilant roadside entrepreneurs. Here we outline that process. How did pizza, a folk food served in the special settings of an ethnic minority, come to be an item of popular food? To what extent and in what ways did place-product-packaging and corporate territoriality foster? In what ways did automobile-convenience contribute? When and in what ways did other Italian foods participate? Who were the entrepreneurs who helped achieve this transformation? How have these foods of Italian origin influenced this most American place, the roadside?

Pizza was very revealing of the way Americans learned to eat at roadside stops. Of all Italy's cuisine adapted to American tastes, pizza has risen to become the most popular road food of ethnic origins, another function of the consumer culture. Historical origins accounted little for the success of New World pizza, contrary to pizza's usual history in America. At the height of Italian immigration into the United States, between 1880 and 1920, slightly more than four million Italians entered the United States, a large percentage of the nation's late-nineteenth- and early-twentieth-century immigrants. But it was not that their numbers in the United States imparted advantage or definitely not that an early arrival imparted the advantages of the Doctrine of First Effective Settlement, that is, the tendency of early immigrants to establish a pattern in an area that the general population in the area adopts thereafter. Most Italian foods initially spread throughout the United States to its urban centers from New York City. Clearly an Italian-American hybrid little recognizable to native Italians, it was pizza, not, for example, spaghetti ala carbonara or braciola that sprung to hungry travelers' minds when contemplating where to get an Italian meal.[1]

Some advantage redounded to pizza in the market as a food of initially poor and eventually prosperous newcomers. Americans champion the underdog and much of the democratic lore defining the nation as the land of opportunity is faith that anyone can rise from a humble background to achieve recognition, and profit, too. In short, a lowly start can end in an exalted finish. Numerous were the ethnic groups come to the United States for opportunity variously defined. If automobile-convenient foods were a function exclusively of the nation's diverse folk foods commercialized, however, road food would be far more diverse than it is. Critics would be hard put to rail, as they could until recently, against a burger-and-fries monopoly. Entrepreneurs wedging small niches of diversity along the roadside in the 1970s would not be settling for returns far smaller than their roadside compatriots of the 1950s. Discovered ethnic foodways would have been recycled as sparkling new investment opportunities in nationalism commodified. If regional hearths suggest themselves, as they have with pizza's initiation among the inhabitants of the East Coast megalopolis, scholars would likely have pursued linkages of proximity into the rural and small-town hinterlands. They have not. Geographer Wilbur Zelinsky's study of foodways stops short of assertion, instead supposing, that Italian food is popular where first- and second-generation Italians lived, and that non-Italians in Peninsular Florida accepted it.[2] What then enabled pizza to rank as the leading ethnic cuisine along the nation's roadside outside these areas, close behind the all-American hamburger and ahead of fried chicken?

Explanation lies in the advent of "fast food" during the 1950s and 1960s—convenience revved higher than before. Richard Pillsbury rightly cautioned against believing fast food's appearance represented a radical cleavage with the past. Yet, we can refer to a profound transformation of the way Americans learned to eat in mid–twentieth century, one in which the automobile was a primary catalyst. To be sure, restaurants served 60 million meals daily in 1947, roughly one meal for every two and one-half Americans. By 1982, which is safely reckoned after the fast-food transformation, 40 million Americans daily ate at fast-food restaurants and their average customer ate there 9 to 10 times per month. Roughly one-fifth of America, thus, often ate a kind of food and in formats that hardly existed before midcentury, although its antecedents captured disproportionate attention due to their novelty and entrepreneurs' ballyhoo. Most notably, beef consumption, risen 76 percent between 1910 and 1976, jumped 90 percent between 1950 and 1976: an impact of the roadside's burger chains. Hard cheese consumption, due largely to the mozzarella used on pizzas, jumped from 8.3 pounds to 17.4 pounds per person between 1960 and 1978. Ending fast food's rapid growth was a backlash in favor of sit-down dining with more personalized ambiance beginning in the 1970s. Fast food and its places seemed too "plastic," to use the word the post–World War II generation took to symbolize progress through technology, only to have it returned as a taunt by a later generation. Acceptance was gained nonetheless for fast food. Business opportunities there were aplenty for it. Moreover, the arbiters of propriety ultimately found a role for fast food, for example, *Good Housekeeping* magazine's report in 1975 on the seven largest fast-food chains—Pizza Hut included—in terms of nutrition, quality, and cost. The suggestion was implicit that discriminating customers could make a worthy selection among fast foods.[3]

Culture encouraged the adoption. By the 1950s, roadside commerce was an agreeable new element of American life with fast-food places a part of it. If McCarthyism early in the decade revealed ardent disagreement about past social remedies, and African-Americans and their supporters reasserted a long quiescent racial item in the agenda for American opportunity, the Federal Aid Highway Act of 1956, which established the interstate system, helped perpetuate the majority's preferred ethos of one happy nation. President Eisenhower, instrumental in the interstate program's adoption, explained it in terms of "greater convenience, greater happiness, and greater standards of living."[4] Resolution through superabundance, as if everyone could routinely obtain their fair share of the growing wealth: the automobile and the roadside configured for its convenience were the foremost inducement and symbol of this enduringly hearty national faith. It was the hegemonic value system in which individuals—consumers and entrepreneurs alike—determined what and how America's roadside eateries served.

Robust self-confidence peculiar to the 1950s encouraged new entrepreneurs to try to satisfy more fully popular expectations for reliable roadside food. Adoption of pizza—a food of once reviled new stock immigrants with negligible presence in America before the fast-food transformation—would be an index of the extent and ways by which national habits of eating out could be reformed in the process.[5]

Pizza's origins traced to distant times and various firsts confirm two varieties, the older Italian substantially distinct from the newer American. Pizza's legendary history has been traced to the flat leavened breads of the Mediterranean, possibly to the ancient Etruscans and Greeks. John Mariani authoritatively held that the name "pizza" originated with the Neapolitan dialect for *pizzicare,* meaning "pinch" or "pluck." The first printed reference to it is claimed for a seventeenth-century cookbook. The first pizzeria or place for eating pizza in Italy opened in 1830 and in the United States in either 1888, 1895, or 1905. In 1995, a visit to the United States from a Neapolitan trade deputation pontificating about the proper ways to make pizza nonetheless underscored American pizza's separate identity.[6]

Mariani guides us to its introduction, American soldiers returning after World War II from southern Italy where they learned of the Neapolitan folk food as well as a hit song of 1953, which included the line, "When the moon hits your eye like a big pizza pie." Still, pizza's demand was restricted to a few big cities where Italian-Americans sought familiar food and others sought culinary adventures.[7]

Pizza's potential as a popular food, however, meshed well with some key traits of the 1950s, family life, teen life, more casual eating, and the centrality of television entertainment, according to Harvey Levenstein. Diners could gather around the television while eating pizza, a food undemanding of side dishes and popular with Mom, Dad, and the kids alike. Or its consumption could be the occasion of exclusively teenage gatherings.[8] Facilitating these practices, convenience gave pizza welcome entree.

Pizza Hut

Pizza Hut is the company that initially popularized pizza as fast food. In the process, pizza's association with small family-owned and -operated pizzerias was replaced with place-product-packaged chain restaurants. By 1990, Pizza Hut ranked fourth in sales among all chain restaurants, a remarkable break in the otherwise solid fast-food leadership by the hamburger chains.[9]

Pizza Places

An apparent anomaly, Pizza Hut started in 1958 in Wichita, Kansas, hardly a center of the Italian immigrants who were most of pizza's initial customers. But the time was conducive, the start of the fast-food transformation. The city, too, was right; Wichita had been one of the nation's principal fast-food hearths, White Castle having started there a generation earlier. Neither time nor place was trammeled by pizza's traditional recipes and format.[10]

Frank and Daniel Carney borrowed $600 from their mother, purchased second-hand equipment, and opened the first Pizza Hut, a small brick building near U.S. 54. Their family owned a grocery store and the brothers sought income to pay for the college education they believed would lead to a better life. Frank, the younger brother, was a college freshman when he realized Pizza Hut's profit potential and quickly abandoned his college education to pursue the fast-food business.[11] Neither blueprint for expansion nor vision of pizza for everyman, however, motivated Carney. He took an opportunity with consequences far exceeding his initial dreams.

Pizza did promise profit. Only two other pizza places existed in Wichita when Pizza Hut opened. Many of Carney's employees and investors incessantly asked how they could purchase an operation like Carney's. As a result, Pizza Hut began franchising in 1959. A year later, a would-be franchisee reneged on the purchase and started a competitive chain in Oklahoma City. Drawn into an expansion-or-die strategy, Pizza Hut launched its own chain in Oklahoma City. Operating from four "old, cruddy buildings," according to Carney's characterization, Pizza Hut was eventually forced to close in Oklahoma City but Carney came to appreciate the importance of a positive architectural image for his chain. In 1965 a uniform architecture and musical jingle ("Putt-Putt to Pizza Hut") were adopted. Units increased: 42 in 1963, 68 in 1964, 85 in 1965, 140 in 1966, 190 in 1967, and 299 in 1968. Within a decade, Carney had a thriving fast-food enterprise with seemingly unlimited capacity for expansion. Pizza Huts featured indoor seating for approximately 80 people although 50 percent of the business through takeout attested to the possibility of even greater profit through lower cost operations. Eleven different "pizza pies," as they were called, were available to Pizza Hut customers. Thus did Midwesterners newly introduced to a once-ethnic specialty foster another generic variation in fast food.[12]

Carney's roadside pizza, however, reached the limits of popularity when it expanded beyond its midwestern base into the Northeast where customers had preexisting pizza expectations. Still reflecting amazement at foodways' considerable variation, despite his company's successful adaptation to them, Carney recalled that "the revision we did in Connecticut was a totally different revision than in Long Island. Just within 100 miles we had two totally different tastes in pizza." Long Islanders disparaged Pizza Hut's thin and crispy pizza—"this stuff isn't pizza, it's matzoh with cheese on it"—until the company shifted to a thicker pizza that customers could fold.[13] Even then, Carney was unable to penetrate the Northeast's market to his satisfaction. Upstate New Yorkers, however, thrived on what Carney called "traditional Pizza Hut pizza." In another culinary twist of fate for the homogenizing fast-food pizza empire, Carney learned that Chicago's pan-style pizza could be profitable throughout his market.[14] In these ways regional pizzas came to vary the Pizza Hut menu.

Philip Langdon has outlined the emergence of Pizza Hut's accompanying architecture, blandly colored walls highlighting a red roof swept to a high ridge (see fig. 12.1). Strong visual cues to speeding drivers had proven standard repertoire for roadside businesses. Certainly these uniform places were in diametric opposition to the neighborhood pizzerias where the traditional food was served and a generic Italian setting was avoided. By the late 1960s, abstract form and bright colors also replaced Pizza Hut's ethnic vestige, a stereotyped Italian chef displayed on the company's first roadside signs.[15] The readily identifiable pizza hut—one of the most enduring items of fast

FIG. 12.1 A typical Pizza Hut restaurant, here shown in West Lafayette, Ind., in 1996, replicated state to state to establish a uniform identity for the corporation in America.

food—is classic roadside place-product-packaging and a dramatic illustration of pizza's Americanization.

Following a successful reformation of franchisees under Pizza Hut's central authority in the late 1960s, Carney directed his business toward further expansion. Food again proved secondary to financial considerations except to speed pizza's production through infrared conveyor ovens introduced by the late 1970s. Seeking security through financial diversification, he acquired several small taco, hamburger, and steak chains. Failing to achieve the desired profits from these new ventures, Carney concentrated again on Pizza Hut, forming a joint venture with a beef producer in food processing and a Japanese company interested in creating a pizza chain in Tokyo. Pizza Hut operated 1,246 units and its franchisees 1,075 units by the mid-1970s. Seeking even greater investment capacity through association with a big corporation, Carney invited PepsiCo's purchase in 1977 of stock worth some $300,000,000. The soft-drink giant, in turn, welcomed Pizza Hut as a further diversification of its own empire. One year later, Carney convinced PepsiCo to purchase Taco Bell, Pizza Hut's Mexican fast-food counterpart.[16]

Ceaseless in pursuit of ever-greater profits, Carney's further life exemplified fast food's self-perpetuating impersonality. When PepsiCo hired Burger King's Donald Smith to lead the food division, Carney resigned, restless for new entrepreneurial challenges. He went on to become one of the most successful franchisees in Chi-Chi's, a family-style Mexican chain, and ruminated about a future niche for ethnic restaurants. His honesty permits a candid view into the dynamics of the automobile-convenient restaurants come to serve Americans by the end of the twentieth century. Explaining to the incredulous Chi-Chi's executives why the multimillionaire Carney approached the company for a franchise, "I said to them that the people who made the most money from Pizza Hut were the franchisees who sold their stores to us, left and got more territory, built up another group of stores, sold them again and got still more territory to do it again. I said I want to be one of those guys. And I told them that if, in the process, you want to acquire whatever it is I'm doing, it's for sale anytime."[17]

Consistent with Carney's philosophy, Pizza Hut's history under PepsiCo continued as a series of financial machinations. And pizza's further development along the roadside was an undertaking for another round of nouveau riches.

Domino's

Pizza spawned a rare innovation in automobile-convenience when Domino's pioneered pizza for mass consumption through home delivery. The second largest pizza chain in number of units at this writing, Domino's capitalized on pizza's unusual capacity for fast food. Although pizza required specialized preparation, initially raising some doubt about its adaptability to fast food, it retained its taste far longer after cooking than many fast foods. French fries might be soggy after sitting under a heat lamp for 15 minutes, but pizza's tastes blended after preparation. Pizza, too, could be a tasty leftover warmed up. Home delivery was one of the standard pizza venues when the Monaghan brothers, Tom and Jim, opened their business in Ypsilanti, Michigan, in 1960, but Tom's entrepreneurship transformed it into a roadside food empire.

Thomas Dicke has fully chronicled Domino's history but we emphasize here aspects especially relevant to the fast-food transformation. Typical of very successful business people, Tom Monaghan was possessed of a vaguely defined desire for great material wealth justified in terms of public service and self-expression. In addition, he was willing to work hard at the menial requirements for his business and implement innovations others questioned. As did other successful fast-food entrepreneurs, he worked to perfect the taste of his product but he was as much concerned to push its profit potential. Monaghan's emphasis on ever-greater profit may seem curious in the food industry because of the belief that cooking originated and should remain a craft incompatible with mass production. Monaghan's autobiography revealed the dynamics of the fast-food transformation through the eyes of one of its foremost devotees.[18]

Tom Monaghan had virtually no business experience and harbored the belief that a college education—in his case, a degree in architecture—would yield the life he wanted when he and his brother started their pizza business. His model was P. T. Barnum, who "stressed the importance of economy, the value of maintaining a balanced budget, of being systematic, and of 'being polite and kind to your customers.'" Denying the humbuggery at the heart of Barnum's philosophy, Monaghan preferred to think of his model as an "advertising genius" (4, 17).

Intrigued with his fledgling pizza business and discouraged by courses at the University of Michigan which he was attending, Monaghan dropped out of college when his brother left the business. Tom delighted in every detail required for his business and

> any extra time I had went into making improvements in the store. My chief concern was with the layout of the oven and the counters. I kept rearranging them, trying to cut a few steps and shave fractions of seconds off the time it took to make pizzas. . . . I could control the assembly of raw materials, and I was obsessed with finding ways to speed up this end of the process. I was constantly on the run. (63)

Deductive thinking, pragmatism, production refinement, emphasis on and exhilaration in speed: the automobile-convenient pizzeria was another application of assembly-line efficiency.

Pizza was a secondary consideration. Monaghan did spend 12 years on and off before he blended pizza sauce to his liking. He visited New York's legendary pizzerias for comparison. But it was the process of production, food delivery, and territorial expansion that occupied the bulk of his talent. Reluctantly at first, Monaghan dropped the small, six-inch pizza for one person's consumption. But he was pleased when few customers complained and he made more money from the exclusive sale of the larger pizza. "This revelation was a major breakthrough in the history of Domino's Pizza." Who but an entrepreneur could be thrilled with learning the economy of scale principle in practice? Fast food's emphasis on a simplified menu came next with the elimination of submarine sandwiches one evening, yielding more profit by exclusive concentration on pizza. "Less, in this case, gave us more, and it was one of the most important lessons I ever learned" (58, 64– 65, 87–88).

Reminiscent of Ray Kroc's epiphany at San Bernardino in 1954, Tom Monaghan recalled the thrill of repeated experiences refined as a system of rapid mass production:

> Each step is clearly defined and logical. Its real beauty, though, is in the thrill of working as a team when the pace gets really frantic, when the phones are ringing without letup and the drivers are running back out the door right after they come in. Each member of the team has to employ manual dexterity, economy of movement, speed, and quick thinking. If you make a mistake, confuse an order, have a driver unable to find an address, or forget any of the little details that go into making a perfect pizza, you can mar a whole night's work.

The crowning achievement was to be a "Dominoid," employees exhilarated by the "game" of "handling the rush" (18).

During the fast-food transformation ending in the 1970s, Domino's basic elements were created, business structure among them. A typical fast-food company, Domino's offered a limited menu—only pizza and Coke—but in 1972 emphasized convenience even more—30-minute guaranteed home delivery. Refusing orders outside its delivery zones permitted its advertised reputation for 95 percent delivery on time. Speed became a liability in the late 1980s, however, when several Domino's deliveries ended in deaths that drew national notoriety. Domino's responded with driver's training for all company-owned units and, in 1993, officially began stressing quality above quick service. Not until 1989 was a new menu item added, a thick-crust pizza.[19]

Although indisputably responsible in a large measure for America's taste for pizza, Domino's exact influence is hard to measure. Many of its units were located in towns with a military installation or college where palates may have been predisposed to mass-produced food. Monaghan boasted that Domino's sold more pizza than his leading competitor, Pizza Hut, but Domino's sold only pizza. This is not to say Domino's growth was easy. Loss of the headquarters in a fire in 1969 and a lawsuit through the late 1970s from Amstar, owner of Domino Sugar, for infringement on the name "Domino's," made trouble. But the 1980s were boom years. Although franchising began in 1967, it was not until 1978 that unit 200 opened. By 1983, however, unit 1,000 opened and by 1993 unit 2,200.[20]

Strangely for an owner interested in architecture, Monaghan never en-

FIG. 12.2 So well inscribed in the market's memory is Domino's place-product-packaging, namely, home delivery and domino game pieces, that one competitor did not need to mention Domino's by name to define itself by opposition in its roadside advertising. Convenience could also mean the competitor's prepackaged pizza to be baked at home.

forced full place-product-packaging in his enterprise. Place instead became an abstract association of product through a logo without any promise of dining experience. Domino's distinctive red-and-white motif with the image of a piece from a domino game clearly signaled a Domino's unit to the passerby and on a Domino's box of pizza delivered to a customer (see fig. 12.2). But unit stores remained a heterogeneous collection of compact kitchens with counters for driver pickup. Minimal architecture was another result of Monaghan's efficiency calculation, no need for totally integrated design necessary so long as Domino's continued printing its logo in the yellow pages of telephone books.

Having innovated the pizza home-delivery venue, Monaghan was unthreatened by competitive advertisements but planned to reach the full potential of his system while he remained in control. Word of mouth was the best advertising, according to Monaghan, whose staunch Catholic faith led him to believe that "God meant me to be a pizza man."[21] The roadside's saturated restaurant market brought Monaghan's essential conservatism to the fore now that the fast-food transformation was achieved.

In the 1980s, pizza's plateau in the fast-food market was a significant fact with important implications for all roadside restaurants. Financial fast-food analyst Robert Emerson pointed out the small—and for some companies the declining—sales growth per store. Pizza was no longer as lucrative as it had been in the 1960s through the 1970s. Symptomatic of the trends in pizza, the leader, Pizza Hut, copied second-place Domino's home-delivery venue

FIG. 12.3 Postcard advertising used by Pizza Inn, 1974.

FIG. 12.4 Shakey's early lured franchisees with prospects of great income as illustrated in this advertisement in the *Franchise Journal* 3 (December–January 1970): 44.

with consequent smaller and cheaper unit operations. Little Caesar's, a privately owned company founded in Farmington Hills, Michigan, in 1959, operated profitable take-home units by selling two pizzas for the price of one. Pizza Inn used the same sales gimmick in opening new outlets (see fig. 12.3). But Little Caesar's two-for-one sales made it pizza's exciting profit-maker of the mid-1980s. The once aggressive Shakey's Pizza Parlors (see fig. 12.4), begun in Burlingame, California, in 1954 with banjo players in each restaurant, dropped that gimmick and, beginning in 1978, converted many units to buffets with pizza a prominent adjunct. From 464 units in 1980, Shakey's fell to 185 units in 1993. Chuck E. Cheese opened the children's pizza market with animated life-size puppets to entertain while eating at ShowBiz Pizza Time with video-game rooms. Here was an origin of the concept restaurants to become fully popular in the 1980s. Mom-and-pop enterprises took advantage of Pizza Hut's introduction of pizza in the Midwest and grew very competitive with the chains beginning in the late 1970s.[22]

In the face of the chains' expensive advertising of large-sized pizzas for bargain prices (Pizza Hut's "Big Foot," Little Caesar's "Big! Big! Cheese," and Domino's "Dominator"), small-scale operations thrived on loyal customers returning for meal after meal. Mom-and-pop owners explained variously and with gusto the superiority of their food and settings. Some mothers, surveilling the opportunities to eat out yet watchful of their family's health, considered pizza more nutritious than other fast foods. It was acknowledged, too, that pizza was a food around which family settings customarily convened, both adults and children agreeing on pizza's tastiness and the shared experiences while eating together. Pizza's added virtue for families was that its cost as a sit-down meal was lower than other foods. Boosting consumption, too, were men accompanying it with TV and radio sportscasts, a carryover from their teen years when they learned to like pizza because its portability and lack of need for dinnerware satisfied their sense of convenience.[23]

A resounding symptom of the entire fast-food industry's malaise in the 1990s, PepsiCo spun off Pizza Hut in 1997 due to the Italian fast-food pioneer's declining income. International growth, however, glimmered at the same time, ranking Pizza Hut and Domino's third and eighth respectively among American restaurant chains abroad.[24]

Other Italian Foods

Italian food investors then moved in two other directions, one to upscale pizza. PepsiCo's California Pizza Kitchen, for example, offered a variety of pizza virtually unrecognizable to eaters of now-traditional roadside pizza. In fact, California Pizza Kitchen served an open-face sandwich on crispy bread with "lite" toppings appealing to a health-conscious clientele (see fig. 12.5). Despite the earnings of California Pizza Kitchen, it too was to be spun off at this writing, another victim of the parent company's classification of 22 percent of its profits from its restaurants as too little.[25]

Other investors took up those Italian foods that pizza left behind in the

FIG. 12.5 California Pizza Kitchen restaurants in 1996. Leading counties were: Los Angeles (Los Angeles), Calif. (13 locations); Fairfax (Falls Church), Va. (7); and Orange (Santa Ana), Calif. (5).

FIG. 12.6 The Olive Garden restaurants in 1995. Leading counties were: Los Angeles (Los Angeles), Calif. (14 locations); Harris (Houston), Tex. (10); Orange (Orlando), Fla. (10); Maricopa (Phoenix), Ariz. (9); Cook (Chicago), Ill. (8); Orange (Santa Ana), Calif. (7); Dallas (Dallas), Tex. and Tarrant (Fort Worth), Tex. (6 each).

TABLE 12.1 Leading Italian Food Chains, 1996

Chain	Headquarters	Units Worldwide	Sales (in millions)	Sales Rank Top 300
Pizza Hut	Dallas	12,335	$7,481	4
Domino's Pizza	Ann Arbor, Mich.	5,500	2,800	9
Little Caesar's	Detroit	4,470	2,000	11
The Olive Garden	Orlando	477	1,300	21
Papa John's	Louisville	1,160	619	48
Sbarro	Commack, N.Y.	816	437	63
Round Table Pizza	Walnut Creek, Calif.	561	370	66
Chuck E. Cheese	Irving, Tex.	314	265	85
Godfather's Pizza	Omaha, Neb.	520	250	92
Pizzeria Uno Chicago Bar and Grill	West Roxbury, Mass.	149	246	93
Romano's Macaroni Grill	Dallas	84	226	99
Piccadilly Circus Pizza	Milford, Iowa	600	220	104
Fazoli's	Lexington	256	219	105
Pizza Inn	Dallas	498	204	111
California Pizza Kitchen	Los Angeles	79	176	122
Mazzio's	Tulsa, Okla.	204	150	133
Hungry Howie's Pizza and Subs	Madison Heights, Mich.	360	140	141
Bertucci's Brick Oven Pizzeria	Wakefield, Mass.	80	128	151
Papa Gino's	Dedham, Mass.	180	128	152
Mr. Gatti's	Kerrville, Tex.	201	115	158
Donato's Pizza	Columbus, Ohio	107	92	181
The Spaghetti Warehouse	Garland, Tex.	39	87	186
Shakey's	Irvine, Calif.	145	85	194
LaRosa's Pizzerias	Cincinnati	58	83	196
Peter Piper Pizza	Phoenix	120	82	198
Old Spaghetti Factory	Portland, Ore.	43	81	201
Mozzarella's American Café	Mobile, Ala.	48	75	211
Italian Oven	Latrobe, Pa.	70	65	236
East Side Mario's	Dallas	45	63	238
Bice	New York, N.Y.	24	57	251
Noble Roman's	Indianapolis	85	54	264
Il Fornaio	San Francisco	129	50	270
Fox's Pizza Den	Pittsburgh	160	50	273
Valentino's	Lincoln, Neb.	46	50	274
The Pasta House Company	St. Louis	27	49	277
Breadeaux French-Style Pisa	St. Joseph, Mo.	92	45	287
Giovanni's Pizza	Ashland, Ky.	100	44	300

Source: Restaurants and Institutions 107 (July 15, 1997): 66.

earlier fast-food transformation. Theming now entered. Olive Garden led these Italian residuals into a health market based on pasta (see fig. 12.6). Avoiding competition with mom-and-pop enterprises, whose Italian food remains very popular, General Mills' Olive Garden, founded in 1982, aimed at diners seeking Italian food at the roadside's typically low prices and served in a comfortable place.[26] Diners could order such Italian favorites as veal marsala, fettucine alfredo, and cannoli, but the company boasted instead of "larger than standard restaurant tables" and chairs "made more comfortable . . . with rollers." General Mills researched and tested every aspect of the restaurant's contrived setting rather than adapting an existing chain. Naming indicated the loose association with folk tradition on which road food typically profited: "While it [Olive Garden] did not say 'this is an Italian restaurant,' the name gave the concept the desired positive name-image. This included the 'garden' image that is an important part of The Olive Garden dining experience."[27]

Observers of American foodways report a rising appetite for ethnic cuisine, Italian leading the way.[28] But it is pizza that leads the Italian segment of the restaurant market. The chains launched with names like Pasquale, Casano's, Dino's, Pizza Inns, and Straw Hat were numerous. Most folded in the face of aggressive competition from the likes of Pizza Hut and Domino's. Of the chains promoting an Italian food orientation today, pizza venues dominate (see Table 12.1).

Italian roadside food in the form of pizza was rendered appropriate to automobile-convenient restaurant formats, including delivery by automobile, and laid a base for other Italian fare. Commodified, pizza represented a kind of cultural amnesia endemic to roadside eateries. Pretending to be one thing, it was, in fact, something else. Promoted as traditionally Italian, the new pizza was distinctly American, standardized for speed of production and speed of consumption and bland enough to appeal to a mass market. Recipes adjusted to localized tastes were really variations on highly standardized venues.

No Italian entrepreneurs and no centers of Italian ancestry explain Pizza Hut's and Domino's development of pizza into an automobile-convenient food favorite across the nation. More than irony is apparent, however. Pizza was redefined in the fast-food transformation as a pre-eminently American food, one involving greater quantities of meat—especially pork and beef—and of thin crust unrecognizable to Italians who can claim only the food's naming as a result. This is one of the principal ways in which the roadside worked on American culture, entrepreneurs sensing lucrative opportunities by rekindling loose associations for which revival is a misnomer. Results are indeed substantially reworked practices hastily changed for whatever suggests the latest commercial advantage.

Nothing more transformed roadside pizza as American fast food than its venues. Convenience reigned. Pizza started as sustenance patiently prepared for consumption in small quantities. Then it was sold to customers arriving by car, the more the better. Contact with these customers turned from restauranteurs hosting diners seated in leisure to employees rushing carry-out, drive-through, and—the format most peculiar to pizza—home delivery to customers in distant remove from the kitchens where the pizza was prepared. So completely altered as final product as well as sense of place did pizza become through automobile convenience that, despite nominal continuity with the past, it largely divided from the past. In the reformation, pizza sustained broad currents of modern American culture.

Big portions of meat drizzled with cheese for a low price have long been the pitchman's stock in trade in restaurants beside the American road. Pizza turned the formula around—cheese drizzled with meat, consumers little heeding the threat of such fatty foods. Pizza lovers, like fast-food customers generally, went to the road for gratification, seeking degrees of indulgence. Pizza served to the strains of Shakey's banjos fit right in. Why not make pizza an excuse for theater at places like Chuck E. Cheese and ShowBiz Pizza Time?

Place-product-packaging yet seldom ran to ethnic theming. Italian place identity was submerged early in Pizza Hut's national expansion and Domino's apparently never contemplated it. It waited until the 1990s for new companies, the return of sit-down dining away from home, and the coincidence of emphasized multiculturalism. At the same time, the pizza innovators having saturated the American market, they began to export their formulas abroad.

CHAPTER 13

Taco Places and Mexican "Cantinas"

After Italian cuisine, Mexican was the next ethnic cuisine to come to the American roadside. Mexican food came north of the border and principally to the American Southwest with the large influx of Mexican immigrants beginning in the 1950s. At first Mexican restaurants were simple, intended only to provide familiar food and comradery among the newcomers (see fig. 13.1). Strong theming via architectural reference to Mexican heritage came later when restauranteurs reached out to a broader "Anglo" market (see fig. 13.2). Daniel Arreola's study of Mexican restaurants in Tucson illustrates. By the 1960s, stucco walls, red-tile roofs, wrought-iron grills, gates, or lamps, and arched entrances signaled the truly Mexican restaurant as a distinctive kind of place among the city's eateries.[1] Convenience increased in importance as Mexican folk foodways were transformed for mass consumption.

Tacos emerged from the wide array of Mexican cuisine—enchiladas, chilaquiles, tostados, frijoles refritos, for example—to be most heartily adopted by Americans. Labeled the "bread of Mexico," the tortilla literally gave form to many Mexican foods. Tortillas were cakes of boiled and kneaded corn made flat, grilled, and used to hold or scoop up mixtures of sauces, meats, beans, chilies, and tomatoes. Made of any food that could be folded into a tortilla, the taco became especially popular with peasants, who filled them with chilies, beans, and sauce. Tacos required none of the comparatively elaborate preparation of the other foods. Was it the taco's simplicity, adaptability, and effectiveness—after all, its convenience became a defining American trait—that permitted this Mexican sandwich rather than any other Mexican food to capture so huge a portion of America's fast-food dollar?[2]

As roadside fare, what happened to chili, another food with some Mexican origins? Chili is a "Tex-Mex" creation unknown to Mexico except along its border with the United States. Chili may seem plebeian to many Americans, but given its high content of beef, a comparatively costly food, it is not the food of poor folk. Named for the chili pepper, its other contents and flavor—

hot or mild—vary considerably. It has been speculated that hot chili became popular to mask the beef tainted without refrigeration on long cattle drives. *Ristras* or strings of chili peppers have stereotyped Mexican restaurant decoration. Crumbled or chopped beef has come to be popularly equated with chili, verification of its Tex-Mex origins where beef was comparatively plentiful. Popular throughout the United States and suitable for fast-food cooking and service notwithstanding, chili has curiously remained a secondary menu item in roadside eateries. Perhaps the habitual suspicion about food whose ingredients could be disguised plagued chili's potential. Perhaps, too, as the main item of many chili joints catering to a night-time clientele in the dubious parts of many towns doubts were multiplied about chili as food, an aura of corruption foreclosing chili's chances as popular fare except in special places. A major one was Cincinnati, a specific locale where the Empress, Dixie, and Skyline chains have established credibility for their products with resulting great popularity.[3]

One of the first documented restaurants to serve tacos was the Xochitl Mexican restaurant at 146 West Forty-Sixth Street in New York City. There, since 1938, Juvenal Maldonado served tacos to celebrities and tourists—portentously—tourists who wanted food they could eat quickly. But such places like Maldonado's remained the exception.[4]

Trade journals in the late 1950s treated tacos as if discovering something startlingly new. Here was a novel taste that could, like hamburgers, be rapidly assembled.[5] Not similarity to American sandwiches, therefore, but compatibility with assembly-line production hastened tacos' adoption as road-

FIG. 13.1 Yet anchoring the burgeoning Mexican food segment were neighborhood stands in the barrios of many American cities, as here in Pepe's Number 2 on the outskirts of San Antonio, 1996.

FIG. 13.2 Straining to advertise its high standing, the reverse of this La Placita Dining Rooms postcard explains at length the virtues of its food and place: "On the Plaza—Old Town—Albuquerque, New Mexico. Built originally in 1706. . . . There are six beautiful and authentically characterized dining rooms to serve you the very finest in genuine Mexican dishes, choice steaks and other delicious American foods in a romantic, candle-lit atmosphere of year-round completely air-conditioned comfort. Troubadours play nightly for added pleasure."

side food. Donald Roland, owner of Don's Drive-In in San Diego, explained in 1958 he had sold nearly one-half million tacos yearly at his fast-food facility along with typical drive-in fare such as hamburgers and fried shrimp. "Speed of service and quality" were the reasons. A day's supply of taco shells was filled with meat in advance, then placed in the refrigerator, ready to grill. Working in advance, the grill man could have as many as 80 tacos on the grill and steam table, ready to be topped with lettuce and sauce, bagged and served through the window.[6]

Rush hour demanded fast food and fast food profited from as many customers as possible. The two parts of the system reciprocated. Tacos were as dazzling a prospect in the technologically smitten fast-food transformation pursuing ever more convenience as were hamburgers. Tacos attracted investors additionally because the low cost of ingredients and mechanized operations yielding to mass production could produce fast food's typically high profit margin. The taco's similarity to pizza—both flattened doughs on which the main foods were served—also made it possible for the taco to gain acceptance in the wake of pizza's opening the ethnic fast-food market.[7]

Taco Bell

Taco Bell was more responsible for the transformation of Mexican food into popular roadside fare than any other chain. Taco Bell achieved this

FIG. 13.3 A large Taco Bell unit under construction in 1996 in Santa Barbara, Calif., symptomized the company's ambitious designs on growth.

in two steps. The first spanned the 16 years between Taco Bell's creation in 1962 and 1978, when PepsiCo purchased the company. Owner first of Bell's Hamburger Stand (1952) in San Bernardino, California, and then partner in the three-unit Taco-Tia chain (1954), Glen W. Bell Jr. was another experienced and aggressive fast-food entrepreneur experimenting with a new option in the automobile-convenient restaurant trade of Southern California when he broke with his partner in Taco-Tia in the hope of franchising a more lucrative taco chain. Thus founding Taco Bell and naming it for himself, Bell carefully oversaw every aspect of its growth. Bell carefully targeted college students, traveling salesmen, and military people—all customers away from home potentially in reach of inexpensive food, but open as well to novelty. Tacos spoke of an American region—the Southwest—but in ways inherently safe while seeming exotic.[8]

Bell required a distinctive building prototype to symbolize his intentions. Drawing on the stereotype of the California mission as quintessentially Mexican architecture, Bell personally directed the theming of a standardized building of low profile with tile roof and brick walls. A bell hung inside an opening in the front facade, a symbol of the company's very name yet a reinforcement to the mission image. A standardized taco was developed, too. Bell worked with a canning company to develop a prepared taco mix. Customers could rely on a uniform taste and franchisees were spared experimentation.[9] In 1964, two years after opening, Bell started franchising, the common strategy for rapid restaurant expansion. Within a decade, Taco Bell outstripped numerous taco competitors to dominate the market, albeit with 673 units by 1975, small by contrast with the hamburger giants.[10]

PepsiCo launched the second stage of Taco Bell's history, entering the ethnic segment of the fast-food industry through purchase both of Pizza Hut and Taco Bell. Immediately, the push was on to expand Taco Bell from a southwestern regional chain into a national one. Building format was reformed while the company's earlier architectural elements were retained to take advantage of the company's hard-won image. No longer hazarding a format but responding to popular impressions, a consumer survey resulted in retention of arched windows and red-tile roof but the bell was replaced with a logo applied to the facade. Symptomatic of the substitution of American popular culture for Mexican folk culture was the new "Mainstream Mansard," as Taco Bell called it, instead of the original arcade. As with Pizza Hut's simultaneous abandonment of the Italian chef sign, Taco Bell readied for growth at the expense of its original ethnic iconography.[11]

The campaign to achieve "mainstream status" affected the menu. Persuaded that Taco Bell's customers came from the same group as the hamburger chains', an effort was made to attract them with more fast food and less Mexican food. Nachos and taco salads, American novelty foods, were added. Then, "commercials as slick as those of the top hamburger chains" were called for by Taco Bell's leadership. Further borrowing from the hamburger chains, Taco Bell added drive-throughs in 1981.[12]

John Martin's direction of Taco Bell to legendary sales ($1.7 billion in 1990) and expansion (3,500 units by 1990) for an ethnic fast food typified the forgetfulness of the past often used to establish roadside empire. Without appreciation for Glen Bell's pioneering entrepreneurship, Martin characterized Taco Bell as originally "a small regional player with an inferiority complex," its 75-units-per-year growth an index. Cheap units built for a market niche of people seeking an occasional dietary change of pace further convinced Martin of his predecessor's inferiority complex (see fig. 13.3). Ever greater profit in roadside Mexican food lay in convincing customers it was nothing new.

FIG. 13.4 Taco Bell pursued the small hamburger entrepreneur's double drive-through format as illustrated here in Indianapolis, Ind., in 1996.

FIG. 13.5 Named for the small shelters, often icehouses, where San Antonians historically socialized while eating, Taco Cabana, begun in 1978, founded patio dining in the Mexican fast-food segment. Despite its leisurely dining image, it catered to carryout and, as shown here in San Antonio in 1996, drive-through.

"What's a burger? Ground beef, cheese, tomato, lettuce, and sauce on a bun. Not very different from a taco." Reasoning like this led to Taco Bell's admission into the roadside market as a hamburger variant, ethnic in name only. Mass production of tacos further excited Taco Bell's executives, typical of fast food's assembly-line production. Borrowing again from the hamburger trade, the company bought the double drive-through pioneer, Hot 'n Now, to learn how to achieve 15-second service (see fig. 13.4).[13]

In 1985, one fast-food executive estimated Mexican fast food was roughly where hamburgers had been 15 years earlier, many mom-and-pop restaurants thriving but many selling out to growing regional chains.[14] Tabulation of the Mexican food segment in 1996 (see Table 13.1) revealed one chain, Taco Bell, towering over all others, which were small in unit numbers and earnings. Taco Bell yet ranked no higher than twelfth in sales among chain restaurants. Mexican roadside fare earned a firm but small niche.

Taco-named fast-food outlets led the way (see fig. 13.5). Taco John's, once priding itself on the title of the number two Mexican food franchiser, began in 1969 and headquartered in Cheyenne, Wyoming. Taco Time's angle was prefabricated restaurants for franchisees programmed to small details like napkins and utensils. Taco Time was founded in 1959 in Eugene, Oregon. Uncommon for its early origins (1940 in Dallas), El Chico required successively remodeled restaurant motifs to keep abreast of the changing competition. By the early 1990s, El Chico's prototype restaurants featured tile roofs, extensive glazing, and simulated adobe walls (see fig. 13.6). By the 1990s, a tortilla derivative—the wrap—gave new impetus to eating out as dashboard dining. Functioning and looking like tortillas, wraps were introduced to hold chicken, fish, and, for the health conscious, vegetables.[15]

When Taco Bell's profits began to sag in the 1990s, however, PepsiCo spun off the Mexican fast-food pioneer in 1997. Taco Bell rallied with another PepsiCo spinoff, KFC, to operate together in many stores. Their bundling benefited from diversification and convenience by offering in one location two different foods complementing each other. As did other big American restaurant chains, Taco Bell also opened stores internationally.[16]

With tacos having launched the roadside market in Mexican food, investors were intrigued to attempt other Mexican foods. Hence, residuals of Mexican cuisine entered the market but at the level of sit-down format and wider menus, potentially more lucrative than the humble taco. The Mexican segment, thus, followed the pattern of pizza and the Italian residuals.

Chi-Chi's

With the popularity of tacos well established by the roadside, attention turned back to the "Mexican cantina." These were restaurants with broad menus featuring Mexican, Tex-Mex, and other related fare housed in popularized Mexican settings.

Chi-Chi's was the largest chain among the Mexican dinner houses. In 1976, restauranteur Marno McDermott and investor Max McGee began Chi-Chi's in Minneapolis, further reinforcing the Midwest's title as a roadside restaurant hearth. Rapid expansion generated 195 units by 1987, 131 company-owned and 64 franchised. Typical of rapidly expanding restaurant chains, operations at the store level were overlooked. Chi-Chi's nonetheless built a firm reputation with a menu occupying middle ground between the two extremes of Mexican food, Tex-Mex and West Coast style. Margaritas at reduced prices were a signature item underlining the chain's stereotypical Mexican food and level above fast food. Further liberties were taken with buffalo wings and Mexican pizza as accompaniments to drinks at the bar.[17]

Festive colors—bright yellow, yellow-green, and pink—signaled Chi-Chi's unmistakable restaurants to passersby, associating Mexican food with

FIG. 13.6 El Chico, the oldest Mexican restaurant chain, appealed to historical and contemporary motifs. Note glass's prominence, a modernizing trait, as seen in Murfreesboro, Tenn., 1997.

popular symbols of Mexican fun and romanticism (see fig. 13.7). Broad and low, massing was complemented with details of stereotyped Mexican architecture, battered walls, vigas, and textured concrete simulating adobe. Inside open-air dining was suggested, lighting and tables divided by low walls adding to the airy feeling. Murals, pinatas, and striped walls supported the festive atmosphere. Servers in stereotypical Mexican peasant costumes completed the illusion of Mexican authenticity.[18]

FAST FOOD

Foodmaker, Inc., owner of the hamburger chain Jack in the Box, purchased Chi-Chi's in 1988, seeking diversification. In 1994 Chi-Chi's merged with El Torito, a dinner-house chain specializing in Mexican food. Their territories complemented, El Torito mainly in California and Chi-Chi's eastward from the Midwest with a few outlets in the South (see fig. 13.8).[19]

Feasibility of marketing ethnic cuisines became calculable by the time Mexican cuisine emerged popular. Authenticity was not the aim for many chain customers. One restauranteur was forced to close his Mexican restaurant in Denver, a city where Mexican food was very popular, and explained: "The problem was we were offering a *real* Mexican regional cuisine, not the cheese-laden, American-style Mexican menu people were familiar with. They didn't understand the full, ethnic flavors or even the concept itself." Echoed were the complaints of the Northeast's pizza lovers of 20 years earlier. The insatiable taste for novelty forced "splintering," genuine regional variations. But restauranteurs despaired, one exclaiming that "the fickle public doesn't give many points for longevity and consistency; its attention span is

TABLE 13.1 Leading Mexican Food Chains, 1996

Chain	Headquarters	Units Worldwide	Sales (in millions)	Sales Rank Top 300
Taco Bell	Irvine, Calif.	6,867	$4,416	6
Chi-Chi's	Irvine, Calif.	184	294	76
Del Taco	Laguna Hills, Calif.	300	235	97
El Torito	Irvine, Calif.	104	229	98
Taco John's	Cheyenne, Wyo.	466	166	127
Chevy's Mexican Restaurants	San Francisco	72	162	129
Taco Cabana	San Antonio	121	151	132
El Chico	Dallas	95	142	140
Don Pablo's	Bedford, Tex.	63	133	147
Taco Time	Eugene, Ore.	346	106	165
Acapulco Restaurants	Long Beach, Calif.	46	77	208
Pancho's Mexican Buffet	Ft. Worth	65	71	219
Taco Bueno	Carrollton, Tex.	107	69	227
Rio Bravo Cantina	Marietta, Ga.	30	66	230
Casa Olé Restaurants	Houston	49	65	232
The Green Burrito	Newport Beach, Calif.	134	46	284
Azteca Mexican Restaurants	Seattle	31	45	289

Source: Restaurants and Institutions 107 (July 15, 1997): 66.

FIG. 13.7 Chi-Chi's in Springfield, Ill., in 1996.

Taco Places and Mexican "Cantinas"

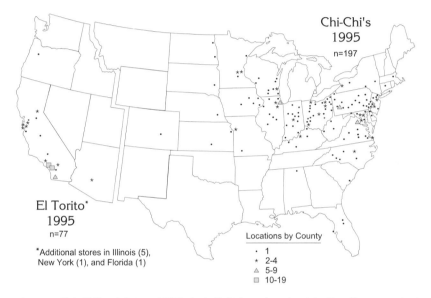

Chi-Chi's
1995
n=197

El Torito*
1995
n=77

*Additional stores in Illinois (5), New York (1), and Florida (1)

Locations by County

·   1
★   2-4
△   5-9
▢   10-19

FIG. 13.8 Chi-Chi's (*right*) and El Torito's (*left*) locations in 1995. Leading counties in the Chi-Chi's chain were: Cook (Chicago), Ill. (6 locations); Fairfax (Falls Church), Va. (6); Franklin (Columbus), Ohio (4); Hennepin (Minneapolis), Minn. and Marion (Indianapolis), Ind. (4 each). Leading counties in the El Torito chain were: Los Angeles (Los Angeles), Calif.; Orange (Santa Ana), Calif. (19 each); and San Diego (San Diego), Calif. (8).

a year or two at the best. More like six months. Then it craves novelty and excitement."[20]

Typical of some entrepreneurs to clone the latest promising initiatives, Chi-Chi's has been followed by a host of would-be competitors in the 1980s. Cantina del Rio in Columbus, Ohio, owned by Bob Evans, typified those intending to diversify existing chains. Tumbleweed Mexican Food and Grill in Louisville, Rio Bravo in Atlanta, Cucos in Metairie, Louisiana, and Casa Gallardo in St. Louis typified independent chains. In their implementation of a broad menu, sit-down dining, and inclusion of liquor, these casual Mexican restaurants rekindled some aspects of the original cantinas.[21]

Tacos and other Mexican foods pale in profit and popularity by comparison with pizza and other Italian foods. Yet they rank second in ethnic cuisine, both in eateries beside the road and at other restaurants. The hamburger directly sustained by America's love of beef continues to leave ethnic food, such as tacos, comparatively unintegrated into the roadside appetite. Hamburgers so predominate that tacos and other foods like pizza are, in the larger scheme of American restaurant eating habits, more like variety-offering alternatives than sound competitors.

Convenience and theming allied to ease Mexican cuisine—also denatured of its genuine ethnicity—into the American diet. The taco, a food of lowly origin and easily adapted to mass production, led the way to Mexican cuisine for Americans spending their discretionary income in roadside eateries. Tacos became another variation on America's beloved meat and cheese sandwich quickly prepared and quickly served in drive-ins and drive-throughs. Following the small-scale operators' pioneering of the market, huge corporate investors seized the initiative to dominate, standardizing the product. But with consumers ceaselessly seeking novelty, small entrepreneurs have continued their presence, introducing other Mexican fare. As the nation's Hispanic communities grew in size and affluence, "real" Mexican restaurants increasingly have come to the fore to drive more sophisticated preferences that may yet impact the roadside directly. For now the chain "cantina," with its highly standardized food venue, pitched for its suggestive qualities—mainstream tastes given an "ethnic" spin none too deviant and thus none too threatening.

FAST
FOOD

CHAPTER 14

Steak Places

W̶e turn here to the most elite yet popular American food—steak. Cheaper foods, comparatively easily prepared and more readily adapted to mass consumption—all those treated above—underwent substantial redefinition in the fast-food transformation to yield a new way to eat and in new place types. Was steak also converted to convenience? Who led the way? What was accomplished? Did theming assist?

Steak has long been immensely popular with Americans, the choicest cut of beef still Americans' favorite. Across the social spectrum, when most Americans envisioned a dining treat, steak was the feature around which the special occasion was structured. Its pretentious implications yet had normative meaning. Assuring its readers that newly inaugurated President Harry Truman was a "representative U.S. citizen," *Life* pointed out his love of steak. Perhaps it was another expression of a democratic culture also grasping for things upscale.[1] A steak dinner verified that the diner "had arrived." Americans tend not to brag over chicken and seafood consumed, but do recollect their steaks with gusto.

Despite its national appeal, however, steak has experienced a curious career as a food for the automobile traveler. Steak comprised a comparatively high-priced meal and never gained serious consideration by the hamburger chains pushing the fast-food transformation, although they could have had ready access as part of their beef supply. Commencing simultaneously with the hamburger chains in the 1950s, entrepreneurs launched separate steakhouse chains.[2] Although riding the franchise stampede to expansion along with other roadside entrepreneurs in the 1950s and 1960s, units neither multiplied as quickly nor achieved the total number they did among the other food chains.

Dinner Houses

Steak was upscale food associated with courses served in sit-down dining, hardly fit for the contrasting declassé drive-in, drive-through, or carry-

FAST FOOD

FIG. 14.1 Ollie Hammond's foreshadowed the venue of steakhouses 20 years hence. The reverse side of the chain's postcard promised high-quality steak guaranteed to suit the discriminating diner of the time by serving speedily, efficiently, and courteously.

out formats. Speed coupled with hash houses' minimum decor were not leading criteria. Propriety often dictated that steakhouses at least look expensive. Ollie Hammond's Steak Houses in California during World War II, for example, displayed chic streamlined modern architecture (see fig. 14.1). Many trying to minimize the cost of the steakhouses by seating customers in large rooms at tables not separated by partitions, a mess hall ambiance, initially were paid back in poor sales.

Dinner houses might have provided the model for inquiring steakhouse entrepreneurs, for dinner houses often featured steak in their menus to draw customers. Dinner houses emerged in America beginning in the nineteenth century and were a uniquely American format. The East Coast's seafood houses but especially Chicago's steakhouses after the Civil War pioneered the format.[3] Contrary to the frequent continental travelers' disdain for American ways of tasteless fare and eating as hurried, dinner houses were upscale places, seldom chains, serving a varied menu of fish and meat—often highlighting steak—and encouraging leisurely dining among intimates. Dinner houses ranked between restaurants and hotel dining rooms appealing to aristocratic tastes with foreign-sounding entrees in formal settings and the quick-meal venues making pretense neither to graceful dining nor fine cuisine. Especially with the automobile, dinner houses came of age beginning in the 1920s as Americans grew more affluent. Often situated just outside city limits, they might serve liquor without fear of the city's police surveillance. At the same time travel to them conjured a sense of outing for the diners. Their grilling or broiling preference perpetuated the national tradition for easy preparation, broiling especially delectable for those who chose to see what they would consume. Dinner-party members were commonly encouraged to select the cut of meat each would eat as part of the custom associated with this venue (see fig. 14.2). Often an open charcoal flame for the broiling enhanced the atmosphere, perhaps vestigial reference to the travelers' shared campfire. Sight and sound of one's meal in the making certainly unleashed a fuller sensory experience than preparation removed to a kitchen, whether staffed by aristocratic servants or fast-food wage earners. Dancing to a band or listening to piano music complemented in some places. Dinner houses gave fuller play to one's eating as more than physical necessity.

FIG. 14.2 Here George Diamond's epitomized the dinner houses' orientation, high-quality food—mostly steak—in plain view of cooking by the diner's own chef. George Diamond's also long bolstered Chicago's reputation for fine steakhouses.

FIG. 14.3 At the Flying M Café in Panguitch, Utah, travelers could dine on "de luxe juicy steaks" as well as "homemade biscuits and pies" asserted advertising on the reverse of this postcard.

By the 1950s dinner houses, however, were challenged as steak places. Gone with the automobility's mass appeal was the dinner house's tantalizing upscale vanity. In some locations steak could be eaten at unpretentious cafés (see fig. 14.3). No single format fully satisfied any longer. How could a costly food be made widely accessible without jeopardizing its pretentious association? The proper formula for a steak house, thus, puzzled investors.

Steaks were expensive food, too. In 1963, driven to low prices at Ponderosa's first restaurant, a nine-ounce steak with an eight-ounce baked potato, salad, and a dinner roll cost $1.39. This was in the era of fast-food giants transforming roadside consumption with 15-cent hamburgers and 12-cent french fries. McDonald's did not increase prices until early 1967 when its hamburgers were raised to 18 cents apiece, still far below any steak. Steak, thus, eventually renewed roadside competition with the prefix "budget," as in "budget steakhouse," affixed to its segment of the restaurant industry.[4]

Bonanza and Ponderosa

Bonanza (see fig. 14.4) and Ponderosa pioneered the successful budget steakhouses and long led them in annual profit. Each started in the Northeast, Bonanza in 1962 in Eastchester, New York, and Ponderosa in Westport, Connecticut, in 1963. Steak entrepreneurship, thus, did not begin in beef-growing country. Nor did many of its most profitable companies headquarter there. Entrepreneurs who profited from automobile-convenient customers often seemed unreflective about their market's regional preferences so long as they maneuvered entrance into the market and managed growth, to wit the pizza as well as the steakhouse barons.[5]

Popular culture begat popular culture and both Bonanza and Ponderosa took their names from the popular television show of the early 1960s, Bonanza for the series itself and Ponderosa for the cattle ranch in the series. Indicative of their big profit ambitions, the two chains began franchising soon after their founding, Bonanza in 1963 and Ponderosa in 1966. With 16 steakhouses throughout the East Coast by 1964, Diversa acquired the Bonanza chain and relocated its corporate offices to Dallas in 1965. Purchased by the Wyly Corporation in 1967, made a public stock company a year later, and numbering 602 units by 1976, Bonanza seemed to be an entrepreneurial brainchild likely to earn ever more profit. Attention to history at Bonanza's competitor, Ponderosa, however, revealed the often improvised and quixotic nature of steakhouse development also characteristic of automobile-convenient food services.

Dan R. Lasater, a Ponderosa founder, told it all in a 1973 interview. Like many founders of the American roadside services, Lasater bypassed a college education when he graduated from high school. Living in a trailer in Kokomo, Indiana, the son of a "poor" family, to use Lasater's own word, he gladly worked for a 60-cents-an-hour wage at McDonald's while learning its system as he moved from unit to unit helping revitalize them. "McDonald's

FIG. 14.4 Bonanza unit number 811 characterized the chain's motif. Upon entrance into a large open space, customers entered a cafeteria line with menu board from which they could order before dining at rugged wooden tables set with steak sauce and ketchup. In this view, several diners eat from their cafeteria tray, heedless of the lighting fixtures and decorations which alluded to the Old West. Budget steakhouses were spartan places in more than their fare.

was my way of life when I graduated. I didn't have anything else I wanted to do, and I really got into it."[6] Echoes of Fred Turner. Eager for his own business and sensing his capacity for greater income through ownership than earned wages, he persuaded a local auto dealer to open a hamburger stand on the city's bypass and let him manage it. Lasater and his patron profited and investigated a franchise with a national steakhouse chain. Dissatisfied with the chain's terms, Lasater's patron financed their own budget steakhouse. An architect joined as partner to design the building and Lasater managed the operations. Characteristic of budget steakhouse origins, Lasater's challenge spurred Bonanza to trademark the name "Ponderosa." Lasater countered by trademarking "Bonanza." Agreeing to settle their differences, the companies exchanged trademarks and returned to their original name. The duel was over.

While extending his hamburger chain as hedge, Lasater began franchising Ponderosa. No advertising was necessary in the speculative heyday of the 1960s' franchise boom; the interested asked Lasater for their opportunity. Wise in operations, but inexperienced in financing, Lasater's management drove Ponderosa into cash-flow problems. Although disaster was averted, Lasater quit to pursue leisure with his $30-million bounty.[7] Between mid-1971 and early 1975, Ponderosa's units had jumped from 118 to 497.[8]

Budget steakhouses improvised a niche just above the hamburger chains. Then, in the mid-1970s, due to high beef prices and the 1974 recession, customers stopped coming. Emerson explained that the steakhouse niche had begun with customers who moved up to budget steak from fast-food hamburgers when the economy permitted. With increased prices, however, fast-food converts returned to hamburgers. Thus the precarious budget steakhouse niche developed a boom and bust cycle.[9]

Bonanza and Ponderosa survived the crisis by appealing to slightly more affluent customers. With prices raised, Bonanza's chief executive explained, "Our check average is now $2.75 [$2.40 in the early 1970s] which is high for a Bonanza restaurant of the past and brings us more into the middle income base. We have expanded the menu. Our target market is a stable base, not price consciousness." Salad bars—not the red meat favorite of the original budget steakhouse customers—was the principal addition on which Bonanza hung its recovery. Shades of upscale dining were suggested when beer and wine were tested at several units in the late 1970s.[10] They were not added as regular features, however. By 1979, Ponderosa's most expensive items (chiefly, T-bone, prime rib, and extra-cut sirloin) earned 31 percent of the company's sales, whereas four years before they earned 8 percent. Middle- and lower-priced entrees decreased at the same time respectively from 44 to 32 percent and 48 to 37 percent.[11] Ponderosa's answer to the steakhouse puzzle, thus, was a niche clearly separate from the hamburger lovers. The era of budget steakhouses was in decline. Could the regal steak become everyman's meal by the highway?

Sizzler

Sizzler, the single most profitable steakhouse in 1990, experienced the same initial trajectory as Bonanza and Ponderosa. Founded in 1957, Sizzler was bought 10 years later by Collins Foods International, a food-service company that diversified with 200 Kentucky Fried Chicken units by 1977 to strengthen itself against the volatile steakhouse market. Sizzler further diversified by adding inexpensive lunches for cheaper customers and more expensive steak cuts for wealthier customers, the whole intended to broaden the chain's appeal. In 1976 Sizzler also installed place-product-packaging that was more "refined," as it was termed, to appeal through flattery. By 1978, Sizzler numbered 55 company-owned and 240 franchised units. Initiated also was a formal education for new staff, its director emphasizing a system that was fast and produced consistent results. Fast-food techniques were being applied to a venue disdaining lower social implications.[12]

Victoria Station

Some steakhouses attempted to mask the industrialized system of fast food they adopted by staging an "experience" for diners. The illusion of participating in an extraordinary circumstance was an old roadside ploy, but systematized at a new level of themed ambiance. Victoria Station offered a good example. Its founders were graduates of Cornell University's Hotel and Restaurant Administration course who added experience in brokerage

Steak Places

FIG. 14.5 The nostalgic lure of a railroad dining car—an exotic foreign one at that—beckoned to customers approaching a Victoria Station.

Locations by County

· 1
★ 2-3

n=22

FIG. 14.6 Victoria Station targeted big city markets as shown in this map of its locations in 1973. Leading counties were: San Francisco (San Francisco), Calif. (3 locations) and Alameda (Oakland), Calif. (2).

and airline management before they opened their chain in San Francisco in 1969. Prime rib served in railroad cars with decor from the British Railways of the 1890s was their venue and format (see fig. 14.5). Old baggage carts became room dividers and salad bars. Customers were greeted at the door by large refrigerated cases of the prime rib from which they would order. Dining cars were carpeted from wall to wall to make the experience amenable to domestic standards of comfort. Borrowing from the motel industry which earlier appreciated the quest for casual access, Victoria Station provided large parking lots (not valets) and coatracks near tables (not coat-check rooms). Victoria Station garnered considerable comment in the trade literature for its stunning contrivances (see fig. 14.6).[13]

Victoria Station was pitched to singles, couples, and families who could not afford high prices yet hungered for cooking they did not want to do themselves, but its prices proved relatively high for the clientele. A dinner including salad and wine cost $15 per couple and the average luncheon was $4. Lower-priced roast-beef dinners—$4.75 to $5.75—sold the most, not the advertised prime rib. By the early 1980s, Victoria Station failed, victim mostly to boredom with the limited menu and format that were initially so attractive. A diversified menu did not salvage the chain because customers refused to think of it except in its original terms.[14] Themed steakhouses, thus, originally proved short-lived gambits, the more frequent their change, the shorter their customers' attention (see fig. 14.7).

FIG. 14.7 Old San Francisco, a survivor of the once-popular themed steakhouse, began in San Antonio in 1968. The chain played on the stuff of popular culture, dedicated to the memory of a Texas Ranger and his sweetheart with the format of an Old West dance hall. (*Source:* Courtesy: Old San Francisco.)

FIG. 14.8 Early Mr. Steaks were direct, their postcards advertising that the "menu features luncheons, sandwiches and USDA choice steaks at popular prices."

Mr. Steak

Few pioneering budget steakhouse chains escaped the niche's volatility. Mr. Steak's founder, defining the niche succinctly as "that untapped market of middle-income family dining, without liquor or a high tab," kept expenses low by advertising franchises on the restaurant's placemats and building restaurants with plain decor. Some referred euphemistically to Mr. Steak's long and low buildings with unadorned picture windows, red and black interiors, and mansard roofs as having "masculine qualities." They were, in fact, indistinguishable from most roadside sprawl except for their logo (a steer in a chef's hat). Customers arrived at Mr. Steak to a severe format, reinforcing the chain's inexpensive menu ($1.39 to $3.79 for a steak dinner) (see fig. 14.8).[15] Peaking at about 300 units in the late 1970s, Mr. Steak declined thereafter, never able to adjust to the changed market.[16] Following the 1970s' combined onslaught of recession and rising beef prices and the 1980s' decline in beef consumption (from 88.9 pounds per capita consumption in 1976 to 65 pounds in 1989),[17] Mr. Steak diversified its menu with "lite" fare and introduced more contemporary architecture. Chicken, seafood, and salads complemented the new interiors' softer and richer colors of beiges and browns, ceiling beams, plants, and pictures. Gone was the interior look of the rugged ranchhouse's great hall. Appreciating that its niche was won from the child-driven hamburger chains, Mr. Steak was the only prominent steakhouse chain to assault that competition in its advertisements, one showing a happy child surrounded by premiums from a hamburger chain while the parents were upset with their dictated dining. Customers could not accept the redefinition and by the 1990s Mr. Steak all but vanished. By 1996 Mr.

Steak shrank to 13 units (two in Denver; and one each in Broomfield, Colorado; Columbus Heights, Minnesota; Bloomington, Minnesota; St. Charles, Missouri; Independence, Missouri; Yuba City, California; Lafayette, Indiana; Fargo, North Dakota; Rapid City, South Dakota; Strongville, Ohio; and Coeur d'Alene, Idaho).[18] Sizzler followed the same trajectory despite its earlier described redefinition and filed for bankruptcy in 1996.[19]

Other Chains

By contrast, Golden Corral, begun in 1972, just before the onset of troubles in the roadside restaurant trade, sustained a fairly evenly distributed national chain by 1995 (see fig. 14.9). A good deal of its success was attributable to the long tenure of its uppermost management; founder James H. Maynard and his director since 1984 Theodore M. Fowler were still at their jobs in the early 1990s. With their patient leadership, Golden Corral had been able to shift from a budget steakhouse to a buffet with budget steak.[20]

Testifying to others' leadership were the steakhouse clones. Hoping to balloon profits through a rapidly franchised empire of budget operations in the 1960s were Bahama Steak House, Blaz'r Steaks, Buffalo Bill's, Char-Steak House, Golden West Steaks, Long Horn Steak Pits, Maverick Steak Houses, Sir Loin's, and Tad's Steak Houses, to name a few. Exemplifying was Golden West's steak for adults and souvenir horseshoe coins, wooden nickels, cowboy hats, games, and coin purses to placate children less interested in food. Golden West Steaks promised franchisees no more than four weeks' training and the on-site instruction at the start. Western Sizzlin' Steak House emerged

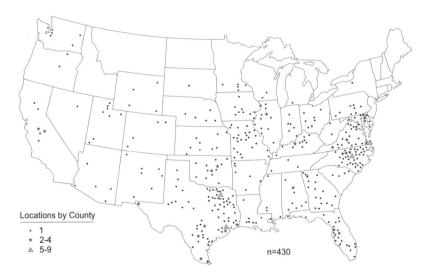

Locations by County

- · 1
- ★ 2-4
- △ 5-9

n=430

FIG. 14.9 Except for New England, New Jersey, North Dakota, Montana, and Idaho, Golden Corral's distribution in 1995 was national. Leading counties were: Harris (Houston), Tex. (7 locations); Chesapeake (Virginia Beach), Va.; Dallas (Dallas), Tex.; and Wake (Raleigh), N.C. (5 each).

TABLE 14.1 Leading Steak Chains, 1996

Chain	Headquarters	Units Worldwide	Sales (in millions)	Sales Rank Top 300
Outback Steakhouse	Tampa	373	$1,077	29
Sizzler	Los Angeles	404	750	38
Golden Corral	Raleigh, N.C.	440	710	40
Ponderosa	Dallas	566	633	47
Ryan's Family Steak Houses	Greer, S.C.	281	597	49
Lone Star Steakhouse and Saloon	Wichita	225	471	58
Western Sizzlin'	Roanoke, Va.	260	330	69
Tony Roma's Famous for Ribs	Dallas	182	321	73
Quincy's Family Steakhouses	Spartanburg, S.C.	199	259	88
Stuart Anderson's Restaurants	Los Altos, Calif.	102	255	89
Damon's the Place for Ribs	Columbus, Ohio	115	250	91
Steak and Ale	Dallas	144	206	109
Ruth's Chris Steak House	Metairie, La.	55	175	123
Bonanza	Dallas	156	140	142
Longhorn Steaks	Atlanta	82	136	145
Morton's of Chicago	Chicago	34	116	157
Western Steer	Claremont, N.C.	86	110	162
Sirloin Stockade	Hutchinson, Kan.	73	93	178
Hoss's Steak and Sea House	Duncansville, Pa.	40	80	204
Roadhouse Grill	Ft. Lauderdale	38	71	220
Hungry Hunter	San Diego	38	70	226
Palm Restaurants	Washington, D.C.	15	65	233
Mountain Jack's	San Diego	36	63	239

Source: Restaurants and Institutions 107 (July 15, 1997): 66.

from the clones as one of the more successful, employing with many a simplified residential architecture housing cafeteria and carryout. Some of these clones failed while holding firm to their original venues; some continued as clones following new directions for steakhouses.[21]

Steak's incredible volatility among the roadside restaurant chains reared again in the 1990s. At the decade's dawn, Bonanza and Ponderosa, as budget steakhouses, clung to their leadership because an adventurous multimillionaire, John Werner Kluge, bought them as reasonable investment risks. Compared to his electronics and media business, the two steak chains required unskilled labor while promising a traditionally high profit-to-investment ratio. Budget steakhouses, however, declined in mid-decade as the new casual dining group moved up, drawing on upscale customers, yet below the highest paying. Outback Steakhouse, staging a faux-Australian theme, ranked number one in sales at this writing (see Table 14.1), one of several spectacular members of the casual group barely recognizable a decade earlier as a group. Perhaps an enduring formula for steak's mass consumption along the roadside had been devised.[22]

Small-scale steakhouses, meanwhile, flourished through the chains' restless search for big profit. They were 35 percent of the steak restaurant market in the early 1990s despite the downturn in red-meat consumption among Americans. The reason remained—steak was rich people's food. Those who went out to eat a good steak dinner were able to overlook the chains' cheaper prices and disdained their plebeian formats. They expected instead distinguished service of a distinctive meal. As the owner of a successful Chicago steakhouse explained, his customers liked to be greeted at the door, served each course of their meal, and be introduced to their chef. Clinching the aristocratic deference to individualized taste, the restauranteur ordered the chef to cook another steak if the customer was not satisfied with the order.[23]

Steak's curious roadside career followed a boom-and-bust cycle. Entrepreneurs of speculative impulse came and went without intention of long-term commitment to steak as roadside fare. Mass consumption seemed possible only when good economic conditions sustained budget venues. No Kroc, Thomas, Sanders, Galardi, DeLuca, or Monaghan was to be found in the chronicles of steakhouse chains. Steaks proved to be a high-priced food for high-priced speculation unsympathetic to the plebeian roadside. High-priced places serving those on an elegant outing remained a persistent strata of the market helping to define the chain's format and venues by contrast. At the time of this writing, the newest push by chains for a steakhouse niche was casual dining, a combination of upscale appeal with moderate prices. Nearly extinct were the original budget operations with their cafeteria lines and mess hall seating. Can the new wave win a permanent niche with the chains that provided other road food? The question will be taken up in the following chapter.

CHAPTER 15

Concept Restaurants

ost of America's roadside restaurants have been configured around quick service, from wayside stands to sit-down places incorporating soda fountains, tables, and booths, to indoor and outdoor walk-ups, to double drive-throughs. The hamburger was central to the creation of roadside restaurants, and, accordingly, the proliferation of restaurant chains. As we have seen, however, various other foods also thrived on the road-side—ice cream, breakfast food, chicken, seafood, pizza, tacos, and steaks. And not all restaurants were quick service in orientation for, as we have described in previous chapters, some restauranteurs went upscale to create "destination" restaurants, places that attracted for decor as well as for food.

We should not be surprised that such entrepreneurs, seizing on various themes or concepts, drove forward chain development built around place-concepts—chains featuring signature food but, more important, attractive restaurant ambiance. Concept restaurants offered distinctive "place experience" symbolized by layout and decor, but reflected as well in the kinds of patrons attracted as consumers of distinctive lifestyles.[1] Concept restaurants have been categorized variously—casual dining (usually moderately priced), formal dining (usually high-priced), and ethnic (ranging in price). Ethnic foods invite decors reminiscent of national origins. So also has region played a role, restaurants configured to represent one or another section of the United States.

The special packaging of place is a form of commodification.[2] Places are created to appeal to specific appetites defined not only in terms of food, but also in terms of environment. Consumed is a place package—food, service, and entertainment. Included is the "self-entertainment" of people watching and being watched by others. The whole is encapsulated and signified by visual, aural, tactile, and even olfactory surrounds. Patrons are linked with others in their consumption of food, but, more importantly, they are linked with each other by their mutual experiencing of a novel context. In these places, eating becomes more a means to an end, a way of being placed or located in a context of social significance. Food and place are consumed as status symbols.

Concept restaurants are a part of a larger trend in American marketing called "theming" by various commentators. Sociologist Mark Gottdiener, in his *Theming of America: Dreams, Visions, and Commercial Spaces,* focuses on the shopping mall and the theme park.[3] Consumers are seen as buying experiences and not just products and services. Where one buys is as important as, if not more important than, what one buys. Geographers David Bell and Gill Valentine describe eating places as "total consumption packages" with the "act of eating out . . . a container of many social and culture practices, norms and codes."[4] They emphasize the performance aspect of food service centered on personnel who perform in carefully scripted "place ballets," server dress and decorum carefully related to restaurant decor and food.

Programmatic Architecture

Decor may be the most important dimension of place packaging. Through the organization, furnishing, and decoration of interior space a sign system is created conducive to particular behaviors. Architectural structuring, in other words, functions to facilitate if not encourage specific programs—food production, food delivery, and various forms of related socializing. Especially important is the manipulation of space through sensory perception. Important as well is the play with symbols, the use of simile and metaphor. Is the restaurant to seem quiet, restful, private, contemplative? Is anonymity to be encouraged? Or is it to be hyperactive, inviting to physical activity, exciting to social interaction? Or is the restaurant to be a mix of the two, different activities in separate zones perhaps?[5] Wrote one designer:

> If the restaurant is romantic, the feeling is conveyed from the specially chosen wooden panels to the custom-crafted light fixtures. Sophisticated lighting systems add theatrical touches, flooding chosen objects with intense colors, dimming automatically as the sky grows dark. If fun is the emphasis, electric colors shout the idea: murals emerge—literally—from the walls. Noise is strategically reverberated off hard surfaces so that it even sounds like everyone's having a good time.[6]

We have already seen Langley's Marine Grill in Portland, Maine, its interior contrived as the deck of a sailing ship (see fig. 11.6). Witness here the Lucca Restaurant in Los Angeles, its dining room configured like an Italian street festooned for a holiday (see fig. 15.1). Witness also the Brown Derby Restaurant, haunt in the 1930s and 1940s of Hollywood celebrities (see fig. 15.2). The Brown Derby took programmed architecture to its fullest development, its theme presented forcefully both inside and outside. The building stood as a sign of itself—a giant derby hat. Produced was an icon of place very legible in the city scene, and, accordingly, memorable as a landmark. Once

FIG. 15.1 Lucca Restaurant, Los Angeles, ca. 1930. The postcard caption reads: "One of the most colorful restaurants in America, with the charm of the old world in a new world setting."

FIG. 15.2 The Brown Derby Restaurant, Los Angeles, ca. 1950. The Brown Derby became one of the city's major landmarks, a symbol of its movie industry.

celebrity status attached, however, the restaurant became an icon of social connection, a place to be for those seeking and pretending social status. One went to the Brown Derby not so much for food as to see and be seen. Few programmed places were ever so successful.

Whimsical contrivances characterized all manner of restaurants from roadside stands to dinner houses. Southern California's mild climate, which sustained year-round automobility and encouraged light construction inviting to architectural experimentation, led the way. Los Angeles was the leader in exotica, borrowing from Hollywood movie lots with set designers contributing directly to restaurant design. Jim Heimann and Rip Georges's *California Crazy: Roadside Vernacular Architecture* offers vivid testimony with its photos of log cabins, Hansel and Gretel cottages, Chinese pagodas, giant coffeepots, and so on.[7] Will the Hoot Hoot Ice Scream stand (configured as a giant owl) or the Tail O' The Pup stand (configured as a giant hot dog) or Randy's Donut Stand (with its giant donut atop) ever be forgotten?

We hasten to re-emphasize, however, that such exaggerated whimsy was the exception and not the rule. Banks and other lenders resisted the financing of purpose-built commercial buildings that could not be easily reused in cases of business failure. Even the carefully built, more durable buildings of roadside commerce were difficult to finance let alone the flimsy exotic windmills, tepees, and lighthouses. Place-product-packaging embraced more customary architecture, building forms that were at once functional and more flexible—buildings that could be altered readily to meet changing needs. Programmatic architecture attracted because of its novelty, but novelty was something that needed always to change, yesterday's enthusiasms giving way to today's and tomorrow's. Restauranteurs needed to upgrade constantly—to appear progressive by being responsive to changing fads and fashions. Central to place-product-packaging was standardization. A chain's restaurants needed to be distinctive, but within narrow ranges of acceptability—"difference in sameness."

Ethnic Orientations

Ethnic food clearly invited reinforcement through specially stylized restaurant decors. Brought to the fore were not only design vocabularies reminiscent of foreign lands, but also simulated restaurant formats typical abroad. We have visited taco and Mexican restaurants, noting the Spanish "cantina" themes operative in such chains as Taco Bell and Chi-Chi's. And so

FIG. 15.3 Ye English Inn, Hollister, Mo., ca. 1960.

also have we noted Mediterranean inspirations playing out across America's pizza and Italian restaurant chains such as the Olive Garden. Tacos and pizza proved very popular by the roadside, whereas other foods of ethnic association have had but modest or no impact, including English, German, Scandinavian, and Greek food, as well as Chinese and other Oriental cuisines.

England's food tastes, never held in high esteem in America, played out most vigorously with the 1960s' enthusiasm for fish and chips. Many servicemen returned from Britain at the end of World War II, and many postwar tourists as well, were enamored with English pubs and old coaching inns. Elite tastes in American domestic architecture favored English revival ornamentation in the 1920s and 1930s. Not surprisingly, more than a few restaurants with "Olde English" decor appeared in affluent suburbs around every American city, and in upscale resorts also. One such English transplant was Ye English Inn on Lake Taneycomo in the Ozarks of Missouri (see fig. 15.3). Chains were launched around the pub idea, for example Chicago-based Barnaby's English Pub which, despite the name, featured American food—hamburgers and pizza—in addition to draft beer.

German-Americans once comprised large self-conscious communities in many of America's largest cities, and in large rural sections of Pennsylvania, the midwestern states, and Texas. Indeed, more American families today claim a German background than claim English or any other origin. The likes of sauerbraten and wiener schnitzel were once quite prevalent in many American homes at special occasions. Undoubtedly, the early popularity of the hot dog in the United States derived from the dependence of German families of modest means on the likes of bratwurst and other sausages. Important wherever there were German speakers in large numbers were beer gardens and music halls, restaurant venues all but eliminated from the American scene by the "culture cleansing" of World War I and the national Prohibition that followed. After World War II, however, dinner houses built around German cuisine enjoyed limited popularity, especially in areas with residual German, Austrian, and Swiss communities. At Frankenmuth, Michigan, for example, success with fried chicken prompted the Zehnder family to double their food-service capacity with the Bavarian Inn (see fig. 15.4). There food and architecture spoke of southern Germany as did the costumes worn by service personnel.

Each immigrant group to come to the United States spawned its own restaurants, some venues popularized across the general population, but most not. In the 1950s and 1960s, an enthusiasm for the Swedish smorgasbord swept the country, a variation on the cafeteria line, and a predecessor of today's buffet restaurants (see fig. 15.5). Some groups, like the Greeks, moved substantially into restaurant ownership. We have already discussed the Greek-American influence in developing the nation's confectionery stores and soda fountains. Large numbers of Chinese-Americans also used restaurant ownership as a means of economic advancement. Many dishes, like chop suey, were contrived and promoted for American tastes—rather like the development of pizza later on. But, unlike pizza, Chinese food has had

FIG. 15.4 Frankenmuth
Bavarian Inn, Franken-
muth, Mich., ca. 1960.

FAST
FOOD

FIG. 15.5 Bit of Sweden
of Hollywood, Los
Angeles, ca. 1955.

only minimal impact on the roadside. Family-owned mom-and-pop operations primarily, Chinese restaurants have favored traditional storefronts in
central cities and on small-town main streets, and in shopping centers.
The highest densities are in the nation's "Chinatowns" with tourism supporting their concentration.

Traditionally, the delivery of Chinese food in restaurants has been highly
personalized, restaurant success hinging on the competency of the chef
and the friendliness of its wait staff. By employing relatives, labor costs are
kept very low. Consequently, attempts to franchise Chinese cuisine have
not proven successful. Early attempts at roadside orientation included John-
ny Quong's Chinafood Kitchen Drive-In chain in Salt Lake City. Out front

FIG. 15.6 Woo's Pagoda Restaurant, Eau Claire, Wis., ca. 1950.

FIG. 15.7 Moon Temple Restaurant, Seattle, ca. 1950.

loomed a great sign with the figure of a Chinese doll advertising "Quickee Chickee."[8] May Loo's Chop Chop chain, featuring precooked food, was launched in Los Angeles. Rickshaw Boy originated in Denver and the Chopsticks System in Utica, New York. San Antonio's Quik Wok and Youngstown, Ohio's Charlie Chan's were both owned by General Mills for short periods as that company experimented with various restaurant foods. In 1988, there were approximately 80,500 outlets operated by the top 100 restaurant chains, but only 26 restaurants were classified as Oriental. At the same time, there were some 17,800 independent Oriental restaurants operating.[9] Chinese restaurants ran the gamut from gaudily ornamented decors (see fig. 15.6) to crisply simplistic formats (see fig. 15.7). Both could be distinctly "Oriental"

TABLE 15.1 Leading Asian Food Chains, 1996

Chain	Headquarters	Units Worldwide	Sales (in millions)	Sales Rank Top 300
Panda Express	S. Pasadena, Calif.	228	$145	138
Benihana	Miami	59	118	154
Manchu Wok	Ontario, Calif.	215	80	203
Yoshinoya Beef Bowl	Torrance, Calif.	90	56	254

Source: Restaurants and Institutions 107 (July 15, 1997): 66.

in implication. Most of America's Chinese food was Cantonese, being introduced initially in San Francisco during the Gold Rush days.

Japanese cuisine, unlike Chinese, did lend itself to chain development—everything from quick service to dinner-house formats—but on a very limited basis. Japanese food was viewed as more upscale. Several restaurant chains were launched by Japanese corporations, for example the Yoshinoya Company's Beef Bowl chain opened in Los Angeles and Denver in 1979. One of the chain's largest franchisees was Kikkoman, the American soy sauce manufacturer.[10] Japanese-Americans were also active. Rocky Aoki's Benihana National Corporation introduced Miami Noodle Time to south Florida, a chain quickly renamed Teriyaki USA. Offered were chicken, beef, and vegetable teriyaki, Japanese dumplings (filled with shrimp or crab), and a teriyaki hamburger (a burger patty dipped in teriyaki sauce and served with cooked onions).[11] Benihana scored its biggest success, however, with its steakhouses, which combined "good food with an unusual atmosphere and a theatrical and entertaining style of service." By 1986, Benihana of Tokyo had grown to 37 company-owned and 10 franchised locations. Offered was the "teppanyaki" style of cooking with customers seated around large grills. "A Japanese chef makes a show of twirling knives while chopping vegetables and slicing meats at the table, before grilling the customer's dinner in front of him."[12]

After World War II, Polynesian themes, if not food, made their appearance as a kind of restaurant exotica. Don the Beachcomber in Hollywood featured exotic rum cocktails and suggestive South Pacific decor with palm trees. Trader Vic's opened in 1937 in San Francisco, but spread after the war into big-city downtown hotel locations, and eventually into the suburbs as well. Trader Vic's offered a kind of theater, its Polynesian orientation having little to do with food and much to do with visual excitement. With the Korean and Vietnam wars came Korean and Vietnamese restaurants introduced by new immigrants, many displaced by war.

Despite such ventures as the Bombay Palace chain launched in New York City in 1979, Indian food and decor has not been successfully franchised. Indeed, even small independent Indian restaurants are few and far between outside the nation's largest metropolises, and its university or college towns. Middle Eastern cuisine is similarly restricted geographically. Exceptions, of course, can always be noted. Near San Jose State University in the 1970s thrived the Queen of the Orient Drive-In offering falafel, shish-kabob, and other Middle Eastern specialties. But fundamental to the restaurant's success was its hamburger emphasis as a quick-service place oriented to students.[13] Asian food is purveyed in the United States primarily by small family-owned and operated restaurants. Large corporate chains built around Asian food concepts remain underrepresented among the nation's largest restaurant operations (see Table 15.1).

Destination Restaurants

Concept Restaurants

Restaurant chains, most oriented to fast food, were in full swing by the mid-1980s. In 1985, 1,446 chains with more than 11 units under the same name operated 102,000 of the nation's approximately 301,000 restaurants.[14] Thus the vast majority of American restaurants were independently operated. They were not chain-affiliated. Included were the host of mom-and-pop operations, but included also were the giants like the two Zehnder restaurants at Frankenmuth, Michigan. In 1994, the top 100 independents accounted for some $850 million in sales.[15] Most of the largest independents were located in the nation's big cities (see fig. 15.8). Most operated in the upscale dinner-house mode, profits engendered substantially through the sale of alcoholic beverages. Important in many sections of the nation, especially in the upper Middle West, were the supper clubs. Usually located beyond the jurisdiction of municipal liquor laws, supper clubs thrived by the roadside as a kind of weekend entertainment destination (see fig. 15.9).

Many highway dinner houses started from wayside stands. Knott's Berry Farm was by no means alone. Angelo Xidis's short-order restaurant at Gulfport, Mississippi, was another example (see fig. 15.10). Angelo's Place grew from an outdoor barbecue pit and adjacent lunch counter into a large

Locations by County

- · 1
- ★ 2-4
- △ 5-9
- ◉ 20 or more
- *Sales in $ millions

FIG. 15.8 One hundred largest independent restaurants, 1994. (*Source:* Jeff Weinstein, "R&I Top 100," *Restaurants and Institutions* 104 [March 15, 1994]: 34-44.)

FIG. 15.9 Jim and Rudy's Riverside Club, Iron Mountain, Mich., ca. 1950.

FIG. 15.10 Angelo's Place, Gulfport, Miss., ca. 1930.

FIG. 15.11 Angelo's Place, Gulfport, Miss., ca. 1950.

FIG. 15.12 Kapok Tree Inn, Clearwater, Fla., ca. 1960.

FIG. 15.13 Kapok Tree Inn, Clearwater, Fla., ca. 1960.

dining room (see fig. 15.11). The restaurant's postcard boasted: "Nationally famous for its spaghetti, flounders, steaks, and delicious salads. This huge building is one of the finest constructions in the South, built entirely of steel, tile and glass." North of Clearwater, Florida, also in a resort area, the Kapok Tree Inn grew to a giant complex of dining rooms, gift shops, outdoor gardens, and parking lots (see figs. 15.12 and 15.13). Here was an extraordinary tourist attraction in its own right, the excesses of classical Athens, Pompeii, and Renaissance Venice all wrapped into one.

Not all "independents" were independent. Some of the largest restaurant companies in the 1990s operated either different restaurants under different names or several very small chains each with distinctive packaging. Some functions, like financing, franchising, accounting, purchasing, and training, were coordinated centrally, with each restaurant carefully configured according to its local market. Specialty Restaurants Corporation, founded in 1959 with a single Polynesian-themed restaurant, expanded into a wide array of dinner houses with names like Dockside Broiler, Ports O'Call, Pieces of Eight, Baby Doe's Matchless Mine. Perhaps the company's most novel formats involved airport locations with World War II aviation themes—the 94th Aero Squadron, the 57th Fighter Group, the 101st Bomb Group.[16] Lettuce Entertain You Enterprises operates with such names as Bub City, Cafe Ba-Ba-Reeba, Ed Debevic's, R. J. Grunts, and Scoozi.

The 1990s saw maturation of a new food and adult-entertainment segment in the restaurant industry. New was Eeerie Entertainment's Jekyll and Hyde in New York City, offering an adult haunted house where patrons were urged to "eat, drink and be wary," the menu built around such offerings as the "Mummy Burger." In Los Angeles the company opened Dive, a submarine theme restaurant that took guests on an underwater voyage through a fantasy world of computer-controlled video animation, animatronics, and special effects.[17] True to its theme, the restaurant featured big-bun "submarine" sandwiches. In Seattle, the Entros Restaurant opened with its sophisticated computer games intended to prompt "unstructured mingling" among patrons. Sought were "the best elements of a dinner party, salon, art commune, and Kiwanis club," the whole billed as an "intelligent amusement park."[18]

Perhaps the most successful of all the theme restaurant chains is the Hard Rock Café, where hamburgers mix with music and memorabilia from Elvis Presley to John Lennon. First opened in London in 1970 to attract homesick expatriate Americans, the chain spread worldwide. A 1950s roadside ambiance prevails at its Los Angeles location. "Bolstering the rock-and-roll theme is a roadside-diner menu, faithfully served up by waitresses dressed in white diner uniforms and bobby socks," wrote one journalist. "The menu focuses on burgers, sandwiches, and other diner staples like pork chops and chili. The back of the menu is reserved for soda fountain items."[19] Rock-and-roll had a highway implication in the dress and gyrations of such performers as Elvis Presley, rooted, as they were, in the 1950s biker culture. At places like the Hard Rock Café, the concept-based restaurant reached a peak of perfection. Eating provided excuse to see and be seen in swirls of theater, much of the excitement coming from the patrons themselves.

Casual Restaurants

The successes scored by the large "independents" as destination restaurants, and the demonstrated value of theme decors generally, prompted a new kind of restaurant chain—the casual restaurant. Several underlying currents came to the surface simultaneously. First came the baby boomers, swelling the young adult population. Second came the rise of the "singles" market, reflecting substantial change in American lifestyles, the traditional family-based household no longer so prevalent. Third came increased informality in dress and behavior in public places, reflecting the increased affluency of Americans generally as the lower middling classes came into their own as consumers of leisure time. Casual informality also reflected a desire to slow down the pace of life pushed to the fast track by corporate America's squeezing of efficiencies from office workers and other employees. Within the restaurant industry entrepreneurs searched for a middle ground between the economy and functionality of fast food and the extravagance and formality of upscale dining.

Concept Restaurants

Restaurants built around an enlarged and often centrally located bar became a new formula. Restaurant patrons were encouraged to "mingle" and, whether actively interacting or merely watching, to be entertained. Carefully integrated were color, lighting, seating arrangement, and other design details to engender environments of social connectivity. The idea was to contain an evening's recreation. "It used to be that people would go out to eat and then to a show," observed one restaurant designer. "But now . . . the eating out is becoming the customer's entertainment event. So he has to be provided with an exciting environment." Designers sought to give customers "a pleasing combination of hurly-burly and intimacy." "When the customer stands up, he should feel a part of the crowd. When he sits down, he should have his privacy."[20] Restaurants were conceptualized like theaters—stages for acting out with smiles and engendered good humor all around.

Casual restaurants evolved out of two venues, the singles' bar and the "gourmet" hamburger restaurant. The T.G.I. Friday's chain illustrates the former and the Ground Round chain the latter. The first Friday's opened in 1965 on Manhattan's Upper East Side, the inspiration of Alan Stillman, a New York businessman. He viewed his restaurant as a place for young singles to gather, a place built around quality hamburgers and a high-volume liquor business. Into the neighborhood's high-rise apartments had come an influx of young unmarrieds with good jobs and thus money to spend.[21] There, as the stereotyping of times emphasized, young lawyers and advertising account executives could meet attractive fashion models and airline stewardesses. In 1972, Dan Scoggin acquired franchising rights to several western cities where he perfected the Friday's format. Decorations ran to the eclectic, everything from moose heads to racing sculls, or what Scoggin termed "elegant litter."[22] Featured were staged antics like waiters in gorilla suits celebrating the start of each weekend. In 1975, Friday's was sold to the Minneapolis-based Carlson Companies, developer of the Radisson hotel chain. Stillman left the company with Scoggin staying on as the chain's chief executive officer. The chain continued its expansion primarily through build-to-suit, freestanding units on leased land, with property owners providing half of the cost of building construction. Favored were suburban shopping-center locations. By 1987 there were 116 restaurants open, and

TABLE 15.2 Leading Casual Restaurant Chains, 1996

Chain	Headquarters	Units Worldwide	Sales (in millions)	Sales Rank Top 300
Applebee's	Overland Park, Kan.	819	$1,540	18
T.G.I. Friday's	Dallas	394	1,145	26
Chili's	Dallas	519	1,104	27
Ruby Tuesday	Mobile, Ala.	319	546	53
Bennigan's	Dallas	226	448	61
Hooters	Atlanta	189	325	71
Red Robin	Englewood, Colo.	130	293	77
Ground Round	Braintree, Mass.	189	285	79
Houlihan's	Kansas City, Mo.	91	241	94
Fuddrucker's	Danvers, Mass.	208	236	95
Planet Hollywood	Orlando	55	222	102
Hard Rock Café	Orlando	76	216	107
Black-Eyed Pea	Scottsdale, Ariz.	126	189	117
Houstons	Atlanta	41	177	120
O'Charley's	Nashville	74	163	128
Chart House	Solana Beach, Calif.	64	160	130
Cheesecake Factory	Calabasas Hills, Calif.	17	139	143
The Cooker	W. Palm Beach, Fla.	47	110	161
Champs Americana	Wayzata, Minn.	21	103	167
Grady's American Grill	South Bend, Ind.	42	100	172
Claim Jumper	Irvine, Calif.	18	93	179
Max and Erma's	Columbus, Ohio	39	79	206
On the Border Cafés	Dallas	30	68	228
McCormick and Schmicks	Portland, Ore.	16	65	231
Garfields	Oklahoma City	53	64	237
Darryl's	Kansas City, Mo.	28	61	241
Slimm's	Los Angeles	23	60	242
Mimi's Café	Tustin, Calif.	25	59	245
Old Chicago	Louisville, Colo.	35	58	247
Cheddars	Arlington, Tex.	25	58	249
Islands	Solana Beach, Calif.	27	55	259
Rock Bottom Brewery	Louisville, Ky.	14	50	268
Charlie Brown's	Mountainside, N.J.	24	50	269
Dave and Buster's	Dallas	9	48	278
Rainforest Café	Hopkins, Minn.	6	48	279
Copelands	Metairie, La.	16	45	288
California Café	Corte Madera, Calif.	19	44	299

Source: Restaurants and Institutions 107 (July 15, 1997): 66.

311 by 1996. As its original customers married and started families, Friday's adjusted to keep pace. "These days, alcohol consumption is down, discos are out, kids are in, and the food profile is way up," reported one trade journal.[23]

The Ground Round represented the Friday's story somewhat in reverse. Started by Howard Johnson's in 1969 as an upscale hamburger restaurant for families, the chain catered to children. Cartoons and "old movies" played, popcorn was served at every table, video games were immediately at hand. Bingo the Clown made periodic visits. The chain grew to 210 locations in 1985, 176 company-owned and 34 franchised.[24] But by 1986 it had declined to 189 units.[25] The Ground Round had penalized itself by too strong a focus on children. The customer mix consisted of too many kids chaperoned by too few adults to the point where some family business was driven away and the singles' crowd absolutely repulsed. Dan Scoggin, hired away from Friday's, was charged with resuscitating Ground Round in the Friday's image. Out went the giant-screen TVs, the popcorn, and the clowns.

Concept Restaurants

Other upscale hamburger chains included Hamburger Hamlet with its 14 gourmet toppings. "One burger is topped with sauteed mushrooms, sour cream, and scallions; another with caviar and Russian dressing; yet another with fried oysters and salted peanuts; and still another with melted brie and toasted almonds."[26] Fuddrucker's, started in 1979 in San Antonio, grew to 150 locations in 1985.[27] Emphasized was "entertaining exhibition." "At Fuddrucker's, the first things customers see as they enter are crates of ketchup bottles, ice cream cones, and cheese sauce just inside the door. Bags of flour and sugar are stacked in the middle of the floor, and crates of lettuce, tomatoes, and onions stand next to the condiment display. Fuddrucker's oversized buns are baked in public view, and forequarters of beef hang in the butcher shop, visible through plate-glass windows. Customers can watch butchers deboning and grinding beef."[28]

A host of chains crowded into the casual restaurant market—Bennigan's, Applebee's, Ruby Tuesday, Chili's. Norman Brinker, developer of Pillsbury's Steak and Ale chain, experimented with several additional restaurant ideas—Bennigan's, Orville Bean's Flying Machine Restaurants, and the Juan 'n Only Mexican Restaurants, all with a casual flair. Bennigan's lasted with its "Super Chopper" hamburger steak topped with sauteed onions and mushrooms. The chain was sold to the Metromedia Restaurant Group (Ponderosa and Bonanza) when Metropolitan purchased Pillsbury. In 1996, it operated at some 220 locations, calling itself Bennigan's Irish American Grill and Tavern. Gone were the frozen, preprepared ingredients in favor of freshly prepared entrees like Turkey O'Toole and Flanigan's Fish Sandwich.[29]

W. R. Grace's T. J. Applebee's (now Applebee's Neighborhood Grill and Bar) was launched in 1968 in Atlanta. Sold in 1988, the chain grew quickly to 361 locations during six years of independent management (see fig. 15.14).[30] Morrison's, the cafeteria operator, bought the 16-unit Ruby Tuesday chain in 1982 and by 1994 it was operating at 276 locations (see fig. 15.15). With its tile floors and Tiffany lamps, the chain favored shopping-mall and

FIG. 15.14
Applebee's,
Terre Haute,
Ind., 1995.

shopping-center locations. Founded in 1975 in Dallas, Chili's grew to 25 locations in 1983, 146 in 1989, and 405 in 1996 (see fig. 15.16). Expansion was directed by Norman Brinker who, forming an investor group, left Bennigan's to buy out Chili's founders Larry and Jack Levine. Hamburgers (with 13 different toppings) were combined with Mexican-inspired dishes including chili. Decorations ran to "junkyard Mexican" upgraded with ceiling fans, potted plants, and wicker chairs.[31]

Into the casual segment also moved several steakhouse chains, prime among them Outback Steakhouse of Tampa with its Australian theme (297 locations in 1995), Lone Star Steakhouse and Saloon of Wichita with its Texan theme (160 locations), and Longhorn Steaks of Atlanta (64 locations) also with Texas "roadhouse" implication.[32] Lone Star began in North Carolina expanding into the mid-Atlantic and midwestern states as well as across the Southeast. The chain was noticeably absent from Texas where its theme or concept base would certainly have loomed as redundant if not artificial.

The casual restaurant, now sometimes referred to in industry publications as the dinner house, is one of the fastest-growing market segments in the United States. Some 37 chains now count among the nation's top 300 restaurant companies, 3 within the top 30 (see Table 15.2). Informal atmosphere inviting to informal dress and behavior, moderately priced meals, and the self-entertainment implications of the centrally located bar, among other attributes, offer a venue reflective of and substantially contributory to today's emergent lifestyles.

Fast Food and Theme Development

Programmatic architecture and the adoption of restaurant themes were by no means lacking from quick-service roadside eateries as previous chapters have established. From the Dutchland Farms windmills to Bob Evans's steamboat gothic buildings to Cracker Barrel's country stores, a few chains thrived by promoting the unusual. But most failed, including the Country School chain (with buildings shaped and decorated like rural one-room schoolhouses) and the Moon Burger chain (with buildings shaped like

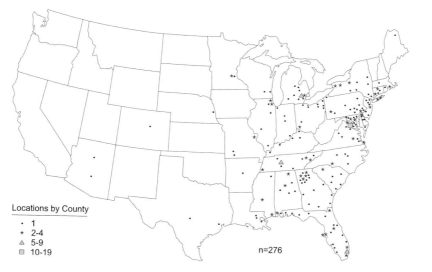

FIG. 15.15 Ruby Tuesday, 1994. Leading counties were: Fairfax, Va. (11 locations) and Broward (Fort Lauderdale), Fla., and Davidson (Nashville), Tenn. (6 each).

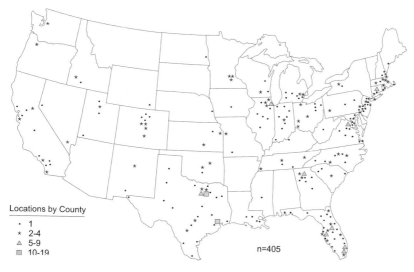

FIG. 15.16 Chili's, 1996. Leading counties were: Dallas, Tex. (18 locations), Harris (Houston), Tex. (15), and Broward (Fort Lauderdale), Fla., and Gwinnett, Ga. (8 each).

flying saucers and food delivered by robots). So also did Mammy Yokum's fail with its rustic shack-like buildings inspired by cartoonist Al Capp's Li'l Abner. Such promotions invariably sought to attract families with small children.

Many chains, foregoing extraordinary architectural motifs, appealed to children through special menus, take-home souvenirs, and, most important, playground equipment. Market research showed that children under 12 made over one-third of all family dining-out decisions, and in fast-food restaurants they constituted one-fifth of all sales.[33] McDonald's led the way as one of television's largest advertisers. Created was a fantasy world called

McDonaldland. Big Mac, the chief of patty police, drove around in a black paddy wagon and tended the security system which included a Burger Alarm. Chief among his targets was the "Hamburglar."[34] More enduring was Ronald McDonald, the prince of McDonaldland. During the 1990s, many McDonald's locations were enlarged with indoor playlands replacing earlier outdoor facilities.

Pizza provided another venue for marketing to children. The Pizza Time Theatre chain was launched in 1979. As described by one journalist,

> the main dining area is a cavernous room filled with long rows of picnic tables that can seat several hundred. At some of the tables children sit wearing party hats, holding balloons and eating pizza. Periodically, the lights dim. On a stage in front of the room large computer-operated stuffed animals begin singing and telling jokes. A quartet of guitar-playing, six-foot dogs called "the Beagles" play old Beatles hits.[35]

Capt. Andy's River Town chain, started in suburban Washington, D.C., featured an indoor theme park grafted onto a restaurant. Besides robotic entertainers (animatronics), children were offered rides and video games. The "interior has a shadowy, sleepy atmosphere reminiscent of the Southern-style river town on which the concept is based," reported one trade journalist.[36] "Main Street" comprised separate "storefronts" containing a coat-check room, a gift shop set up like a country general store, an order counter for pizza, sandwiches and chicken, a salad bar, an ice cream parlor, and a beverage booth.

Concept restaurants not only offered food but, equally (if not more) important, they offered a distinctive sense of place or themed environments. Emphases varied. In some instances it was programmatic architecture that carried the restaurant's image. Elsewhere it was ethnicity, decor tied to distinctive cuisine. In other instances it was entertainment, including the "self-entertainment" of patrons "seeing and being seen." Some concept restaurants were configured to cater to adults. Other restaurants catered to children's tastes not only in food but in fun. Concept restaurants very clearly were more than mere containers—places where people consumed food. Rather they were intended to be consumed as places also, food and place both contributing to customer satisfaction.

Concept restaurants were highly symbolic in intent. Of course, all restaurants carried symbolic value, but by specially packaging restaurant formats place concepts could be substantially amplified. Restaurants could be made to signify lifestyle, social class, generational and other orientations. They could be seen as synthesizing localities into global cultures or, conversely, as sustaining regional diversity in the face of universality. The consumption of food in places of distinction enabled patrons to variously reinforce self-identities, to relate variously to society at large while boosting self-esteem. Adult-oriented packaging of place encouraged a whole new market niche— the "casual" segment of the restaurant industry. Casual restaurants are spatially organized around enlarged bars, to engender kinds of sociability especially attractive to singles. Child-oriented packaging has wrought change in traditional restaurant formats, especially through the addition of play equipment. In various ways have restaurants become places of entertainment as much as eateries.

Concept
Restaurants

CHAPTER 16

The Roadside Restaurant in Springfield, Illinois

How did eating out develop along the streets in and the highways to and from a specific city? What did its customers expect? What options did owners serve and in what kinds of places? In what intracity locations did restaurants cluster over time? Specifically, how did automobility come to figure in an American city's restaurant scene? We turn to answering these questions in this chapter, exploring how processes of change outlined in foregoing chapters actually play out in the geography of a specific place.

Springfield, Illinois, state capital since 1837, offers a good case study. "Springfield is a restaurant town," its denizens and travelers commonly remark. By this is paid the grandest compliment about eating out in the consumer culture: you can find almost every kind of food in almost every setting at various prices—a diner's delight. Legislators and lobbyists attracted to Springfield alone have a fairly cosmopolitan perspective, legitimizing the assessment of the city's restaurant establishment. But the city's farthest reaching renown comes as "Mr. Lincoln's Hometown." Abraham Lincoln's home and satellite landmarks draw regular pilgrimages by international and national tourists alike. To politics and tourism add two insurance companies, three colleges, and a large medical center. In addition, the city stands as the crossroads of two interstate highways, primary among them I-55, Route 66's replacement as the principal Chicago–to–St. Louis connection. Travelers, workers, managers, executives, teachers, students, and patients are part of Springfield's public life; the demands for eating they create are large.

The food served throughout the city is broadly representative of the nation's various appetites. But there is local distinctiveness also. Chili and the "horseshoe sandwich" are the two foods for which Springfield notes itself as an exemplar and source. Characteristic, too, of most American cities, no single restaurant or type of restaurant casts a shadow of superiority over any other. Springfield has developed consistently; it is not a town of boom and bust cycles. Springfield has become familiar to both of us authors over

the last 25 years. Intimate knowledge of the place made possible through immediate accessibility and daily living there lessens the likelihood of overly
facile assessment. Springfield, Illinois, is not a typical American city (for
there is no such thing), but the processes of urban change characteristic of
America have played out here in typical ways. This is especially true of the
coming of the automobile and the changes that automobility has wrought.

In order to outline geographical change in the twentieth century, the chapter is organized around a series of maps depicting restaurants at 20-year intervals—1915, 1935, 1955, 1975, and 1995. The histories of individual restaurants and restauranteurs, including chain developments, flesh out the story
told by the maps.

The Roadside Restaurant in Springfield, Illinois

Before the Automobile

Located on the gently rolling prairie of central Illinois and with the Sangamon River and its tributaries' ample watershed into the Illinois River,
Springfield was favorably situated for rapid growth after it became the
state capital in 1837. By 1912, eight railroads and three interurbans served
the city. Small industries and coal mining buoyed the local economy by the
original population comprised of Upland Southerners, with substantial
numbers of central and southern Europeans and a few African-Americans.
Population increased by a third to 51,678 between 1890 and 1910, the era
seen in retrospect as Springfield's boom years. A medium-sized American
city with numerous eating establishments evolved.[1]

Springfield was a racially and socially divided city by 1915. Following the
nationally renowned race riot of seven years before, African-Americans began constituting an economically depressed minority residing in a segregat-
ed east side just beyond the central business district. To the north and south
of this area lived the large white working-class population whose males
labored chiefly in factories and mines near their homes. Germans lived in
the northeast quadrant, the Irish to the east of the African-American community. Upper-class residents lived on the south and west side. Southside
and westside subdivisions matured into the city's affluent neighborhoods
throughout the twentieth century.[2]

Business centered in two locations, the state capitol attracting, some several blocks west of the Chicago and Alton railroad depot. Two blocks east of
the depot the county courthouse in the remodeled previous state capitol,
however, was the public pivot for most Springfieldians and people come to
town for business. Upper-floor offices and ground-floor stores occupied
most of the buildings surrounding the courthouse on four sides.

City government, headquartered several blocks to the southeast at Seventh and Monroe, was a bipartisan machine permitting an extensive saloon
and gambling trade. Its most glaring expression, the infamous "levee" or
red-light district, flourished a few blocks directly east of the central business
district. Not until 1917 did reformers drive the levee out of business. Local
prohibition's enactment that year assisted. Early twentieth-century Spring-

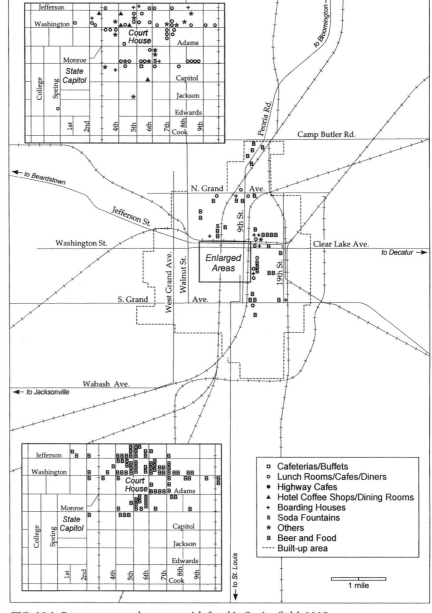

FIG. 16.1 Restaurants and taverns with food in Springfield, 1915.

field enjoyed a vibrant and colorful public life in the several blocks around the square, typical of many contemporary cities.[3]

There nested almost all of Springfield's eating establishments (see fig. 16.1), serving the numerous people passing through the city but principally its denizens working outside their homes. Street vendors may also have intermingled. They certainly were features of sidewalk life in bigger cities. Ed Crastos, who in 1899 began selling tamales and chili garnished with crackers served on tin pans from a cart one block south of the courthouse, perhaps

FIG. 16.2 Rollet's Restaurant in the late 1920s. (*Source:* Courtesy of James Rollet and the Sangamon Valley Collection.)

typified in Springfield. The city's fondness for chili seems to have started in this early era. Taverns furnishing food as a loss leader were spread from the central business district toward the east, and at locations around the coal mines mostly north of the business district. Walking to and from work or public business at the courthouse, pedestrians could patronize various kinds of places, mostly lunchrooms, cafés, and diners.[4]

What did those places look like? The earliest interior photographs of the city's main-street restaurants or cafés date from 1912 and show lunch counters and tables and booths in spaces organized perpendicular to outside sidewalks. In 1924 Rollet's Restaurant opened two blocks south of the courthouse (see fig. 16.2). Remove the tables and stools from these lunchrooms and the container of pressed-metal ceiling, tiled floors, and unadorned plaster walls could be occupied comfortably by numerous other kinds of retail businesses.[5] Here was generic space to be rented variously in response to the city's changing economic fortunes.

At the upper end of the restaurant scale ranked the Leland Hotel's dining room, an important part of the hotel's business since it opened in 1867. Typifying early hotel location, it helped anchor the downtown. Three blocks east of the statehouse, the Leland had been built to help secure Springfield's hold on the seat of state government against a rival claimant, and an impressive dining room with good service had been an important bidding chip. Remodelings brought the dining room up to prevailing standards throughout the turn-of-the-century period such that in 1898 it maintained a spare ambiance in a space 75 by 40 feet wide (see fig. 16.3). The lobby, through which every visitor had to pass, was palatial by contrast. Except in its larger size, the Leland appeared hardly different than the city's lunchrooms, cafés, and diners.[6]

FAST FOOD

FIG. 16.3 Springfield's Leland Hotel dining room. (*Source: Springfield in 1892: Souvenir Supplement* [Springfield, Ill.: Illinois State Journal, 1892], 71. Courtesy of the Sangamon Valley Collection.)

Food quality or novelty seemed to figure little, at least judging from newspaper advertising of the period. Random sampling of Springfield's two newspapers in 1915, 1920, and 1925 indicates the Leland's café featured an orchestra in the evenings for dinner or "after theater parties" in 1915. More innovative was Strong's Cafeteria which advertised in 1920 "Fast, Efficient Service and a Desire to Serve as We Would Be Served." Menu was not advertised. In 1925 two Springfield dance rooms did specify barbecue sandwiches and chicken dinners as menu items, but doubtless as secondary attractions for customers.[7]

Early intracity development of roadside restaurants for automobile travelers was slow. Focusing on South Grand Avenue and West Grand Avenue, with its Wabash Avenue extension, in 1915 (see fig. 16.1), later to become two of the city's primary routes of automobile travel, is instructive. No restaurants were located on West Grand Avenue–Wabash Avenue, then tracking along the city's western residential extremity. Traversing the evolving residential west side and the city's principal southern boundary, South Grand Avenue had little call for serving food to people away from home. Several small establishments offering beer and snacks, but not full meals, were the most common eating establishments along the street's east side between Eighth and Twentieth Streets, where streetcar passengers were the primary customers. Notably, no restaurants located on the west end of South Grand where the streetcar served stylish suburbs.

Neither distinctive settings nor distinctive food lured customers before the mid-1920s. Eating out was, perhaps, a necessary evil of low social status implication. Only those who were not part of traditional family households depended on restaurants for principal meals. Others patronized eateries "on the fly" in response to work schedules—the impulse to "fast food" operating then as now. Symptomatic of the automobile's future influence was a tiny advertisement for Henry Scharf's store which appeared in 1925, one of 45 in a omnibus advertisement for neighborhood grocers: "When out driving, drive around, between First and Second on Calhoun, for a good dish of ice cream or a glass of cold buttermilk."[8] Automobiles appeared in Springfield just after the turn of the century and became increasingly common between 1909 and 1912.[9]

The Roadside Restaurant in Springfield, Illinois

The Automobile's Landscape

Automobile highways connected Springfield early to other cities, for, in the 1920s, Illinois built one of the nation's first statewide trunk highway systems, the legacy of Governor Len Small (1921–29) who leveraged roadbuilding to maximum political advantage. By 1924 Springfield had excellent paved road connections with cities immediately to the east and southwest and, with the exception of five miles of gravel, "hard road" connections with Chicago and St. Louis as well.[10]

Each was part of the new system of automobile access along numbered routes substantially following roads preceding the automobile. Route 4 tying Chicago and St. Louis was the one significant new road. Tracking diagonally between the two cities to satisfy the automobilist's impatience for the shortest distance between two points, Route 4 was designated Route 66 in Illinois when the federal highway system started in 1926. By the early 1920s, more than 50,000 visited Springfield every year, many to the Lincoln sites rediscovered, as historic sites were in almost every American locale at the dawn of mass automobility. In 1937, the same year a four-lane improvement of Route 66 north of the city was opened to ensure travel at once rapid and safe, state highway engineers planned a bypass for Route 66 around the east and south side of the city. While diverting traffic otherwise congesting the city, Bypass 66 would prove to be the first step in drawing automobile-convenient business outward to the city's margins. For a time business thrived downtown, its electrically lighted and fully paved streets symbolizing bold progress beyond the horse-and-buggy past. The local economy and population, however, settled into slow and steady growth until the 1960s, population, for example, plateauing at growth rates between 5 and 8 percent through the 1950s.[11]

Opportunistic entrepreneurs sought the new automobile trade, Teddy Gray's Sugar Bowl exemplifying. Claimed to be the Illinois capital's first drive-in, Gray's business sold candy and ice cream at the Sugar Bowl on the northeast corner of Eleventh and South Grand Avenue, a busy intersection on the city's near southeast side, between 1919 and 1936, and at least by 1926 provided curb service. A jog in the street survey handed Gray an unusual advantage, a wedge-shaped piece of land between the side of his store and the

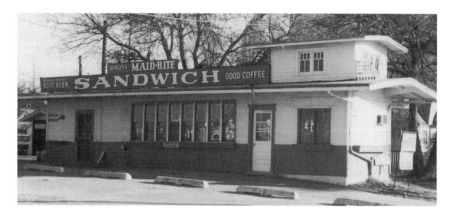

FIG. 16.4 The Maid-Rite, 1982.

FAST
FOOD

street, big enough for two to three cars at a time to pull off the street and wait for service from a boy hired for that reason. Here was the nationally developing pattern of confectionaries' and soda fountains' curb service showing up in Springfield. And characteristic of later places of automobile convenience, like the notorious intersections anchored by a gas station on each corner, Gray's Sugar Bowl was one of four small retailers occupying the intersection's corners.[12]

Maid-Rite, on the southeast corner of Jefferson and Pasfield, long survived as a landmark showing how the new venue looked. Built in 1924 as an independent sandwich shop and converted in 1930 to a member of the Maid-Rite chain, the facility provided a parking lot for motorists to alight and walk to the windows along the shop's sides (see fig. 16.4).[13]

In 1935, intracity restaurant locations reflected both the traditional pedestrian city and the emerging landscape of automobile convenience (see fig. 16.5). Traditional storefront restaurants, on the one hand, reached their highest number of all the intervals years in 1935 and they were, as in most cities, concentrated principally throughout the central business district, the blocks around the county courthouse square being the epicenter (see fig. 16.5). A few centered on neighborhood streetcorner intersections in the city's southern, eastern, and northern peripheries (see fig. 16.5). The affluent west side sustained no pedestrian restaurants, their inhabitants presumably eating either at home or in the storefront restaurants downtown, near their work. Only four of the 222 restaurants in 1915 survived with the same name at the same location in 1935. The 1935 total of 169 includes the largest number of beer and food establishments registered in any of the years studied, likely the consequence of Prohibition's end three years earlier. Taverns with food concentrated throughout the city's older working-class neighborhoods on the east side and north side and newer ones on the southside. Adjacent there to the railroad lines serving the warehouse and factory districts, a coal mine, and railroad shops, taverns with light meals provided workers respite in comradery as well as food. Taverns with food were evenly dispersed downtown, a function of its pedestrian-based commerce and court-

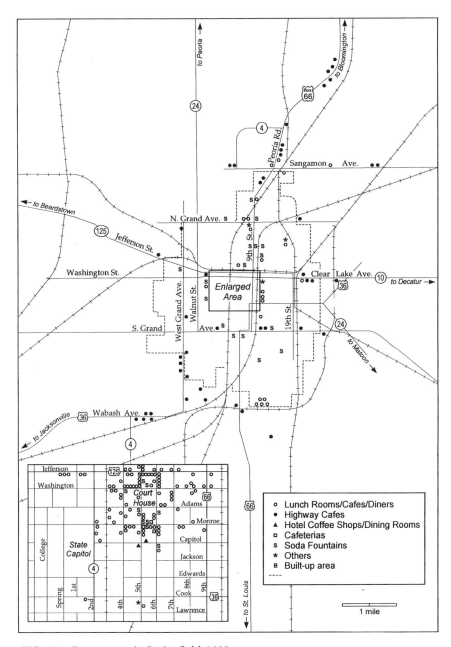

FIG. 16.5 Restaurants in Springfield, 1935.

house business (see fig. 16.6). Automobile-convenient restaurants, on the other hand, were evenly dispersed along the city's major traffic thoroughfares outward to the city's peripheries, including the west side. It was along peripheral highways especially that out-of-town travelers in automobiles stopped to eat.

Attention to West Grand Avenue with its Wabash Avenue extension and South Grand Avenue in 1935 (see fig. 16.5) discloses the substantial emergence of roadside restaurants since 1915. Wabash and West Grand Avenue

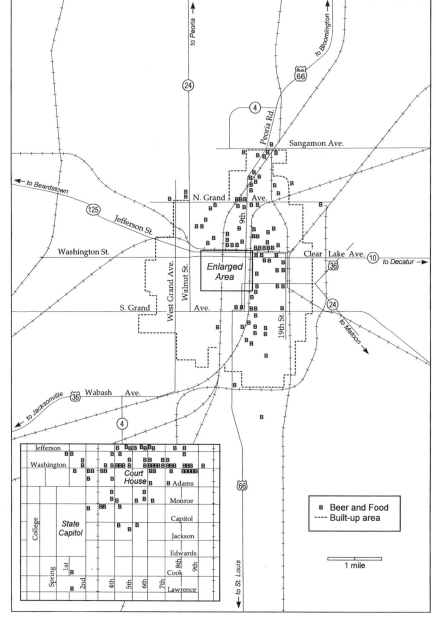

FIG. 16.6 Taverns with food in Springfield, 1935.

began functioning as a single street for travelers entering or exiting the city along Routes 4 and 36. As the westernmost street for automobile traffic going north or south, West Grand Avenue was the location for a collection of highway eateries, especially south of South Grand. An artery of automobile commerce by 1935, including a portion of Route 66, South Grand Avenue's locations to eat spread evenly along the street east to west, no longer bunched in groups as they had been in 1915 and on the east side only. Here were the automobile's rhythms of convenience at work. With sufficient

FIG. 16.7 The Jack Robinson System's lone survivor in Springfield, 1980.

separation between competitors, roadside restaurants had a better chance of being seen and drawing customers than if they remained clustered together, thus rendering themselves less distinguishable to the hurrying travelers. The South Grand Avenue eateries were also principally highway cafés and soda fountains. The streetcar, which ended service in 1937, had fallen behind the automobile in helping locate convenient places to eat. As in 1915, the avenue's streetcar service to the west side's elite suburbs necessitated no places for those eating out. Roadside restaurants had clear social implications by 1935. Those who could afford to travel or had to for their work ate out. Laborers to and from work did, too, but the professional and managerial classes still preferred eating at home most of the time.

Following national trends, hamburger places were the first roadside restaurants to make an enduring mark in Springfield although they began to operate in the mid-1930s, approximately a decade behind other cities such as Wichita. The Jack Robinson System was the first, the enterprise of Jack Robinson, a young businessman from southern Illinois. He had failed in a barbecue restaurant in Peoria, and so tried hamburgers in Springfield. In 1934 he opened a diner in a storefront on Monroe Street just east of the central business district. Seeing the quickened pace of business along city streets dispersing trade outward from the city's center, Robinson opened three hamburger joints between 1935 and 1937 on streets rich in automobile traffic, the first in Decatur (approximately 40 miles east of Springfield) and the last two in Springfield (see fig. 16.7). His purchase of porcelain enamel–clad diners (which White Castle manufactured) for his expanding chain reflected his fascination with images of mobility, as did the Depression decade. His diners' black-and-white motif, few seats, short and cheap menu emphasizing the hamburger, and street-side locations along streets of high traffic volume emulated White Castle's place-product-packaging. Jack Robinson's, confronted with the homogenizing aspects of other chains, brought not only a sense of the modern but a feel of standardization to the American scene. When Robinson's interests turned to the greater profit of drilling and pumping oil wells between Decatur and Springfield following World War II, the small, remnant chain survived under a former manager's ownership until the 1980s.[14]

The Steak 'n Shake chain became the leading advocate of place-product-packaging in the city. The Icy Root Beer Stand in Springfield, remembered as a "small, screened-in place that had drive-up service and sold root beer and hamburgers," gave Steak 'n Shake's founder the notion for the venue he developed. Four years later, in 1939, the Stuller family of Springfield launched the oldest franchised Steak 'n Shake by converting a failing walk-up in the capital's downtown to takeout and sit-down eating. The following year, adding to the ripple of restaurant profit reorientation to automobile travelers away from the city's center, the Stullers opened their first drive-in.[15]

Through the 1930s, 1940s, and 1950s, Springfield developed a penchant for unpretentious middlebrow restaurants offering foods palatable to travelers as well as clericals and factory workers. In an article in 1947 for the *Saturday Evening Post,* Elise Morrow passed judgment on Springfield from her eastern urban vantage point (a staff writer for the *Philadelphia Inquirer* and her husband a *Washington Post* editor). She called it "an overgrown prairie village" that happened to be inhabited by 85,000 people; the city's indigenous "horseshoe sandwich is an indigestible but satisfying collection of toast, fried egg, ham and French-fried potatoes, covered with a thick, rich Welsh rarebit and served on a sizzling oval platter."[16] The Leland Hotel's chef had created the horseshoe in 1928.[17] Here was a city where roadside restaurants could thrive—where friendly service and ordinary but reliable food in sizable portions passed for good eating.

Mom-and-pop operations yet reigned but automobile convenience was relocating many of them. Fazi's and The Poplars, which it succeeded, illustrated. These were on one of Springfield's oldest locations for roadside food, about one mile north of the city limits on the main highway and featured not only a restaurant but as well a gas station and motel. Richard Fazi started his business there in the late 1920s when the highway was designated U.S. 66. An Italian immigrant who had worked up from coal mining to running a boardinghouse and owning a tavern, Fazi was attracted to the site as a highway location and staked his future on it. Although he started with a gas station, it was the restaurant, with a bar serving bootleg whiskey during Prohibition that earned a reputation with travelers and locals alike. He had a dozen cabins cobbled together for complementary overnight lodging and built his own house nearby. "Uncle Dick," as Fazi became known, ascended the social ladder, moving in 1948 to a house on Lake Springfield, one of the city's sylvan suburbs. He sold his roadside establishment to three young Methodist women from Battle Creek, Michigan, who came to Springfield seeking stable income and a decent setting for raising their young family.[18]

Velma Hamilton led the trio, including her sisters Pearl and Opal. Having traveled extensively in her work as a nurse, Pearl advised getting into the motel trade because the nation's new motels always seemed to be filled. Just that innocently, the group bought Fazi's property and, during a blinding snow-

FIG. 16.8 The Poplars just after it was renamed in 1948. Its restaurant is in the left foreground, the gas station on the right, and the cabins behind both.

storm, arrived in a caravan of cars to take possession. The sisters put their own stamp on the place and, after considerable deliberation, began by renaming it "The Poplars," for poplars had sprouted up on the lot as a windbreak (see fig. 16.8). It was their restaurant that triumphed, a business readily amenable perhaps to their domesticating touch. Without any restaurant experience, they hewed to their exacting standards for home cooking. Their restaurant became a haunt for tourists to the Lincoln sites and traveling state workers and truckers, too, learned to count on The Poplars, even after it required a circuitous drive off the Interstate 55 bypass opened a mile to the east in 1963.[19]

The immediate post–World War II years witnessed a continued rise in roadside eateries (see fig. 16.9 and Table 16.1) although traditional store-front restaurants were prominent. The Cozy Dog Drive-In opened in 1950 alongside Route 66. Recently this place has come to symbolize Springfield's drive-in era, part of a nostalgia boom for Route 66. Named for its specialty, a batter-dipped and deep-fat fried hot dog on a stick, the Cozy Dog mirrored the national tendency for generic roadside food to be promoted as if it were novel—elsewhere people recognized a Cozy Dog as a corn dog. Demonstrating the typically quixotic fortunes of serving roadside patrons, however, is Mimi's Fountain, no trace of which survives today. In business for only two years, 1949–50, along Route 66, only a few blocks north of the Cozy Dog, Mimi's nonetheless was featured in the trade magazine *Fountain Service* in December 1949, a distinction that even its owners forgot. The rapid rise of similar, cheaply built, usually predictable eateries on the roadside seemingly enforces a virtual amnesia often causing the less-popular places to be dismissed as totally trivial when, in fact, taken together they represent an important part of America's common roadside business reorientation.[20]

By 1955, individual locally owned restaurants still made up the vast majority. Chains were only slightly better represented since 1935, totaling

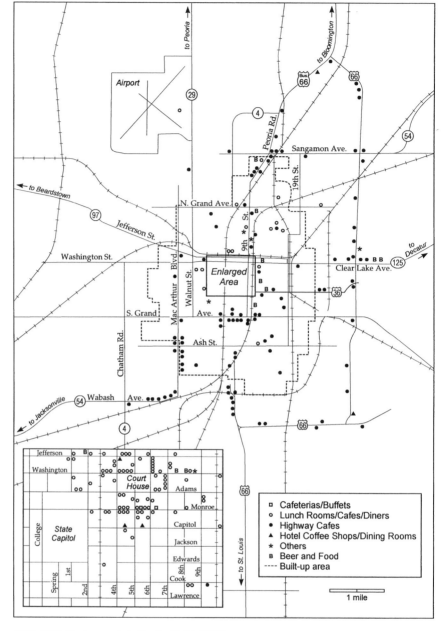

FAST FOOD

FIG. 16.9 Restaurants in Springfield, 1955.

only 15 restaurants, less than 1 percent. The largest chain was still Jack Robinson's, which comprised three restaurants still locally owned. Two other chains, Martin Way, which a former Jack Robinson employee started, and Icy Root Beer Stand, with two stores apiece, were also local enterprises.[21] Hamburger places led the way so far as the chains were concerned—six of the fifteen regional and national chains in the city (see Table 16.2). Twelve of 228 restaurants survived in 1955 from 1935, each with the same name located at the same address.

TABLE 16.1 Restaurant Types in Springfield

Type	1915	1935	1955	1975	1995	
Hotel / motel coffee shops / dining rooms	5	2	2	12	10	
Cafeterias / buffets	1	3	2	4	3	
Lunchrooms / cafés / diners	50	118	100	32	21	
Highway cafés	0	46	107	149	235	
Boardinghouses	12	0	0	0	0	
Beer and food	139	169	12	8	4	*The Roadside*
Soda fountains	2	26	0	0	0	*Restaurant in*
Others	13	4	5	0	11	*Springfield,*
TOTAL	222	368	228	205	284	*Illinois*

Beer and food places dropped precipitously overall by 1955 (see Table 16.1 above). This most obvious change in Springfield's pattern of eating out was attributable to two reinforcing trends, primarily the decline of the industrial economy common to much of America but also Springfield's own campaign for middle-class decency in public life from the late 1940s through the late 1950s. Although the establishment's target was the bars, whose gambling and prostitution made the capital notorious, it is probable working-class bars disappeared, too, an innocent yet peripheral casualty of a reformist ethos.[22]

The intracity restaurant orientation toward the automobile, however, grew apparent in the spatial expanse of the city's restaurants outward from the city's center (see fig. 16.9). Whereas no substantial expansion of the city's built-up area had occurred since 1935, many more restaurants were situated on its margins by 1955. Most noticeable was the era's fast-food boom along the Route 66 bypass on the city's eastern edge. Henceforth, Bypass 66 would grow to rival the older restaurant corridors along South Grand and West Grand (renamed MacArthur Boulevard in 1942)–Wabash Avenue. Restaurants did grow in numbers along the MacArthur Boulevard–Wabash Avenue corridor where they merged with Illinois Route 4 and U.S. 36 at the southwestern edge of town, but not to the same extent as the new Route 66 fast-food corridor. By 1955 numerous small businesses convenient to automobile customers, roadside restaurants chief among them, changed South Grand from its earlier residential bastion. Serving travelers on state highways and for a portion of Route 66, South Grand's roadside restaurants were located near the areas where these highways intersected, between Second and Ninth. Places serving beer and food to travelers had shrunk significantly along South Grand, catering to the trade of neighborhoods off the motorists' busiest paths.

In the city's central business district restaurants still thrived, catering to the courthouse, statehouse, and shopping trade (see fig. 16.9). Almost all of these downtown restaurants were one of a kind. A substantial evening trade contributed (see fig. 16.10). The incipient chains dotted the city's arteries but were not yet poised along arteries serving the growing suburbs and

TABLE 16.2 Chain Restaurant Categories in Springfield

Type	1955	1975	1995
Sandwiches			
A&W Root Beer	1	1	1
Arby's	0	1	3
Dog "N" Suds	1	0	0
Jax	0	1	0
Maid-Rite	1	1	1
Schlotzsky's	0	0	1
Other	2	3	3
Hamburgers			
Burger Chef	0	2	0
Burger King	0	2	2
Jack Robinson System	3	2	0
McDonald's	0	3	9
Sandy's / Hardee's	1	5	9
Steak 'n Shake	2	3	2
Wendy's	0	0	4
Other	2	2	2
Breakfast			
Steak 'n Egg Kitchen	0	0	2
Casual			
Applebee's	0	0	1
Bombay Bicycle Club	0	0	1
Chili's	0	0	1
Fuddrucker's	0	0	1
Ground Round	0	0	1
Ruby Tuesday	0	0	1
Chicken			
Kentucky Fried Chicken	0	3	3
Lee's Famous Recipe	0	0	2
Popeye's	0	0	1
Other	1	2	1
Family			
Baker's Square	0	0	1
Bob Evans	0	0	1
Denny's	0	0	2
Cracker Barrel	0	0	1
Howard Johnson's	1	2	0
Perkins	0	0	1
Shoney's	0	0	1
Fish			
Long John Silver's	0	1	4
Red Lobster	0	0	1
Ice Cream			
Baskin-Robbins	0	2	4
Bressler's	0	0	1

continued

FAST
FOOD

TABLE 16.2 *Continued*

Type	1955	1975	1995
Dairy Queen	0	5	4
Larry's Dairy Swirl	0	2	0
TCBY	0	0	1
Tacos and Mexican			
Chi-Chi's	0	0	1
Taco Bell	0	1	3
Other	0	0	5
Pizza and Italian			
Chuck E. Cheese	0	0	1
Domino's	0	0	4
Godfather's	0	1	1
Little Caesar's	0	0	6
Olive Garden	0	0	1
Pizza Hut	0	2	6
Shakey's	0	0	1
Other	0	5	8
Steak			
Bonanza	0	1	0
Ponderosa	0	2	0
Ryan's	0	0	1
Other	0	0	4
Other	0	0	14
TOTAL	15	55	130

The Roadside Restaurant in Springfield, Illinois

helping encourage roadside investment in intercity routes. Suburban reorientation began in the 1960s with small, neighborhood-oriented shopping centers. Supermarkets and department stores anchored several of these early shopping centers. Initially they effected cooperation between small- and medium-sized local merchants and large outside investors and retailers.[23] Ultimately, large out-of-town-administered corporations dominated.

Springfield followed national trends toward automobile convenience in the 1950s and 1960s, as, for example, reflected in Russell's Pizza Drive-Inn, which also illustrated how Springfield's considerable ethnic minorities—in this case, Italians—contributed. This was notwithstanding Springfield's reputation in other aspects of public life as a place of lethargy. Angelo and Fred Yannone, respectively owner and manager, opened their remodeled drive-in in 1961, on Bypass 66 gorged with locals and travelers and soaring to a popular icon (see fig. 16.11). Russell's was featured in a 1962 article in the *Drive-In Restaurant* magazine. Angelo and Fred were highlighted as role models for other entrepreneurs seeking innovation through savvy business practices. It is interesting that the Yannones continued doing business under the Anglicized "Russell" name given by the first primary owner, also an Italian (Russell Saputo), even though Italian food, and especially pizza, was to be emphasized. The Yannones helped convert pizza into a fast food and also

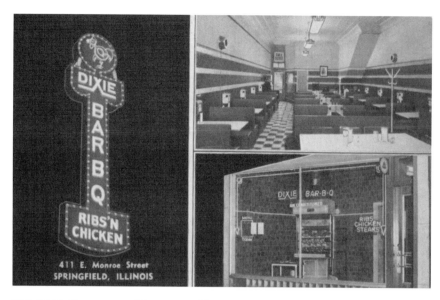

FIG. 16.10 The reverse of the postcard from the Dixie Bar-B-Que (411 E. Monroe) heralded its barbecued chicken and ribs, lunches and dinners, and hours, from 11 A.M. to 3 A.M. daily. Attesting to the city's growing trade in outlying areas, however, the postcard added "Delivery Service in the City Limits."

FIG. 16.11 The Yannones' advertisement for their Russell's Drive-In in the nearby high school's annual for 1962 featured teenagers. (*Source: The Log,* Feitshans High School [(Springfield:) n.p., 1962], 133. Courtesy of *The Log,* Feitshans High School, 1962, Springield, Ill. and the Sangamon Valley Collection.)

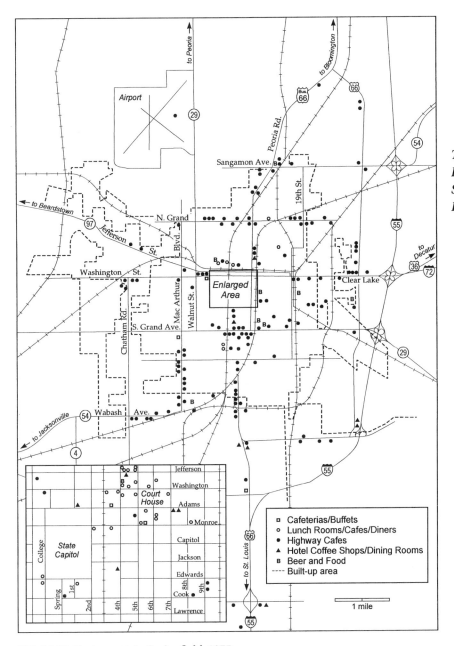

Legend:

□ Cafeterias/Buffets
○ Lunch Rooms/Cafes/Diners
● Highway Cafes
▲ Hotel Coffee Shops/Dining Rooms
B Beer and Food
---- Built-up area

1 mile

FIG. 16.12 Restaurants in Springfield, 1975.

contributed significantly to Bypass 66's pull on the capital's would-be entre-preneurs.[24]

Springfield's population increased by 10 percent during the 1960s and 1970s, primarily as a result of expanded state government, a new university, and a state medical college.[25] New restaurants were created to feed the now more thoroughly automobile-oriented public, leaving traditional storefront restaurants far behind in the competition. In a radical break with the past, chains seized the creative initiative. The shift was clearly obvious in 1975 (see fig. 16.12). While the number of restaurants declined by 23 between 1955 and 1975, automobile-convenient ones jumped by almost half, from 107 to 149, and traditional storefront restaurants (lunchrooms, cafés, and diners) plummeted by two-thirds from 100 to 32 (see Table 16.1 above). The dislocation is ironic in light of the fact that many employees of Springfield's "growth industries" of the 1960s–1970s worked downtown and resided on the burgeoning west side. It was likely they who kept the downtown restaurants in business even while retailing was moving nearer their homes, especially after 1977 when the regional White Oaks Mall opened in the city's far southwest corner. A tiny fraction of Springfield's restaurants persisted from 1955; seven restaurants of 205 retained the same name at the same location.

Centrifugal dispersal to Springfield's highway margins continued apace. Automobile-convenient restaurants clustered in the same areas and in roughly the same numbers in 1975 as they had in 1955 (see figs. 16.9 and 16.12 above). Downtown storefront restaurants declined in numbers. Chain restaurants increased in number, crowding into the city itself by 1975 in pursuit of new investment opportunities. Chain expansion was dramatically different in 1955 and 1975; in the latter year, chains accounted for one-fourth of all Springfield's restaurants (see Tables 16.1 and 16.2 above). The chain store was also made larger, occupying longer lots, and entailed, accordingly, far greater sums of money than in the past. All of the chain-food segments were well represented and not just hamburgers. Regional and national chains fully asserted aggressively to challenge mom-and-pop enterprise.

Between 1935 and 1975, the MacArthur Boulevard–Wabash Avenue and South Grand Avenue corridor experienced no significant changes. Continuing to function as an important line of automobile travel, roadside restaurants located in approximately the same location, in the same numbers, and were of the same type as they had been 20 years earlier. Given the low density of previous residential development between the expanding roadside services on Wabash Avenue, however, that former extension of the MacArthur Boulevard roadside corridor began to take on the look of a classic automobile strip. Brightly painted and lighted signs pointing toward restaurants in formula architecture beneath bombarded passing motorists' sight. Place-product-packaging converted Wabash Avenue into the prophet of Springfield's seemingly inarguable destiny to grow southwestward.

From the late 1970s through the mid-1990s, Springfield's restaurant typicality was reaffirmed in a series of characterizations. Locals summed up in 1990 with self-deprecation for a *Chicago Sun-Times* article, "It's all meat and potatoes."[26] Fairness, however, requires not only tribute to those Springfield restaurants aiming at distinctive dining and diversified menus, but acknowledgment that most Springfieldians hungered for plain cooking like that served by the roadside. The Fleetwood was a microcosm.

At the start of 1957, Tony and Opal Lauck opened the 135-seat Fleetwood (see fig. 16.13) on Bypass 66 on the city's northeast side, then teeming with a mix of intra- and intercity travelers. The Fleetwood became a truckstop

The Roadside Restaurant in Springfield, Illinois

FIG. 16.13 The Fleetwood distinguished itself from many ephemeral roadside restaurants by its promotion with postcards, such as this one.

well publicized by word of mouth up and down Route 66. Other travelers, especially tourists, complemented the trade. Broasted chicken became the house specialty, added in 1959 after trial and error confirmed its popularity among other alternatives. Undaunted when in 1963 Interstate 55 diverted much of their trade off Route 66, the Laucks reinvented their restaurant to serve Springfield and vicinity families. They enlarged the Fleetwood's seating capacity, remodeling it in the early 1970s and again in the mid-1980s. The Fleetwood prospered with only 20 percent of its trade representing travelers. Traditional fare at reasonable prices was emphasized. Symptomatic of mom-and-pop restaurant fortunes nationally by the late 1980s, successive family generations made a comfortable living at the Fleetwood. It peaked with 1,000 daily customers, seating for 300, and 96 employees. Rising costs and the franchise revolution in Springfield restaurant trade, however, brought an abrupt end to the business in late 1993. Increased operating costs and scarcer labor exacerbated.[27] Symbolic of the Bypass 66 corridor's decline, the Fleetwood's hulk housed a low-intensity operation, a T-shirt factory, at the time of this writing.

Restaurant investment had shifted dramatically toward Springfield's far southwest side, to the intersection of Veterans Parkway and Wabash, and southward beside Veterans Parkway's western edge. A dense constellation of restaurants was evident in the citywide map for 1995 (see fig. 16.14). The year 1992 was recounted in the city's major paper as "the year of the restaurant in Springfield." True, a dozen restaurants had opened in 1992, some of them individually owned, but it was the fast-food and family restaurant chains at White Oaks shopping center and the new strip malls, Southwest Plaza and Parkway Point, that impacted most. Place-product-packaged chains stand side to side arrayed in service to the demand for automobile convenience (see fig. 16.15). Themed restaurants contributed to a large portion of this influx.

It was not only the menu and speedy service but settings grown familiar through traveling elsewhere that attracted local customers to the new chain

FAST
FOOD

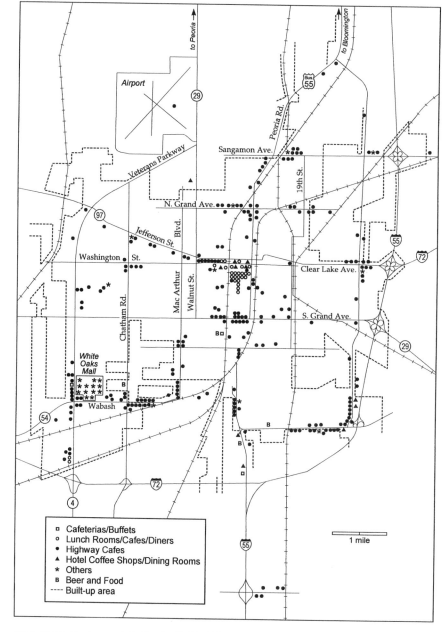

FIG. 16.14 Restaurants in Springfield, 1995.

offerings. Objects of format franchising, each chain's Springfield representative looked like all the others in distant locations. Despite each chain's distinctiveness, they looked as a group rather all alike—the place-product-packaged roadside restaurant now Springfield's dominant venue for eating out. Polychromatic and brightly lit by night in contrast with earlier roadside restaurants, these new restaurant venues seek visual excitement, equating same, it is hoped, with gustatory satisfaction. Inside, the casual restaurants' thinly partitioned booths encouraged a general din, repelling others. They

The Roadside Restaurant in Springfield, Illinois

FIG. 16.15 Chain casual restaurants stood side by side at White Oaks Mall.

are made to be places of excitement—places of entertainment and not just eateries.

Liquor with food also reappeared in Springfield eateries en masse through this format popular with the newly affluent working-class young. Centrally located bars were focal points of the layout in many chain restaurants by the malls. Absent through the ascendance of reformist middle-class values at midcentury, drinking in moderation came again to be deemed acceptable as Springfield shared in the nation's liberalizing culture by the end of the century. Despite their liquor service, food was the main menu item; hence, the new roadside chain restaurants are not tabulated as beer and food.

Restaurants were uncommon in shopping malls nationwide until the 1980s. Not to be left behind, White Oaks was remodeled in 1993 and a food court with seven chain restaurants added. And so the mall became not only a place to shop, but a place in which to be entertained through eating. The renewed mall with restaurant enhancement greatly increased Springfield's locus for an 11-county hinterland of a half-million people with an estimated buying power of $7.5 million. Although the fast-food impulse was moved off the highway into the mall, it still echoed in the automobile's rapid mobility and overall domination. Chain restaurants clustered at the city's interstate highway interchanges, representing another restructuring of the city's restaurant geography (see fig. 16.16).[28]

Another of the capital's most recent innovations in automobile-convenient eating is the new drive-through restaurants. Characteristic of the format, both small and large companies have probed the city's drive-through market. PepsiCo's Hot 'n Now operated for 18 months in 1992–93 at three locations adjacent to existing constellations of fast-food eateries. Two are being remodeled into Rally's and another is up for sale at this writing. At

FAST FOOD

FIG. 16.16 Signs for chain restaurants pulled hungry travelers off Interstate 72 to the dynamic strip malls in the mid-1990s.

the opposite end of the investment scale was Burger Park, one of six nationwide when opened. Headquartered in Hagerstown, Maryland, Burger Park featured a menu, mostly hamburgers, playing on a baseball theme, for example, a bunt (49 cents). Operating in 1994 and 1995 on the southwest corner of Seventh and South Grand, it also closed. Both before and after Burger Park, Rally's occupied that corner in two separate episodes, 1989–94 and 1996 through the time of this writing. Pioneered by Steak 'n Shake in 1951, the southwest corner of Seventh and South Grand was a bellwether site for new hamburger venues in Springfield.[29] On this corner novelty has repeatedly played out in changing fashions.

Rally's was the largest chain of double drive-throughs when Springfield became the second Illinois city that the company entered. Their store grew with auspicious declarations about how its "limited menu" and absence of indoor seating made possible lower operating costs with lower prices, accordingly, passed on to customers; 70 to 75 people were to be employed, a community asset in its own right.[30] A cofranchisee, however, refused to detail what was wrong with Rally's "direction," as he called it, when he changed over to Burger Park. A new franchisee, Rally's largest, reopened after the property had stood idle. The new franchisee also operated several franchise pizza restaurants in Illinois and Indiana.[31] This one location characterizes the sort of volatility long endemic to the restaurant industry. Distant in time and place is the congenial lunch counter with its direct sociability. Activity is frenetic at Rally's (see fig. 16.17).

As Interstate 55's intersections with Springfield's principal arteries drew new businesses, so also did the intersection of Dirksen Parkway and Stevenson Drive at the southeast end of town. Investment downtown looked to "niche investment" serving customers but solely for breakfast and for lunch. Only a few were chains,[32] faintly echoing the national trend to renewed inner-city development.

Automobility still acts centrifugally in Springfield, not only away from the inner city but away from restaurants as eating places themselves. In addition to the practice of home delivery, which individual restaurants long have offered, 1994 witnessed the start of common delivery service for several individual and chain restaurants throughout the city.[33]

The last look here at roadside eateries along MacArthur Boulevard–Wabash Avenue and South Grand Avenue discloses important continuities and discontinuities over time (see fig. 16.14 above). Most significant was Wabash Avenue's extension into the virtual second city around the malls southwest. Driving south along MacArthur to those malls, one experienced ever bigger, ever more visually raucous places in tow to car culture. Serving almost exclusively automobile travelers from within Springfield, South Grand Avenue had neither suffered decline in roadside restaurant numbers nor witnessed their relocation in the two decades before 1995. Compared to 1915, however, no longer did affluent travelers and hungry laborers generate demand exclusively while the west side's establishment ate at home. Springfieldians alone sustained a vibrant restaurant trade along South Grand Avenue even while the travelers' interstates spawned key commercial vortexes, continuing thus to make South Grand Avenue an important focus for future analysis of the capital's roadside restaurants. Where cars passed in great numbers restaurants readied for convenient service.

By 1995, restaurant chains embracing automobile convenience seemed to have matured in Springfield. No lengthy discussion of market saturation surfaced in the Springfield press, but the increased density of locations corroborated in the jump of restaurant numbers by almost 40 percent—to 284—suggested that the city was experiencing trends evident nationwide: proliferation of nontraditional households with changed eating habits favoring eating out and more working women considering it a necessity to eat out. Out of 205 restaurants existing in 1975 26 carried over to 1995 with the same name at the same address. Chains accounted for virtually all of the

The Roadside Restaurant in Springfield, Illinois

FIG. 16.17 Rally's small building was made to seem large with shiny horizontal red and silver trim, the ensemble bedecked with fluttering flags. Customers could pause to sit and eat at canopy- or umbrella-shaded tables but they only surveyed traffic moving in the street or cars lined up adjacent, waiting to be served.

79 restaurants added since 1975. Only three restaurants had survived with the same name at the same address for 60 years—one pedestrian-oriented downtown, Maldaner's, a fern-bar restaurant refashioned from an old eatery, and two automobile-convenient along the streets immediately beyond downtown, the Dew Chilli Parlor and Maid-Rite. The restaurant business in Springfield, as across the nation, had been repeatedly remade, this remaking continuing apace with new products and restaurant forms coming to the fore.

FAST FOOD

Mr. Lincoln's Hometown is a city he would and would not recognize certainly, with respect to its restaurants. He and Mary Todd Lincoln once lived in and took their meals at the Globe Tavern, a public boardinghouse. Even in 1947, when journalist Elise Morrow maligned the city as little changed since the Great Emancipator walked its streets, there were signs of the progress Springfieldians coveted in, of all places, its lowly eateries. The changes, we suspect, Lincoln would not only have noticed, but with his proclivity to Whig Party economic policies, would have approved. If Lincoln's young family ate and lodged comfortably at the Globe Tavern before buying their own home, they would have found in 1947 the equivalent in one of the hotels downtown. By 1967 their temporary place of residence and their eating places likely would have been first a motel and then chain-restaurant businesses nearby on the outskirts of town, just off the new interstates. Today he might sleep downtown and eat at one of the new posh motor hotels, but more likely his practical sense would incline him outward to the roadside and its new democratic variety—Mary Lincoln left to the enticements of the Hilton and the Renaissance. One might imagine Lincoln at his best, perhaps, seated at a stool of a 1930s diner telling stories and cracking jokes.

Springfield is now a decentralized city spread out along its thoroughfares, tied together largely by moving automobiles and motor trucks. Gone is the tyranny of the railroad tying people closely to the city's center. The map of 1915 disclosed a pedestrian place (see fig. 16.1 above). Small-scale enterprise generated the most eateries in a constellation of storefront locations downtown. Hotels principally, also downtown, beckoned upscale dining.

Throughout the city's entire history its public cuisine, however, gravitated substantially to the commonplace. Entrepreneurs entered the marketplace in search of profit if not ease of operation. Aristocratic individuality was pretended, seldom practiced. Springfield gained a modest reputation outside for its hometown food—chili and the horseshoe, but that was little more than the provincial testing of recipes known popularly nationwide.

Springfield advanced materially because it shared such averageness. By 1935, the highways built to and from the capital a decade before began reconfiguring its retail landscape, including its restaurants. A balance between downtown eateries and those along the highways to and from it prevailed through 1955 but chain restaurants wrought a breach with the past by 1995. The automobile clearly had swept over Mr. Lincoln's hometown by the twentieth century's end. That trend, however, accelerated and multiplied in magnitude because of the cultural forces that Springfieldians had set in motion to create the Illinois capital's landscape since its inception. Eluding easy explanation, Lincoln as a lawyer influential in the state's young and malleable business law would likely have enjoyed many consequences of the city's automobility. Chains tentatively sought downtown opportunities and, in this way, were unrepresentative of national trends in larger cities. Springfield's characteristic pragmatism and circumspection about rapidly installed novelty persisted.

Convenience inured. To get on with earning a living wage or building one's business to a desired profit level, the people of Springfield left themselves little opportunity for the casual. Eating, itself one of the most common satisfactions away from work, was also prey to convenience. People settled for simple fare easily obtained because other demands waited. Travelers' experiences paralleled. Time and space, the twin inconveniences, were hurdled through improved transportation technologies—automobiles the most widely appealing.

The Roadside Restaurant in Springfield, Illinois

Conclusion

Disappointing meals dominate the pleasure trips of millions of motorists, and the memory of bad cooking, instead of magic scenery, remains," wrote journalist Ted Shane in the early 1950s in decrying the hazards of "roadside indigestion."[1] The nation's highways had become "ulcer traps" with "highly priced, badly mauled food," he argued. Southern fried chicken provided clear evidence that the South was still trying to win the War Between the States "by poisoning the North." Was it true? Many thought so. How did America's roadside restaurants earn such reputation? What might be done about culinary indifference? Was it something implicit in the nation's new automobility? Was speed somehow the culprit? Were motorists too impatient to demand quality of product and service? Was the nation doomed to something soon to be termed "fast food"?

Eating fast in America has a long history. Frederick Marryat, traveling in 1837, observed:

> At every fifteen miles of the railroads there are refreshment rooms; the cars stop, all the doors are thrown open, and out rush the passengers like boys out of school, and crowd round the tables to solace themselves with pies, patties, cakes, hard-boiled eggs, ham, custards and a variety of railroad luxuries, too numerous to mention.[2]

When departure bells rang, passengers hurried off "their hands and mouths full." Americans have long been a hurried people, a circumstance devolving, perhaps, from the nation's preoccupation with business—time spent without profit being time wasted. A nation set in rapid motion by railroading seemingly demanded "quick service." As travel switched to motorized highways, the impulse was amplified.

Roadside Restaurants

The automobile quickened quick service. Adopting frying and other fast cooking techniques (the foods themselves amenable to such speedy prepa-

322

ration), restaurants were configured around lunch counters and takeout windows, and, more important, provisioned with off-street parking lots. Early wayside eateries spoke clearly of automobile convenience. And such convenience spoke loudly of speed. Then came "drive-ins" with food delivered to waiting cars, "walk-ups" where customers queued in multiple lines to speed food purchase, and, ultimately, "drive-throughs" with food handed out to motorists in waiting cars. Reflecting the age of industrial assembly lines, food preparation and delivery were engineered, fully rationalized in time and motion. Americans took immediately to automobile-convenient food as a logical extension of their general mania for quickening life.

America's consumer culture of apparent release, as Jackson Lears has instructed, involves an important dimension of producer control.[3] Consumers vote with their dollars, but do so only with the arrays of goods and services entrepreneurs make available. Early on, varied menus were not an effective marketing strategy. Most road food was by nature inherently simple, easily prepared, and not exotically garnished with sauces or seasonings. What counted most was food fried or otherwise quickly prepared with flavor restored through standard toppings. Being long partial to foods held in the hand, Americans took readily to the likes of hamburgers, hot dogs, and tacos.[4] Fried chicken and fried fish served in baskets also could be picked up and readily eaten, and so also pizza, the latter a kind of open-faced sandwich. Made possible, for those so inclined, was a kind of dashboard dining whereby drivers could eat while driving, the ultimate in speed-induced convenience. Such food was quite inexpensive. Thus the predominant road food insured that the vast majority of Americans could afford to eat out, most doing so, of course, by leaving their cars to dine.

Dave Thomas, Wendy's founder, recalled his early attraction to restaurants, and, by extension, to restaurant work. He mused, "Sure, I liked the food, but the big thing for me was eating out. It was a special event."[5] Eating out offered change of pace from domestic routine. Roadside restauranteurs hit not only on new ways to speed service but, in so doing, on new forms of recreation and entertainment. At the new drive-ins, customers were invited to stay seated in their cars, to relax, and to watch the show as carhops went their rounds. At the new drive-throughs there was the novelty of remote ordering and the innovation of joining a parade of cars (see figs. C.1 and C.2). Drive-through service represented the entrepreneur's complete obedience to customer satisfaction defined in terms of automobile convenience. The customer remained attached to his or her car. The restaurant was made part of the customer's "open road" with implications for amplified personal power through mobility.[6] Place, coupled with movement, offered not only novelty but also ego enhancement through automobile ownership and use.

But the roadside also proved congenial to customers whose sense of satisfaction derived more from lingering than from speeding. Restauranteurs were responsive to those wanting to savor place if not food. Giant signs and sign-like buildings—both calculated to slow and stop speeding motorists—were joined by structures programmed more deliberately to detain. Programmed indoors and out, concept restaurants were designed for more

FAST FOOD

FIG. C.1 McDonald's, Collinsville, Ill., 1996. Drive-throughs have supplanted the drive-ins for convenience.

complex kinds of sociability beyond mere ordering and consuming of food. Upscale roadside eateries sought to provide distinctive decors linked variously to distinctive menus. They were elaborated as places of entertainment. Concept restaurants remained automobile-convenient in that customers arrived by car to park close by. But in format they were not automobile-oriented in the fullest sense. Customers left their cars to enjoy leisure in settings variously supportive of lifestyle aspirations. These places offered antidote to the open road. They offered an alternative to life's fast pace. They offered invitation to rest and reenergize. They have assumed fully the role of what Ray Oldenburg has called "the great good place."[7]

Restaurants, like gas stations and motels, are places defined at the scale of the retail store. They are contained in buildings signed and otherwise configured as readily identifiable behavior settings. They open and close, functioning over set durations of time. They have location, being proximate to other things, while having, as well, their own spatial extent. They engender or invite sets of ongoing behaviors. They facilitate the activities of certain kinds of people engaged variously in acts of production and consumption. Restaurants are furnished to encourage expected behaviors, being programmed, in other words, to encourage some kinds of social interaction and discourage other kinds. They have physical substance; but, equally as important, they symbolize. They carry social meaning.

When successfully contrived and located, restaurants turn profits as commercial or business propositions. Some function singly. Others are linked— networked into a restaurant system, an essence of corporate territoriality. In restaurant chains, place meanings are carefully replicated location to location through place-product-packaging, each link in a chain designed to function like all the others. Each restaurant chain promotes for itself some sense of distinctive personality (see fig. C.3). Customers come to know what to expect and are attracted (or, conversely, repelled) accordingly. Substantially, success in the restaurant business hinges on successful chain formatting—on successful place-making through cloning.

Roadside restaurants, taken in the aggregate, also contribute to another sense of place—that of the roadside itself, those linear landscape arrays marginal to highways. The roadside is as much a kind of experience as a kind of place. Being "on the road" carries with it clear place implication—actual places defined at various scales nest along linear trajectories of movement. What is anticipated, and what is remembered, is not so much physical reality as the feelings of release, excitement, and adventure that movement by automobile excites, especially in leisure time. The roadside completes the road as an overall context for experience. The roadside encapsulates and stimulates with sets of opportunities both supporting of and diverting from movement. It can be held in the distance as mere visual display, or it can be directly engaged toward some satisfaction.

Roadside America helps to anchor life quite apart from travel. The road (and the roadside) serves as a source of metaphor helpful in conceptualizing modern life. Remembering the roadside as it used to be provides not just the stuff of nostalgia, but the stuff of personal history whereby Americans measure themselves in time. A rendezvous for teenagers in the 1950s and 1960s, drive-ins and diners were places for convening a generational subculture built substantially around cars. Teenagers could meet in drive-in parking lots beyond parental surveillance and adult authority, coming and going on their own initiatives. Being there was a means of legitimating oneself as a teenager, and thus of inserting oneself into a community of peers.[8] The movies *Diner* and *American Graffiti* showed the roadside restaurant as a conventional place of mooring, a metaphoric refrain in daily routine and, consequently, a literally comfortable place. Participants relaxed in familiar roles. Such places have taken on mythical import for several generations continuing to indulge belief in unique needs. Owners of classic fifties cars, for example, seek out remaining drive-ins as places for socializing in their road rallies with generational peers.

Conclusion

FIG. C.2 The queue of cars moves forward, the restaurant made part of the road itself.

FIG. C.3 Billboard advertising the Maverick Family Steak House, Springfield, Ill., 1996.

FAST
FOOD

Historical relevance evolves and dissipates by stages, we suspect. Roadside restaurants in various forms evolved as commonplace. Older forms gave way to new, victim to functional and physical obsolescence. A nostalgic "gee whiz" has been attached to certain categories of roadside relic. Diners and glitzy 1950s drive-ins have especially come to symbolize early automobility. This has prompted impulses to study, preserve, and even restore vestiges of roadside Americana. Already at hand are impulses to imitate and replicate traditional roadside places in new design. One anticipates the day not long coming when restorations and replications will seem commonplace, the cycle of changing apprehension completed.

There are two principal emphases to be recommended in undertaking landscape study. First, the built environment needs to be assessed for typicality. What is normative? What reaches out to other places as a base of similarity? Second, what is distinctive, even unique? What is it that distinguishes a place from other places? Place meaning involves a conjoining of both—the search for commonality and the search for distinctiveness. In the ephemeral world of roadside landscape, distinctiveness results from things old and new. Constant change through such related processes as place-product-packaging and corporate territoriality produces commonplaceness—the substantial homogenization that makes one roadside very much like another. What gives distinctive personality to a locale is the relic feature somehow residual from a past era and, as well, the new innovation freshly introduced anticipating times coming. Most students of roadside America emphasize the unique, especially the kitsch. The celebration of relic uniqueness found in 1920s and 1930s programmed architecture is given vivid play in coffee-table picture books. We have tried, however, to search for the normative as well. We have tried to understand the processes of homogenization—to focus more on the relics of standardization, the evidences of modernization that have actually prevailed decade to decade.

Like the other elements of the roadside, restaurants carry both cultural and personal meaning as places to be consumed. Our emphasis in this book,

however, has not been the consuming of places so much as place production—the creation of places for consumption. Our emphasis has been on
the entrepreneur—the restauranteur—as the creator of place. The roadside
may be a place for individuals to variously seek fulfillment, but it is also a
place for capitalists to profit—a place for entrepreneurs to experiment in
the development of restaurant formats and food emphases conducive to
customer satisfaction. The American roadside sustains a tension between
consumer needs and demands and the entrepreneur's ability to satisfy. *Conclusion*
Place-making along the roadside plays out as business gamble, whether
the small-scale experiments of mom-and-pop operators or the large-scale
contrivances of giant franchisors. The roadside is a place of negotiated transaction between producers and consumers, the former always constrained by
the latter's tastes.

   The American roadside has represented a kind of frontier for capitalism.
Highways substantially reorganized the nation, geographically turning cities,
for example, essentially "inside out" as people and activities decentralized.
Customers could be captured in novel ways—products and services packaged around automobility. Systems for selling were devised and replicated
across networks for selling, instilling substantial degrees of sameness from
one roadside to another, from one part of the country to another. We have
emphasized the rise of place-product-packaging and related corporate territoriality in the restaurant industry as it played out primarily along the nation's highways. We have not attempted to tell the whole story of the changing restaurant business in America, but we have, we feel, sketched its
outlines, focusing on dominant architectural formats and dominant food
emphases associated with the nation's emergent automobility.

   Laboring in roadside restaurants is one of the most revealing aspects of
the restaurant industry's embracing of automobile convenience. Of the
three primary roadside services—gas, lodging, and food—restaurant workers are those most clearly in view. Customers deal directly with servers and
cashiers, but often can see the kitchen help at work as well. Only cursory observation suffices to establish that power relationships prevailing in society
off the road are reinforced along the road as well. White middle-aged men
most often own and manage while women, minorities, the young, and
increasingly, seniors labor. Low-paid, temporary teenaged workers carry
much of the restaurant industry's labor requirements, especially in fast-
food places. Food production and delivery have been fully rationalized, but
primarily in ways to reduce labor costs.

   While speed is a virtue for consumers, it can be a curse for workers. Their
work is hard. The pace is fast and workers are on their feet throughout the
workday. Rewards amount to minimum wage or little more, waitresses and
waiters counting on tips to augment. Customers can be irritating, expecting
speedy service and making servers feel that they are accountable for unsat-
isfactory food. Few restaurant workers covet a lifelong career in such circumstances although exceptional people have emerged to be celebrated for their
saintly dedication and patient manner. The constant advertisement for

"workers needed" testifies to the overwhelming majority of employees who are dissatisfied with menial restaurant work. High turnover rates among workers remain a critical problem for the industry. Even the idealized carhops of the past, the most glamorous of all roadside workers ever, were functionally independent vendors, quite vulnerable because they essentially purchased food from their employers and resold it to customers.[9] Exploitation is one cost of automobile-induced speed in eating.

Throughout the roadside restaurant experience runs the theme of a world divided. Pleasantly distracting illusions mask serious and often distasteful realities. Modernity presents itself in full flower. Advertising and mass marketing play a leading hand. No question of the warnings nutritionists sound about fast-food threats to health. These are proven. But consider the dangerous illusions perpetuated in a Malthusian world too little contemplated. While low food supplies and intermittent starvation suggest deadly answers about the future in many places, Americans on the road are invited to follow only their impulses in eating. So it is that the realities of restaurant work, played out literally before customers' eyes, generate little critical assessment.[10]

Entrepreneurs, particularly the big corporate players, bridge the divide of illusion and reality by amplifying the sense of social good through feeding the masses. They see their industry in a missionary light. Management also convinces that it can do well as well as good. Opportunities for self-respect and clear pathways to progress, all measurable in awards and profits, are spread before graduates from in-house corporate training schools, all pointed toward subsequent profit tallies. Through franchising, small-business people sense shortcuts to success; franchisors benefit from pyramiding success through investment networks. The restaurant industry champions faith in the American dream. As autobiographies authored by successful players attest, it is not all myth.

Restaurants contribute significantly to the opportunistic character of the American roadside. Individual hard work and perseverance substitute for forethought and planning in the mythology promoted. Early on, the simple foods expected by consumers required little to no specialization or little technical expertise to prepare. "Try it and see if it works!" That was the motto followed by most. If ventures disappointed, then "sell out and move on." Although we will likely know little about the many who despaired and quit, we know from the biographies of the successful that success hinged on starting over several times in the face of repeated failure. We know that faith in self-ability played an important role, especially when close associates chose to give up. Family members at Domino's and Pizza Hut, and business partners at White Castle and A&W, for example, dropped out early, leaving the most determined to succeed. Business savvy served, but so also did bald obsession. Ray Kroc, Harland Sanders, Dave Thomas: they proved to be persisting exceptions, and thus are enshrined in the pantheon of roadside restaurant greats. From their enshrinement belief is sustained that almost anything was and is possible on the roadside.

By the late 1980s, nearly 90 percent of Americans ate at least once a week in restaurants, and 40 percent on a daily basis.[11] So convinced of a fundamental shift in the nation's way of eating was the U.S. Department of Agriculture that it produced the first in-depth study of eating out in America in 1989.[12] Several facts emerged. Whereas Americans spent 34 percent of their food dollars away from home in 1970, the percent rose to nearly 46 percent in 1989. Eating out in 1989 occurred most often in fast-food places (some 41 percent of the total spent) followed by family-type restaurants (some 25 percent). But family-type restaurants captured the largest share of expenditures (29 percent) followed by fast-food places with 27 percent. Americans were spending some $118 billion in restaurants.[13] In 1996, Americans spent over $200 billion.[14]

Place-product-packaging and its use by large corporations in creating large trade territories underlie much of the nation's shift from home food consumption to "eating out." Standardized, prepackaged food, merchandised under corporate brand names, already dominated grocery-store merchandising by the 1920s. The rise of the supermarket chains only intensified the American food shopper's reliance on branded products. Chain restaurants represent nothing more than a further extension of such practice. In chain restaurants, standardized food is prepared on-site and packaged under corporate logo for on-site consumption or carryout. In addition, added to the packaging of the food is the packaging of the restaurant itself as merchandising surround. As similar places are linked in geographical systems for selling, clear trade territories are defined.

The petroleum industry led the way in configuring the American roadside through place-product-packaging and corporate territoriality. Beginning around 1910 and accelerating rapidly in the 1920s, gasoline station chains evolved under the careful scrutiny of the Justice Department, the Supreme Court having mandated industry competition in its 1911 breakup of the Standard Oil Trust. Today the federal government continues to referee a level playing field where a dozen or so major petroleum companies compete, no single corporate entity dominating the nation's gasoline supply.[15] Nonetheless, gasoline retailing remains organized from the top down. Corporate investments in petroleum exploration, refining, and transportation bring a generic gasoline product to the market through networks of wholesale jobbers and local retailers all carefully orchestrated from on high.

The hospitality industry remained more the domain of local entrepreneurship, small-business people operating outside of corporate influence. Although big-city hotels required sizable capital investments and demanded modern management techniques, most of the newly emergent motels during the 1920s and 1930s remained mom-and-pop operations capitalized through "sweat equity" and operated often by trial and error.[16] Motel chains launched in the late 1930s were mostly "associations"—networks of small-business people referring customers to one another through guidebooks and other advertising. Motel chains, in other words, were initially organized from the bottom up. In the 1950s, as motels evolved into large, multimillion-dollar highway hotels, the corporate chains finally came to the fore largely through franchising. Investor syndicates were easier to organize, and banks and other financial institutions easier to tap, when proposed motels linked readily into place-product-packaging systems.

Selling food by the roadside remained even longer the province of the small operator. And, indeed, today the small independent restauranteur remains an important part of the roadside scene. It was not until the 1960s that place-product-packaging arrived in force in the restaurant industry through the instrument of business format franchising. Especially in the purveying of "fast food" (where low price remains perhaps the most important competitive advantage) is the corporate chain dominant. In the refueling of cars, automation has come to the fore. In motels, checking in and checking out is becoming increasingly streamlined and may yet be automated. But personalized service through the "human touch" remains essential to the serving of restaurant food. In restaurants, individualized attention remains an important customer expectation. Consequently, machine vending in restaurants has enjoyed only very limited success.

Early on critics could editorialize about the threat of roadside restaurants to landscape aesthetics (see fig. C.4). But, as the 1920s cartoon reminds, it was not the chain restaurant that initially participated in the creation of commercial strips, but small operators. The cartoon reminds just how far roadside restaurants have come both as architecture and as symbol. They have changed from unsightly shacks symbolizing cheapness, mercenary

FAST
FOOD

FIG. C.4 The threat of roadside restaurants. (*Source: Los Angeles Times,* April 6, 1924. Copyright 1924 Los Angeles Times. Reprinted with permission.)

opportunity, and landscape degradation to credible architecture signifying speed, convenience, and lifestyle. Thus corporate dominance of the
American roadside grows. Major changes are being introduced from the
top down in all areas of retailing. Today bundling appears to be an important trend. Certain restaurant chains have begun combining their stores
with those of other chains at selected locations. Different brands, and the
different foods that they represent, are conjoined to give customers complementary choice. Fast-food brands have been conjoined with gasoline brands *Conclusion*
in enlarged convenience stores. Will the combining of branded restaurant
and motel venues also see an increase?

A Role for Preservationists?

With change accelerating, and increasingly corporate driven, we should
ask: what is to become of redundant restaurant forms? What is or is not
worth preserving? Of late, historic preservation's impact on the American
scene has become more dramatic, inviting participation of more groups
with varied affinities. Appreciation of popular culture has joined appreciation of polite culture. But what about the ephemerality of popular culture as
expressed in roadside landscapes? Where is value to be found? Will it be the
comfortable categorization of particular roadside places according to architectural style? Can we move beyond the purity of particular roadside places
frozen in physical integrity to accept the jerried and continually remodeled
as worthy candidates for preservation also? What does not have significance?
What honestly can be excluded from preservation? Does elitism still mas-
querade behind anxious efforts to select just the right roadside places to
designate as landmarks? Must an example embody elements of an accepted
architectural style to win preservationist sentiments? What is to be learned
from the forces giving rise to architectural forms? Is it not the very process
of roadside development that should win intellectual recognition, however
much roadside entrepreneurship has been at odds with landscapes orderly
managed by professionals?

A Role for Landscape Historians

It has been argued that objects of mass culture are truly indistinguishable, their apparent novelty based on essentially skin-deep details alone.
Recent scholarship, less judgmental, has suggested that the systems yielding
these mass-culture objects require more than dismissal as the *deux ex
machina* of the hegemonic elite. The production of popular culture deserves
attention. For better or worse, media, for example, create a single audience
of many groups for whom the skin-deep and ephemeral are acceptable as
common denominator.[17] How is it that the visual titillation of roadside adventure engages ever-higher levels of interest and spending? We cannot just
dismiss this popular excitement as benighted and as awaiting education.
Scholars would do so at risk of their own irrelevance.

Future writing focused on both the entrepreneur's and the consumer's use of roadside places is to be encouraged. We have outlined the entrepreneurial roots of roadside commerce—focusing on roadside restaurants here, and, in previous work, on gasoline stations and motels. Indeed, this book completes an intended trilogy on the roadside encompassing refueling, sleeping, and eating in roadside America. But what does the roadside fully mean in today's consumption-oriented society? What cultural meaning does the roadside carry above and beyond the immediacy of the functional? At best, we have only been able to speculate, using our speculations to justify focus on entrepreneurship.

Roadside restaurants have been places promotive of social transformation, often without approbation. For every image conjured of joyful teenagers passing the rites of youth at drive-ins or of a nuclear family sitting down to the blissful experience of a dinner out, mother freed from the kitchen and participating as an equal, there are also images of social deviance. At roadhouses, liquor and light meals were sequences to illicit relationships beyond the bonds of daylight surveillance. Automobility's multifaceted workings have, perhaps, too exclusively been remembered in terms of society's normative cases. Liberalizing the social patterns of the past, not only conserving them in some regards, roadside eateries have substantially redefined opportunities for self-expression and exploration in consumer culture wherein preoccupation with one's own development is a consequence of choice.

Do not restaurants, especially those by the roadside, hold potential for symbolizing social change in America? Roadside restaurants may have helped catalyze some profound aspects of national identity. Closing off worker prerogatives has been one of the principal influences of the fast-food industry's routinization of labor. As a byproduct of its outstanding profits, McDonald's has delineated for consumers a way of feeling. One scholar has identified the "McDonald's experience" where friendliness, deference, diligence, and good cheer are mass-produced just like hamburgers.[18] Perhaps customers benefit. But what of the worker's sense of honesty and self-worth? How does alienation from one's own feelings, in keeping up marketing pretense, influence in the long term? Can civility, trust, and personal liberty be written into the fast-food experience? Surely exchanges at work accrue as cultural values in society at large.

The power of the roadside as a place of popular entertainment puts at risk serious efforts to define a scholarly agenda—thus to grasp more fully the roadside's cultural significance. Focus is easily distracted by the roadside's protean qualities, for example, the glitz of roadside restaurant formats. Scholarly work is further confounded by the variable quality of resources upon which to base comprehension. Data sources are not fully adequate. Trade magazines are dedicated to the latest trends, the persistent efforts for news reporting leaving untreated the stories of what failed or how innovations were adopted as commonplace. Corporate archives frequently amount to random collections of press releases and publicity-inspired photographs regularly purged for advertising campaign assemblages absent any archivist's oversight. Surveys documenting consumer preferences remain precious industrial secrets jealously guarded from eyes outside, scholars included. Historical society collections often contain splendid photographs but also ones safely historical, separated from a past no longer in competition except for nostalgic affection.

Oral history projects are imperative to recording roadside history and its pageant of personalities, of entrepreneurs and consumers alike. On happy occasions persistent scholars are presented with opportunities to interview figures important in past decisionmaking, and, in combination with scrutiny of documents, to reconstruct a past circumstance. The scholar becomes not only analyst but curator of his/her own archive. Past consumer response can only be inferred, except insofar as customer reminiscences come into play. As regards the historic roadside, the record is too often nonexistent, too much ephemeral like the gas stations, motels, and restaurants themselves. One is left, thus, with the task at once intriguing but challenging, sometimes even frustrating: how to write the past of a central American place type without the convenience of the resources known to be essential?

Conclusion

Disparate audiences hunger for understanding of the roadside, further complicating the view of the past. Various academic disciplines lend their insights but often overlook or dismiss the work of other disciplines seen as competitive to the "one best" viewpoint. In a postmodern environment at once appreciative of the underlying powerplays in differing perspectives and the wide range of helpful views, no one of which can be objectively authoritative, many still insist on the primacy of their view rather than inviting a collegial investigation from different perspectives in an intellectual landscape of shared interest. For others, the roadside is just too damn obvious to require rigorous contemplation. "It's in plain view. Enjoy!": so recommend many aficionados. We are surprised at how many of this mindset persist in "dumbing down" scholarly treatment of the roadside. For many people in the common walk of life it is often merely sufficient to affix personal recognition. Asserting overreaching societal significance looms as scholarly pretension. In a culture of automobile convenience, few lack fond memories of road trips taken with their refreshments, refuelings, and lodgings along the way. So many have so much they want to say that in effect no one can say it adequately for everyone's satisfaction. Surely in this very discordance we have the identifying trait of an essential place—the roadside—which many can agree to focus on and enjoy in many ways. While the roadside yet evolves, we should remain open to new insights. The roadside's dynamism should engender a supple and sensitive intellectual poise yet one guided by dialectical hypotheses. An open-handed acceptance of fellow travelers is in order for the road ahead.

Notes

INTRODUCTION

1. John A. Jakle and Keith A. Sculle, *The Gas Station in America* (Baltimore: Johns Hopkins University Press, 1994), and John A. Jakle, Keith A. Sculle, and Jefferson Rogers, *The Motel in America* (Baltimore: Johns Hopkins University Press, 1996).

2. Ray Oldenburg, *The Great Good Place: Cafés, Coffee Shops, Community Centers, Beauty Parlors, General Stores, Bars, Hangouts, and How They Get You through the Day* (New York: Paragon House, 1989), 9.

3. Ibid., 11.

4. John A. Jakle, "Roadside Restaurants: The Evolution of Place-Product-Packaging," *Journal of Cultural Geography* 3 (1982): 76–93.

5. John A. Jakle, *The Tourist: Travel in Twentieth-Century North America* (Lincoln: University of Nebraska Press, 1985).

6. James Hurt, "Images of Chicago," in *Illinois: Its History and Legacy,* ed. Roger D. Bridges and Rodney O. Davis (St. Louis: River City Publishers, 1984), 172.

7. Keith A. Sculle, "Finger-Licking Landmarks: Pioneer Fast Food Places," *Illinois Magazine* 21 (1982): 13–15; and Sculle, "Diners," *Historic Illinois* 5 (1983): 1–4.

8. This idea has been explored by Ruth Reichl in "When Going Out Is In, We Are Where We Eat," *New York Times,* April 2, 1995, 6e. The phrase "we are what we eat" is attributable to the French gourmand Anthelme Brillat-Savarin. See Warren J. Belasco, *Appetite for Change: How the Counterculture Took on the Food Industry* (Ithaca, N.Y.: Cornell University Press, 1993), 15.

9. Richard Pillsbury, *From Boarding House to Bistro: The American Restaurant Then and Now* (Boston: Unwin Hyman, 1990); John Mariani, *America Eats Out* (New York: William Morrow, 1991); John Baeder, *Diners* (New York: Harry N. Abrams, 1978); Richard J. S. Gutman, *American Diner, Then and Now* (New York: Harper Perennial, 1993); Paul Hirshorn and Steven Izenour, *White Towers* (Cambridge: MIT Press, 1979); Alan Hess, *Googie: Fifties Coffee Shop Architecture* (San Francisco: Chronicle Books, 1985); Michael Karl Witzel, *The American Drive-In: History and Folklore of the Drive-In Restaurant in American Car Culture* (Osceola, Wis.: Motorbooks International, 1994); Jim Heimann, *Car Hops and Curb Service: A History of American Drive-In Restaurants, 1920–1960* (San Francisco: Chronicle Books, 1996); Philip Langdon, *Orange Roofs, Golden Arches: The Architecture of American Chain Restaurants* (New York: Knopf, 1986); Stan Luxenberg, *Roadside Empires: How the Chains Franchised America* (New York: Penguin Books, 1985).

10. For an excellent introduction to the landscape concept, see George F. Thompson, ed., *Landscape in America* (Austin: University of Texas Press, 1995).

11. John B. Jackson, *Discovering the Vernacular Landscape* (New Haven: Yale University Press, 1984), 5. For definition of common or vernacular landscapes also see D. W. Meinig, ed., *The Interpretation of Ordinary Landscapes* (New York: Oxford University Press, 1979).

12. For an overview of the place concept embracing landscape visualization as well as function or utility, see John A. Jakle, *The Visual Elements of Landscape* (Amherst: University of Massachusetts Press, 1987).

13. See Erving Goffman, *The Presentation of Self in Everyday Life* (Garden City, N.Y.: Doubleday Anchor Books, 1959). For a discussion of front and back regions in touristic contexts, see Dean MacCannell, *The Tourist: A New Theory of the Leisure Class* (New York: Schocken Books, 1976).

14. Erving Goffman, *Relations in Public: Microstudies of the Public Order* (New York: Basic Books, 1971); Roger G. Barker, *Ecological Psychology: Concepts and Methods for Studying the Environment of Human Behavior* (Stanford, Calif.: Stanford University Press, 1968); Irwin Altman, *The Environment and Social Behavior* (Monterey, Calif.: Brooks/Cole, 1979).

15. John A. Jakle, "Small Towns as Historical Places: A Symbolic Interactionist Approach to Structuration Theory Through the Study of Landscape," in *Marginalized Places and Populations: A Structurationist Agenda*, ed. David Wilson and James O. Huff (Westport, Conn.: Praeger, 1994), 61–83.

16. Robert D. Sack, *Place, Modernity, and the Consumer's World* (Baltimore: Johns Hopkins University Press, 1992), 1, 3.

17. Mark Gottdiener, *The Theming of America: Dreams, Visions, and Commercial Spaces* (Boulder, Colo.: Westview Press, 1997), 4.

18. M[ark]. Gottdiener, *Postmodern Semiotics: Material Culture and the Forms of Postmodern Life* (Oxford, U.K.: Blackwell, 1995), 74.

CHAPTER 1. THE RISE OF THE QUICK-SERVICE RESTAURANT

1. Mariani, *America Eats Out*, 25.

2. *Webster's New International Dictionary*, 2nd ed. (Springfield, Mass.: G. and C. Merriam, 1949), 2124.

3. U.S. Bureau of the Census, *1982 Census of Retail Trade;* discussed in Robert L. Emerson, *The New Economics of Fast Food* (New York: Van Nostrand Reinhold, 1990), 33.

4. "The U.S. Eating-Out Market," *Cornell Hotel and Restaurant Administration Quarterly* 7 (August 1967): 2.

5. Emerson, *New Economics of Fast Food*, 3.

6. Mariani, *America Eats Out*, 174.

7. The number of "eating and drinking places" in 1985 was estimated at 297,536, with "limited menu restaurants" numbering 121,645. See "20th Annual RGI [restaurant growth index] Industry Summary," *Restaurant Business* 86 (Sept. 20, 1987): 107.

8. "24th Annual Industry Report," *Restaurant Business* 90 (Sept. 20, 1991): 74.

9. Christopher C. Muller and Robert H. Woods, "An Expanded Restaurant Typology," *Cornell Hotel and Restaurant Administration Quarterly* 35 (June 1994): 27.

10. Daniel P. Puzo, "Industry Forecast," *Restaurants and Institutions* 107 (Jan. 1, 1997): 29. This statistic includes quick-service and fuel-service restaurants. When expanded to include all forms of food service, the industry generated some $330 billion in sales in 1996.

11. "Nutrition: Fast Foods," *Current Health* 2 (May 1979): 15.

12. See Bettye Rice Hughes, "A Negro Tourist in Dixie," *The Reporter* 26 (April 26, 1962): 20–21; "Civil Rights: Discriminating Taste," *Time* 92 (Aug. 30, 1968): 36.

13. Warren J. Belasco, *Americans on the Road: From Autocamp to Motel, 1910–1945* (Cambridge: MIT Press, 1979), 59.
14. *Hotel Planning and Outfitting: Commercial, Residential, and Recreational* (Chicago: Albert Pick-Barth Companies, 1928), 15. See Karl B. Raitz and John Paul Jones, "The City Hotel as Landscape Artifact and Community Symbol," *Journal of Cultural Geography* 9 (Fall/Winter 1988): 17–36; and Jakle, Sculle, and Rogers, *Motel in America,* 26.
15. Paul Dickson, *The Great American Ice Cream Book* (New York: Atheneum, 1972), 89.
16. J. A. Silander, "The Soda Fountain Story," *Ice Cream Trade Journal* 47 (June 1951): 30.
17. Langdon, *Orange Roofs, Golden Arches,* 9.
18. "How the Hot Soda Fountain Is Advertised," *The Soda Fountain* 15 (February 1916): 47.
19. Robert S. Merrill, "Spreads Unjust Criticism of Fountain Lunch," *The Soda Fountain* 23 (June 1924): 37.
20. Frederick Allen, *Secret Formula* (New York: Harper Business, 1994), 21.
21. Ibid., 213.
22. "Pop Culture: Soft Drinks Have Been an Integral Part of the American Landscape since the 1800s," *Restaurant Business* 93 (March 1994): 136.
23. Witzel, *American Drive-In,* 168.
24. Mariani, *America Eats Out,* 113.
25. Langdon, *Orange Roofs, Golden Arches,* 10.
26. "New York's 'Goldstone' Cost $83,000," *The Soda Fountain* 14 (September 1915): 25.
27. Frank G. Shattuck, "We Found Quality the Shortest Road to Volume," *System: The Magazine of Business* 43 (March 1923): 409.
28. F. H. Sinclair, "Schrafft's Success Is Based on Quality," *The Soda Fountain* 33 (April 1934): 14.
29. "Advertising: Schrafft's Gets with It," *Time* 92 (Oct. 25, 1968): 98.
30. Elmer A. Lundberg, "Put Up a Good Front," *Restaurant Digest* (September 1947): 9.
31. Sinclair Lewis, *Oil!* (New York: Grosset and Dunlap, 1926), 18.
32. Gary Thatcher, "Are True, Down-Home Southern Restaurants Gone with the Wind?" *Christian Science Monitor,* Sept. 11, 1986, 7.
33. William Least Heat Moon, *Blue Highways: A Journey into America* (Boston: Little, Brown, 1982), 26.
34. Pillsbury, *From Boarding House to Bistro,* 46.
35. Ibid.
36. Ruth Kedzie Wood, *The Tourist California* (New York: Dodd, Mead, 1914).
37. Mariani, *America Eats Out,* 119.
38. Jane Stern and Michael Stern, "Cafeteria," *New Yorker Magazine,* Aug. 1, 1988, 37–54.
39. Tom Mahoney and Mort Weisinger, "Everybody's Clubhouse," *Restaurant Digest* (November 1950): 11; see Langdon, *Orange Roofs, Golden Arches,* 16.
40. "White Tower Opens First Automatic Restaurant," *American Restaurant* (January 1962): 5.
41. The early history of the diner has been well documented. See John Hunter, "The Diner in Worcester, 1890–1970: Mass Cultural Elements in an Urban Landscape," *Monadnock* 52 and 53 (1978–79): 45–54; Joseph T. Manzo, "From Pushcart to Modular Restaurant: The Diner on the Landscape," *Journal of American Culture* 13 (Fall 1990): 13–21; Mariani, *America Eats Out;* Gutmann, *American Diner.*
42. Mariani, *America Eats Out,* 108.
43. Gutman, *American Diner,* 113.
44. "'Coffee and' in the Doggy Dog-Wagon," *Literary Digest* 112 (Feb. 20, 1932): 42.
45. "The Diner Business," *Fortune* 46 (July 1952): 167.
46. Manzo, "From Pushcart to Modular Restaurant," 19. See also Andrew Hurley, "From Hash House to Family Restaurant: The Transformation of the Diner and Post–World War II Consumer Culture," *Journal of American History* 83 (March 1997): 1282–1308.
47. "The Lunch Wagon Settles Down," *New York Times,* Oct. 19, 1941, 20.

48. See E. W. Ingram, *"All This from a 5-cent Hamburger!": The Story of the White Castle System* (New York: Newcomen Society in North America, 1964); Andy Siering, "The Castle, No One Escapes Its Spell," *St. Louis* 16 (February 1984): 55–57, 72–74.

49. Langdon, *Orange Roofs, Golden Arches*, 30.

50. Ingram, *"All This from a 5-cent Hamburger!"* 10.

51. Hirshorn and Izenour, *White Towers*, 1.

52. Ibid., 22.

53. Mariani, *America Eats Out*, 126.

CHAPTER 2. QUICK-SERVICE RESTAURANTS IN THE AGE
OF AUTOMOBILE CONVENIENCE

1. U.S. Department of Transportation, Federal Highway Administration, *Highway Statistics: Summary to 1985* (Washington, D.C.: U.S. Government Printing Office, n.d.), Table MV-201.

2. U.S. Department of Transportation, Federal Highway Administration, *Selected Highway Statistics and Charts, 1990* (Washington, D.C.: U.S. Government Printing Office, n.d.), Table ss90-4, ss90-17.

3. Effie Price Gladding, *Across the Continent by the Lincoln Highway* (New York: Brentano's, 1915), 228.

4. Warren J. Belasco, "Toward a Culinary Common Denominator: The Rise of Howard Johnson's, 1925–1940," *Journal of American Culture* 2 (Fall 1979): 506.

5. Ibid., 507.

6. Jan Whitaker, "Catering to Romantic Hunger: Roadside Tea Rooms, 1909–1930," *Journal of American Culture* 15 (Winter 1992): 21. See also Cynthia Brandimarte, "To Make the Whole World Homelike: Gender, Space, and America's Tea Room Movement," *Winterthur Portfolio* 30 (January 1995): 1–19.

7. Josephine Ware and Jeannette Ware, "The Tea-Room Business," *Journal of Home Economics* 1 (October 1924): 565.

8. "Coney Island's Soda Fountains," *The Soda Fountain* 14 (October 1924): 565.

9. W. Dwayne Jones, "In Search of the Vernacular Twentieth-Century Drive-In Restaurant," in *Preserving the Recent Past*, ed. Deborah Slaton and Rebecca A. Shiffer (Washington, D.C.: Historic Preservation Education Foundation, 1995), 2:31.

10. "Drive-Ins: A Chronology," in *Drive-In Management Guidebook*, ed. Lawrence Witchell (New York: Harcourt Brace, 1968), 9. See also Jones, "In Search of the Vernacular," 32.

11. Cecil Roberts, *Gone Sunward* (London: Hodder and Stoughton, 1936), 205.

12. "Unusual Places That Get the Business," *The Soda Fountain* 30 (February 1931): 23.

13. Ibid.

14. Jim Heimann and Rip Georges, *California Crazy: Roadside Vernacular Architecture* (San Francisco: Chronicle Books, 1980), 20; David Gebhard, "Programmatic Architecture: An Introduction," *Society for Commercial Archeology Journal* 13 (Spring/Summer 1995): 2.

15. "The New Outlet—Roadside Refreshment Stands," *Printers' Ink* 135 (April 22, 1926): 127.

16. Leslie Childs, "'Hot Dog Kennels' as Nuisances to Adjoining Property Owners," *American City* 38 (February 1928): 137.

17. "Elevating the Standing of the 'Hot Dog Kennel,'" *American City* 38 (May 1928): 99; see also "Winning Designs in the Wayside Refreshment Stand Competition," *American Builder* 45 (July 1928): 92; and Graves and Epps, Architects, "Journal Roadside Stands," *Ladies Home Journal* 29 (August 1932): 46–47.

18. Waldon Fawcett, "Roadside Merchants Organize to Study Mutual Problems," *Sales Management and Advertising Weekly* 15 (Sept. 1, 1928): 480.

19. Lord Kinross, *The Innocents at Home* (New York: Morrow, 1959), 193.

20. John Steinbeck, *The Wayward Bus* (New York: Viking Press, 1947), 5.

21. "Cafes Operated by 47 Per Cent of Courters: Becoming Vital Part of the Industry," *Tourist Court Journal* 2 (June 1939): 5.

22. "Motel Food Service," *Restaurant Digest* (July 1956): 28.

23. "10,000 Motorists' Dollars Help Howard Johnson Build Up Chain of 130 Company-Owned Shops," *Ice Cream Review* 23 (July 1940): 25.

24. See Chris Gould, "Howard Johnson's and the Standardizing of Roadside Architecture," *North American Culture* 7 (1991): 3–18.

25. Stephen A. Kurtz, "Howard Johnson's Elevating the Host," in *Wasteland: Buying the American Dream* (New York: Praeger, 1973), 23.

26. Hess, *Googie,* 61, 67.

27. Langdon, *Orange Roofs, Golden Arches,* 121.

28. Mariani, *America Eats Out,* 181.

29. "Houston's Drive-In Trade Gets Girl Show with Its Hamburgers," *Life* (Feb. 26, 1940): 84.

30. "Winstead's of Kansas City: Where Hamburgers and Shakes Are King and Queen," *Drive-In Magazine* 21 (September 1957): 15.

31. "Where the Drive-Ins Are," *Drive-In Restaurant* 28 (April 1964): 16.

32. Jones, "In Search of the Vernacular," 35; see also Michael Karl Witzel, *The American Drive-In* (Osceola, Wis.: Motorbooks International, 1994), 128.

33. Langdon, *Orange Roofs, Golden Arches,* 63; see also Harry E. Werner, "Designing Modern Drive-Ins," *Architecture* 30 (January 1953): 96–103.

34. "Free Movies Keep 'Em Comin' to Casey's Drive-In," *Fountain Service* 47 (November 1948): 26.

35. "World's Largest Drive-In," *Restaurant Digest* (May 1953): 25.

36. "The Drive-In That Jack Built," *Restaurant Management* 83 (December 1958): 53.

37. Lon Fanald, "A Robot Takes the Car Hop Out of the Track's Service," *Fountain Service* 49 (November 1950): 31; James Forton, "A Telephone Speeds Service," *Fountain Service* 49 (July 1950): 28; "For Labor Saving Speed Service, Customers Phone the Orders at Bill's Seattle Drive-In," *Fountain Service* 49 (November 1950): 31–32; Langdon, *Orange Roofs, Golden Arches,* 72; "Drive-In Service Goes Automatic," *American Restaurant Magazine* (September 1953): 89.

38. Theodore Goldberg, "The Automobile: A Social Institution for Adolescents," *Environment and Behavior* 1 (December 1969): 157–85.

39. "What Makes the Teenager Tick?" *Drive-In Magazine* 23 (September 1959): 10–15, and 23 (October 1959): 9–12; "A Drive-In's Program for 'Juvenile Adult' Control," *Drive-In Restaurant* 28 (August 1964): 16–17.

40. David G. Orr, "The Ethnography of Big Mac," in *The World of Ronald McDonald,* ed. Marshall Fishwick (Bowling Green, Ohio: Bowling Green State University Popular Press, 1978), 382.

41. Joseph F. Trimmer, "Enter the Wizard," in *World of Ronald McDonald,* ed. Fishwick, 349.

42. "Self-Service Works When There Is Money to be Saved by Customers," *Fast Food* 63 (May 1964): 93.

43. Trimmer, "Enter the Wizard," 350, 352.

44. Ralph L. Blaikie, "Remodeling a Drive-In around Its New Take-Home Department," *Fountain and Fast Food* 53 (March 1954): 44.

45. "How Burger Chef Speeds Service," *Fast Food* 58 (January 1959): 33.

46. Bruce A. Lohof, "Hamburger Stand: Industrialization and the American Fast-Food Phenomenon," *Industrial Archaeology Review* 2 (1978): 272–76.

47. "Biff Burger Experimenting to Come Up with 'The Best,'" *Fast Food* 63 (May 1964): 166.

48. E. Christine Jackson, "Ethnography of an Urban Burger King Franchise," *Journal of American Culture* 2 (Fall 1979): 534–39.

49. "The Growing American Appetite for Inexpensive Food," *Restaurant Business* 78 (May 1979): 159.

50. Max Boas and Steve Chain, *Big Mac: The Unauthorized Story of McDonald's* (New York: Mentor Books, 1976), 48.

51. Carol Lynn Tiegs, "Burger Chef Carving Out an Image," *Restaurant Business* 79 (March 1, 1980): 162.

52. Robert L. Emerson, *Fast Food: The Endless Shakeout* (New York: Lebhar-Friedman, 1979), 113.

53. "Restaurants Follow Them Home," *Business Week* (May 3, 1952): 44–47.

54. Carol Casper, "Food-to-Go: Market Segment Report," *Restaurant Business* 90 (Nov. 1, 1991): 122.

55. Witzel, *American Drive-In,* 28.

56. "Pick a Good Location and Then Merchandise It!" *American Restaurant Magazine* 38 (October 1954): 71.

57. "Six Serve Sixty Cars an Hours . . . Without One Car Hop!" *Fast Food* 55 (February 1957): 50–51.

58. Emerson, *Fast Food,* 91.

59. Rona Gindin, "Drive Thru-Only Revs Up," *Restaurant Business* 85 (May 20, 1986): 148.

60. Emerson, *Fast Food,* 92.

61. Deb Reichman, "Fast-Food Technologists Work to Make Their Products Safe for Motorists," *Centre Daily Times,* July 11, 1997, 9A.

62. "The Post House New Fountain Sanitation Rating Plan," *Fountain Service* 46 (October 1947): 30.

63. "Post House Uses an Auxiliary Fountain," *Fountain Service* 47 (September 1948): 30–31.

64. "Tourists and Your Business," *Restaurant Digest* (August 1960): 1–3.

65. "Horne's—What It Takes to Get Rich," *Restaurant Management* 92 (July 1963): 25–26.

66. Kenneth Lelen, "Stuckey's: Still Kicking," *Restaurant Business* 93 (Nov. 1, 1994): 70–71.

67. I. J. Nickerson, quoted in postcard caption.

68. "Food and Fuel: Four Approaches to One-Stop Service," *Fast Food* 68 (July 1969): 103.

69. "Truckstop: Multi Billion-Dollar Business," *National Petroleum News* 66 (October 1968): 71, 77.

70. John Radford, "Fast Food along the 427-Mile New York State Thruway," *Fountain and Fast Food* 53 (August 1954): 34–35.

CHAPTER 3. RESTAURANT CHAINS

1. Thomas S. Dicke, *Franchising in America: The Development of a Business Method, 1840–1980* (Chapel Hill: University of North Carolina Press, 1992); Charles L. Vaughn, *Franchising: Its Nature, Scope, Advantages, and Development* (Lexington, Mass.: Lexington Books, 1979), 34.

2. *Franchising in the U.S. Economy: Prospects and Problems,* Committee on Small Business, House of Representatives, 101st Congress, 2nd sess. (Washington, D.C.: U.S. Government Printing Office, 1990), 9.

3. Dicke, *Franchising in America,* 129.

4. Charles L. Vaughn, "Survey of Fast Food Franchising," *Cornell Hotel and Restaurant Administration Quarterly* 11 (November 1970): 24.

5. John F. Love, *McDonald's: Behind the Arches* (Toronto: Bantam Books, 1986), 57.

6. Emerson, *New Economics of Fast Food,* 59.

7. "Cramping the Business Style of Franchisors," *Business Week* (June 16, 1975): 82.

8. Ray Kroc, *Grinding It Out: The Making of McDonald's* (New York: Berkley, 1977), 178.

9. Robert Metz, *Franchising: How to Select a Business of Your Own* (New York: Hawthorn Books, 1969), 139.

10. Ibid., 140; David Shulman, "Food Franchising," *Franchise Journal* 2 (July/August 1969): 33.

11. Metz, *Franchising,* 158.

12. Carol Jouzaitis, "Franchises Shrug Off Recession," *Chicago Tribune,* Jan. 11, 1983, sec. 3, p. 7.

13. "Restaurant Franchising in the Economy," *Restaurant Business* 81 (March 15, 1982): 109.

14. Kevin Farrell, "Burger King: 'Making It Special,'" *Restaurant Business* 80 (Oct. 1, 1981): 102.

15. W. Charles Thor Jr., "Profile of a Franchise," *Modern Franchising* 13 (February / March 1971): 10.

16. Love, *McDonald's,* 372.

17. "Toward a Black Middle Class," *Fast Food* 68 (November 1969): 129.

18. Vaughn, *Franchising,* 25.

19. Belasco, "Toward a Culinary Common Denominator," 511.

20. "Howard Johnson's New Flavor," *Business Week* (Oct. 19, 1963): 109.

21. "Giant British Firm Buys Hojo for $630 Million," *Institution* 85 (Oct. 15, 1979): 3.

22. John Merwin, "The Sad Case of the Dwindling Orange Roofs," *Forbes* (Dec. 30, 1985): 77.

23. "Meet the Big Boys from Big Boy," *Restaurant Business* 74 (June 1975): 65.

24. "Big Boys of America—A Sleeping Giant Wakes Up," *Institutions* 82 (May 15, 1979): 46.

25. "Cities on the Move: Fort Wayne," *Fast Food* 63 (February 1964): 71.

26. "Cultivating a Strong Comeback," *Restaurant Business* 80 (June 1, 1981): 132.

27. See Howard Schlossberg, "Elias Bros.' Goal, Keep Big Boy Big," *Restaurant Business* 87 (July 1, 1988): 152–54.

28. Charles Bernstein, *Great Restaurant Innovators: Profiles in Success* (New York: Lebhar-Friedman, 1981), 135.

29. Luxenberg, *Roadside Empires,* 239.

30. Rona Gindin, "Shoney's Shows Who's Boss," *Restaurant Business* 84 (Aug. 10, 1985): 194.

31. "Shoney's Bid Values TPI Enterprises at $160 Million," *New York Times,* Sept. 6, 1995, C4.

32. "Denny's: 'Strong Guidance from Our Office Paves the Way for Uniformity and Profit,'" *Fast Food* 63 (May 1964): 72.

33. "Denny's Stalks Billion Dollar Biz by 1980s," *Institutions* 80 (Feb. 1, 1977): 12.

34. Denise Garbedian-Brennan, "Vern Curtis' Grand Slam Market Strategy," *Restaurant Business* 81 (June 1, 1982): 125.

35. Joe Baer, "Sambo's Turns Managers into Tigers," *Fast Food* 65 (December 1966): 39.

36. Emerson, *New Economics of Fast Food,* 192.

37. "Sambo's Serves Its Managers an Extra Slice," *Business Week* (Jan. 26, 1974): 82; "Sambo's Many Problems: Morale, Image," *Newsweek* (March 6, 1978): 88.

38. Kevin Farrell, "Sambo's: What Went Wrong?" *Restaurant Business* 79 (May 1, 1980): 158.

39. Abby Mendelson, "Sambo's: What Really Happened?" *Fast Service/Family Restaurants* 41 (March 1982): 46.

40. Jacque W. Kochak, "Does VICORP Have a Tiger by the Tail?" *Restaurant Business* 85 (Jan. 20, 1986): 115.

41. See, e.g., D. Daryl Wyckoff and W. Earl Sasser, *The Chain-Restaurant Industry* (Lexington, Mass.: Lexington Books, 1978), xxvii; Mark J. Lawless and Christopher W. Hart, "Forces That Shape Restaurant Demand," *Cornell Hotel and Restaurant Administration Quarterly* 24 (November 1983): 7–17.

42. Luxenberg, *Roadside Empires,* 223.

43. "Mirror, Mirror on the Wall," *Forbes* 106 (Nov. 1, 1970): 21.

44. Greer Williams, "Good Mormons Don't Go Broke," *Saturday Evening Post* (June 10, 1950): 48–49, 157–60.

45. "Marriott Corporation," *Fast Food* 69 (November 1970): 93.

46. "Marriott Merger," *Restaurant Business* 81 (March 1, 1982): 30–31.

47. Peter Belinski and Denise Brennan, "Marriott Broadens Business Horizons," *Restaurant Business* 81 (June 1, 1982): 117.

48. Christopher Muller, "The Marriott Divestment: Leaving the Past Behind," *Cornell Hotel and Restaurant Administration Quarterly* 31 (February 1990): 8.

49. Robin Ashton, "Why Are Food Service Chains Selling? And Why Are Food Companies Buying Them?" *Institutions/Volume Feeding* 82 (April 15, 1978): 56.

50. Ibid., 68.

51. See Lisa Raflo and Jeffrey Durbin, "Teal Roofs and Pecan Logs: A History of Stuckey's Pecan Shoppes," *Journal Society for Commercial Archeology* 13 (Fall 1995): 2–8.

52. Pete Belinski and Sharon Pavlista, "Franchise Entrepreneurs: The Chain's Crucial Links," *Restaurant Business* 75 (Oct. 1, 1976): 108.

53. Ibid., 109.

54. George Lazarus, "Big Franchise Holder Nearing Burger King Crown," *Chicago Tribune,* Feb. 28, 1996, sec. 3, p. 3.

55. Emerson, *New Economics of Fast Food,* 7.

56. Ibid., 123.

CHAPTER 4. HAMBURGER PLACES, PART 1

1. Richard Ohmann, "Magazine Culture, ca. 1900," *Reviews in American History* 24 (1996): 52.

2. James J. Flink, *The Automobile Age* (Cambridge: MIT Press, 1988), 234–35; David Riesman, *The Lonely Crowd: A Study of the Changing American Character* (Garden City, N.Y.: Doubleday, 1955).

3. Stuart Ewen, *Captains of Consciousness: Advertising and the Social Roots of the Consumer Culture* (New York: McGraw-Hill, 1976); Roland Marchand, *Advertising the American Dream: Making the Way for Modernity, 1920–1940* (Berkeley: University of California Press, 1985); David M. Potter, *People of Plenty: Economic Abundance and the American Character* (Chicago: University of Chicago Press, 1954); Thomas Hine, *The Total Package: The Evolution and Secret Meanings of Boxes, Cans, and Tubes* (Boston: Little, Brown, 1995).

4. Elyce J. Rotella, *From Home to Office: U.S. Women at Work, 1870–1930* (Ann Arbor, Mich.: UMI Research Press, 1981), 3–7; Lynn Langway, Thomas Nicholson, Barbara Graustark, Dewey Grum, and Howard Lucy, "America: Out to Eat," *Newsweek* (Oct. 3, 1977): 86; Mariani, *America Eats Out,* 49–50; Pillsbury, *From Boarding House to Bistro,* 35–48, 51–53.

5. Ingram, *"All This from a 5-cent Hamburger!"* 17; Lohof, "Hamburger Stand," 272; Mary Etzel, interview by Keith A. Sculle in Galesburg, Ill., Aug. 24, 1995 (worked for Steak 'n Shake, 1941–72); Everett Roberts, telephone interview by Keith A. Sculle, March 21, 1983 (worked for Snappy Service, 1929–44).

6. Howard Kelley, interview by Keith A. Sculle, in Bloomington, Ill., Nov. 8, 1994 (worked for Steak 'n Shake, 1938–50). For an example of the slogan in a printed advertisement, see *Bloomington (Ill.) Daily Pantagraph,* July 4, 1934, 6.

7. James E. Brownell, "How Safe Is the Roadside Restaurant?" *Hygenia* 17 (July 1939): 590–91.

8. Langdon, *Orange Roofs, Golden Arches,* 5–25. For some exemplifying early roadside restaurants, see Clyde G. Bartel, "Getting the Motorist's Money!" *The Soda Fountain* 29, no. 8 (August 1930): 34, 36, 38; Arthur R. Herrmann, "Speed Spells Success," *The Soda Fountain* 30, no. 11 (November 1931): 28–30, 33; A. L. Lyman, "Light Out in Front Sales Stimulator," *The Soda Fountain* 32, no. 3 (March 1933): 16–19.

9. For example, see John Goodspeed, "Little Taverns," *Baltimore Magazine* (June 1986): 47.

10. Letitia Brewster and Michael F. Jacobson, *The Changing American Diet* (Washington, D.C.: Center for Science in the Public Interest, 1978), 4; Jeremy Rifkin, *Beyond Beef: The Rise and Fall of the Cattle Culture* (New York: Dutton, 1992), 56–59, 89, 155, 166.

11. Bill Bryson, *Made in America: An Informal History of the English Language in the United States* (New York: Avon Books, 1994), 196–97; J. Anthony Lukas, "As American as McDonald's on the Fourth of July," *New York Times Magazine,* July 4, 1971, 22; Mitford M. Mathews, ed., *A Dictionary of Americanisms on Historical Principles* (Chicago: University of Chicago Press, 1951), 769; Pillsbury, *From Boarding House to Bistro,* 49; Witzel, *American Drive-In,* 49; Harvey Levenstein, *Paradox of Plenty: A Social History of Eating in Modern America* (New York: Oxford University Press, 1993), 46. For a good popular

history of the hamburger, see Jeffrey Tennyson, *Hamburger Heaven: The Illustrated History of the Hamburger* (New York: Hyperion, 1993).

12. William Morris and Mary Morris, *Morris Dictionary of Word and Phrase Origins* (New York: Harper and Row, 1971), 269; Marvin Harris, "The Revolutionary Hamburger," *Psychology Today* 17 (October 1983): 6; Roderick Nash, *The Nervous Generation: American Thought, 1917–1930* (Chicago: Rand McNally, 1970), 142–46; Robert Sklar, Introduction, in *The Plastic Age (1917–1930)*, ed. Robert Sklar (New York: George Braziller, 1970), 1–24; William Saroyan, *Short Drive, Sweet Chariot* (New York: Phaedra, 1966), 127.

13. Bryson, *Made in America*, 182; Mathews, ed., *A Dictionary of Americanisms on Historical Principles*, 665; Morris and Morris, *Morris Dictionary of Word and Phrase Origins*, 230.

14. For examples, see Henry S. Ehle, "The Customers Approve," *American Restaurant Magazine* 35 (March 1951): 109; Phil Dessauer, "Fried Chicken Champ," *Coronet* 29 (March 1951): 150; Al P. Nelson, "Walkie-Talkie Drive-In," *American Restaurant Magazine* 35 (September 1951): 40; "Pick a Good Location and Then Merchandise It!" 72.

15. Levenstein, *Paradox of Plenty*, 46; Duncan Hines, *Food Odyssey* (New York: Thomas Y. Crowell, 1955), 100; "One Million Hamburgers and 160 Tons of French Fries a Year," *American Restaurant Magazine* 36 (July 1952): 44–45.

16. "Milk Shakes Yesterday and Today," *Drive-In Fast Service* 31 (April 1972): 53; John Russell Ward, "Legalized Beer Affect Fountain Volume?" *Soda Fountain Magazine* 32, no. 2 (February 1933): 11. For an example of how new soda fountains and curb service could drive an older drugstore's business, see E. Roy Albright, "Building Drug Store Business Around a Soda Fountain," *The Soda Fountain* (February 1934): 26–27, 35.

17. For a well-documented history of White Castle, putting it into the larger context of changed American eating in the twentieth century, see David Gerard Hogan, *Selling 'Em by the Sack: White Castle and the Creation of American Food* (New York: New York University Press, 1997).

18. Kroc, *Grinding It Out*, 96.

19. Ingram, *"All This from a 5-cent Hamburger!"* 10.

20. Ibid.; Langdon, *Orange Roofs, Golden Arches*, 30.

21. Ingram, *"All This from a 5-cent Hamburger!"* 21–22, 25; Langdon, *Orange Roofs, Golden Arches*, 30–31.

22. Langdon, *Orange Roofs, Golden Arches*, 30; Ingram, *"All This from a 5-cent Hamburger!"* 13–14, 17–19.

23. Ingram, *"All This from a 5-cent Hamburger!"* 14–15. For a brief overview of Betty Crocker, see Karal Ann Marling, *As Seen on TV: The Visual Culture of Everyday Life in the 1950s* (Cambridge: Harvard University Press, 1994), 206–13.

24. Ingram, *"All This from a 5-cent Hamburger!"* 15–16, 20, 23–24.

25. Ibid., 26.

26. Siering, "The Castle," 56.

27. W. Ray Luce, "White Castle and Preservation," *Society for Commercial Archeology News Journal* 2, no. 4 (September 1984): 4–6; Luce, "Kent State, White Castles and Subdivisions," in *Preserving the Recent Past*, ed. Slaton and Shiffer, 2:17; W. Ray Luce and Barbara Powers, "Porcelain Steel White Castle Restaurants in Columbus [Ohio]," National Register of Historic Places Inventory—Nomination Form, November 1983; U.S. Department of the Interior, National Park Service, National Register of Historic Places Evaluation/Return Sheet, "Porcelain Steel White Castle Restaurants, Franklin County, Ohio," May 4, 1984; W. Ray Luce, telephone interview with Keith A. Sculle, June 10, 1996; Kristin L. Wilson and Nella L. Bean, "White Castle Building #8," National Register of Historic Places Inventory—Nomination Form, June 1986.

28. Emma H. Fisher, telephone interview with Keith A. Sculle, Aug. 4, 1994 (Fisher is Hill's daughter) (hereafter Fisher interview); Merle Davis, telephone interview with Keith A. Sculle, June 12, 1983 (worked for Snappy Service, 1925–61) (hereafter Davis interview); Don Hill, telephone interview with Keith A. Sculle, Aug. 9, 1994 (Don Hill is Paul Hill's

son) (hereafter Don Hill interview); Grady Copeland, telephone interview with Keith A. Sculle, July 18, 1983 (worked for Snappy Service, 1930–50) (hereafter Copeland interview).

29. *Trenton (Missouri) Daily Republican and Tribune,* Oct. 8, 1925, 7.

30. Arabella Hill, telephone interview with Keith A. Sculle, Aug. 5, 1994 (Arabella is Don Hill's wife) (hereafter Arabella Hill interview); Davis interview; Merle Davis, letter to Keith A. Sculle, June 29, 1983 (hereafter Davis letter); Fisher interview.

31. *Trenton (Missouri) Republican Times,* Jan. 19, 1929, comic section, p. 2; Forrest Niedholt, telephone interview with Keith A. Sculle, Jan. 4, 1995 (Niedholt has been a Trenton area resident since 1918); Davis interview. For example of Hill's advertising in Chillicothe, Missouri, see *Cressant* 22 (1928), 142 (Chillicothe high school annual); *Polk's Memphis City Directory, 1927* (n.p.: R. L. Polk and Co., 1927), 1759; *R. L. Polk's Memphis City Directory* (n.p.: R. L. Polk and Co., 1928), 1779; *Polk's Memphis City Directory* (n.p.: R. L. Polk and Co., 1929), 1741; *Polk's Memphis (Tennessee) City Directory 1930* (Memphis: R. L. Polk and Co., 1930), 1706; *Polk's Memphis (Shelby County, Tenn.) City Directory, 1940* (n.p.: R. L. Polk and Co., 1940), 1492; Ralph Tandy, interview by Keith A. Sculle in Canton, Ill., Sept. 22, 1994 (worked for Snappy Service, 1932–34); Don Hill interview.

32. Jon C. Teaford, *Cities of the Heartland: The Rise and Fall of the Industrial Midwest* (Bloomington: Indiana University Press, 1993), xvii, 174.

33. Fisher interview.

34. *Kokomo (Indiana) Tribune,* July 31, 1931, 3; Davis letter; *Terre Haute Star,* Jan. 10, 1928, 1; Jan. 1, 1929, 4; May 11, 1929, 4; June 12, 1929, 4; June 16, 1929, 2, 8. For an economic overview of Terre Haute in the 1920s, see Robert M. Taylor Jr., Errol Wayne Stevens, Mary Ann Ponder, and Paul Brockman, *Indiana: A New Historical Guide* (Indianapolis: Indiana Historical Society, 1989), 270.

35. *Terre Haute Star,* Dec. 15, 1928, 4, and June 18, 1928, 4.

36. For example, see ibid., July 8, 1929, 29.

37. For various restaurant types exemplified, see ibid., March 22, 1928, 28; April 5, 1928, 9; July 19, 1928, 5. For coffee shops exemplified, see ibid., Sept. 13, 1928, 6.

38. Ibid., March 22, 1928, 14.

39. For example, see March 22, 1928, 14; Sept. 30, 1928, 21.

40. For June Brown's, see ibid., Feb. 14, 1929, 14. For free parking exemplified in advertising, see ibid., June 23, 1929, 25. For an example of a restaurant's cook advertised, see ibid., May 19, 1928, 12.

41. Ibid., Oct. 25, 1929, 24.

42. Davis interview; Everett Roberts, telephone interview with Keith A. Sculle, Oct. 19, 1994; *Oxford English Dictionary* 16: Soot-Styx, 2nd ed. (Oxford: Clarendon Press, 1989), 489.

43. *Terre Haute Star,* July 30, 1929, 12; "Way Back When," *Marion (Indiana) Chronicle-Tribune Magazine,* Jan. 29, 1972, 8.

44. Davis interview.

45. Cy Copra, telephone interview with Keith A. Sculle, Oct. 18, 1994 (worked for Snappy Service, 1932–61).

46. Don Hill, letter to Keith A. Sculle, Aug. 9, 1994 (hereafter Hill letter); Everett Roberts, telephone interview with Keith A. Sculle, March 21, 1983.

47. Cy Copra, telephone interview with Keith A. Sculle, Oct. 24, 1994.

48. Davis interview; Vic Abshier, telephone interview with Keith A. Sculle, July 22, 1983 (Abshier worked at the restaurant Hill sold in Owensboro, Ky.); Robert Knowles, telephone interview with Keith A. Sculle, July 14, 1983; Aug. 3, 1994 (Knowles is son of one of the founders of Snappy Service in Illinois); Don Hill interview; *Caron's Anderson, Ind. City Directory for 1933–1934* (Louisville, Ky.: Caron Directory Co., [1934]), 816; *Polk's Marion (Grant County, Ind.) City Directory, 1938* (Indianapolis: R. L. Polk and Co., 1938), 187; Nedra Bloom, "Crawfordsville Shanty Stands the Test of Time," *Indianapolis Star,* Jan. 18, 1984, sec. 1, p. 10. The only printed history of Hill's early business is "Hamburger

Now U.S. Sandwich," unidentified Terre Haute newspaper article in the possession of Robert Knowles. For a history of the Illinois branches of Snappy Service, see Keith A. Sculle, "A Family Business Affair: 'Snappy Service' in Central Illinois," *Historic Illinois* 18, no. 3 (October 1995): 3–6.

49. Don Hill interview.
50. Copeland interview; "Modern Homes and Schools in Evansville Vicinity Designed and Supervised by Jacob S. McCutchan, Who Has Great Faith in Kosnos" (advertising flyer in Jacob S. McCutchan manuscripts in authors' possession).
51. Copeland interview; Don Hill interview.
52. Arabella Hill interview; Hill letter.
53. Hill letter; Emma Fisher, letter to Keith A. Sculle, Sept. 9, 1994; Jacob McCutchan, telephone interview with Keith A. Sculle, March 26, 1984; Everett Roberts, telephone interview with Keith A. Sculle, Oct. 25, 1994; Davis interview; Sue Loughlin, "After 55 Years Here, Service to Snap at Cafe Famous for 5-cent Burgers," *Terre Haute Tribune-Star,* March 6, 1983, A10; Copeland interview.
54. James Van Meter, telephone interview with Keith A. Sculle, Aug. 16, 1990 (Van Meter worked for Snappy Service, 1940–54, 1956).
55. Don Hill interview.
56. Arabella Hill interview; Don Hill interview; "Marion Will Lose an 'Institution,'" unidentified Marion, Ind., newspaper article in authors' possession.
57. Loughlin, "After 55 Years Here, Service to Snap at Cafe Famous for 5-cent Burgers," A1; Pasquale Rocchio, "Hill's Snappy Service Here Is Last of 16-Diner Chain," *Kokomo (Indiana) Tribune,* May 29, 1983, 9.

CHAPTER 5. HAMBURGER PLACES, PART 2

1. "Hamburger: Still Profit King and Growing Bigger," *Food Service Magazine* 28 (September 1968): 25–27.
2. Emerson, *Fast Food: The Endless Shakeout* (New York: Lebhar-Friedman Books, 1979), 61; Ada Louise Huxtable, "Architecture for a Fast-Food Culture," *New York Times Magazine,* Feb. 12, 1978, 30; "Jack in the Box Proves Huge Success," *Drive-In Restaurant* 25, no. 6 (June 1961): 6–7.
3. Gary Hoover, Alta Campbell, and Patrick J. Spains, eds., *Hoover's Handbook of American Business* (Emoryville, Calif.: Publishers Group West, 1990), 452; "Jack v. Mac," *Newsweek* 105 (May 5, 1975): 71–72; Jacque White, "At Jack in the Box, Only the Name Is the Same," *Restaurant Business* 82 (Feb. 1, 1983): 172.
4. "Ralston Purina to Drop 232 Jack in the Box Fast-Food Restaurants," *Institutions Magazine* 85 (November 1979): 3; Delores Long, "Jack in the Box: A Strategy for Menu Superiority," *Restaurant Business* 86 (May 20, 1987): 124, 126; White, "At Jack in the Box, Only the Name Is the Same," 172, 174, 176; Kevin Farrell, "California Chain Casts Menu Stars," *Restaurant Business* 87 (Aug. 10, 1988): 106; "Ralston Purina Company," *Restaurants and Institutions* 98 (Oct. 28, 1988): 44; Emerson, *New Economics of Fast Food,* 9.
5. Farrell, "California Chain Casts Menu Stars," 107, 116; Steve Brooks, "The Long Road Back," *Restaurant Business* 93 (May 20, 1994): 48.
6. Langdon, *Orange Roofs, Golden Arches,* 93–94; "41 in Florida: All 41 Units Built on Insta's Pattern of Proven Success," *Drive-In Restaurant and Highway Cafe Magazine* 19 (June 1955): 19. For an autobiographical perspective by one of Burger King's founders on Burger King's history, see James W. McLamore, *The Burger King: Jim McLamore and the Building of an Empire* (New York: McGraw-Hill, 1998).
7. Lohof, "Hamburger Stand," 266, 269; "Franchising Success Means Constant Market Development," *Cornell Hotel and Restaurant Administration Quarterly* 11 (November 1970): 36; Pillsbury, *From Boarding House to Bistro,* 95–96; Love, *McDonald's,* 53.
8. Joe J. Haszonics, "Inside a Franchise," *Restaurant Magazine* 69, no. 3 (July 1962): 33–34, 37–38, 40; "Initial Capital, Plus the Desire to Succeed Is All We Ask of Franchisees," *Fast*

Food 63 (May 1964): 68–71; Ester Reiter, *Making Fast Food: From the Frying Pan into the Fryer* (Montreal: McGill-Queen's University Press, 1991), 64.

9. Marilyn Alva, "Can They Save the King?" *Restaurant Business* 93 (May 1, 1994): 104–7, 112–14; Reiter, *Making Fast Food,* 64; "From Neon to Brass," *Best: The Magazine of Pillsbury* (Autumn 1986): 6.

10. Langdon, *Orange Roofs, Golden Arches,* 148; Reiter, *Making Fast Food,* 64–65; "The Man Who McDonaldized Burger King," *Business Week* (Oct. 8, 1979): 132; "Burger King," in *International Directory of Company Histories,* ed. Lisa Mirabile (Chicago: St. James Press, 1990), 2:614.

11. "The Man Who McDonaldized Burger King," 132.

12. "Burger King," 614.

13. Emerson, *New Economics of Fast Food,* 66; "Burger King," 614.

14. Alva, "Can They Save the King?" 111–12, 114; "Burger King Buys 57 Restaurants for $55.6 Million," *New York Times,* Feb. 1, 1996, C4.

15. "How Burger Chef Speeds Service," 33–34.

16. Pillsbury, *From Boarding House to Bistro,* 139.

17. "How Burger Chef Speeds Service," 33.

18. "Franchised Drive-Ins," *Food Service* 27 (May 1965): 39.

19. Love, *McDonald's,* 62.

20. Tiegs, "Burger Chef Carving Out an Image," 158, 160.

21. Emerson, *Fast Food;* Emerson, *New Economics of Fast Food,* 8–9.

22. "Squeeze in Fast Food," *Time* (March 26, 1979): 63; "Fast Food Feast," *Time* (Nov. 30, 1981): 69; Dan Dorfman, "McDonald's Sizzling Out?" *Esquire* 91 (March 13, 1979): 10; Love, *McDonald's,* 281; "Hardee's Gets Burger Chef," *Restaurant Business* 81 (Feb. 1, 1982): 23.

23. "Top 400," *Restaurants and Institutions* 107 (July 15, 1997): 66.

24. Carole Marsh, *The Hardee's Heritage,* Hardee's Food Systems, Inc., Rocky Mount, N.C., 1976, 2–3 (repr. from *Hardee's News* 4, no. 5 [December 1976]).

25. Ibid., 6–7, 9, 11, 18; "Hardee's," *Fast Food* 67, pt. 2 (November 1968): 85–86; Timothy K. Nielsen, "Spartan Food Systems: The Professional Franchise," *Fast Food* 71 (May 1971): 194, 196.

26. Richard E. Hattwick, "Gust E. 'Brick' Lundberg," photocopy, Kewanee Business History Series 1, Illinois Business Hall of Fame, Center for Business and Economic Research, Western Illinois University, August 1976, 14–15; "Hardee's Honcho Has Roots in Q-C Area," *Davenport (Iowa) Quad-City Times,* Dec. 31, 1995, 3M; *Hardee's Food Systems, Inc., Annual Report 1972,* 8; Ralph Raffio, "Jack Laughery," *Restaurant Business* 82 (May 15, 1983): 148; *Hardee's Food Systems, Inc., Annual Report 1976,* 14; "Hardee's," *Restaurant Business* 78 (Jan. 1, 1979): 102.

27. Langdon, *Orange Roofs, Golden Arches,* 169–71; "Coming to Terms with Change," *Food Service Marketing* 40 (September 1978): 117.

28. "Hardee's Restructures," *Restaurant Business* 82 (February 1983): 26; Kevin Farrell, "Hardee's Burger Battle Plan," *Restaurant Business* 85 (Oct. 10, 1986): 212–13; *Imasco Annual Report,* 1988 (hereafter *IAR*), 10, 14–15.

29. *IAR,* 1994, 6; *IAR,* 1990, 10; *IAR,* 1991, 25; *IAR,* 1992, 12.

30. "Hardee's Is Set to Sell Its Roy Rogers Restaurants," *New York Times,* Dec. 16, 1995, 19; "Pact Set on Buying Roy Rogers Sites for $74 Million," *New York Times,* Aug. 3, 1996, Y-19.

31. "Top 400," 88; Anne Chamberlain, "A Live Show Daily at Hamburger Hamlet," *Fortune* 95 (March 1977): 209.

32. Chamberlain, "A Live Show Daily," 209, 217, 219.

33. Ibid., 212, 217; Frank P. Piontek (librarian, Beverly Hills Public Library), letter to Keith A. Sculle, July 5, 1996.

34. R. David Thomas, *Dave's Way: A New Approach to Old-Fashioned Success* (New York: Putnam, 1991); Thomas, *Well Done!: The Common Guy's Guide to Everyday Success* (Grand Rapids, Mich.: Zondervan, 1994). For an example of the popular literature about

Thomas, see Steven J. Austin, "America's Favorite 'Hamburger Cook,'" *Mississippi 55 & Fine* (May–October 1994): 4–7.

35. Wendy's Old-Fashioned Hamburgers information package, "R. David Thomas: How Wendy's Founder Worked His Way to Success," Wendy's International, Granville, Ohio [1995], 101.

36. Ibid., 2.

37. Ibid., 3. For Thomas's account of his part in creating Colonel Sanders's image and what Thomas learned from Sanders in return, see Thomas, *Dave's Way,* 79–86.

38. Austin, "America's Favorite 'Hamburger Cook,'" 4.

39. Bernstein, *Great Restaurant Innovators,* 9–10.

40. Ibid., 10–12; Langdon, *Orange Roofs, Golden Arches,* 144; Emerson, *Fast Food,* 60–61; Emerson, *New Economics of Fast Food,* 9.

41. "Wendy's Homes In on Young Adults," *Business Week* (July 11, 1977): 60–61.

42. Bernstein, *Great Restaurant Innovators,* 18–19.

43. Ibid., 16; Gary Hoover, Alta Campbell, and Patrick J. Spain, eds., *Hoover's Handbook of American Business* (Emoryville, Calif.: Publishers Group, 1995), 1112; Kevin Farrell, "Super Bar, Says Wendy's Will Position the Concept Outside of Competition's Way and Provide Continuing Flexibility," *Restaurant Business* 88 (Jan. 1, 1989): 83; James Scarpa, "Combo Deluxe," *Restaurant Business* 91, no. 7 (May 1, 1992): 115–16; Wendy's Old-Fashioned Hamburgers information package, "Wendy's Profits Up 20% in Second Quarter," [1995].

44. Pillsbury, *From Boarding House to Bistro,* 74; Langdon, *Orange Roofs, Golden Arches,* 35; "Krystal's Mini-Burger a Southern Tradition," *Jackson (Miss.) Clarion-Ledger,* Jan. 6, 1984, 5B.

45. "Krystal's Mini-Burger a Southern Tradition," 8A; "'Rekrystalized,'" *Fast Service/Family Restaurant* (March 1982): 37, 42; "Krystal Acquires Po Folks," *Restaurant Business* 81 (November 1982): 50, 55; Sean Mehegan, "In the Shop," *Restaurant Business* 94 (Oct. 10, 1995): 73.

46. "Karcher: Business Sense Plus Humanism Promotes Success," *Food Service and Chain Executive* 6, no. 9 (September 1978): 151; Rona Gindin, "The Karchers' Synergistic Growth Scheme," *Restaurant Business* 83 (Sept. 1, 1984): 162.

47. "Karcher," 151.

48. Gindin, "Karchers' Synergistic Growth Scheme," 165.

49. "Karcher," 159.

50. Gindin, "Karchers' Synergistic Growth Scheme," 162, 165–66.

51. Ibid., 162–64.

52. Alexa Bell, "Carl's Quandry," *Restaurant Business* 91 (July 1, 1992): 56, 57.

53. "The Name's the Same—But a Carrol's Franchisee Is Now the Franchiser," *Fast Food* 68 (March 1969): 160; Love, *McDonald's,* 55; "1977 Chain Executives Forum," *Food Service Marketing* 39 (December 1977): 39.

54. Emerson, *New Economics of Fast Food,* 90–91; Gindin, "'Drive Thru-Only' Revs Up," 149.

55. "Breaking with Brick," *Restaurant Business* 92 (Sept. 30, 1993): 134; Gindin, "'Drive Thru-Only' Revs Up," 147.

56. Rally's Hamburgers information package, "The Rally's Story," [1995]; "Checkers to Buy Rally's Hamburgers," *New York Times,* January 30, 1999, B3.

57. Emerson, *New Economics of Fast Food,* 94.

58. B. M., "The International Agenda," *Restaurants and Institutions* 105 (July 1, 1995): 146.

59. Emerson, *Fast Food,* 59.

CHAPTER 6. MCDONALD'S

1. For a financial analysis see "McDonald's Grinds Out Growth," *Dun's Review* 110 (December 1977): 50–52.

2. The Popular Culture Center, Bowling Green State University, has periodically studied McDonald's; especially see their anthologies: Marshall Fishwick, ed., *The World of*

Ronald McDonald (Bowling Green, Ohio: Bowling Green University Popular Press, 1978), and Fishwick, ed., *Ronald Revisited: The World of Ronald McDonald* (Bowling Green, Ohio: Bowling Green University Popular Press, 1983). For an anthropologist's insights, see Conrad P. Kottak, "Rituals at McDonald's," *Natural History* 87 (January 1978): 75–82. For a biography of Kroc ending in praise, see Ted C. Hinkley and Roderick C. Johnson, "Ray Kroc, Embodiment of Mid-Twentieth-Century America," *Journal of the West* 25, no. 1 (January 1986): 94–102.

3. Mariani, *America Eats Out,* 164.

4. Boas and Chain, *Big Mac,* 1–16; Love, *McDonald's,* 30–47; "Appealing to a Mass Market," *Nation's Business* 56 (July 1968): 71–72.

5. J. Ronald Oakley, *God's Country: America in the Fifties* (New York: Dembner Books, 1986), 238; Kroc, *Grinding It Out,* 108; Boas and Chain, *Big Mac,* 24, 27; Love, *McDonald's,* 278, 281, 470–71.

6. Oakley, *God's Country,* 120–21, 228, 249; Elaine Tyler May, *Homeward Bound: American Families in the Cold War Era* (New York: Basic Books, 1988), 137. For a social history of the family-oriented restaurant's replacement of the working-class diner after World War II, see Hurley, "From Hash House to Family Restaurant," 1282–1308.

7. Douglas T. Miller and Marion Nowak, *The Fifties: The Way We Really Were* (Garden City, N.Y.: Doubleday, 1977), 155; May, *Homeward Bound,* 145–49.

8. Clifford Edward Clarke Jr., *The American Family Home, 1800–1960* (Chapel Hill: University of North Carolina Press, 1986); Kenneth Jackson, *The Crabgrass Frontier: The Suburbanization of the United States* (New York: Oxford University Press, 1985), 203–13; Oakley, *God's Country,* 134–35; May, *Homeward Bound,* 16–36.

9. Miller and Nowak, *The Fifties,* 134; James Howard Kunstler, *Geography of Nowhere: The Rise and Decline of America's Man-Made Landscape* (New York: Simon and Schuster, 1993), 10.

10. Siegfried Gideon, *Mechanization Takes Command* (New York: Norton, 1948), 41–49; Cecelia Tichi, *Shifting Gears: Technology, Literature, and Culture* (Chapel Hill: University of North Carolina Press, 1987); Miller and Nowak, *The Fifties,* 128, 139.

11. William L. O'Neill, *American High: The Years of Confidence, 1945–1960* (New York: Free Press, 1986), 32; Karal Ann Marling, "America's Love Affair with the Automobile in the Television Age," *Design Quarterly* 146 (1989): 5–19.

12. "Service Is the Byword at White Hut," *Drive-In Restaurant and Highway Cafe Restaurant* 20, no. 8 (August 1956): 13, 17.

13. Ernest W. Fair, "Denver," *American Restaurant Magazine* 31 (August 1947): 26; Fair, "Salt Lake City," *American Restaurant Magazine* 31 (September 1947): 26; Fair, "Tulsa," *American Restaurant Magazine* 32 (May 1948): 30.

14. Kroc, *Grinding It Out,* 65.

15. For example, see "Circular Drive-In Includes Commissary," *Architectural Record* 100, no. 3 (September 1946): 101; "Shrine to the Hamburger," *Popular Mechanics* 91 (January 1949): 101–3; "Eating Goes On Assembly-Line at California Drive-In," *Business Week* (July 23, 1949): 22–23; "Tray on Trestle Serves at Drive-In," *Popular Mechanics* 92 (September 1949): 127.

16. Nelson, "Walkie-Talkie Drive-In," 40–41, 103.

17. Howard Kelley, interview with Keith A. Sculle in Bloomington, Ill., Nov. 8, 1994; Howard Kelley's untitled work manual, copy in authors' possession.

18. "Restaurant Blues," *Business Week* (April 5, 1947): 30.

19. "Restaurants Follow Them Home," 47.

20. Rifkin, *Beyond Beef,* 264–65.

21. Love, *McDonald's,* 15–16; Mariani, *America Eats Out,* 167; Oakley, *God's Country,* 267–90.

22. Love, *McDonald's,* 25–27; "One Million Hamburgers and 160 Tons of French Fries a Year," *American Restaurant Magazine* 36 (July 1952): 44. For the best account of the McDonald brothers' adventures in the emerging fast-food industry, see Love, *McDonald's,* 9–27. Too many antecedents, both businesspeople and cultural values, contributed to

fast food's development, however, to accept Love's claim (16–19) that the McDonald brothers invented fast food.

23. Luxenberg, *Roadside Empires,* 74; Witzel, *American Drive-In,* 106.

24. Sinclair Lewis, "Adventures in Autobuming—The Great American Frying Pan," *Saturday Evening Post* (Jan. 3, 1920): 62.

25. Kroc, *Grinding It Out,* 111–12, 173–74. Subsequent references appear by page number in the text.

26. Levenstein, *Paradox of Plenty,* 229, implies that Kroc viewed the suburbs simply as the richest treasure to take.

27. Kroc, *Grinding It Out,* 25–26, 57, 80, 112, 166.

28. Ibid., 7; Love, *McDonald's,* 85–86.

29. Kroc, *Grinding It Out,* 7–8.

30. Chain and Boas, *Big Mac,* the first serious history of McDonald's, was published the year before Kroc, *Grinding It Out.* Without the advantage of Kroc's account of his observations at the McDonald brothers' drive-in, Chain and Boas, *Big Mac,* explains Kroc's visit to the McDonald brothers' drive-in purely in terms of profit potential (10–13). Love, *McDonald's,* the best history of McDonald's, curiously ignores the extended anecdotal account of Kroc's epiphany at the McDonald brothers' restaurant in July 1954 (38–41). Perhaps the omission is due to a "linear" approach to business history which gives no meaning to things subjective, in this case Kroc's feelings about the business, instead focusing on the flow of logic toward Kroc's creation of the McDonald's empire.

31. Kroc, *Grinding It Out,* 9.

32. Ibid., 10, 71–73, 95–96, 131, 137; Emerson, *Fast Food,* 72.

33. Ibid., 73; Mariani, *America Eats Out,* 9.

34. Love, *McDonald's,* 275–300.

35. Ibid., 48, 72, 74, 78–85; Kroc, *Grinding It Out,* 79–80, 82–83, 146–47; "Appealing to a Mass Market," 72; "McDonald's Makes Franchising Sizzle," *Business Week* (June 15, 1968): 102–3.

36. "McDonald's Makes Franchising Sizzle," 102–3.

37. Kroc, *Grinding It Out,* 168.

38. "McDonald's Makes Franchising Sizzle," 102.

39. Ibid.; Love, *McDonald's,* 153–58.

40. "McDonald's Makes Franchising Sizzle," 102.

41. Ibid.

42. Ibid.; Kroc, *Grinding It Out,* 97; Love, *McDonald's,* 290–91.

43. Love, *McDonald's,* 147–49; Nancy Fraser, "Hamburger University," *Life* (Oct. 21, 1966): 100; [Mary Alice Kellogg], "Making the Grade at Hamburger U," *Newsweek* 80 (Sept. 25, 1972): 78.

44. [Kellogg], "Making the Grade at Hamburger U," 78.

45. Love, *McDonald's,* 101.

46. Kroc, *Grinding It Out,* 88. Also see "The Big Burger Boss," *Time* (Dec. 17, 1973): 100.

47. Kroc, *Grinding It Out,* 5–6; W. Earl Sasser and Samuel H. Pettway, "Case of Big Mac's Pay Plans," *Harvard Business Review* 52 (July–August 1974): 30–32, 36, 40, 44–45; "McDonald's Makes Franchising Sizzle," 102; Love, *McDonald's,* 142, 291–92, 394–95.

48. Love, *McDonald's,* 203–5, 219–21, 247.

49. Alan Hess, "Golden Architecture," *Journal: A Contemporary Art Magazine* 4, no. 36 (Spring 1983): 28–30; Hess, *Googie,* 97–107; Hess, "The Origins of McDonald's Golden Arches," *Journal of the Society of Architectural Historians* 54 (March 1986): 60–67; Alan L. Hess and John Beach, "McDonald's Drive-In Restaurant and Sign," National Register of Historic Places Inventory—Nomination Form, Aug. 3, 1983; U.S. Department of the Interior, National Park Service, National Register of Historic Places, Evaluation / Return Sheet, "McDonald's Restaurant and Sign," Los Angeles County, California, Dec. 8, 1983.

50. Kroc, *Grinding It Out,* 142–43; Love, *McDonald's,* 136–37; Langdon, *Orange Roofs, Golden Arches,* 90, 139–41.

51. Kroc, *Grinding It Out,* 138–39, 163; Love, *McDonald's,* 294.

52. Love, *McDonald's,* 187–201, 275; Fishwick, ed., *Ronald Revisited,* 8.

53. For example see "Burgers: Bracing for Battle," *Restaurant Business* 77 (March 1978): 128; "Jack v. Mac," *Time* (May 5, 1975), 71–72; Jeffrey Madrick, "A Cautious Approach to Fast-Food Chains," *Business Week* (March 28, 1977): 85; "Eating Out: A Binge That Defies Recession," *U.S. News and World Report* (Feb. 19, 1979): 62; Judith B. Gardner, "A Burger Battle—With Everything," *U.S. News and World Report* (Nov. 8, 1982): 76.

54. Kroc, *Grinding It Out,* 168; "Fast-Food Franchisers Invade the City," *Business Week* (April 27, 1974): 92.

55. Love, *McDonald's,* 358, 368–69; "An Academic Twist to the Sale of Hamburgers," *Ebony* 29 (October 1974): 72.

56. Reiter, *Making Fast Food,* 48; Rick Fantasia, "American Commodities as Cultural Goods: The 'Place' of Fast-Food in France," unpublished paper, Smith College, Northampton, Mass., cited in Robin Leidner, *Fast Food, Fast Talk: Service Work and the Routinization of Everyday Life* (Berkeley: University of California Press, 1993), 222; "Not For Export?" *Forbes* (Oct. 15, 1975): 23–24; "Bull in the Hamburger Shop," *Forbes* (May 15, 1973): 130; Love, *McDonald's,* 416.

57. Love, *McDonald's,* 297–99, 340–43; "Broader Menus for Fast Foods," *Business Week* (July 14, 1975): 118.

58. For example, see "How Nutritious Are Fast-Food Meals?" *Consumer Reports* (May 1975): 278.

59. "Fast-Food War: Big Mac Under Attack," *Business Week* (Jan. 30, 1984): 45.

60. Luxenberg, *Roadside Empires,* 168, 172, 174–75, 284; Reiter, *Making Fast Food,* 164–65; Joan Oleck, "Minimum Wage: How High?" *Restaurant Business* 93 (Dec. 10, 1994): 70; Michael Romano, "Minor Characters," *Restaurant Business* 92 (May 1, 1993): 56 [46, 50, 56].

61. Emerson, *Fast Food,* 263–70; Boas and Chain, *Big Mac,* 89–97; "The Burger That Conquered the Country," *Time* (Sept. 17, 1973): 90.

62. "The Fast-Food Furor," *Time* (April 21, 1975): 49, 51; Michael A. Lev, "Ronald's *Clowna Non Grata* to Some Lake Forest Residents," *Chicago Tribune,* April 28, 1994, 1, 6; Lukas, "As American As McDonald's on the Fourth of July," 27.

63. Lukas, "As American as McDonald's on the Fourth of July," 27; Antoinette McAllister, "Cities OK Fast-Food Chains—But Hold the Golden Arches," *Planning* 42 (October 1976): 20; Margaret J. King, "McDonald's and the New American Landscape," *USA Today* (January 1980): 48.

64. R.M.K., "Letter from the Country," *Country Journal* 6 (March 1979): 27.

65. For example, see "Commentary/Opinions," *Ferdinand (Indiana) News,* Aug. 8, 1996, 2; Wes Smith, "Small Town Fends Off an Attack by Big Mac," *Chicago Tribune,* Aug. 15, 1996, 1, 14; R.M.K., "Letter from the Country," 27.

66. Shelly Branch, "McDonald's Strikes Out with Grownups," *Fortune* (Nov. 11, 1996): 157–58, 160, 162; Kathy Bergen, "Franchisees Attack McDonald's," *Chicago Tribune,* May 22, 1997, 1, 4; Barnaby J. Feder, "Where Have You Gone, Ray Kroc?" *New York Times,* June 5, 1997, C1, C6; Feder, "Third Management Shake-Up at McDonald's in Two Years," *New York Times,* July 10, 1997, C2.

67. B.M., "The International Agenda," 142; Feder, "Where Have You Gone, Ray Kroc?" C1.

CHAPTER 7. SANDWICH PLACES

1. American Heritage editors, *The American Heritage Cookbook and Illustrated History of American Eating and Drinking* (New York: Simon and Schuster, 1964), 2:495 (hereafter *American Heritage Cookbook*); "The Hotdog," *Restaurants and Institutions* 99 (May 29, 1989): 108, 112.

2. *American Heritage Cookbook,* 2:495; "The Hotdog," 112.

3. *American Heritage Cookbook,* 2:495; "The Hotdog," 112; Bryson, *Made in America,* 198–99.

4. Bryson, *Made in America,* 198. A specific claim for the hot dog's early introduction has been advanced in Murray Handwerker, *Nathan's Famous Hot Dog Cookbook* (New York: Gramercy Publishing, 1983), xvii–xviii, which holds Charles Feltman served the first hot dog in a roll in the United States on Coney Island in 1867.

5. Bryson, *Made in America,* 198.

6. "Frankfurters Grab Bigger Share of Market," *Food Service Magazine* 28 (September 1966): 31–32; Handwerker, *Nathan's Famous Hot Dog Cookbook,* xxi–xxii.

7. Helen Christie Bennett, "'Pinkie's Pantry' Took the Cake," *American Magazine* (June 1928): 66; J. M. Bennett, *Roadsides: The Front Yard of the Nation* (Boston: Stratford Co. Publishers, 1936), 165; Childs, "'Hot Dog Kennels' as Nuisances to Adjoining Property Owners," 137–38; "'Coffee and' in the Doggy Dog-Wagon," 42; "Elevating the Standing of the 'Hot Dog Kennel,'" 99–100; Anne O'Hagan, "The Hot Dog Trail," *The Woman's Journal* 13 (May 1928): 12–15; P. K. Marsh, "Shooting the Market on the Wings," *Printer's Ink* (Feb. 20, 1932): 36.

8. Handwerker, *Nathan's Famous Hot Dog Cookbook,* xxvi; "Nathan Sells Famous Hot Dogs," *Food Service and Marketing* 38 (July 1976): 65.

9. "Growth Companies," *Restaurants and Institutions* 99 (Oct. 2, 1989): 86; Anthony Ramirez, "Advertising," *New York Times,* June 30, 1995, D4.

10. "'Hot Dogs' on Wane," *Terre Haute Star,* July 17, 1929, 4.

11. "The Hot Dog," 127.

12. Florence Fabricant, "The Geography of Taste," *New York Times Magazine,* March 10, 1996, 40–41.

13. Padriac Burke, "Rolling Carts and Songs of Plenty: The Urban Food Vendor," *Journal of American Culture* 2 (1979): 483; James Scarpa, "Chicago's Wurst," *Restaurant Business* 87 (Oct. 10, 1988): 48.

14. Handwerker, *Nathan's Famous Hot Dog Cookbook,* xxvi.

15. American Entrepreneurs' Association, *Hot Dog Stand: AEA Business Manual No. 73* (Santa Monica, Calif.: American Entrepreneurs' Association, 1979), 4.

16. Emerson, *Fast Food,* 64.

17. Handwerker, *Nathan's Famous Hot Dog Cookbook;* "The Hotdog," 116.

18. Langdon, *Orange Roofs, Golden Arches,* 59–60; Witzel, *American Drive-In,* 30–31; "Let's Be Frank about Franchises," *Drive-In Magazine* 21, no. 6 (June 1957): 8; Love, *McDonald's,* 49. For a brief history of an A&W mimic, see Steven R. Hoffbeck, "The Barrels: Root Beer Stands of the Upper Midwest," *Minnesota History* 53, no. 7 (Fall 1993): 254–65.

19. "Let's Be Frank about Franchises," 8; "Matched to Metro Market," *Fast Food* 67 (1968): 132; "A Root-Beer Franchiser Regains Its Fizz," *Business Week* (Oct. 20, 1973): 54.

20. "Lynch Pumps New Fizz Into A&W Int'l.," *Institutions* 79 (Oct. 15, 1976): 25.

21. Luxenberg, *Roadside Empires,* 271; Marilyn Alva, "El Sid," *Restaurant Business* 94 (March 1, 1995): 38.

22. Alva, "El Sid," 38.

23. "Hotdogs Are Not Passe: Cheatham Designs Chain to Prove It," *Nation's Restaurant News* 19 (May 27, 1985): 35; Scarpa, "Chicago's Wurst," 48; Laurie Bain, "Hot Dog Concepts: Can They Cut the Mustard?" *Restaurant Business* 85 (Feb. 10, 1986): 191–98; "Hot Dogs Go Gourmet," *Independent Restaurants* 48 (May 1986): 26, 28.

24. Michael Roark, "Fast Foods: American Food Regions," *North American Culture* 2, no. 1 (1985): 26, 34; Pillsbury, *From Boarding House to Bistro,* 215.

25. "Dog n Suds Merging with Chicago Firm," *Franchise Journal* 2 (July–August 1969): 18; Kirby Pringle, "'World's Creamiest Root Beer' May Be Foaming Its Way Back," *Champaign-Urbana (Illinois) News-Gazette,* April 28, 1993, C-1.

26. "Dog 'n Suds," *American Restaurant Magazine* (June 1958): 63; "Dog n Suds," *Drive-In Magazine* 24, no. 10 (October 1960): 6; "Dog n Suds Sees Right Spot as Key to Franchisee's Success," *Fast Food* 63 (May 1964): 134, 141.

27. "Dog n Suds Merging with Chicago Firm," 18; Pringle, "'World's Creamiest Root Beer'" C-1.

28. Langdon, *Orange Roofs, Golden Arches,* 97; "Concept 80 at der Wienerschnitzel," *Institutions* 78 (March 1, 1976): 53.

29. Alexa Bell, "Wienerschnitzel: Hot Dogs with Relish," *Restaurant Business* 87 (Nov. 20, 1988): 78.

30. John F. Rooney Jr., Wilbur Zelinsky, and Dean R. Louder, eds., *This Remarkable Continent: An Atlas of United States and Canadian Society and Cultures* (College Station, Tex.: Texas A&M University Press, 1982), 127; Mariani, *America Eats Out,* 66, 114; John Egerton, *Southern Food at Home, on the Road, in History* (New York: Knopf, 1987), 39.

31. "Subway Restaurant's Fred DeLuca—The Man Behind the Sandwich," Information package (Milford, Conn.: Subway, n.d.).

32. Langdon, *Orange Roofs, Golden Arches,* 49.

33. John Birmingham, "What Now?" *Restaurant Business* 91 (July 20, 1992): 86.

34. Jacque Kochak, "Sandwich: Market Segment Report," *Restaurant Business* 88 (Nov. 20, 1989): 196.

35. "Subway Restaurants Lead Convenience Store Industry" (Milford, Conn.: Subway, 1996).

36. Carol Casper, "Hot Heroes," *Restaurant Business* 93 (Jan. 20, 1994): 110.

37. "C-Stores' Stampede to Subway Keeps Gaining Speed" (Milford, Conn.: Subway, n.d.).

38. Peter Romeo, "RB's Top 50 Growth Chains," *Restaurant Business* 94 (1995): 102.

39. Birmingham, "What Now?" 86–87.

40. "Get a Fresh Start with a Recognized Leader" (Milford, Conn.: Subway, n.d.).

41. B.M., "International Agenda," 146.

42. Jacque White Kochak, "Regional Chains Dominate Barbecue Segment," *Restaurant Business* 84 (March 1, 1985): 102; Fabricant, "Geography of Taste," 40; Jacque Kochak, "Barbecue: The Accent Is on Regional Growth," *Restaurant Business* 83 (Aug. 10, 1984): 108.

43. W. Dwayne Jones with Roni Morales, "Pig Stands: The Beginning of the Drive-In Restaurant," *Society for Commercial Archeology News Journal* 12, no. 1 (Winter 1991–92): 2–5; Jones, "In Search of the Vernacular," II-31–39.

44. Egerton, *Southern Food at Home,* 47, 149–50.

45. Pillsbury, *From Boarding House to Bistro,* 116.

46. Kochak, "Regional Chains Dominate Barbecue Segment," 102.

47. Romano, "RB's Top 50 Growth Chains," 28.

48. Kochak, "Regional Chains Dominate Barbecue Segment," 102.

49. "Love's: Back from the Brink," *Restaurant Business* 86 (July 1, 1987): 122.

50. Michael Romano, "Still Smoking," *Restaurant Business* 93 (March 20, 1994): 24, 28.

51. James Scarpa, "Rax Rebounds," *Restaurant Business* 89 (Aug. 10, 1990): 82, 84, 87; Jacque White Kochak, "Rax Revamps Roast Beef Concept," *Restaurant Business* 82 (Aug. 10, 1983): 138–39; "Top 400," 88.

52. Sylvia Riggs, "Marriott Makes Lean Years a Season to Grow," *Restaurants and Institutions* 91 (Aug. 18, 1982): 70; Sean Mehegan, "Picking Up the Pieces of a Once-Proud Franchise," *Restaurant Business* 95 (Jan. 20, 1996): 18.

53. Metz, *Franchising,* 183–84.

54. "Raffel: Arby's Projects Quality, Concentrates on Nutrition," *Food Service Chain Executive* 6, no. 9 (August 1978): 93–94; "Arby's," *Restaurant Business* 78 (Jan. 1, 1979): 98.

55. "Arby's," 98–99; Glenn Collins, "Owner of Arby's to Buy Long John Silver's Chain," *New York Times,* Sept. 22, 1994, C4; Steve Brooks, "The Trials of Chairman Posner," *Restaurant Business* 91 (May 20, 1992): 98; B.M., "The International Agenda," 146.

56. W. F. Angell, letter to Keith A. Sculle, March 1, 1982; "Your Future Maid-Rite" ([Muscatine, Iowa:] Maid-Rite, n.d.)

57. Runza placemat, in authors' possession, [1986]; "The Heartland's Best-Kept Secret" (Lincoln, Neb.: Runza Restaurants, n.d.).

58. Kochak, "Sandwich," 200.

1. Fabricant, "Geography of Taste," 41.
2. "The Interesting Story of Ice Cream," *The Soda Fountain* 16 (June 1917): 41.
3. Anne Cooper Funderburg, *Chocolate, Strawberry, and Vanilla: A History of American Ice Cream* (Bowling Green, Ohio: Bowling Green State University Popular Press, 1995), 17.
4. Quoted in Waverly Root and Richard de Rochemont, *Eating in America: A History* (New York: Morrow, 1976), 427.
5. M. T. Fussell, "1851, the Beginning of the Wholesale Ice Cream Industry," *Ice Cream Trade Journal* 47 (May 1951): 40.
6. Brewster and Jacobson, *Changing American Diet,* 33.
7. "Where the Industry Sells Its Ice Cream Gallonage," *Ice Cream Trade Journal* 45 (May 1949): 43.
8. "Thirteenth Annual Survey of Industry Trends," *Ice Cream Field* 85 (March 1965): S-5.
9. Dickson, *Great American Ice Cream Book,* 66–70. See also Funderburg, *Chocolate, Strawberry, and Vanilla,* 117–23.
10. "How the Cone Was Born," *Ice Cream Field* 63 (June 1954): 39.
11. Dickson, *Great American Ice Cream Book,* 65.
12. "The Isaly Story," *Ice Cream Review* 36 (May 1953): 90.
13. "Latest Bonnie Doon Unit Designed for Speedy Service," *Ice Cream Review* 34 (January 1951): 44.
14. "Franchise Drive-In Stores," *Ice Cream Review* 38 (February 1956): 46.
15. V. E. Moynahan, "'He Who Serves Best' . . . Profits Most," *The Soda Fountain* 34 (June 1935): 10.
16. "Roadstands Reap Rich Rewards," *The Soda Fountain* 36 (April 1937): 27, 56.
17. Dickson, *Great American Ice Cream Book,* 74.
18. Edward Thom, "Ice Cream Bar on a Stick," *Ice Cream Review* 33 (March 1950): 134–39.
19. "Good Humor Finds Its Customers on the Highways," *Ice Cream Review* 14 (August 1930): 40.
20. Dickson, *Great American Ice Cream Book,* 81.
21. Funderburg, *Chocolate, Strawberry, and Vanilla,* 132.
22. Dickson, *Great American Ice Cream Book,* 83.
23. "Mister Softee Increasing Sales Goal for '58," *Ice Cream Review* 41 (January 1958): 34.
24. "What about This Mobile Soft Serve Market?" *Ice Cream Review* 43 (June 1960): 24–26, 60, 62.
25. Correspondence between Edward L. Cornils and Keith A. Sculle, Aug. 11, 1996.
26. "'Women Managers Are Top-Notch' Says Prince Castle," *Fountain Service* 47 (August 1948): 28.
27. "Franchise Drive-Ins Pay Off for Bresler as Ice Cream Dealers," *Ice Cream Review* 40 (September 1956): 98.
28. Franchise Company Data, U.S. Department of Commerce, Washington, D.C., 1965, 41.
29. Love, *McDonald's,* 117.
30. Funderburg, *Chocolate, Strawberry, and Vanilla,* 145.
31. Ibid., 147.
32. "Dairy Queen Operators Celebrate 13th Year: Have $60 Million Business," *Ice Cream Review* 37 (November 1953): 84, 86.
33. "Dairy Queen Stores Put on a 'New Hat,'" *Ice Cream Review* 45 (June 1962): 42.
34. Jacque Kochak, "Ice Cream and Yogurt," *Restaurant Business* 90 (May 1, 1991): 230.
35. Eric N. Berg, "Dairy Queen Bracing for Battle," *New York Times,* Nov. 19, 1990, Y-C2.
36. "2,500,000 Gals. of Mix for Soft-Serve Products Sold by Tastee Freez in 1952," *Ice Cream Trade Journal* 19 (July 1953): 38.
37. Langdon, *Orange Roofs, Golden Arches,* 91.

38. Carol Casper, "Ice Cream and Yogurt: Market Segment Report," *Restaurant Business* 91 (May 1, 1992): 224.

39. "Expanding Carvel Chain an American Success Story," *Ice Cream Review* 35 (July 1958): 48.

40. Franchise Company Data, 23.

41. "Ice Cream Franchises," *Franchise Journal* 2 (May / June 1969): 26.

42. Alfred Lansing, "Cold Licks and Hot Profits," *Collier's* (Aug. 3, 1956): 30.

43. "Gas Station Sites with Leased Retail Ice Cream Stores Is the Newest Development," *Ice Cream Trade Journal* 46 (August 1950): 30–31, 96.

44. "Eat Up and Fill Up," *Ice Cream Review* 37 (May 1954): 62.

45. See Judith W. Meyer and Lawrence A. Brown, "Diffusion Agency Establishment: The Case of Friendly Ice Cream and Public-Sector Diffusion Processes," *Socio-Economic Planning Sciences* 13 (1979): 242–49.

46. Kochak, "Ice Cream and Yogurt," 248.

47. "Ice Cream," *Restaurant Business* 79 (March 1, 1980): 125.

48. Kochak, "Ice Cream and Yogurt," 244.

49. Marc Bittman, "Ben and Jerry's Caring Capitalism," *Restaurant Business* 89 (Nov. 20, 1990): 132.

50. "Franchising: Maturing Menus and Markets," *Restaurant Business* 83 (March 20, 1984): 160.

51. Kochak, "Ice Cream and Yogurt," 248.

52. "Hot Growth: Frozen Yogurt Chain," *Restaurant Business* 87 (May 1, 1988): 110.

CHAPTER 9. BREAKFAST PLACES

1. Bryson, *Made in America*, 185; Floyd M. Henderson, "Foodways," in *This Remarkable Continent*, ed. Rooney, Zelinsky, and Louder, 231.

2. Helen Sanstadt, "Doughnuts: A $300,000,000 a Year Bonanza," *Food Service* 25 (May 1961): 52; "How to Make Your Donuts Sell," *Drive-In Restaurant* 26 (June 1962): 34.

3. Clifford Krauss, "Police Officers. (Quick, Which Food Comes to Mind?)," *New York Times*, Oct. 22, 1996, B-1.

4. "Who Eats Donuts Anyway?" *Drive-In Restaurant* 26 (June 1962): 37.

5. "Spudnut," *Modern Franchising* 8 (March / April 1966): 23.

6. Robert E. Bond, *The Source Book of Franchise Opportunities* (Homewood, Ill.: Dow Jones–Irwin, 1985), 286.

7. Risto Laulajainen, *Spatial Strategies in Retailing* (Dordrecht: D. Reidel, 1987), 89.

8. Garbedian-Brennan, "Verne Curtis' Grand Slam Market Strategy," 120.

9. Mary Timmins, "Winchell's Donut Chain Rises Again," *Restaurant Business* 82 (Sept. 15, 1983): 62–70.

10. Emerson, *New Economics of Fast Food*, 2.

11. "Canadians Sweet on Doughnuts," *Toronto Globe and Mail*, July 4, 1995, B 10. See also A. Victoria Bloomfield, "Tim Horton's: Growth of a Canadian Coffee and Doughnut Chain," *Journal of Cultural Geography* 14 (Spring / Summer 1994): 1–16.

12. Seth Mydans, "From Cambodia to Doughnut Shops," *New York Times*, May 26, 1995, Y A-8.

13. Metz, *Franchising*, 123.

14. P. Berman, "Lessons Not Learned in School: Dunkin' Donuts," *Forbes* (July 15, 1977): 78.

15. Ralph Raffio, "Dunkin' Donuts Upgrades, Expands," *Restaurant Business* 85 (March 10, 1986): 228.

16. Harry Kursh, *The Franchise Boom* (Englewood Cliffs, N.J.: Prentice-Hall, 1968), 2.

17. Henderson, "Foodways," 232.

18. James Joseph, "Uncle John's Glamorizes the Lowly Flapjack!" *Food Service* 20 (May 1958): 28.

19. "Impact of Speed," *Restaurant Management* 92 (October 1963): 32.

20. James Scarpa, "Perkins Gears for Growth," *Restaurant Business* 89 (Jan. 1, 1990): 67.
21. "A Chain Is Born," *Fast Food* 63 (November 1964): 80–87.
22. "'Country-Style' Breakfast Key to Bob Evans Success," *Food Service Chain Executive,* no. 2 (December 1978): 27.
23. "Bob Evans: Country Chain Eyes Urban Markets," *Institutions* 83 (Sept. 1, 1978): 27.
24. "The Top 50 Franchises," *Restaurants and Institutions* 100 (July 25, 1990): 28.
25. "Bruegger's Bagel Bakery," *Restaurants and Institutions* 105 (Aug. 1, 1995): 82.
26. "Quality Dining to Buy Bruegger's Bakeries," *New York Times,* Feb. 23, 1996, Y-C4.
27. Gianna Jacobson, "Let Them Eat Bread, Especially at $4 a Loaf," *New York Times,* Nov. 18, 1995, Y-19.
28. Jolie Solomon, "Not in My Backyard. Starbucks Is Doing Great, but Is a Backlash Beginning?" *Newsweek* (Sept. 16, 1996): 65.
29. Carol Casper, "Caffeine Rush," *Restaurant Business* 95 (Jan. 1, 1996): 103.
30. "Fast Food Blitz Boosts Outlook for Pork Bellies," *Champaign-Urbana (Illinois) News Gazette,* Aug. 10, 1996, A-10.

CHAPTER 10. CHICKEN PLACES

1. Brewster and Jacobson, *Changing American Diet,* 78.
2. Jane E. Brody, "Study Finds a Three-Decade Gain in American Eating Habits, But a Long Way to Go," *New York Times,* Sept. 5, 1996, Y A-9.
3. Fabricant, "Geography of Taste," 40.
4. Ibid.
5. "Midwest Millionaires," *Restaurant Business* 79 (Jan. 1, 1980): 109.
6. Knott's Berry Farm and Ghost Town menu, 1962.
7. M. L. Graham, "$100 Capital in 1925—$1,000,000 Gross Sales in 1936," *The Soda Fountain* 35 (December 1936): 10–13.
8. "Franchising Was His Road to Fame and Fortune," *Food Service* 26 (February 1964): 62.
9. Dessauer, "Fried Chicken Champ," 150.
10. "Franchise Challenge," *Fast Food* 63 (May 1964): 75.
11. Kursh, *Franchise Boom,* 262.
12. Bond, *Source Book of Franchise Opportunities,* 314.
13. William Whitworth, "Kentucky-Fried," *New Yorker* 45 (Feb. 14, 1970): 42.
14. Vaughn, *Franchising,* 28.
15. Whitworth, "Kentucky-Fried," 43.
16. "Franchising: Too Much, Too Soon?" *Business Week* (June 27, 1970): 54.
17. James Stewart-Gordon, "Saga of the 'Chicken' Colonel," *Reader's Digest* 106 (February 1975): 143–46.
18. Emerson, *Fast Food,* 189.
19. Stuart Watson, chairman of Heublein, Inc., quoted in Joan Bakos, "Finds KFC Not a Quick Fix," *Restaurant Business* 79 (May 1, 1980): 191.
20. "KFC Conversions in Full Gear," *Restaurant Business* 85 (Sept. 20, 1986): 39.
21. "Today's KFC," promotional brochure, KFC Corporation, Louisville, Kentucky, 1994.
22. "Ron's Krispy Fried Chicken Looks to Market Penetration for Successful Growth," *Food Service* 71 (March 1971): 40.
23. Milton Werner, "The Unlimited Chicken Unlimited," *Fast Food* 71 (March 1971): 90–95.
24. Bond, *Source Book of Franchise Opportunities,* 325.
25. "The Powerful Punch of Popeye's," *Fast Service* 40 (July 1981): 20.
26. Elizabeth Rhein, "Popeye's Flexes Its Muscles," *Restaurant Business* 86 (May 20, 1987): 117.
27. Philip B. Fitzell, "At Church's Fried Chicken the Growing Pains Are Over," *Fast Food* 72 (April 1973): 84.
28. "Church's," *Food Service Marketing* 39 (December 1977): 1.

29. Laurie Bain, "Manufacturing Program Builds Revenues for Church's," *Restaurant Business* 85 (Nov. 20, 1986): 126–28.

30. "Transforming Gas Stations Into Fast Food Restaurants," *Fast Service* 40 (May 1981): 30.

31. "Bojangles': A Spicy Appeal," *Restaurant Business* 80 (Sept. 1, 1981): 106.

32. "The Allure of a Hot Chicken Chain," *Fortune* (Feb. 6, 1984): 129–30.

33. Bond, *Source Book of Franchise Opportunities,* 315.

34. Mary Timmins, "Chicken George Cracks Urban Market," *Restaurant Business* 82 (Jan. 1, 1983): 111–12.

35. Carol E. Curtis, "Born Again Chicken," *Forbes* (June 9, 1980): 69.

36. Judith H. Dobrzynski, "Chicken Done to a Golden Rule," *New York Times,* April 3, 1996, Y C-1.

37 "Grandy's: The Market Pioneer," *Restaurant Business* 80 (Aug. 1, 1981): 101.

38. Don Jeffrey, "Upscale Chicken on the Wings of Change," *Restaurant Business* 87 (July 20, 1988): 105.

39. "Mrs. Winner's: Playing for First Place in the Southeast," *Restaurant Business* 80 (Oct. 1, 1981): 110.

40. Tom Strenk, "Broader Menus Spice Up Chicken Sales," *Restaurant Business* 84 (Jan. 20, 1985): 108.

41. Marilyn Alva, "Crazy for Chicken," *Restaurant Business* 94 (March 1, 1996): 84.

42. Bill McDowell, "A Game of Chicken," *Restaurants and Institutions* 104 (Nov. 15, 1994): 42.

43. "Growth Chains," *Restaurant Business* 93 (July 20, 1994): 74.

44. Marilyn Alva, "Brown's Bag," *Restaurant Business* 94 (April 10, 1995): 42.

CHAPTER 11. SEAFOOD PLACES

1. Brewster and Jacobson, *Changing American Diet,* 24; "Rough Waters," *Restaurant Business* 92 (Oct. 10, 1993): 121.

2. Jacque White Kochak, "Seafood Operators Take a Fresh Approach," *Restaurant Business* 84 (July 1, 1985): 93.

3. Carol Casper, "Keeping Afloat," *Restaurant Business* 93 (July 1, 1994): 136.

4. Ray Moseley, "Sea's Riches a Dwindling Infinity," *Chicago Tribune,* Sept. 2, 1996, 1.

5. Brewster and Jacobson, *Changing American Diet,* 3.

6. For a discussion of America's changing dietary habits, see Levenstein, *Paradox of Plenty.*

7. Carol Casper, "All in the Family," *Restaurant Business* 92 (Oct. 10, 1993): 134.

8. Wyckoff and Sasser, *Chain-Restaurant Industry,* 47.

9. "Red Lobster," *Restaurant Business* 78 (Aug. 1, 1979): 85.

10. Kochak, "Seafood Operators Take a Fresh Approach," 98.

11. Casper, "Keeping Afloat," 152.

12. Bernstein, *Great Restaurant Innovators,* 53–54.

13. "Barnacle Bill's," *Franchise Journal* 2 (July/August 1969): 84.

14. "Fish and Chips," *Franchise Journal* 3 (May 1970): 39.

15. Dan Bearth, "Yankee Clipper Runs Up Distress Signal, Steers Course to Pizza," *Wichita Eagle Beacon,* March 15, 1976, 26.

16. "Kentucky Fried Chicken to Market H. Salt Esq.," *Franchise Journal* 2 (September 1969): 52; "Food Franchises," *Franchising Journal* 3 (July 1970): 46.

17. James Cataland, quoted in Jeff Blyskal, "Fat-Fryer Alchemy," *Forbes* (Dec. 6, 1982): 131.

18. Rona Gindin, "Can Cataland's Confidence Turn around Arthur Treacher's?" *Restaurant Business* 85 (Jan. 1, 1986): 119.

19. "Wall Street Bets on Long John Silver's," *Institutional/Volume Feeding* 76 (April 15, 1975): 49.

20. "Why Some Analysts Worry about Jerrico," *Business Week* (Sept. 27, 1976): 76.

21. "Seafood: Costs Are Eroding Profits," *Restaurant Business* 77 (March 1, 1978): 137.

22. "Market Report: Seafood," *Restaurant Business* 92 (Oct. 10, 1993): 139; "Market Report: Seafood," *Restaurant Business* 93 (July 1, 1994): 154.

23. Kochak, "Seafood Operators Take a Fresh Approach," 93.

24. Luxenberg, *Roadside Empires,* 239.

25. Gindin, "Shoney's Shows Who's Boss," 194.

CHAPTER 12. PIZZA PLACES

1. Giovanni E[rmenegildo] Schiavo, *The Italians in Chicago: A Study in Americanization* (1928; repr., New York: Arno Press, 1975), 141; Wilbur Zelinsky, *The Cultural Geography of the United States* (Englewood Cliffs, N.J.: Prentice-Hall, Inc., 1973), 13–14; Mariani, *America Eats Out,* 68–69.

2. Roark, "Fast Foods," 28.

3. Pillsbury, *From Boarding House to Bistro,* 156–59; "Restaurant Blues," 30; Isadore Barmash, "Fast Food Restaurants—How They Grew and Grew," *Good Housekeeping* 195 (November 1982): 114; Brewster and Jacobson, *Changing American Diet,* 4; "GH Goes to 7 Popular Fast-Food Chains and Tells How They Rate in—Nutrition, Quality, and Cost," *Good Housekeeping* 181 (November 1975): 170, 172.

4. Cited in Phil Patton, *Open Road: A Celebration of the American Highway* (New York: Simon and Schuster, 1986), 88.

5. O'Neill, *American High,* 105, 175, 291.

6. Nancy Ross Ryan, "Pizza," *Restaurants and Institutions* 99 (Sept. 4, 1989): 104; Mariani, *America Eats Out,* 65–66; Herbert Mitgang, "For the Love of Pizza," *Collier's* (March 7, 1953): 67; Pillsbury, *From Boarding House to Bistro,* 50; Florence Fabricant, "The Italian Pizza Police Are Offering Rules for the Real Thing," *New York Times,* June 7, 1995, B6.

7. Mariani, *America Eats Out,* 66; Levenstein, *Paradox of Plenty,* 51–52.

8. Levenstein, *Paradox of Plenty,* 230.

9. Pillsbury, *From Boarding House to Bistro,* 158; Alan M. Kraut, "Ethnic Foodways: The Significance of Food in the Designation of Cultural Boundaries Between Immigrant Groups in the U.S., 1840–1921," *Journal of American Culture* 2 (1979): 415.

10. Pillsbury, *From Boarding House to Bistro,* 158.

11. Pizza Hut information package, sheet: "Our Heritage" (Dallas: Pizza Hut, [1995]), [p. 1]; John A. Byrne, "Pizza to Tacos to Pasta," *Forbes* (Oct. 11, 1982): 172; Emerson, *Fast Food,* 230.

12. Emerson, *Fast Food,* 230, 235; Byrne, "Pizza to Tacos to Pasta," 172; Pizza Hut information package, sheet: "Historical Highlights" (Dallas: Pizza Hut, [1995]), [p. 1]; *Moody's Industrial Manual* (New York: Moody's Investors Service, 1969), 3326.

13. Emerson, *Fast Food,* 205–6, 234; Byrne, "Pizza to Tacos to Pasta," 174.

14. Emerson, *Fast Food,* 234; Byrne, "Pizza to Tacos to Pasta," 174.

15. Langdon, *Orange Roofs, Golden Arches,* 148–49.

16. *Moody's Industrial Manual* (New York: Moody's Investors Service, 1974), 2270; *Moody's Industrial Manual* (New York: Moody's Investors Service, 1977), 3775; Emerson, *Fast Food,* 237; Warren J. Belasco, "Ethnic Fast Foods: The Corporate Melting Pot," *Food and Foodways: Explorations in the History and Culture of Human Nourishment* 2, no. 1 (1987): 18.

17. Byrne, "Pizza to Tacos to Pasta," 174, 177.

18. Dicke, *Franchising in America,* 117–49; Tom Monaghan with Robert Anderson, *Pizza Tiger* (New York: Random House, 1986) (subsequent references to *Pizza Tiger* appear by page number in the text).

19. Dicke, *Franchising in America,* 148; Ron Sympson, "Can Monaghan Deliver?" *Restaurant Business* 91 (April 10, 1992): 81; Bernice Kranner, "Pizza Wars: A Bigger Slice of the Market," *New York* 20, no. 37 (Sept. 21, 1987): 20; D.K., "Domino's Drivers Cited For Poor Safety Record," *Restaurant Business* 89 (May 1, 1990): 280; Hoover, Campbell, and Spain, eds., *Hoover's Handbook of American Business* (1995), 440; Domino's Pizza infor-

mation package, "Domino's Pizza: Important Dates," Domino's Pizza, Ann Arbor, Mich., 1994, [p. 2].

20. Monaghan with Anderson, *Pizza Tiger* 4, 263–64.

21. Bruce Horovitz, "Domino's Theory: Toss Old Image, Get Back to Top," *USA Today* (June 13, 1996): 12B.

22. Emerson, *New Economics of Fast Food,* 67, 70, 74; Rona Gindin, "A Fight to Stay on Top," *Restaurant Business* 89 (July 1, 1986): 152–54; "Franchising: How Fertile Its Future?" *Restaurant Business* 79 (March 1, 1980): 117; Metz, *Franchising,* 170–74; Carol Casper, "Pizza," *Restaurant Business* 92 (Feb. 10, 1993): 138.

23. "Discounting Discounting," *Restaurant Business* 93 (May 1, 1994): 170; Judy Wiley, "Pizza," *Institutions* 82 (May 15, 1978): 32; Jacque White Kochak, "Pizza Turns Chic as Sales Soar," *Restaurant Business* 83 (Feb. 10, 1984): 134; Michael J. Weiss, *Latitudes and Attitudes: An Atlas of American Tastes, Trends, Politics, and Passions* (Boston: Little, Brown and Company, 1994), 11.

24. Glenn Collins, "Left Alone at the Food Fight," *New York Times,* July 16, 1997, C1, C4; B.M., "International Agenda," 146.

25. Glenn Collins, "PepsiCo to Spin Off Its Restaurant Business," *New York Times,* Jan. 24, 1997, C2.

26. Cheryl Turi Coutts, "The Olive Garden: Ripe for Growth," *Restaurant Business* 86 (May 1, 1987): 122.

27. Olive Garden information package, "A History: How The Olive Garden Started," Olive Garden, Orlando, Fla., n.d., [1, 2]

28. Michael Sanson, "Splintering Ethnic," *Restaurant Hospitality* 80 (February 1986): 47; Wilbur Zelinsky, *Exploring the Beloved Country* (Iowa City: University of Iowa Press, 1994), 459–92.

CHAPTER 13. TACO PLACES AND MEXICAN "CANTINAS"

1. Daniel D. Arreola, "Mexican Restaurants in Tucson," *Journal of Cultural Geography* 3, no. 2 (Spring/Summer, 1983): 110–11.

2. Jonathan Norton Leonard and the editors of Time-Life Books, *Latin American Cooking* (New York: Time-Life Books, 1968), 50–51; Reay Tannahill, *Food in History* (New York: Stein and Day, 1973), 249–50.

3. Mariani, *America Eats Out,* 80; Arreola, "Mexican Restaurants in Tucson," 112; *American Heritage Cookbook,* 1:230, 233; Jane Stern and Michael Stern, *Way Out West* (New York: HarperCollins, 1993), 315; Calvin Trillin, *American Fried: Adventures of a Happy Eater* (New York: Doubleday, 1974), 130–32.

4. "Tacos Going Faster—Everywhere!" *Fast Food* 57 (January 1958): 36.

5. "Mexican Tacos to Give Hot Dogs a Run for the Money," *Drive-In Magazine* 24, no. 6 (June 1960): 8, 14.

6. "Speedy Tacos by the Millions," *Fast Food* 57 (November 1958): 46.

7. "Tacos from the Franchising Firing Line," *Fast Food* 57 (January 1958): 34; Emerson, *Fast Food,* 119; Levenstein, *Paradox of Plenty,* 234.

8. Chris Shovey, librarian, San Bernardino Public Library, letter to Keith A. Sculle, Nov. 19, 1996; Cindy Friday, "New Manager Has Taco-Tia Cooking," *San Bernardino Sun,* March 28, 1989, B8; Debra Lee Baldwin, "How Green Is His Valley," *San Diego Union-Tribune,* Sept. 29, 1996, H-17; "Taco Bell Put Their Work into Building and Let the Rest Come Naturally," *Fast Food* 66, pt. 2 (November 1967): 90.

9. "Taco Bell Put Their Work into Building," 90–91.

10. Bryce Webster, *The Insider's Guide to Franchising* (New York: American Management Association, 1986), 268.

11. Langdon, *Orange Roofs, Golden Arches,* 177–80.

12. Mariani, *America Eats Out,* 81; Marjorie Thomas, "Taco Bell Rings in a New Image," *Restaurant Business* 83 (October 1984): 218.

13. Brian Quinton, "John Martin's Common-Sense Miracle," *Restaurants and Institutions* 101 (July 10, 1991): 11; Don Nichols, "Taco Machine Proves a Big Hit in Its Test Run," *Restaurant Business* 92 (March 1, 1993): 16.

14. Jacque White Kochak, "Mexican Fast Food Moves Into the Mainstream," *Restaurant Business* 84 (Nov. 1, 1985): 133.

15. Bond, *Source Book of Franchise Opportunities,* 384; "Taco Time Goes PRE-FAB," *Fast Service* 36 (June 1977): 46, 48–50; "El Chico Cooks Up a Turnaround," *Restaurants and Institutions* 104 (March 1, 1994): 16–17.

16. Collins, "Left Alone at the Food Fight," C1, C4; Barbara Sullivan, "Eateries' New Trend: Bundling," *Chicago Tribune,* Dec. 25, 1996, 1, 4; B.M., "International Agenda," 146.

17. James Scarpa, "The Changing Face of Chi-Chi's," *Restaurant Business* 87 (March 1, 1988): 156, 147.

18. Scarpa, "Changing Face of Chi-Chi's," 157.

19. Farrell, "California Chain Casts Menu Stars," 116; Brooks, "Long Road Back," 54.

20. Sanson, "Splintering Ethnic," *Restaurant Hospitality* 80 (February 1996): 50, 54.

21. Carol Casper, "A Whole New Enchilada," *Restaurant Business* 93 (Oct. 16, 1994): 158.

CHAPTER 14. STEAK PLACES

1. Margaret Cussler and Mary L. De Give, *'Twixt the Cup and the Lip: Psychological and Socio-Cultural Factors Affecting Food Habits* (New York: Twayne Publishers, 1952), 156; Noel F. Busch, "A Year of Truman," *Life* (April 8, 1946): 96.

2. Nancy Ross Ryan, "Great American Food Chronicles: Steak," *Restaurants and Institutions* 99 (Oct. 2, 1989): 114.

3. Root and de Rochemont, *Eating in America,* 135, 207.

4. "Dan Lasater: How to Make $30 Million in Twelve Years," *Dun's* 101 (May 1973): 16.

5. "Thomson Outlines Changes in Bonanza Operations," *Food Service Chain Executive* 4, no. 11 (November 1976): 81; Ryan, "Great American Food Chronicles," 114.

6. Bryce Webster, *The Insider's Guide to Franchising* (New York: American Management Association, 1986), 263; "Dan Lasater," 15.

7. "Dan Lasater," 15–17, 133.

8. Emerson, *Fast Food,* 196.

9. Ibid., 196–98.

10. "Thomson Outlines Changes in Bonanza Operations," 82.

11. Emerson, *Fast Food,* 200.

12. "New Design, Menu Items Upgrade Sizzler Image," *Food Service Chain Executive* 5, no. 2 (February 1977): 73; "1977 Chain Executives," 31; "Effective Training Program Keeps Pace with Sizzler Growth," *Food Service Marketing* 40 (September 1978): 52.

13. Wyckoff and Sasser, *Chain-Restaurant Industry,* 1; Langdon, *Orange Roofs, Golden Arches,* 159.

14. Wyckoff and Sasser, *Chain-Restaurant Industry,* 7; Emerson, *New Economics of Fast Food,* 15.

15. Advertisement, *Franchise Journal* 2 (March/April 1969): 13; Metz, *Franchising,* 176; "Changes Prepare Mr. Steak for the Coming Decade," *Chain Executive* 8 (January 1980): 80.

16. Michael Romano, "Mr. Steak Wants to Be a Steakhouse Again," *Restaurant Business* 92 (Sept. 20, 1993): 37.

17. Carol Casper, "Steak," *Restaurant Business* 90 (July 20, 1991): 160.

18. "Changes Prepare Mr. Steak for the Coming Decade," 81; Stewart Kull, telephone interview with Keith A. Sculle, Aug. 29, 1996. (Kull was Mr. Steak's director of marketing, 1972–74.)

19. Glenn Collins, "Changing Tastes Put End to Sizzler's Salad Days," *New York Times,* June 22, 1996, 19.

20. B.M., "Golden Corral Sees Golden Opportunities with Its New Metro Market Unit," *Restaurants and Institutions* 102 (July 22, 1992): 110.

21. Kursh, *Franchise Boom,* 284; "Golden West Steaks," *Franchise Journal* 2 (July/August 1969): 86.

22. Casper, "Steak," 160; Steve Brooks, "Round Up," *Restaurant Magazine* 91 (Oct. 10, 1992): 88–89, 94; Nancy Brumback, "Taking the Prime Cut: Casual Chains Have Carved Out the Lucrative Mid-Priced Section of the Steak Segment," *Restaurant Business* 95 (Jan. 20, 1996): 109–10, 112, 114, 116, 124–25.

23. Rona Feldman, "Steak: Market Segment Report," *Restaurant Business* 91 (June 10, 1992): 172; Ryan, "Great American Food Chronicles," 120.

CHAPTER 15. CONCEPT RESTAURANTS

1. Keith Goldman, "Concept Selection for Independent Restaurants," *Cornell Hotel and Restaurant Administration Quarterly* 34 (December 1993): 59–72.

2. For a discussion of place commodification see Sack, *Place, Modernity, and the Consumer's World.*

3. Gottdiener, *Theming of America.* See also Gottdiener's *Postmodern Semiotics.*

4. David Bell and Gill Valentine, *Consuming Geographies: We Are Where We Eat* (London: Routledge, 1997), 125.

5. Robert Ladau and Richard Nininger, "Programmed Environment: The Art of Sensory Deception," *Fast Food* 68 (October 1969): 116–21.

6. Rona Gindin, "Restaurants by Design," *Restaurant Business* 86 (July 1, 1987): 177.

7. Heimann and Georges, *California Crazy.*

8. "Chinese Drive-In in Salt Lake City," *Drive-In Restaurant* 25 (September 1961): 37.

9. Jacque White Kochak, "Oriental: Despite Its Popularity . . . ," *Restaurant Business* 87 (March 1, 1988): 178.

10. "A U.S. Beachead for Japanese Fast Food," *Business Week* (July 2, 1979): 23–24.

11. Ralph Raffio, "Fast Food," *Restaurant Business* 83 (May 20, 1984): 190–95.

12. Kochak, "Oriental," 184; Webster, *Insider's Guide to Franchising,* 262.

13. "Mid-Eastern Specialties in San Jose," *Drive-In Fast Service* 33 (May 1974): 48.

14. "Independents Dominate Majority of U.S. Restaurant Categories," *Independent Restaurants* 46 (June 1985): 36.

15. Jeff Weinstein, "R&I Top 100," *Restaurants and Institutions* 104 (March 15, 1994): 34.

16. Langdon, *Orange Roofs, Golden Arches,* 180–81.

17. Rajan Chaudhry, "That's Eat-ertainment," *Restaurants and Institutions* 104 (April 1, 1994): 19.

18. "Seattle Restaurant Has a Game Plan," *Chicago Tribune,* July 29, 1996, sec. 4, p. 8.

19. Alexa Bell, "Rockin' and Rollin'," *Restaurant Business* 87 (June 10, 1988): 182.

20. G. "Skip" Downing, quoted in "Creating an Entertaining Environment," *Fast Service* 40 (January 1981): 28, 29.

21. Mariani, *America Eats Out,* 202.

22. Joan Lang, "T.G.I. Friday's Continues to Flourish," *Restaurant Business* 83 (Nov. 1, 1984): 108.

23. "Theme Dining," *Restaurant Business* 80 (June 10, 1987): 178; Carol Casper, "Staying Power," *Restaurant Business* 95 (Sept. 1, 1996): 90, 81.

24. Kevin Farrell, "Ground Round Carves Out a Turnaround," *Restaurant Business* 84 (May 1, 1985): 126.

25. Carol Casper, "The Ground Round Comes on the Scene Again," *Restaurant Business* 85 (July 1, 1986): 177.

26. Jacque Kochak, "Behind the Gourmet Burger Boom," *Restaurant Business* 83 (Nov. 11, 1984): 127.

27. Don Nichols, "A New Take on Fuddruckers," *Restaurant Business* 87 (May 20, 1988): 86.

28. Langdon, *Orange Roofs, Golden Arches,* 188.

29. Casper, "Staying Power," 90.

30. Romeo, "RB's Top 50 Growth Chains," 82.

31. Elaine Raffel, "What Makes Chili's Hot?" *Restaurant Business* 82 (Oct. 1, 1983): 148; "Best-Run Companies," *Restaurants and Institutions* 99 (May 29, 1989): 50.

32. Brumback, "Taking the Prime Cut," 109.

33. Denise M. Brennan, "The Name of the Game: Kidding Around," *Restaurant Business* 90 (June 10, 1991): 98.

34. Boas and Chain, *Big Mac,* 111.

35. Luxenberg, *Roadside Empires,* 117.

36. Mary Timmins, "Capt. Andy's Charts Course for National Expansion," *Restaurant Business* 82 (Feb. 1, 1983): 112.

CHAPTER 16. THE ROADSIDE RESTAURANT IN SPRINGFIELD, ILLINOIS

1. Clinton L. Conkling, *Encyclopedia of Illinois and History of Sangamon County,* vol. 2, ed. Newton Bateman and Paul Selby (Chicago: Munsell Publishing, 1912), 770–78; Edward J. Russo, *Prairie of Promise: Springfield and Sangamon County* (Woodland Hills, Calif.: Windsor Publications, 1983), 24–26, 33–35; James Krohe and Cullom Davis, "Springfield: An Evolving Capital," in *The Middle-Size Cities of Illinois: Their People, Politics, and Quality of Life,* ed. Daniel Milo Johnson and Rebecca Monroe Veach (Springfield, Ill.: Sangamon State University, 1980), 191–99.

2. Jane E. Knepler, "Up and Out of the East End: The Irish in Springfield," *Bulletin of the Illinois Geographical Society* 17, no. 1 (July 1976): 25–32; Russo, *Prairie of Promise,* 36, 42–43.

3. Russo, *Prairie of Promise,* 48–50; James Krohe Jr., *A Springfield Reader: Historical Views of the Illinois Capital, 1818–1976* (Springfield, Ill.: Sangamon County Historical Society, 1976), 12–13.

4. For a good introduction to urban street vendors, see Burke, "Rolling Carts and Songs of Plenty," 480–87. V. Y. Dallman, "Lighter Vein," *Illinois State Register,* Jan. 21, 1947, 6; Victoria Pope, "The Man Who Gave Chili Its Second 'L,'" *Illinois Times,* Feb. 5, 1976, 4–5, 24–25; Charlyn Fargo, "Chilli Central," *Heartland* (Nov. 5, 1993): 4A-6A.

5. Russo, *Prairie of Progress,* 44; Albert Walter Lewis, compiler, *Springfield: The Capital of the State of Illinois* (Springfield, Ill.: [Springfield Commercial Association,] 1912), [79].

6. Conkling, *Encyclopedia of Illinois and Sangamon County,* 654; *Springfield in 1892: Souvenir Supplement* (Springfield, Ill.: Illinois State Journal, 1892), 71, 85; *The Illinois Capital Illustrated* (Springfield, Ill.: Press of the Illinois State Register, 1898), 138.

7. *Illinois State Journal,* June 1, 1915, 14; June 4, 1920, 4; June 1, 1925, 7; *Illinois State Register,* June 1, 1915, 8; June 4, 1920, 11.

8. *Illinois State Register,* June 5, 1925, 16.

9. Russo, *Prairie of Promise,* 47.

10. Donald F. Tingley, *The Structuring of a State: The History of Illinois, 1899–1928* (Urbana: University of Illinois Press, 1980), 241–42; State of Illinois, Department of Public Works and Buildings, Division of Highways, "Illinois Roads" (map), October 1, 1924.

11. Russo, *Prairie of Promise,* 53, 55; Keith A. Sculle, "Some Musings about the Way Between Sherman and Springfield, Illinois," *Bulletin of the Illinois Geographical Society* 37, no. 1 (Spring 1995): 4, 6; Krohe and Davis, "Springfield," 196.

12. "Do You Remember?" *Illinois State Register,* April 19, 1972, 38; *Jefferson's Directory of the City of Springfield, Illinois, 1926* (Springfield, Ill.: Jefferson's Printing Co., 1926), 1356; Estelle B. Marlowe, "Selling at the Curb," *The Soda Fountain* 30, no. 6 (June 1931): 33.

13. Frank Mitchell, "Maid-Rite the Oldest Springfield Drive-In," *State Journal-Register,* Aug. 14, 1971, 3A; Sculle, "Finger-Licking Landmarks," 13–14; *Jefferson's Directory of the City of Springfield, Illinois, 1930* (Springfield, Ill.: Jefferson's Printing and Stationery, 1930), 1040.

14. Sculle, "Finger-Licking Landmarks," 14–15; Bob Sampson, "Jack Robinson Restaurant Sticks with Simplicity—And Survives," *Decatur Daily Review,* Aug. 8, 1979, 36.

15. Kirby Pringle, "When You Say Steakburger, You've Said It All," *(Champaign, Ill.) News-Gazette,* Jan. 30, 1991, C-1; Andy Lindstrom, "It All Began with 'Mother,'" *State Journal-Register,* Oct. 16, 1979, 8A–11A; Michael Murphy, "A Family Affair: The Stullers Keep a Tradition Alive," *State Journal-Register,* July 15, 1988, 8A–12A.

16. Elise Morrow, "Springfield, Illinois," *Saturday Evening Post* (Sept. 27, 1947): 112.

17. Joanne Long, "Springfield's Sandwich of Distinction," *State Journal-Register,* Feb. 19, 1972, 9A.

18. Sculle, "Some Musings about the Way Between Sherman and Springfield," 3–11; Lucille Falzone (Richard Fazi's daughter), interview with Keith Sculle, Springfield, Ill., April 2, 1996; Armando and Lucille (Mr. and Mrs.) Falzone, interview with Keith Sculle, Springfield, Ill., April 3, 1996.

19. Velma (Hamilton) Kelley, interview with Keith A. Sculle, Springfield, Ill., Jan. 7, 1996; Velma Kelley and Pearl Ahrenkiel (Velma's sister), interview with Keith A. Sculle, Springfield, Ill., Jan. 14, 1996.

20. "Mimi's Dispensers Make 'Em Feel Patronage Is Appreciated," *Fountain Service* 48 (December 1949): 24–25; Dominic Vitale, telephone interview with Keith A. Sculle, February 16, 1996. For a history of the Cozy Dog see Tom Teague, "Ed Waldmire Passes On," *The 66 News!* (Fall 1993): 4–6.

21. Arthur Hepworth (worked for Jack Robinson, 1938–66), telephone interview with Keith A. Sculle, December 14, 1980; Steve Slack, "The Martin Way," *State Journal-Register,* April 29, 1978, 14A.

22. Russo, *Prairie of Promise,* 67–68; Mary Nolan, "Taming the City," *State Journal-Register,* Oct. 21, 1988, 8A–12A; Jerry Wallace, "Treating Symptoms or Dealing with Principles?" cited in Krohe, *Springfield Reader,* 159–64.

23. George Derwig, "Shopping Center Surge," *State Journal-Register,* July 21, 1961, 1, 18; "Shopping Centers Growing Here," *State Journal-Register,* June 23, 1968, 17.

24. *Polk's Springfield (Sangamon Co., Illinois) City Directory, 1955* (Springfield, Ill.: R. L. Polk and Co., 1955), 109; *Polk's Springfield (Sangamon Co., Illinois) City Directory, 1961* (Springfield, Ill.: R. L. Polk and Co., 1961), 594; "Pizza Drive-In," *Drive-In Restaurant* 26, no. 4 (April 1962): 12–13, 28.

25. Krohe and Davis, "Springfield," 197.

26. Sandra Martin, "Eating in Springfield," *Illinois Times,* Feb. 17–23, 1978, 13; "A U.S. Beachhead for Japanese Fast Food," *Business Week* (July 2, 1979): 24; Anne Taubeneck, "Lincoln's Land Touts Honest Cooking," *Chicago Sun-Times,* April 19, 1990, 6N.

27. Fran Bernard, "It's Good Eating and Lots of Fun at the Fleetwood," *State Journal-Register,* Jan. 17, 1977, 14; "Your Tourist Guide" (Springfield tourism brochure with Fleetwood history on back page), c. 1987; Chris Dettro and Chris Green, "Fleetwood Closed," *State Journal-Register,* Sept. 28, 1993, 1, 3.

28. Chris Dettro, "Mall, Downtown Area to Share Spotlight in '93," *State Journal-Register,* Jan. 31, 1993, 10A–11A; "Food Court a Smash at Mall," *Decatur* (Illinois) *Herald,* Oct. 17, 1993, F-1.

29. *State Journal-Register,* Oct. 4, 1992, 54, and Oct. 18, 1992, 37; "Burger Park Has Replaced Rally's Franchise," Feb. 13, 1994, 37; "Rally's Hamburgers to Open; Fast Service Will Be Stressed," March 22, 1989, 21; *Polk's Springfield (Sangamon County, Illinois) City Directory, 1951* (Springfield, Ill.: R. L. Polk and Co., 1952), 502.

30. "Rally's Hamburgers to Open," 21.

31. "Burger Park Has Replaced Rally's Franchise," 37.

32. Matthew Dietrich, "Changes Revolving around White Oaks Mall Could Turn Within," *State Journal-Register,* Jan. 26, 1992, 65; Chris Dettro, "Restauranteur Turns Failure into Success," *State Journal-Register,* March 13, 1988, 47; Dale J. Diamond, interview with Keith A. Sculle, Springfield, Ill., July 1, 1996.

33. "Express Restaurant Delivery Guide," 3rd ed. (Winter 1996–97) [Springfield: n.p., 1996.]

CONCLUSION

1. Ted Shane, "Fare Warning: Roadside Indigestion," *Reader's Digest* 65 (August 1955): 55.
2. Frederick Marryat, *A Diary in America, with Remarks on Its Institutions, Part Second* (London: Longman, Orme, Brown, Green and Longmans, 1839), 27–28.
3. Jackson Lears, *Fables of Abundance: A Cultural History of Advertising in America* (New York: Basic Books, 1994), 6.
4. Root and de Rochemont, *Eating in America,* 317.
5. Thomas, *Dave's Way,* 28.
6. For discussion of speed as a form of life-affirmation, see Cynthia Golomb Dettelbach, *In the Driver's Seat: The Automobile in American Literature and Popular Culture* (Westport, Conn.: Greenwood Press, 1976), 36–38.
7. Oldenburg, *The Great Good Place.*
8. John Storey, *Cultural Studies and the Study of Popular Culture: Theories and Methods* (Athens: University of Georgia Press, 1996), 107.
9. Heimann, *Car Hops and Curb Service,* 62–63.
10. Stuart Ewen, *All-Consuming Images: The Politics of Style in Contemporary Culture* (New York: Basic Books, 1988); Root and de Rochemont, *Eating in America,* 443–44.
11. Pillsbury, *From Boarding House to Bistro,* 85.
12. Jesus C. Dumagan and John W. Hackett, Food and Consumer Economics Division, Economic Research Service, U.S. Department of Agriculture, *U.S. Trends in Eating Away from Home, 1982–89: A Survey by Eating Occasion, Type of Foodservice Establishment, and Kind of Food,* Statistical Bulletin No. 926 (December 1995).
13. Jesus C. Dumagan and John W. Hackett, "Almost Half of the Food Budget Is Spent Eating Out," *Food Review* 18 (January–April 1996): 37, 38.
14. Puzo, "Industry Forecast," 29.
15. See Jakle and Sculle, *Gas Station in America.*
16. See Jakle, Sculle, and Rogers, *Motel in America.*
17. Diana Crane, *The Production of Culture: Media and the Urban Arts* (Newbury Park, Calif.: Sage Publications, 1992), 3–5.
18. Robin Leidner, *Fast Food, Fast Talk: Service Work and the Routinization of Everyday Life* (Berkeley: University of California Press, 1993), 45–46, 230–31.

Select Bibliography

CITY DIRECTORIES AND STATISTICAL SOURCES

Jefferson's Directory of the City of Springfield, Illinois. Springfield, Ill.: Jefferson's Printing
    Co., 1926, 1930.
Moody's Industrial Manual. New York: Moody's Investors Service, 1969, 1974, 1977.
1987 Springfield, Illinois, City Directory. Taylor, Mich.: R. L. Polk and Co., 1987.
Polk 1992 Springfield, Illinois, City Directory. Taylor, Mich.: Polk and Co., 1992.
Polk's Marion (Grant County, Ind.) City Directory, 1938. Indianapolis: R. L. Polk and Co.,
    1938.
Polk's Memphis City Directory. N.p.: R. L. Polk and Co., 1927, 1928, 1929, 1930, 1940.
Polk's Springfield (Sangamon County, Illinois) City Directory. Springfield, Ill.: R. L. Polk and
    Co., 1952, 1955, 1961, 1963.

GOVERNMENT DOCUMENTS

Hess, Alan L., and John Beach. "McDonald's Drive-In Restaurant and Sign." National Regis-
    ter of Historic Places Inventory—Nomination Form, Aug. 3, 1983.
Luce, W. Ray, and Barbara Powers. "Porcelain Steel White Castle Restaurants in Columbus
    [Ohio]." National Register of Historic Places Inventory—Nomination Form (November
    1983).
U.S. Department of the Interior, National Park Service, National Register of Historic Places,
    Evaluation / Return Sheet. "McDonald's Restaurant and Sign," Los Angeles County, Calif.
    (Dec. 8, 1983).
———. "Porcelain Steel White Castle Restaurants, Franklin County, Ohio" (May 4, 1984).
U.S. Department of Transportation, Federal Highway Administration. *Highway Statistics:
    Summary to 1985.* Washington, D.C.: U.S. Government Printing Office, n.d.
———. *Selected Highway Statistics and Charts, 1990.* Washington, D.C.: U.S. Government
    Printing Office, n.d.
Wilson, Kristin L., and Nella L. Bean. "White Castle Building #8." National Register of His-
    toric Places Inventory—Nomination Form (June 1986).

BOOKS

Allen, Frederick. *Secret Formula.* New York: Harper Business, 1994.
Altman, Irwin. *The Environment and Social Behavior.* Monterey, Calif.: Brooks / Cole, 1979.

American Entrepreneurs' Association. *Hot Dog Stand: AEA Business Manual No. 73.* Santa Monica, Calif.: American Entrepreneurs' Association, 1979.

American Heritage editors. *The American Heritage Cookbook and Illustrated History of American Eating and Drinking,* Vols. 1–2. New York: Simon and Schuster, 1964.

Baeder, John. *Diners.* New York: Harry N. Abrams, 1978.

Barker, Roger G. *Ecological Psychology: Concepts and Methods for Studying the Environment of Human Behavior.* Stanford, Calif.: Stanford University Press, 1968.

Belasco, Warren J. *Americans on the Road: From Autocamp to Motel, 1910–1945.* Cambridge: MIT Press, 1979; Baltimore: Johns Hopkins University Press, 1997.

——. *Appetite for Change: How the Counterculture Took on the Food Industry.* Ithaca, N.Y.: Cornell University Press, 1993.

Bell, David, and Gill Valentine. *Consuming Geographies: We Are Where We Eat.* London: Routledge, 1997.

Bennett, J. M. *Roadsides: The Front Yard of the Nation.* Boston: Stratford Co. Publishers, 1936.

Bernstein, Charles. *Great Restaurant Innovators: Profiles in Success.* New York: Lebhar-Friedman, 1981.

Boas, Max, and Steve Chain. *Big Mac: The Unauthorized Story of McDonald's.* New York: Mentor Books, 1976.

Bond, Robert E. *The Source Book of Franchise Opportunities.* Homewood, Ill.: Dow Jones–Irwin, 1985.

Brewster, Letitia, and Michael F. Jacobson. *The Changing American Diet.* Washington, D.C.: Center for Science in the Public Interest, 1978.

Bryson, Bill. *Made in America: An Informal History of the English Language in the United States.* New York: Avon Books, 1994.

"Burger King." In *International Directory of Company Histories,* ed. Lisa Mirabile, 2:613–15. Chicago: St. James Press, 1990.

Clarke, Clifford Edward, Jr. *The American Family Home, 1800–1960.* Chapel Hill: University of North Carolina Press, 1986.

Conkling, Clinton L. *Encyclopedia of Illinois and Sangamon County.* Vol. 2. Edited by Newton Bateman and Paul Selby. Chicago: Munsell Publishing, 1912.

Crane, Diana. *The Production of Culture: Media and the Urban Arts.* Newbury Park, Calif.: Sage Publications, 1992.

Cussler, Margaret, and Mary L. De Give. *'Twixt the Cup and the Lip: Psychological and Socio-Cultural Factors Affecting Food Habits.* New York: Twayne Publishers, 1952.

Dicke, Thomas S. *Franchising in America: The Development of a Business Method, 1840–1980.* Chapel Hill: University of North Carolina Press, 1992.

Dickson, Paul. *The Great American Ice Cream Book.* New York: Atheneum, 1972.

Drinnon, Elizabeth McCants. *Stuckey: The Biography of Williamson Sylvester Stuckey, 1909–1977.* Macon, Ga.: Mercer University Press, 1997.

Egerton, John. *Southern Food at Home, on the Road, in History.* New York: Knopf, 1987.

Emerson, Robert L. *Fast Food: The Endless Shakeout.* New York: Lebhar-Friedman, 1979.

——. *The New Economics of Fast Food.* New York: Van Nostrand Reinhold, 1990.

Ewen, Stuart. *All-Consuming Images: The Politics of Style in Contemporary Culture.* New York: Basic Books, 1988.

——. *Captains of Consciousness: Advertising and the Social Roots of the Consumer Culture.* New York: McGraw-Hill, 1976.

Fantasia, Rick. "American Commodities as Cultural Goods: The 'Place' of Fast-Food in France." Unpublished paper, Smith College, Northampton, Mass., cited in Leidner, *Fast Food, Fast Talk,* 222.

Fine, Gary Alan. *Kitchens: The Culture of Restaurant Work.* Berkeley: University of California Press, 1996.

Fishwick, Marshall, ed. *Ronald Revisited: The World of Ronald McDonald.* Bowling Green, Ohio: Bowling Green University Popular Press, 1983.

——. *The World of Ronald McDonald.* Bowling Green, Ohio: Bowling Green University Popular Press, 1978.

Flink, James J. *The Automobile Age.* Cambridge: MIT Press, 1988.

Franchising in the U.S. Economy: Prospects and Problems. Committee on Small Business, House of Representatives, 101st Congress, 2nd Sess. Washington, D.C.: U.S. Government Printing Office, 1990.

Funderburg, Anne Cooper. *Chocolate, Strawberry, and Vanilla: A History of American Ice Cream.* Bowling Green, Ohio: Bowling Green State University Popular Press, 1995.

Gideon, Siegfried. *Mechanization Takes Command.* New York: Norton, 1948.

Gladding, Effie Price. *Across the Continent by the Lincoln Highway.* New York: Brentano's, 1915.

Goffman, Erving. *The Presentation of Self in Everyday Life.* Garden City, N.Y.: Doubleday Anchor Books, 1959.

——. *Relations in Public: Microstudies of the Public Order.* New York: Basic Books, 1971.

Gottdiener, M[ark]. *Postmodern Semiotics: Material Culture and the Forms of Postmodern Life.* Oxford, U.K.: Blackwell, 1995.

——. *The Theming of America: Dreams, Visions, and Commercial Spaces.* Boulder, Colo.: Westview Press, 1997.

Gutman, Richard J. S. *American Diner: Then and Now.* New York: Harper Perennial, 1993.

Handwerker, Murray. *Nathan's Famous Hot Dog Cookbook.* New York: Gramercy Publishing, 1983.

Hardee's Food Systems, Inc., Annual Report 1972, 1976.

Hattwick, Richard E. "Gust E. 'Brick' Lundberg." Photocopy, 1–17. Kewanee Business History Series 1, Illinois Business Hall of Fame, Center for Business and Economic Research, Western Illinois University, August 1976.

Heimann, Jim. *Car Hops and Curb Service: A History of American Drive-In Restaurants, 1920–1960.* San Francisco: Chronicle Books, 1996.

Heimann, Jim, and Rip Georges. *California Crazy: Roadside Vernacular Architecture.* San Francisco: Chronicle Books, 1980.

Henderson, Floyd M. "Foodways." In *This Remarkable Continent,* ed. Rooney, Zelinsky, and Louder, 225–33.

Hess, Alan. *Googie: Fifties Coffee Shop Architecture.* San Francisco: Chronicle Books, 1985.

Hine, Thomas. *The Total Package: The Evolution and Secret Meanings of Boxes, Cans, and Tubes.* Boston: Little, Brown, 1995.

Hines, Duncan. *Food Odyssey.* New York: Thomas Y. Crowell, 1955.

Hirshorn, Paul, and Steven Izenour. *White Towers.* Cambridge: MIT Press, 1979.

Hogan, David Gerard. *Selling 'Em by the Sack: White Castle and the Creation of American Food.* New York: New York University Press, 1997.

Hoover, Gary, Alta Campbell, and Patrick J. Spain, eds. *Hoover's Handbook of American Business.* Emoryville, Calif.: Publishers Group, 1995.

——. *Hoover's Handbook of American Business.* Emoryville, Calif.: Publishers Group West, 1990.

Hotel Planning and Outfitting: Commercial, Residential, and Recreational. Chicago: Albert Pick-Barth Companies, 1928.

Hurt, James. "Images of Chicago." In *Illinois: Its History and Legacy,* ed. Roger D. Bridges and Rodney O. Davis. St. Louis: River City Publishers, 1984.

Illinois Capital Illustrated. Springfield, Ill.: Press of the Illinois State Register, 1898.

Imasco Annual Reports. 1988, 1990, 1991, 1992, 1994.

Ingram, E. W. *"All This from a 5-cent Hamburger!" The Story of the White Castle System.* New York: Newcomen Society in North America, 1964.

Jackson, John B. *Discovering the Vernacular Landscape.* New Haven: Yale University Press, 1984.

Jackson, Kenneth. *The Crabgrass Frontier: The Suburbanization of the United States.* New York: Oxford University Press, 1985.

Jakle, John A. "Small Towns as Historical Places: A Symbolic Interactionist Approach to Structuration Theory Through the Study of Landscape." In *Marginalized Places and Populations: A Structurationist Agenda*, ed. David Wilson and James O. Huff, 61–83. Westport, Conn.: Praeger, 1994.

——. *The Tourist: Travel in Twentieth-Century North America*. Lincoln: University of Nebraska Press, 1985.

——. *The Visual Elements of Landscape*. Amherst: University of Massachusetts Press, 1987.

Jakle, John A. and Keith A. Sculle. *The Gas Station in America*. Baltimore: Johns Hopkins University Press, 1994.

Jakle, John A., Keith A. Sculle, and Jefferson Rogers. *The Motel in America*. Baltimore: Johns Hopkins University Press, 1996.

Jones, W. Dwayne. "In Search of the Vernacular Twentieth-Century Drive-In Restaurant." In *Preserving the Recent Past*, ed. Deborah Slaton and Rebecca A. Shiffer, 2:31–39. Washington, D.C.: Historic Preservation Education Foundation, 1995.

Kinross, Lord. *The Innocents at Home*. New York: Morrow, 1959.

Kroc, Ray. *Grinding It Out: The Making of McDonald's*. New York: Berkley, 1977.

Krohe, James, Jr. *A Springfield Reader: Historical Views of the Illinois Capital, 1818–1976*. Springfield, Ill.: Sangamon County Historical Society, 1976.

Krohe, James, and Cullom Davis. "Springfield: An Evolving Capital." In *The Middle-Size Cities of Illinois: Their People, Politics, and Quality of Life*, ed. Daniel Milo Johnson and Rebecca Monroe Veach, 191–213. Springfield, Ill.: Sangamon State University, 1980.

Kunstler, James Howard. *Geography of Nowhere: The Rise and Decline of America's Man-Made Landscape*. New York: Simon and Schuster, 1993.

Kursh, Harry. *The Franchise Boom*. Englewood Cliffs, N.J.: Prentice-Hall, 1968.

Kurtz, Stephen A. "Howard Johnson's Elevating the Host." In *Wasteland: Buying the American Dream*, 19–25. New York: Praeger, 1973.

Langdon, Philip. *Orange Roofs, Golden Arches: The Architecture of American Chain Restaurants*. New York: Knopf, 1986.

Laulajainen, Risto. *Spatial Strategies in Retailing*. Dordrecht: D. Reidel, 1987.

Lears, Jackson. *Fables of Abundance: A Cultural History of Advertising in America*. New York: Basic Books, 1994.

Leidner, Robin. *Fast Food, Fast Talk: Service Work and the Routinization of Everyday Life*. Berkeley: University of California Press, 1993.

Levenstein, Harvey. *Paradox of Plenty: A Social History of Eating in Modern America*. New York: Oxford University Press, 1993.

Lewis, Albert Walter, comp. *Springfield: The Capital of the State of Illinois*. Springfield, Ill.: [Springfield Commercial Association], 1912.

Lewis, Sinclair. *Oil!* New York: Grosset and Dunlap, 1926.

Love, John F. *McDonald's: Behind the Arches*. Toronto: Bantam Books, 1986.

Luce, W. Ray. "Kent State, White Castles and Subdivisions." In *Preserving the Recent Past*, ed. Deborah Slaton and Rebecca A. Shiffer, 2:15–20. Washington, D.C.: Historic Preservation Education Foundation, 1995.

Luxenberg, Stan. *Roadside Empires: How the Chains Franchised America*. New York: Penguin Books, 1985.

MacCannell, Dean. *The Tourist: A New Theory of the Leisure Class*. New York: Schocken Books, 1976.

McLamore, James W. *The Burger King: Jim McLamore and the Building of an Empire*. New York: McGraw-Hill, 1998.

Marchand, Roland. *Advertising the American Dream: Making the Way for Modernity, 1920–1940*. Berkeley: University of California Press, 1985.

Mariani, John. *America Eats Out*. New York: William Morrow, 1991.

Marling, Karal Ann. *As Seen on TV: The Visual Culture of Everyday Life in the 1950s*. Cambridge: Harvard University Press.

Marryat, Frederick. *A Diary in America, with Remarks on Its Institutions, Part Second*. London: Longman, Orme, Brown, Green and Longmans, 1839.

Marsh, Carole. *The Hardee's Heritage.* Rocky Mount, N.C.: Hardee's Food Systems, Inc., 1976.

Mathews, Mitford M., ed. *A Dictionary of Americanisms on Historical Principles.* Chicago: University of Chicago Press, 1951.

May, Elaine Tyler. *Homeward Bound: American Families in the Cold War Era.* New York: Basic Books, 1988.

Meinig, D. W., ed. *The Interpretation of Ordinary Landscapes.* New York: Oxford University Press, 1979.

Metz, Robert. *Franchising: How to Select a Business of Your Own.* New York: Hawthorn Books, 1969.

Miller, Douglas T., and Marion Nowak. *The Fifties: The Way We Really Were.* Garden City, N.Y.: Doubleday, 1977.

Monaghan, Tom, with Robert Anderson. *Pizza Tiger.* New York: Random House, 1986.

Moon, William Least Heat. *Blue Highways: A Journey Into America.* Boston: Little, Brown, 1982.

Morris, William, and Mary Morris. *Morris Dictionary of Word and Phrase Origins.* New York: Harper and Row, 1971.

Nash, Roderick. *The Nervous Generation: American Thought, 1917–1930.* Chicago: Rand McNally, 1970.

Oakley, J. Ronald. *God's Country: America in the Fifties.* New York: Dembner Books, 1986.

Oldenburg, Ray. *The Great Good Place: Cafés, Coffee Shops, Community Centers, Beauty Parlors, General Stores, Bars, Hangouts, and How They Get You through the Day.* New York: Paragon House, 1989.

O'Neill, William L. *American High: The Years of Confidence, 1945–1960.* New York: Free Press, 1986.

Orr, David G. "The Ethnography of Big Mac." In *The World of Ronald McDonald,* ed. Fishwick, 377–86.

Oxford English Dictionary. Vol. 16: Soot-Styx, 2nd ed. Oxford: Clarendon Press, 1989.

Patton, Phil. *Open Road: A Celebration of the American Highway.* New York: Simon and Schuster, 1986.

Pillsbury, Richard. *From Boarding House to Bistro: The American Restaurant Then and Now.* Boston: Unwin Hyman, 1990.

———. *No Foreign Food: The American Diet in Time and Place.* Boulder, Colo.: Westview Press, 1998.

Pizza Hut information package. Dallas: Pizza Hut, [1995].

Potter, David M. *People of Plenty: Economic Abundance and the American Character.* Chicago: University of Chicago Press, 1954.

Reiter, Ester. *Making Fast Food: From the Frying Pan into the Fryer.* Montreal: McGill-Queens University Press, 1991.

Riesman, David. *The Lonely Crowd: A Study of the Changing American Character.* Garden City, N.Y.: Doubleday, 1955.

Rifkin, Jeremy. *Beyond Beef: The Rise and Fall of the Cattle Culture.* New York: Dutton, 1992.

Roberts, Cecil. *Gone Sunward.* London: Hodder and Stoughton, 1936.

Rooney, John F., Jr., Wilbur Zelinsky, and Dean R. Louder, eds. *This Remarkable Continent: An Atlas of United States and Canadian Society and Cultures.* College Station: Texas A&M University Press, 1982.

Root, Waverly, and Richard de Rochemont. *Eating in America: A History.* New York: Morrow, 1976.

Rotella, Elyce J. *From Home to Office: U.S. Women at Work, 1870–1930.* Ann Arbor, Mich.: UMI Research Press, 1981.

Russo, Edward J. *Prairie of Promise: Springfield and Sangamon County.* Woodland Hills, Calif.: Windsor Publications, 1983.

Sack, Robert David. *Place, Modernity, and the Consumer's World.* Baltimore: Johns Hopkins University Press, 1992.

Saroyan, William. *Short Drive, Sweet Chariot.* New York: Phaedra, 1966.

Schiavo, Giovanni E[rmenegildo]. *The Italians in Chicago: A Study in Americanization.* 1928; repr. ed., New York: Arno Press, 1975.

Shelton, Allen, and Joe L. Kincheloe. *The Sign of the Burger: Double Takes on McDonald's.* Boulder, Colo.: Westview Press, 1998.

Shortridge, Barbara, and James R. Shortridge, eds. *The Taste of American Place: A Reader on Regional and Ethnic Foods.* Lanham, Md.: Rowman and Littlefield, 1990.

Sklar, Robert. Introduction. In *The Plastic Age (1917–1930),* ed. Robert Sklar, 1–24. New York: George Braziller, 1970.

Springfield in 1892: Souvenir Supplement. Springfield, Ill.: Illinois State Journal, 1892.

State of Illinois, Department of Public Works and Buildings, Division of Highways. "Illinois Roads" (map), October 1, 1924.

Steinbeck, John. *The Wayward Bus.* New York: Viking Press, 1947.

Stern, Jane, and Michael Stern. *Way Out West.* New York: HarperCollins, 1993.

Taylor, Robert M., Jr., Errol Wayne Stevens, Mary Ann Ponder, and Paul Brockman. *Indiana: A New Historical Guide.* Indianapolis: Indiana Historical Society, 1989.

Tennyson, Jeffrey. *Hamburger Heaven: The Illustrated History of the Hamburger.* New York: Hyperion, 1993.

Thomas, R. David. *Dave's Way: A New Approach to Old-Fashioned Success.* New York: Putnam, 1991.

———. *Well Done!: The Common Guy's Guide to Everyday Success.* Grand Rapids, Mich.: Zondervan, 1994.

Thompson, George F., ed. *Landscape in America.* Austin: University of Texas Press, 1995.

Tichi, Cecelia. *Shifting Gears: Technology, Literature, and Culture.* Chapel Hill: University of North Carolina Press, 1987.

Tierney, James, ed. *1990 Directory of Chain Restaurant Operations.* New York: Lebhar-Friedman, 1990.

Tingley, Donald F. *The Structuring of a State: The History of Illinois, 1899–1928.* Urbana: University of Illinois Press, 1980.

Trillin, Calvin. *American Fried: Adventures of a Happy Eater.* New York: Doubleday, 1974.

Trimmer, Joseph F. "Enter the Wizard." In *The World of Ronald McDonald,* ed. Fishwick, 348–54.

Vaughn, Charles L. *Franchising: Its Nature, Scope, Advantages, and Development.* Lexington, Mass.: Lexington Books, 1979.

Webster, Bryce. *The Insider's Guide to Franchising.* New York: American Management Association, 1986.

Weiss, Michael J. *Latitudes and Attitudes: An Atlas of American Tastes, Trends, Politics, and Passions.* Boston: Little, Brown, 1994.

Witchell, Lawrence, ed. *Drive-In Management Guidebook.* New York: Harcourt Brace, 1968.

Witzel, Michael Karl. *The American Drive-In: History and Folklore of the Drive-In Restaurant in American Car Culture.* Osceola, Wis.: Motorbooks International, 1994.

Wood, Ruth Kedzie. *The Tourist California.* New York: Dodd, Mead, 1914.

Wyckoff, D. Daryl, and W. Earl Sasser. *The Chain-Restaurant Industry.* Lexington, Mass.: Lexington Books, 1978.

Zelinsky, Wilbur. *The Cultural Geography of the United States.* Englewood Cliffs, N.J.: Prentice-Hall, 1973.

———. *Exploring the Beloved Country.* Iowa City: University of Iowa Press, 1994.

PERIODICALS

"An Academic Twist to the Sale of Hamburgers." *Ebony* 29 (October 1974): 64–66, 68, 70, 72.

Albright, E. Roy. "Building Drug Store Business Around a Soda Fountain." *The Soda Fountain* (February 1934): 26–27, 35.

"The Allure of a Hot Chicken Chain." *Fortune* (Feb. 6, 1984): 129–30.

Alva, Marilyn. "Brown's Bag." *Restaurant Business* 94 (April 10, 1995): 40–42, 47.

——. "Can They Save the King?" *Restaurant Business* 93 (May 1, 1994): 104–7, 112–14.

——. "Crazy for Chicken." *Restaurant Business* 94 (March 1, 1996): 84–86, 90.

——. "El Sid." *Restaurant Business* 94 (March 1, 1995): 33, 38.

"Appealing to a Mass Market." *Nation's Business* 56 (July 1968): 71–74.

"Arby's." *Restaurant Business* 78 (Jan. 1, 1979): 96–99.

Arreola, Daniel D. "Mexican Restaurants in Tucson." *Journal of Cultural Geography* 3, no. 2 (Spring/Summer 1983): 108–14.

Ashton, Robin. "Why Are Food Service Chains Selling? And Why Are Food Companies Buying Them?" *Institutions/Volume Feeding* 82 (April 15, 1978): 51–60.

Austin, Steven J. "America's Favorite 'Hamburger Cook.'" *Mississippi 55 & Fine* (May–Oct. 1994): 4–7.

Baer, Joe. "Sambo's Turns Managers Into Tigers." *Fast Food* 65 (December 1966): 37–45.

Bain, Laurie. "Hot Dog Concepts: Can They Cut the Mustard?" *Restaurant Business* 85 (Feb. 10, 1986): 191–98.

——. "Manufacturing Program Builds Revenues for Church's." *Restaurant Business* 85 (Nov. 20, 1986): 126–28.

Bakos, Joan. "Finds KFC Not a Quick Fix." *Restaurant Business* 79 (May 1, 1980): 190–92.

Barmash, Isadore. "Fast Food Restaurants—How They Grew and Grew." *Good Housekeeping* 195 (November 1982): 114, 123–25.

Bartel, Clyde G. "Getting the Motorist's Money!" *The Soda Fountain* 29, no. 8 (August 1930): 34, 36, 38.

Bearth, Dan. "Yankee Clipper Runs Up Distress Signal, Steers Course to Pizza." *Wichita Eagle Beacon*, March 15, 1976, 26.

Belasco, Warren J. "Ethnic Fast Foods: The Corporate Melting Pot." *Food and Foodways: Explorations in the History and Culture of Human Nourishment* 2, no. 1 (1987): 1–30.

——. "Toward a Culinary Common Denominator: The Rise of Howard Johnson's, 1925–1940." *Journal of American Culture* 2 (Fall 1979): 503–18.

Belinski, Pete, and Sharon Pavlista. "Franchise Entrepreneurs: The Chain's Crucial Links." *Restaurant Business* 75 (Oct. 1, 1976): 101–11, 126–27.

Belinski, Peter, and Denise Brennan. "Marriott Broadens Business Horizons." *Restaurant Business* 81 (June 1, 1982): 113–25.

Bell, Alexa. "Carl's Quandry." *Restaurant Business* 91 (July 1, 1992): 53, 56–57.

——. "Rockin' and Rollin'." *Restaurant Business* 87 (June 10, 1988): 182–84.

——. "Wienerschnitzel: Hot Dogs with Relish." *Restaurant Business* 87 (Nov. 20, 1988): 74, 76, 78.

Bennett, Helen Christie. "'Pinkie's Pantry' Took the Cake." *American Magazine* (June 1928): 65–66.

Berg, Eric N. "Dairy Queen Bracing for Battle." *New York Times*, Nov. 19, 1990, Y-C2.

Bergen, Kathy. "Franchisees Attack McDonald's." *Chicago Tribune*, May 22, 1997, 1, 4.

Bernard, Fran. "It's Good Eating and Lots of Fun at the Fleetwood." *State Journal-Register*, Jan. 17, 1977, 14.

"Big Boys of America—A Sleeping Giant Wakes Up." *Institutions* 82 (May 15, 1979): 43–46.

"The Big Burger Boss." *Time* (Dec. 17, 1973): 100.

Birmingham, John. "What Now?" *Restaurant Business* 91 (July 20, 1992): 80–88.

Bittman, Marc. "Ben and Jerry's Caring Capitalism." *Restaurant Business* 89 (Nov. 20, 1990): 132–34.

Blaikie, Ralph L. "Remodeling a Drive-In around Its New Take-Home Department." *Fountain and Fast Food* 53 (March 1954): 44–46.

Bloom, Nedra. "Crawfordsville Shanty Stands the Test of Time." *Indianapolis Star*, Jan. 18, 1984, sec. 1, p. 10.

Bloomfield, A. Victoria. "Tim Horton's: Growth of a Canadian Coffee and Doughnut Chain." *Journal of Cultural Geography* 14 (Spring/Summer 1994): 1–16.

Blyskal, Jeff. "Fat-Fryer Alchemy." *Forbes* (Dec. 6, 1982): 129–31.

Branch, Shelly. "McDonald's Strikes Out with Grownups." *Fortune* (Nov. 11, 1996): 157–58, 160, 162.

Brandimarte, Cynthia. "To Make the Whole World Homelike: Gender, Space, and America's Tea Room Movement." *Winterthur Portfolio* 30 (January 1995): 1–19.

"Breaking with Brick." *Restaurant Business* 92 (Sept. 30, 1993): 132, 134, 139.

Brennan, Denise M. "The Name of the Game: Kidding Around." *Restaurant Business* 90 (June 10, 1991): 98–106.

"Broader Menus for Fast Foods." *Business Week* (July 14, 1975): 118, 120, 122.

Brody, Jane E. "Study Finds a Three-Decade Gain in American Eating Habits, But a Long Way to Go." *New York Times,* Sept. 5, 1996, Y-A9.

Brooks, Steve. "The Long Road Back." *Restaurant Business* 93 (May 20, 1994): 44–54.

———. "Round Up." *Restaurant Magazine* 91 (Oct. 10, 1992): 86–89, 94–96.

———. "The Trials of Chairman Posner." *Restaurant Business* 91 (May 20, 1992): 88, 94–98.

Brownell, James E. "How Safe Is the Roadside Restaurant?" *Hygenia* 17 (July 1939): 590–92.

Brumback, Nancy. "Taking the Prime Cut: Casual Chains Have Carved Out the Lucrative Mid-Priced Section of the Steak Segment." *Restaurant Business* 95 (Jan. 20, 1996): 109–10, 112, 114, 116, 124–25.

"Bull in the Hamburger Shop." *Forbes* (May 15, 1973): 130.

"Burger King Buys 57 Restaurants for $55.6 Million." *New York Times,* Feb. 1, 1996, C4.

"Burger Park Has Replaced Rally's Franchise." *State Journal-Register,* Feb. 13, 1994, 37.

"Burgers: Bracing for Battle." *Restaurant Business* 77 (March 1978): 128–30, 245.

"The Burger That Conquered the Country." *Time* (Sept. 17, 1973): 84–86, 89–90.

Burke, Padriac. "Rolling Carts and Songs of Plenty: The Urban Food Vendor." *Journal of American Culture* 2 (1979): 480–87.

Busch, Noel F. "A Year of Truman." *Life* (April 8, 1946): 94–98, 101–2, 104.

Byrne, John A. "Pizza to Tacos to Pasta." *Forbes* 130 (Oct. 11, 1982): 172, 174, 177.

"Canadians Sweet on Doughnuts." *Toronto Globe and Mail,* July 4, 1995, B10.

Casper, Carol. "Caffeine Rush." *Restaurant Business* 95 (Jan. 1, 1996): 92–109.

———. "Food-to-Go: Market Segment Report." *Restaurant Business* 90 (Nov. 1, 1991): 121–36.

———. "The Ground Round Comes on the Scene Again." *Restaurant Business* 85 (July 1, 1986): 176–78.

———. "Hot Heroes." *Restaurant Business* 93 (Jan. 20, 1994): 109–10, 112, 114, 120.

———. "Ice Cream and Yogurt: Market Segment Report." *Restaurant Business* 91 (May 1, 1992): 209–30.

———. "Keeping Afloat." *Restaurant Business* 93 (July 1, 1994): 135–58.

———. "Pizza." *Restaurant Business* 92 (Feb. 10, 1993): 126, 128, 132, 137–38, 151–52.

———. "Staying Power." *Restaurant Business* 95 (Sept. 1, 1996): 81–90.

———. "Steak." *Restaurant Business* 90 (July 20, 1991): 159–60, 164–66, 170, 172, 194, 198.

———. "A Whole New Enchilada." *Restaurant Business* 93 (Oct. 16, 1994): 157–58, 160–66, 168–69.

"A Chain Is Born." *Fast Food* 63 (November 1964): 80–87.

Chamberlain, Anne. "A Live Show Daily at Hamburger Hamlet." *Fortune* 95 (March 1977): 208–12, 214–15, 217, 219.

"Changes Prepare Mr. Steak for the Coming Decade." *Chain Executive* 8 (January 1980): 80–81.

Chaudhry, Rajan. "That's Eat-ertainment." *Restaurants and Institutions* 104 (April 1, 1994): 18–22, 28.

"Checkers to Buy Rally's Hamburgers." *New York Times,* January 30, 1999, B3.

Childs, Leslie. "'Hot Dog Kennels' as Nuisances to Adjoining Property Owners." *American City* 38 (February 1928): 137–38.

"Chinese Drive-In in Salt Lake City." *Drive-In Restaurant* 25 (September 1961): 37.

"Circular Drive-In Includes Commissary." *Architectural Record* 100, no. 3 (September 1946): 101.

"Cities on the Move: Fort Wayne." *Fast Food* 63 (February 1964): 67–71.

"Civil Rights: Discriminating Taste." *Time* (Aug. 30, 1968): 36–37.

"'Coffee and' in the Doggy Dog-Wagon." *Literary Digest* 112 (Feb. 20, 1932): 42–43.

Collins, Glenn. "Changing Tastes Put End to Sizzler's Salad Days." *New York Times,* June 22, 1996, 17, 19.

———. "Left Alone at the Food Fight." *New York Times,* July 16, 1997, C1, C4.

———. "Owner of Arby's to Buy Long John Silver's Chain." *New York Times,* Sept. 22, 1994, C4.

———. "PepsiCo to Spin Off Its Restaurant Business." *New York Times,* Jan. 24, 1997, C1-C2.

"Coming to Terms with Change." *Food Service Marketing* 40 (September 1978): 112, 117, 119.

"Commentary / Opinions." *Ferdinand (Indiana) News,* Aug. 8, 1996, 2.

"Concept 80 at der Wienerschnitzel." *Institutions* 78 (March 1, 1976): 53–60.

"Coney Island's Soda Fountains." *The Soda Fountain* 14 (October 1924): 565–69.

Coutts, Cheryl Turi. "The Olive Garden: Ripe for Growth." *Restaurant Business* 86 (May 1, 1987): 120–22, 124.

"Cramping the Business Style of Franchisors." *Business Week* (June 16, 1975): 82.

"Creating an Entertaining Environment." *Fast Service* 40 (January 1981): 28–31.

Curtis, Carol E. "Born Again Chicken." *Forbes* (June 9, 1980): 68–70.

"Dairy Queen Stores Put on a New Hat." *Ice Cream Review* 45 (June 1962): 42, 48.

Dallman, V. Y. "Lighter Vein." *Illinois State Register,* Jan. 21, 1947, 6.

"Dan Lasater: How to Make $30 Million in Twelve Years." *Dun's* 101 (May 1973): 15–16, 21, 133–34, 136.

"Denny's: 'Strong Guidance from Our Office Paves the Way for Uniformity and Profit.'" *Fast Food* 63 (May 1964): 72–74.

Derwig, George. "Shopping Center Surge." *State Journal-Register,* July 21, 1961, 1, 18.

Dessauer, Phil. "Fried Chicken Champ." *Coronet* 29 (March 1951): 150, 152, 154.

Dettro, Chris. "Mall, Downtown Area to Share Spotlight in '93." *State Journal-Register,* Jan. 31, 1993, 10A–11A.

———. "Restauranteur Turns Failure Into Success." *State Journal-Register,* March 13, 1988, 47.

Dettro, Chris, and Chris Green. "Fleetwood Closed." *State Journal-Register,* Sept. 28, 1993, 1–3.

Dietrich, Matthew. "Changes Revolving around White Oaks Mall Could Turn Within." *State Journal-Register,* Jan. 26, 1992, 65.

Dobrzynski, Judith H. "Chicken Done to a Golden Rule." *New York Times,* April 3, 1996, Y C-1.

"Dog n Suds." *American Restaurant Magazine* (June 1958): 63.

"Dog n Suds." *Drive-In Magazine* 24, no. 10 (October 1960): 6, 12, 17.

"Dog n Suds Merging with Chicago Firm." *Franchise Journal* 2 (July–August 1969): 18.

"Dog n Suds Sees Right Spot as Key to Franchisee's Success." *Fast Food* 63 (May 1964): 134, 141.

Domino's Pizza information package, "Domino's Pizza: Important Dates." Domino's Pizza, Ann Arbor, Mich. [1994].

Dorfman, Dan. "McDonald's Sizzling Out?" *Esquire* 91 (March 13, 1979): 10–12.

"Do You Remember?" *Illinois State Register,* April 19, 1972, 38.

"The Drive-In That Jack Built." *Restaurant Management* 83 (December 1958): 52–53, 102.

"Eating Goes on Assembly-Line at California Drive-In." *Business Week* (July 23, 1949): 22–23.

"Eating Out: A Binge That Defies Recession." *U.S. News and World Report* (Feb. 19, 1979): 62–63.

"Eat Up and Fill Up." *Ice Cream Journal* 37 (May 1954): 62, 90.

"Effective Training Program Keeps Pace with Sizzler Growth." *Food Service Marketing* 40 (September 1978): 52, 55.

Ehle, Henry S. "The Customers Approve." *American Restaurant Magazine* 35 (March 1951): 50–52, 108–12, 114, 116–17.

"El Chico Cooks Up a Turnaround." *Restaurants and Institutions* 104 (March 1, 1994), 16–17.

"Elevating the Standing of the 'Hot Dog Kennel.'" *American City* 38 (May 1928): 99–100.

"Expanding Carvel Chain an American Success Story." *Ice Cream Review* 35 (July 1958): 48, 60.

"Express Restaurant Delivery Guide," 3rd ed. Winter 1996–97. [Springfield: n.p., 1996.]

Fabricant, Florence. "The Geography of Taste." *New York Times Magazine,* March 10, 1996, 40–41.

———. "The Italian Pizza Police Are Offering Rules for the Real Thing." *New York Times,* June 7, 1995, B6.

Fair, Ernest W. "Denver." *American Restaurant Magazine* 31 (August 1947), 24, 26, 68, 70.

———. "Salt Lake City." *American Restaurant Magazine* 31 (September 1947), 26–28, 66, 68, 70, 74.

———. "Tulsa." *American Restaurant Magazine* 32 (May 1948), 30, 32, 86, 88, 90.

Fanald, Lon. "A Robot Takes the Car Hop Out of the Track's Service." *Fountain Service* 49 (November 1950): 30–31.

Fargo, Charlyn. "Chilli Central." *Heartland,* Nov. 5, 1993, 4A-6A.

Farrell, Kevin. "Burger King: 'Making It Special.'" *Restaurant Business* 80 (Oct. 1, 1981): 97–111.

———. "California Chain Casts Menu Stars." *Restaurant Business* 87 (Aug. 10, 1988): 105–9, 116–17.

———. "Ground Round Carves Out a Turnaround." *Restaurant Business* 84 (May 1, 1985): 126, 129–30.

———. "Hardee's Burger Battle Plan." *Restaurant Business* 85 (Oct. 10, 1986): 211–17.

———. "Sambo's: What Went Wrong?" *Restaurant Business* 79 (May 1, 1980): 158, 163–68, 172–74.

———. "Super Bar, Says Wendy's Will Position the Concept Outside of Competition's Way and Provide Continuing Flexibility." *Restaurant Business* 88 (Jan. 1, 1989): 82–85, 90–91.

"Fast Food Blitz Boosts Outlook for Pork Bellies." *Champaign-Urbana (Illinois) News Gazette,* Aug. 10, 1996, A-10.

"Fast Food Feast." *Time* (Nov. 30, 1981): 69.

"Fast-Food Franchisers Invade the City." *Business Week* (April 27, 1974): 92.

"The Fast-Food Furor." *Time* (April 21, 1975): 49, 51.

"Fast-Food War: Big Mac Under Attack." *Business Week* (Jan. 30, 1984): 44–46.

Fawcett, Waldon. "Roadside Merchants Organize to Study Mutual Problems." *Sales Management and Advertising Weekly* 15 (Sept. 1, 1928): 480–81.

Feder, Barnaby J. "Third Management Shake-Up at McDonald's in Two Years." *New York Times,* July 10, 1997, C2.

———. "Where Have You Gone, Ray Kroc?" *New York Times,* June 5, 1997, C1, C6.

Feldman, Rona. "Steak: Market Segment Report." *Restaurant Business* 91 (June 10, 1992): 155–56, 160, 166, 170, 172, 174, 176.

Fitzell, Philip B. "At Church's Fried Chicken the Growing Pains Are Over." *Fast Food* 72 (April 1973): 84–87.

"Food Court a Smash at Mall." *Decatur (Illinois) Herald,* Oct. 17, 1993, F-1.

"Food Franchises." *Franchising Journal* 3 (July 1970): 34–49.

Forton, James. "A Telephone Speeds Service." *Fountain Service* 49 (July 1950): 28–29.

"41 in Florida: All 41 Units Built on Insta's Pattern of Proven Success." *Drive-In Restaurant and Highway Cafe Magazine* 19 (June 1955): 19, 26.

"Franchised Drive-Ins." *Food Service* 27 (May 1965): 38–39.

"Franchise Drive-Ins Pay Off For Bresler as Ice Cream Dealers." *Ice Cream Review* 40 (September 1956): 96–98.

"Franchise Drive-In Stores." *Ice Cream Review* 38 (February 1956): 46, 80.

"Franchising: How Fertile Its Future?" *Restaurant Business* 79 (March 1, 1980): 109–20.

"Franchising: Maturing Menus and Markets." *Restaurant Business* 83 (March 20, 1984): 133–46, 152–54, 156–60, 163.

"Franchising: Too Much, Too Soon?" *Business Week* (June 27, 1970): 54–55.

"Franchising Success Means Constant Market Development." *Cornell Hotel and Restaurant Administration Quarterly* 11 (November 1970): 35–38.

"Franchising Was His Road to Fame and Fortune." *Food Service* 26 (February 1964): 62–68.

"Frankfurters Grab Bigger Share of Market." *Food Service Magazine* 28 (September 1966): 31–32.

Fraser, Nancy. "Hamburger University." *Life* (Oct. 21, 1966): 100.

"Free Movies Keep 'Em Comin' to Casey's Drive-In." *Fountain Service* 47 (November 1948): 26–27.

Friday, Cindy. "New Manager Has Taco-Tia Cooking." *San Bernardino Sun,* March 28, 1989, B5, B8.

"From Neon to Brass." *Best: The Magazine of Pillsbury* (Autumn 1986): 5–7.

Fussell, M. T. "1851, the Beginning of the Wholesale Ice Cream Industry." *Ice Cream Trade Journal* 47 (May 1951): 40–42.

Garbedian-Brennan, Denise. "Vern Curtis' Grand Slam Market Strategy." *Restaurant Business* 81 (June 1, 1982): 119–30.

Gardner, Judith B. "A Burger Battle—With Everything." *U.S. News and World Report* (Nov. 8, 1982), 76.

"Gas Station Sites with Leased Retail Ice Cream Stores Is the Newest Development." *Ice Cream Trade Journal* 46 (August 1950): 30–31, 96.

Gebhard, David. "Programmatic Architecture: An Introduction." *Society for Commercial Archeology Journal* 13 (Spring/Summer 1995): 2–7.

"GH Goes to 7 Popular Fast-Food Chains and Tells How They Rate in—Nutrition, Quality, and Cost." *Good Housekeeping* 181 (November 1975): 170–72.

Gindin, Rona. "Can Cataland's Confidence Turn around Arthur Treacher's?" *Restaurant Business* 85 (Jan. 1, 1986): 115–25.

———. "D'Lites, Killing the Golden Goose." *Restaurant Business* 86 (July 20, 1987): 121–23.

———. "Drive Thru-Only Revs Up." *Restaurant Business* 85 (May 20, 1986): 146–50.

———. "A Fight to Stay on Top." *Restaurant Business* 89 (July 1, 1986): 152–54.

———. "The Karchers' Synergistic Growth Scheme." *Restaurant Business* 83 (Sept. 1, 1984): 161–69, 172.

———. "Restaurants by Design." *Restaurant Business* 86 (July 1, 1987): 177–81, 188–93.

———. "Shoney's Shows Who's Boss." *Restaurant Business* 84 (Aug. 10, 1985): 194–95.

Goldberg, Theodore. "The Automobile: A Social Institution for Adolescents." *Environment and Behavior* 1 (December 1969): 157–85.

Goldman, Keith. "Concept Selection for Independent Restaurants." *Cornell Hotel and Restaurant Administration Quarterly* 34 (December 1993): 59–72.

"Good Humor Finds Its Customers on the Highways." *Ice Cream Review* 14 (August 1930): 40–41.

Goodspeed, John. "Little Taverns." *Baltimore Magazine* (June 1986): 47.

Gould, Chris. "Howard Johnson's and the Standardizing of Roadside Architecture." *North American Culture* 7 (1991): 3–18.

Graham, M. L. "$100 Capital in 1925—$1,000,000 Gross Sales in 1936." *The Soda Fountain* 35 (December 1936): 10–13.

Graves and Epps, Architects. "Journal Roadside Stands." *Ladies Home Journal* 29 (August 1932): 46–47.

"Growth Chains." *Restaurant Business* 93 (July 20, 1994): 67–118.

"Growth Companies." *Restaurants and Institutions* 99 (Oct. 2, 1989): 86.

"Hamburger: Still Profit King and Growing Bigger." *Food Service Magazine* 28 (September 1968): 25–27.

"Hardee's." *Fast Food* 67, pt. 2 (November 1968): 82–91, 154.

"Hardee's." *Restaurant Business* 78 (Jan. 1, 1979): 100–103.

"Hardee's Gets Burger Chef." *Restaurant Business* 81 (Feb. 1, 1982): 23.

"Hardee's Honcho Has Roots in Q-C Area." *Davenport (Iowa) Quad-City Times,* Dec. 31, 1995, 3M.

"Hardee's Is Set to Sell Its Roy Rogers Restaurants." *New York Times,* Dec. 16, 1995, 19.

"Hardee's Restructures." *Restaurant Business* 82 (February 1983): 26.

Harris, Marvin. "The Revolutionary Hamburger." *Psychology Today* 17 (October 1983): 6–8.

Haszonics, Joe J. "Inside a Franchise." *Restaurant Magazine* 69, no. 3 (July 1962): 33–34, 37–38, 40.

Herrmann, Arthur R. "Speeds Spells Success." *The Soda Fountain* 30, no. 11 (November 1931): 28–30, 33.

Hess, Alan. "Golden Architecture." *Journal: A Contemporary Art Magazine* 4, no. 36 (Spring 1983): 28–30.

———. "The Origins of McDonald's Golden Arches." *Journal of the Society of Architectural Historians* 54 (March 1986): 60–67.

Hinkley, Ted C., and Roderick C. Johnson. "Ray Kroc, Embodiment of Mid-Twentieth-Century America." *Journal of the West* 25, no. 1 (January 1986): 94–102.

Hoffbeck, Steven R. "The Barrels: Root Beer Stands of the Upper Midwest." *Minnesota History* 53, no. 7 (Fall 1993): 254–65.

Horovitz, Bruce. "Domino's Theory: Toss Old Image, Get Back to Top." *USA Today,* June 13, 1996, 12B.

"The Hotdog." *Restaurants and Institutions* 99 (May 29, 1989): 105, 108, 112, 116, 126–28.

"Hotdogs Are Not Passe: Cheatham Designs Chain to Prove It." *Nation's Restaurant News* 19 (May 27, 1985): 35.

"Hot Dogs Go Gourmet." *Independent Restaurants* 48 (May 1986): 26, 28.

"Hot Dogs on Wane." *Terre Haute Star,* July 17, 1929, 4.

"Houston's Drive-In Trade Gets Girl Show with Its Hamburgers." *Life* (Feb. 26, 1940): 84–85.

"How Burger Chef Speeds Service." *Fast Food* 58 (January 1959): 33–34.

"How Nutritious Are Fast-Food Meals?" *Consumer Reports* (May 1975): 278–81.

"How the Cone Was Born." *Ice Cream Field* 63 (June 1954): 34–39.

"How to Make Your Donuts Sell." *Drive-In Restaurant* 26 (June 1962): 34–35.

Hughes, Bettye Rice. "A Negro Tourist in Dixie." *The Reporter* 26 (April 26, 1962): 20–21.

Hunter, John. "The Diner in Worcester, 1890–1970: Mass Cultural Elements in an Urban Landscape." *Monadnock* 52 and 53 (1978–79): 45–54.

Hurley, Andrew. "From Hash House to Family Restaurant: The Transformation of the Diner and Post–World War II Consumer Culture." *Journal of American History* 83, no. 4 (March 1997): 1282–1308.

Huxtable, Ada Louise. "Architecture for a Fast-Food Culture." *New York Times Magazine,* Feb. 12, 1978, 23–25, 30, 32, 36.

"Ice Cream Franchises." *Franchise Journal* 2 (May / June 1969): 22–27, 52–57.

"Independents Dominate Majority of U.S. Restaurant Categories." *Independent Restaurants* 46 (June 1985): 36–38.

"Initial Capital, Plus the Desire to Succeed Is All We Ask of Franchisees." *Fast Food* 63 (May 1964): 68–71.

"Jack in the Box Proves Huge Success." *Drive-In Restaurant* 25, no. 6 (June 1961): 6–7.

Jackson, E. Christine. "Ethnography of an Urban Burger King Franchise." *Journal of American Culture* 2 (Fall 1979): 534–39.

"Jack v. Mac." *Time* (May 5, 1975): 71–72.

Jacobson, Gianna. "Let Them Eat Bread, Especially at $4 a Loaf." *New York Times,* Nov. 18, 1995, Y-19, Y-21.

Jakle, John A. "Roadside Restaurants: The Evolution of Place-Product-Packaging." *Journal of Cultural Geography* 3 (1982): 76–93.

Jeffrey, Don. "Upscale Chicken on the Wings of Change." *Restaurant Business* 87 (July 20, 1988): 104–8.

Jones, W. Dwayne, with Roni Morales. "Pig Stands: The Beginning of the Drive-In Restaurant." *Society for Commercial Archeology News Journal* 12, no. 1 (Winter 1991–92): 2–5.

Joseph, James. "Uncle John's Glamorizes the Lowly Flapjack!" *Food Service* 20 (May 1958): 27–30.

Jouzaitis, Carol. "Franchises Shrug Off Recession." *Chicago Tribune,* Jan. 11, 1983, sec. 3, p. 7.

K., D. "Domino's Drivers Cited for Poor Safety Record." *Restaurant Business* 89 (May 1, 1990): 280.

K., R. M. "Letter from the Country." *Country Journal* 6 (March 1979): 26–27.

"Karcher: Business Sense Plus Humanism Promotes Success." *Food Service and Chain Executive* 6, no. 9 (September 1978): 151–52.

[Kellogg, Mary Alice]. "Making the Grade at Hamburger U." *Newsweek* (Sept. 25, 1972): 78.

King, Margaret J. "McDonald's and the New American Landscape." *USA Today* (January 1980): 46–48.

Knepler, Jane E. "Up and Out of the East End: The Irish in Springfield." *Bulletin of the Illinois Geographical Society* 17, no. 1 (July 1976): 25–32.

Kochak, Jacque [White]. "Barbecue: The Accent Is on Regional Growth." *Restaurant Business* 83 (Aug. 10, 1984): 108, 110, 114, 118, 122, 126, 130.

———. "Behind the Gourmet Burger Boom." *Restaurant Business* 83 (Nov. 11, 1984): 120–37.

———. "Does VICORP Have a Tiger by the Tail?" *Restaurant Business* 85 (Jan. 20, 1986): 115–18.

———. "Ice Cream and Yogurt." *Restaurant Business* 90 (May 1, 1991): 229–38, 246–52.

———. "Mexican Fast Food Moves Into the Mainstream." *Restaurant Business* 84 (Nov. 1, 1985): 133, 138, 142–44, 146–48.

———. "Oriental: Despite Its Popularity . . . " *Restaurant Business* 87 (March 1, 1988): 177–92.

———. "Pizza Turns Chic as Sales Soar." *Restaurant Business* 83 (Feb. 10, 1984): 134, 138, 142, 146, 151, 154.

———. "Rax Revamps Roast Beef Concept." *Restaurant Business* 82 (Aug. 10, 1983): 138–39.

———. "Regional Chains Dominate Barbecue Segment." *Restaurant Business* 84 (March 1, 1985): 97, 100, 102, 106, 108, 110–11.

———. "Sandwich: Market Segment Report." *Restaurant Business* 88 (Nov. 20, 1989): 193–94, 196–98, 200.

———. "Seafood Operators Take a Fresh Approach." *Restaurant Business* 84 (July 1, 1985): 93–103.

Kottak, Conrad P. "Rituals at McDonald's." *Natural History* 87 (January 1978): 75–82.

Kranner, Bernice. "Pizza Wars: A Bigger Slice of the Market." *New York* 20, no. 37 (Sept. 21, 1987): 20, 22, 25.

Krauss, Clifford. "Police Officers. (Quick, Which Food Comes to Mind?)." *New York Times,* Oct. 22, 1996, B-1.

Kraut, Alan M. "Ethnic Foodways: The Significance of Food in the Designation of Cultural Boundaries Between Immigrant Groups in the U.S., 1840–1921." *Journal of American Culture* 2 (1979): 409–20.

"Krystal Acquires Po Folks." *Restaurant Business* 81 (November 1982): 50, 55.

"Krystal's Mini-Burger a Southern Tradition." *Jackson (Miss.) Clarion-Ledger,* Jan. 6, 1984, 5B, 8B.

Ladau, Robert, and Richard Nininger. "Programmed Environment: The Art of Sensory Deception." *Fast Food* 68 (October 1969): 116–21.

Lang, Joan. "T.G.I. Friday's Continues to Flourish." *Restaurant Business* 83 (Nov. 1, 1984): 106, 108, 110, 112, 114, 116.

Langway, Lynn, Thomas Nicholson, Barbara Graustark, Dewey Grum, and Howard Lucy. "America: Out to Eat." *Newsweek* (Oct. 3, 1977): 86–87, 89.

Lansing, Alfred. "Cold Licks and Hot Profits." *Colliers* (Aug. 3, 1956): 30–34.

"Latest Bonnie Doon Unit Designed for Speedy Service." *Ice Cream Review* 34 (January 1951): 44–45.

Lawless, Mark J. and Christopher W. Hart. "Forces That Shape Restaurant Demand." *Cornell Hotel and Restaurant Administration Quarterly* 24 (November 1983): 7–17.

Lazarus, George. "Big Franchise Holder Nearing Burger King Crown." *Chicago Tribune*, Feb. 28, 1996, sec. 3, p. 3.

"Let's Be Frank about Franchises." *Drive-In Magazine* 21, no. 6 (June 1957): 7–11, 13.

Lev, Michael A. "Ronald's *Clowna Non Grata* to Some Lake Forest Residents." *Chicago Tribune*, April 28, 1994, 1, 6.

Lewis, Sinclair. "Adventures in Autobuming—The Great American Frying Pan." *Saturday Evening Post* (Jan. 3, 1920): 20–21, 62, 65–66.

Lindstrom, Andy. "It All Began with 'Mother.'" *State Journal-Register* (Oct. 16, 1979), 8A-11A.
Lohof, Bruce A. "Hamburger Stand: Industrialization and the American Fast-Food Phenomenon." *Industrial Archaeology Review* 2 (1978): 272–76.

Long, Delores. "Jack in the Box: A Strategy for Menu Superiority." *Restaurant Business* 86 (May 20, 1987): 124, 126, 128, 130.

Long, Joanne. "Springfield's Sandwich of Distinction." *State Journal-Register*, Feb. 19, 1972, 8A-9A.

"Love's: Back from the Brink." *Restaurant Business* 86 (July 1, 1987): 120–22.

Lubow, Arthur. "The McDonald's–Burger King Food Fight and the Blurring of American Taste," *New York Times Magazine*, April 19, 1998, 38–43.

Luce, W. Ray. "White Castle and Preservation." *Society for Commercial Archeology News Journal* 2, no. 4 (September 1984): 4–6.

Lukas, J. Anthony. "As American as McDonald's on the Fourth of July." *New York Times Magazine* (July 4, 1971): 5, 22, 24–27, 29.

Lundberg, Elmer A. "Put Up a Good Front." *Restaurant Digest* (September 1947): 8–10.

Lyman, A. L. "Light Out in Front Sales Stimulator." *The Soda Fountain* 32, no. 3 (March 1933): 16–19.

"Lynch Pumps New Fizz Into A&W Intl." *Institutions* 79 (Oct. 15, 1976): 25.

M., B. "Golden Corral Sees Golden Opportunities with Its New Metro Market Unit." *Restaurants and Institutions* 102 (July 22, 1992): 110.

——. "The International Agenda." *Restaurants and Institutions* 105 (July 1, 1995): 142, 146.

McAllister, Antoinette. "Cities OK Fast-Food Chains—But Hold the Golden Arches." *Planning* 42 (October 1976): 20–21.

"McDonald's Grinds Out Growth." *Dun's Review* 110 (December 1977): 50–52.

"McDonald's Makes Franchising Sizzle." *Business Week* (June 15, 1968): 102–3.

McDowell, Bill. "A Game of Chicken." *Restaurants and Institutions* 104 (Nov. 15, 1994): 36–44, 50.

Madrick, Jeffrey. "A Cautious Approach to Fast-Food Chains." *Business Week* (March 28, 1977): 85.

"The Man Who McDonaldized Burger King." *Business Week* (Oct. 8, 1979): 132–36.

Manzo, Joseph T. "From Pushcart to Modular Restaurant: The Diner on the Landscape." *Journal of American Culture* 13 (Fall 1990): 13–21.

"Market Report: Seafood." *Restaurant Business* 92 (Oct. 10, 1993): 121–23, 138–40.

"Market Report: Seafood." *Restaurant Business* 93 (July 1, 1994): 133–34, 152–55.

Marling, Karal Ann. "America's Love Affair with the Automobile in the Television Age." *Design Quarterly* 146 (1989): 5–19.

Marlowe, Estelle B. "Selling at the Curb." *The Soda Fountain* 30, no. 6 (June 1931): 33, 49.

Marsh, P. K. "Shooting the Market on the Wings." *Printer's Ink* (Feb. 20, 1932): 35–36, 99, 101–2

Martin, Sandra. "Eating in Springfield." *Illinois Times*, Feb. 17–23, 1978, 13.

"Matched to Metro Market." *Fast Food* 67 (1968): 132–33, 140.

"Meet the Big Boys from Big Boy." *Restaurant Business* 74 (June 1975): 65–76.

Mehegan, Sean. "In the Shop." *Restaurant Business* 94 (Oct. 10, 1995): 71–73, 76.

——. "Picking Up the Pieces of a Once-Proud Franchise." *Restaurant Business* 95 (Jan. 20, 1996): 18.

Mendelson, Abby. "Sambo's: What Really Happened?" *Fast Service/Family Restaurants* 41 (March 1982): 46–48.

Merwin, John. "The Sad Case of the Dwindling Orange Roofs." *Forbes* (Dec. 30, 1985): 75–79.

"Mexican Tacos to Give Hot Dogs a Run for the Money." *Drive-In Magazine* 24, no. 6 (June 1960): 8, 14.

Meyer, Judith W., and Lawrence A. Brown. "Diffusion Agency Establishment: The Case of Friendly Ice Cream and Public-Sector Diffusion Processes." *Socio-Economic Planning Sciences* 13 (1979): 242–49.

"Mid-Eastern Specialties in San Jose." *Drive-In Fast Service* 33 (May 1974): 48–50.

"Midwest Millionaires." *Restaurant Business* 79 (Jan. 1, 1980): 109–10.

"Milk Shakes Yesterday and Today." *Drive-In Fast Service* 31 (April 1972): 53–55.

"Mimi's Dispensers Make 'Em Feel Patronage Is Appreciated." *Fountain Service* 48 (December 1949): 24–25.

"Mister Softee Increasing Sales Goal for '58." *Ice Cream Review* 41 (January 1958): 34, 61.

Mitchell, Frank. "Maid-Rite the Oldest Springfield Drive-In." *State Journal-Register,* Aug. 14, 1971, 3A.

Mitgang, Harbert. "For the Love of Pizza." *Collier's* (March 7, 1953): 66–69.

Morrow, Elise. "Springfield, Illinois." *Saturday Evening Post* (Sept. 27, 1947): 28–29, 108–10, 112.

Moseley, Ray. "Sea's Riches a Dwindling Infinity." *Chicago Tribune,* Sept. 2, 1996, 1, 8.

"Motel Food Service." *Restaurant Digest* (July 1956): 27–29.

Moynahan, V. E. "'He Who Serves Best' . . . Profits Most." *The Soda Fountain* 34 (June 1935): 10–11.

"Mrs. Winner's: Playing for First Place in the Southeast." *Restaurant Business* 80 (Oct. 1, 1981): 108–13.

Muller, Christopher. "The Marriott Divestment: Leaving the Past Behind." *Cornell Hotel and Restaurant Administration Quarterly* 31 (February 1990): 7–13.

Muller, Christopher C., and Robert H. Woods. "An Expanded Restaurant Typology." *Cornell Hotel and Restaurant Administration Quarterly* 35 (June 1994): 27–37.

Mydans, Seth. "From Cambodia to Doughnut Shops." *New York Times,* May 26, 1995, Y A-8.

"The Name's the Same—But a Carrol's Franchisee Is Now the Franchiser." *Fast Food* 68 (March 1969): 160, 162.

"Nathan Sells Famous Hot Dogs." *Food Service and Marketing* 38 (July 1976): 65.

Nelson, Al P. "Walkie-Talkie Drive-In." *American Restaurant Magazine* 35 (September 1951): 40–41, 103.

"New Design, Menu Items Upgrade Sizzler Image." *Food Service Chain Executive* 5, no. 2 (February 1977): 73–74.

"The New Outlet—Roadside Refreshment Stands." *Printers' Ink* 135 (April 22, 1926): 127–28.

Nichols, Don. "A New Take on Fuddruckers." *Restaurant Business* 87 (May 20, 1988): 86–118, 126–28.

——. "Taco Machine Proves a Big Hit in Its Test Run." *Restaurant Business* 92 (March 1, 1993): 16.

Nielsen, Timothy K. "Spartan Food Systems: The Professional Franchise." *Fast Food* 71 (May 1971): 190, 194, 196, 198.

"1977 Chain Executives Forum." *Food Service Marketing* 39 (December 1977): 29–31, 33–34, 36–40.

Nolan, Mary. "Taming the City." *State Journal-Register,* Oct. 21, 1988, 8A–12A.

"Not for Export?" *Forbes* 116 (Oct. 15, 1975): 23–24.

"Nutrition: Fast Foods." *Current Health* 2 (May 1979): 15–17.

O'Hagan, Anne. "The Hot Dog Trail." *The Woman's Journal* 13 (May 1928): 12–15.

Ohmann, Richard. "Magazine Culture, ca. 1900." *Reviews in American History* 24 (1996): 51–55.

Oleck, Joan. "Minimum Wage: How High?" *Restaurant Business* 93 (Dec. 10, 1994): 66–67, 70–72, 74.

Olive Garden information package. Orlando, Fla.: Olive Garden, n.d.

"One Million Hamburgers and 160 Tons of French Fries a Year." *American Restaurant Magazine* 36 (July 1952): 44–45.

"Pact Set on Buying Roy Rogers Sites for $74 Million." *New York Times,* Aug. 3, 1996, Y-19.

"Pick a Good Location and Then Merchandise It!" *American Restaurant Magazine* 38 (October 1954): 71–73.

"Pizza Drive-In." *Drive-In Restaurant* 26, no. 4 (April 1962): 12–13, 28.

"Pop Culture: Soft Drinks Have Been an Integral Part of the American Landscape since the 1800s." *Restaurant Business* 93 (March 1994): 136–38.

Pope, Victoria. "The Man Who Gave Chili Its Second 'L.'" *Illinois Times,* Feb. 5, 1976, 4–5, 24–25.

"The Powerful Punch of Popeye's." *Fast Service* 40 (July 1981): 19–21, 63.

Pringle, Kirby. "'World's Creamiest Root Beer' May Be Foaming Its Way Back." *Champaign-Urbana (Ill.) News-Gazette,* April 28, 1993, C-1, C-4.

Puzo, Daniel. "Industry Forecast." *Restaurants and Institutions* 107 (Jan. 1, 1997): 29–31.

Quinton, Brian. "John Martin's Common-Sense Miracle." *Restaurants and Institutions* 101 (July 10, 1991): 10–11, 14.

Radford, John. "Fast Food along the 427-Mile New York State Thruway." *Fountain and Fast Food* 53 (August 1954): 34–35.

"Raffel: Arby's Projects Quality, Concentrates on Nutrition." *Food Service Chain Executive* 6, no. 9 (August 1978): 93–94, 102.

Raffel, Elaine. "What Makes Chili's Hot?" *Restaurant Business* 82 (Oct. 1, 1983): 147–58.

Raffio, Ralph. "Dunkin' Donuts Upgrades, Expands." *Restaurant Business* 85 (March 10, 1986): 228–34.

———. "Fast Food." *Restaurant Business* 83 (May 20, 1984): 190–95.

———. "Jack Laughery." *Restaurant Business* 82 (May 15, 1983): 148–49.

Raflo, Lisa, and Jeffrey Durbin. "Teal Roofs and Pecan Logs: A History of Stuckey's Pecan Shoppes." *Journal Society for Commercial Archeology* 13 (Fall 1995): 2–8.

Raitz, Karl B., and John Paul Jones. "The City Hotel as Landscape Artifact and Community Symbol." *Journal of Cultural Geography* 9 (Fall/Winter 1988): 17–36.

Rally's Hamburgers information package. Louisville, Ky.: Rally's Hamburgers, [1995].

"Rally's Hamburgers to Open; Fast Service Will Be Stressed." *State Journal-Register,* March 22, 1989, 21.

"Ralston Purina Company." *Restaurants and Institutions* 98 (Oct. 28, 1988): 44.

"Ralston Purina to Drop 232 Jack in the Box Fast-Food Restaurants." *Institutions Magazine* 85 (November 1979): 3.

Ramirez, Anthony. "Advertising." *New York Times,* June 30, 1995, D4.

Reichl, Ruth. "When Going Out Is In, We Are Where We Eat." *New York Times,* April 2, 1995, 6e.

"'Rekrystalized.'" *Fast Service/Family Restaurant* (March 1982): 34–39, 42.

"Restaurant Blues." *Business Week* (April 5, 1947): 30, 32.

"Restaurant Franchising in the Economy." *Restaurant Business* 81 (March 15, 1982): 109–24.

"Restaurants Follow Them Home." *Business Week* (May 3, 1952): 46–49.

Rhein, Elizabeth. "Popeye's Flexes Its Muscles." *Restaurant Business* 86 (May 20, 1987): 117–18, 120.

Riggs, Sylvia. "Marriott Makes Lean Years a Season to Grow." *Restaurants and Institutions* 91 (Aug. 18, 1982): 69–70, 72, 74, 76.

"Roadstands Reap Rich Rewards." *The Soda Fountain* 36 (April 1937): 27, 56.

Roark, Michael. "Fast Foods: American Food Regions." *North American Culture* 2, no. 1 (1985): 24–36.

Romano, Michael. "Minor Characters." *Restaurant Business* 92 (May 1, 1993): 46, 50, 56.

——. "Mr. Steak Wants to Be a Steakhouse Again." *Restaurant Business* 92 (Sept. 20, 1993): 37.

——. "Still Smoking." *Restaurant Business* 93 (March 20, 1994): 24, 28.

Romeo, Peter. "RB's Top 50 Growth Chains." *Restaurant Business* 94 (1995): 67–68, 70, 74, 78, 80, 82, 88, 90, 96, 100, 102, 107, 110, 114, 118.

"Ron's Krispy Fried Chicken Looks to Market Penetration for Successful Growth." *Food Service* 71 (March 1971): 40–43.

"A Root-Beer Franchiser Regains Its Fizz." *Business Week* (Oct. 20, 1973): 54, 56.

"Rough Waters." *Restaurant Business* 92 (Oct. 10, 1993): 121–22.

Ryan, Nancy Ross. "Great American Food Chronicles: Steak." *Restaurants and Institutions* 99 (Oct. 2, 1989): 103, 106, 110, 114, 118–20.

——. "Pizza." *Restaurants and Institutions* 99 (Sept. 4, 1989): 101, 104, 108, 114, 118, 122.

"Sambo's Many Problems: Morale, Image." *Newsweek* (March 6, 1978): 88.

"Sambo's Serves Its Managers an Extra Slice." *Business Week* (Jan. 26, 1974): 82.

Sampson, Bob. "Jack Robinson Restaurant Sticks with Simplicity—And Survives." *Decatur Daily Review,* Aug. 8, 1979, 36.

Sanson, Michael. "Splintering Ethnic." *Restaurant Hospitality* 80 (February 1996): 47, 50–54.

Sanstadt, Helen. "Doughnuts: A $300,000,000 a Year Bonanza." *Food Service* 25 (May 1961): 52–53, 98–99.

Sasser, W. Earl, and Samuel H. Pettway. "Case of Big Mac's Pay Plans." *Harvard Business Review* 52 (July–August 1974): 30–32, 36, 40, 44–45.

Scarpa, James. "The Changing Face of Chi-Chi's." *Restaurant Business* 87 (March 1, 1988): 145–49, 156–57.

——. "Chicago's Wurst." *Restaurant Business* 87 (Oct. 10, 1988): 48.

——. "Combo Deluxe." *Restaurant Business* 91, no. 7 (May 1, 1992): 114–16.

——. "Perkins Gears for Growth." *Restaurant Business* 89 (Jan. 1, 1990): 60–62, 67.

——. "Rax Rebounds." *Restaurant Business* 89 (Aug. 10, 1990): 82, 84, 87.

Schlossberg, Howard. "Elias Bros.' Goal, Keep Big Boy Big." *Restaurant Business* 87 (July 1, 1988): 152–54.

Sculle, Keith A. "Diners." *Historic Illinois* 5 (1983): 1–4.

——. "A Family Business Affair: 'Snappy Service' in Central Illinois." *Historic Illinois* 18, no. 3 (October 1995): 3–6.

——. "Finger-Licking Landmarks: Pioneer Fast Food Places." *Illinois Magazine* 21 (1982): 13–15.

"Seafood: Costs Are Eroding Profits." *Restaurant Business* 77 (March 1, 1978): 136–39.

"Seattle Restaurant Has a Game Plan." *Chicago Tribune,* July 29, 1996, sec. 4, p. 8.

"Service Is the Byword at White Hut." *Drive-In Restaurant and Highway Cafe Restaurant* 20, no. 8 (August 1956): 13, 17.

Shattuck, Frank G. "We Found Quality the Shortest Road to Volume." *System: The Magazine of Business* 43 (March 1923): 314–17, 408–12.

"Shopping Centers Growing Here." *State Journal-Register,* June 23, 1968, 17.

"Shrine to the Hamburger." *Popular Mechanics* 91 (January 1949): 101–3.

Shulman, David. "Food Franchising." *Franchise Journal* 2 (July/August 1969): 22–38.

Siering, Andy. "The Castle, No One Escapes Its Spell." *St. Louis* 16 (February 1984): 55–57, 72–74.

Silander, J. A. "The Soda Fountain Story." *Ice Cream Trade Journal* 47 (June 1951): 30–32, 102.

Sinclair, F. H. "Schrafft's Success Is Based on Quality." *The Soda Fountain* 33 (April 1934): 14–15, 31.

Slack, Steve. "The Martin Way." *State Journal-Register,* April 29, 1978, 14A.

Smith, Wes. "Small Town Fends Off an Attack by Big Mac." *Chicago Tribune,* Aug. 15, 1996, 1, 14.

Solomon, Jolie. "Not in My Backyard. Starbucks Is Doing Great, but Is a Backlash Beginning?" *Newsweek* (Sept. 16, 1996): 65.

"Squeeze in Fast Food." *Time* (March 26, 1979): 63.

Stern, Jane, and Michael Stern. "Cafeteria." *New Yorker* (Aug. 1, 1988): 37–54.

Stewart-Gordon, James. "Saga of the Chicken Colonel." *Readers Digest* 106 (February 1975): 143–46.

Strenk, Tom. "Broader Menus Spice Up Chicken Sales." *Restaurant Business* 84 (Jan. 20, 1985): 99–112.

"Subway Restaurant's Fred DeLuca—The Man Behind the Sandwich." Information package. Milford, Conn.: Subway, n.d.

Sullivan, Barbara. "Eateries' New Trend: Bundling." *Chicago Tribune,* Dec. 25, 1996, 14.

Sympson, Ron. "Can Monaghan Deliver?" *Restaurant Business* 91 (April 10, 1992): 78–81, 86–88.

"Taco Bell Put Their Work Into Building and Let the Rest Come Naturally." *Fast Food* 66, pt. 2 (November 1967): 88–91.

"Tacos from the Franchising Firing Line." *Fast Food* (January 1958): 34–35.

"Tacos Going Faster—Everywhere!" *Fast Food* 57 (January 1958): 36–37.

"Taco Time Goes PRE-FAB." *Fast Service* 36 (June 1977): 46, 48–50.

Taubeneck, Anne. "Lincoln's Land Touts Honest Cooking." *Chicago Sun-Times,* April 19, 1990, 6N.

Teague, Tom. "Ed Waldmire Passes On." *The 66 News!* (Fall 1993): 4–6.

"10,000 Motorists Dollars Help Howard Johnson Build Up Chain of 130 Company-Owned Shops." *Ice Cream Review* 23 (July 1940): 25.

"Theme Dining." *Restaurant Business* 80 (June 10, 1987): 178–79.

"Thirteenth Annual Survey of Industry Trends." *Ice Cream Field* 85 (March 1965): S-5–S-6.

Thom, Edward. "Ice Cream Bar on a Stick." *Ice Cream Review* 33 (March 1950): 134–39.

Thomas, Marjorie. "Taco Bell Rings in a New Image." *Restaurant Business* 83 (October 1984): 210, 214, 218.

"Thomson Outlines Changes in Bonanza Operations." *Food Service Chain Executive* 4, no. 11 (November 1976): 81–83.

Thor, Charles W., Jr. "Profile of a Franchise." *Modern Franchising* 13 (February / March 1971): 10, 24–25, 27–32.

Tiegs, Carol Lynn. "Burger Chef Carving Out an Image." *Restaurant Business* 79 (March 1, 1980): 158, 160, 162, 164.

Timmins, Mary. "Capt. Andy's Charts Course for National Expansion." *Restaurant Business* 82 (Feb. 1, 1983): 110–14.

——. "Chicken George Cracks Urban Market." *Restaurant Business* 82 (Jan. 1, 1983): 111–12.

——. "Winchell's Donut Chain Rises Again." *Restaurant Business* 82 (Sept. 15, 1983): 62–70.

"Today's KFC." Promotional brochure, KFC Corporation, Louisville, Ky., 1994.

"Top 400." *Restaurants and Institutions* 107 (July 15, 1997), 66–115.

"Tourists and Your Business." *Restaurant Digest* (August 1960): 1–3.

"Toward a Black Middle Class." *Fast Food* 68 (November 1969): 124–35, 173–74.

"Transforming Gas Stations Into Fast Food Restaurants." *Fast Service* 40 (May 1981): 30–31.

"Tray on Trestle Serves at Drive-In." *Popular Mechanics* 92 (September 1949): 127.

"Truckstop: Multi Billion-Dollar Business." *National Petroleum News* 66 (October 1968): 70–76.

"A U.S. Beachhead for Japanese Fast Food." *Business Week* (July 2, 1979): 24.

"The U.S. Eating-Out Market." *Cornell Hotel and Restaurant Administration Quarterly* 7 (August 1967): 2–4.

Vaughn, Charles L. "Survey of Fast Food Franchising." *Cornell Hotel and Restaurant Administration Quarterly* 11 (November 1970): 20–27.

"Wall Street Bets on Long John Silver's." *Institutional/Volume Feeding* 76 (April 15, 1975): 49–51.

Ward, John Russell. "Legalized Beer Affect Fountain Volume?" *Soda Fountain Magazine* 32, no. 2 (February 1933): 11–12, 36.

Ware, Josephine, and Jeannette Ware. "The Tea-Room Business." *Journal of Home Economics* 1 (October 1924): 565–69.

"Way Back When." *Marion (Indiana) Chronicle-Tribune Magazine,* Jan. 29, 1972, 8.

Weinstein, Jeff. "R&I Top 100." *Restaurants and Institutions* 104 (March 15, 1994): 34–44.

"Wendy's Homes in on Young Adults." *Business Week* (July 11, 1977): 60–61.

Wendy's Old-Fashioned Hamburgers information package. Granville, Ohio: Wendy's International [1995].

Werner, Harry E. "Designing Modern Drive-Ins." *Architecture* 30 (January 1953): 96–103.

Werner, Milton. "The Unlimited Chicken Unlimited." *Fast Food* 71 (March 1971): 90–95.

"What about This Mobile Soft Serve Market?" *Ice Cream Review* 43 (June 1960): 24–26, 60–62.

"What Makes the Teenager Tick?" *Drive-In Magazine* 23 (September 1959): 10–15, and 23 (October 1959): 9–12.

"Where the Industry Sells Its Ice Cream Gallonage." *Ice Cream Trade Journal* 45 (May 1949): 40–44.

Whitaker, Jan. "Catering to Romantic Hunger: Roadside Tea Rooms, 1909–1930." *Journal of American Culture* 15 (Winter 1992): 17–25.

White, Jacque. "At Jack in the Box, Only the Name Is the Same." *Restaurant Business* 82 (Feb. 1, 1983): 172, 174, 176.

Whitworth, William. "Kentucky-Fried." *New Yorker* (Feb. 14, 1970): 40–46, 48, 51–52.

Williams, Greer. "Good Mormons Don't Go Broke." *Saturday Evening Post* (June 10, 1950): 48–49, 157–60.

"Winning Designs in the Wayside Refreshment Stand Competition." *American Builder* 45 (July 1928): 92–93.

"'Women Managers Are Top-Notch' Says Prince Castle." *Fountain Service* 47 (August 1948): 28–29.

"World's Largest Drive-In." *Restaurant Digest* (May 1953): 25–26.

"Your Future Maid-Rite." [Muscatine, Iowa:] Maid-Rite, n.d.

Index

LIBRARY OF CONGRESS CATALOGING-IN-PUBLICATION DATA

Jakle, John A.

   Fast food : roadside restaurants in the automobile age / John A. Jakle and Keith A.
Sculle.

         p.   cm. — (The road and American culture)
   Includes bibliographical references and index.
   ISBN 0-8018-6109-8 (alk. paper)
   1. Restaurants—United States—History.   2. Fast food restaurants—United States—
History.   3. Architecture, Modern—20th century—United States.   4. Roadside archi-
tecture—United States.   I. Sculle, Keith A.   II. Title.   III. Series.
TX945.J35   1999
647.9573′0973′0904—dc21   98-49864
                                                                                      CIP